Interpreting the Bible

Historical and theological studies in honour of David F. Wright

Edited by A. N. S. Lane

 APOLLOS

APOLLOS (an imprint of Inter-Varsity Press),
38 De Montfort Street, Leicester LE1 7GP, England

© Inter-Varsity Press, 1997

First published 1997

British Library Cataloguing in Publication Data
A catalogue record for this book is available from the British Library.

ISBN 0-85111-455-5

Typeset in Great Britain by Tyndale House, Cambridge

Printed in Great Britain by Galliard (Printers) Ltd, Great Yarmouth

CONTENTS

Preface

This collection of essays is offered to an esteemed scholar who celebrates his sixtieth birthday on 2nd October, 1997.

A perusal of his bibliograpy indicates not only a prolific and highly creative mind, but also someone who has a breadth and depth of scholarly interests matched by few of his contemporaries. His scholarly publications have spanned a wide diversity of topics. His research studies began in the early church, an interest he has maintained with studies like 'Apocryphal gospels: the "Unknown Gospel" (Pap. egerton 2) and the *Gospel of Peter'*, 'Constantine and the "Mother of God": *Oratio Ad Sanctorum Coetum* 11:9', and '*Tractatus* 20–22 of St. Augustine's *In Iohannem'*. At a later date he moved also into Reformation studies, producing an annotated tanslation of works of Martin Bucer. He has become chief general editor of the new English translation of Calvin's Old Testament commentaries as well as a member of the editorial commission of the critical edition of Calvin's works. He has an interest in the use of the fathers in the sixteenth century, writing on 'Basil the Great in the Protestant Reformers' and other such topics. The modern period has not been neglected with articles like 'The Watershed of Vatican II: Catholic Attitudes Towards Other Religions'. Baptism has been a special interest and he has written on the origins of infant baptism, baptism in the fourth and fifth centuries and in the debates of the sixteenth and seventeenth centuries, as well as examining the important contemporary document *Baptism, Eucharist and Ministry*. Finally, he has also courageously tackled the vexed issue of homosexuality and as well as publishing a number of articles on the topic is in the course of writing a monograph on early Christian attitudes.

David Wright is also a 'collaborative scholar', to which there could be no better testimony than the large number of books that he has edited or coedited with others. Many academics manage to publish by neglecting the interests of their students. Nothing could be further than the truth with David Wright. Apart from his own students, there are a large number of scholars both young and maturing who have been the recipients of warm encouragement, unstinting attention and wise counsel and look back with gratitude to all the help that they have received. They know that his list of publications would have been even more impressive if the time generously devoted to their studies had instead been invested in adding to it.

If reflects the heart of a true Christian scholar and theological educator that he has found time to write for student journals, clergy publication and numerous articles in dictionaries both for the specialist and the lay person. As a churchman and a scholar he epitomises what it means to hold together the head and the heart and to write with integrity for both the academy and the church. In his case the question of Tertullian 'What has the academy to do with the church?' would have received an unexpected reply.

I personally am particularly glad to have the privilege of editing this volume as I owe David Wright a special debt. Our interests coincide doubly in that we have both worked extensively on Calvin and we both have a long-term interest in the question of the use of the early church fathers in the sixteenth century. With many of my own writings he has helped me considerably, both with advice in the course of research and with constructive criticism of the final product. I have always felt more confident in allowing something to proceed to print when it has his *nihil obstat!*

His membership of learned societies also testifies to his breadth of scholarly interests. One such society, the Tyndale Fellowship for Biblical and Theological Research, is deeply indebted to him for his long-standing interest and contributions as a member, as the chairman of a study group and, more recently, as the chairman of its administrative committee. This collection of essays is presented to him with affection and gratitude by a number of colleagues who have over the years been associated with him in the Tyndale Fellowship Doctrine Group.

Tony Lane
4th June, 1997

Selected List of Publications

'*Tractatus* 20-22 of St Augustine's *In Iohannem*,' *Journal of Theological Studies* n.s. 15 (1964) 317-330.

'Clement and the Roman succession in Irenaeus,' *Journal of Theological Studies* n.s. 18 (1967) 144-154.

'Rewards in the Teaching of Jesus,' *Themelios* 4:1 (1967) 24-32.

'Martin Bucer—the First "Ecumaniac"?', *New College Bulletin* V:2 (1970) 10-26.

'The Manuscripts of St Augustine's *Tractatus in Evangelium Iohannis*: A Preliminary Survey and Check-List,' *Recherches Augustiniennes* 8 (1972) 55-143.

'Pelagius the Twice-Born,' *Churchman* 86 (1972) 6-15.

Common Places of Martin Bucer (translated and annotated), Courtenay Library of Reformation Classics 4, (Appleford: Sutton Courtenay, 1972).

'Why were the Montanists Condemned?', *Themelios* 2 (1976-77) 15-22.

'*Piscina Siloa* or *Piscina Salomonis*? (Possidius, *Indiculum* X^6.57),' *Revue des Etudes Augustiniennes* 25 (1979) 47-60.

'Training the Whole Church for Ministry' in Jock Stein (ed.), *Ministers for the 1980s* (Edinburgh: Handsel Press, 1979) 42-53.

'Augustine's Sermons in Vlimmerius's *Editio Princeps* of Possidius's *Indiculum*,' *Revue des Etudes Augustiniennes* 25 (1979) 61-72.

'Soundings in the Doctrine of Scripture in British Evangelicalism in the First Half of the Twentieth Century,' *Tyndale Bulletin* 31 (1980) 87-106.

'The Manuscripts of the "'*Tractatus in Iohannem*:" A Supplementary List,' *Recherches Augustiniennes* 16 (1981) 59-100.

'Christian Faith in the Greek World: Justin Martyr's Testimony,' *Evangelical Quarterly* 54 (1982) 77-87.

'Basil the Great in the Protestant Reformers' in E.A. Livingstone (ed.), *Studia Patristica* 17:3 (Oxford etc.: Pergamon, 1982) 1149-1155.

'Montanism: A Movement of Spiritual Renewal?', *Theological Renewal* 22 (1982) 19-29.

'The Ethical Use of the Old Testament in Luther and Calvin: A Comparison,' *Scottish Journal of Theology* 36 (1983) 463-485.

[Survey of Ecclesiastical History at Edinburgh 1702-1983], *New College Bulletin* 14 (1983) 25-26.

'Homosexuals or Prostitutes? The Meaning of *arsenokoitai* (1 Cor. 6:9, 1 Tim. 1:10),' *Vigiliae Christianae* 38 (1984) 125-153, reprinted in W.R. Dynes and S. Donaldson (eds.), *Homosexuality and Religion and Philosophy*, Studies in Homosexuality 12 (New York and London: Garland Publishing, 1992) 351-379.

'Woman Before and After the Fall: A Comparison of Luther's and Calvin's Interpretation of Genesis 1-3,' *Churchman* 98 (1984) 126-135 (reprinted in R.C. Gamble (ed.), *Calvin's Work in Geneva*, Articles on Calvin and Calvinism 3 (New York and London: Garland Publishing, 1992) 156-165).

'The Lima Report: *Baptism* and *Eucharist* Compared,' *Theology* 87 (1984) 330-336.

'Ordination,' *Themelios* 10 (1985) 5-10.

'War in a Church-Historical Perspective,' *Evangelical Quarterly* 57 (1985) 133-161.

'Apocryphal Gospels; the "Unknown Gospel" (Pap. Egerton 2) and the *Gospel of Peter*' in D. Wenham (ed.), *Gospel Perspectives V: The Jesus Tradition Outside the Gospels* (Sheffield: JSOT Press, 1985) 207-232.

'Papyrus Egerton 2 (the *Unknown Gospel*) - Part of the *Gospel of Peter*?', *The Second Century* 5 (1985-86) 129-50.

'Calvin's Pentateuchal Criticism: Equity, Hardness of Heart and Divine Accommodation in the Mosaic Harmony Commentary,' *Calvin Theological Journal* 21 (1986) 33-50 (reprinted in R.C. Gamble (ed.), *Calvin and Hermeneutics*, Articles on Calvin and Calvinism 6 (New York and London: Garland Publishing, 1992) 213-230).

'Ministry and Priesthood: Further Reflections,' *Anvil* 3 (1986) 195-207.

'Apologetic and Apocalyptic: the Miraculous in the *Gospel of Peter*' in D. Wenham and C. Blomberg (eds.), *Gospel Perspectives VI: The Miracles of Jesus* (Sheffield: JSOT Press, 1986) 401-418.

'Word, Ministry and Congregation in the Reformation Confessions' in N.M.deS. Cameron and S.B. Ferguson (eds.), *Pulpit and People. Essays in Honour of William Still on his 75th Birthday* (Edinburgh: Rutherford House, 1986) 39-50.

'Donatist Theologoumena in Augustine? Baptism, Reviviscence of Sins, and Unworthy Ministers,' in *Congresso Internazionale su S. Agostino nel XVI Centenario della Conversione, Roma 15-20 settembre 1986, Atti* II, Studia Ephemeridis 'Augustinianum' 25 (Rome: Institutum Patristicum 'Augustinianum,' 1987) 213-224.

'Translating ARSENOKOITAI (1 Cor. 6:9; 1 Tim. 1:10),' *Vigiliae Christianae* 41 (1987) 396-398.

'The Origins of Infant Baptism - Child Believers' Baptism?', *Scottish Journal of Theology* 40 (1987) 1-23.

'How Controversial was the Development of Infant Baptism in the Early Church?' in James E. Bradley and Richard A. Muller (eds.), *Church, Word and Spirit: Historical and Theological Essays in Honor of Geoffrey W. Bromiley* (Grand Rapids: Eerdmans, 1987) 45-63.

'One Baptism or Two? Reflections on the History of Christian Baptism,' *Vox Evangelica* 18 (1988) 7-23 [the 1987 Laing Lecture].

'"The Commoun Buke of the Kirke:" the Bible in the Scottish Reformation' in Wright (ed.), *The Bible in Scottish Life and Literature*, 155-178.

'Luther and the Schwärmer' in I.H. Marshall (ed.), *Christian Experience in Theology and Life* (Edinburgh: Rutherford House, 1988) 55-82.

'Introduction,' 'Mary in the New Testament,' '"Mother of God"?', and 'Mary in the Reformers' in Wright (ed.), *Chosen by God: Mary in Evangelical Perspective* (London: Marshall Pickering, 1989) 1-14, 15-33, 120-140, 161-183.

'The Edinburgh Manuscript Pages of Servetus' *Christianismi Restitutio*' in E.A. McKee and B.G. Armstrong (eds.), *Probing the Reformed Tradition. Historical Studies in Honor of Edward A. Dowey, Jr* (Louisville: Westminster John Knox Press, 1989) 263-291.

'Homosexuality: The Relevance of the Bible,' *Evangelical Quarterly* 61 (1989) 291-300.

'Early Christian Attitudes to Homosexuality' in E.A. Livingstone (ed.), *Studia Patristica* 18:2 (1989) 329-334.

'The Meaning and Reference of "One Baptism for the Remission of Sins" in the Niceno-Constantinopolitan Creed' in E.A. Livingstone (ed.), *Studia Patristica* 19 (Leuven: Peeters, 1989) 281-285.

'The Nativity of Christ in Calvin's Commentaries' in I. Backus and F. Higman (eds.), *Théorie et pratique de l'exégèse. Actes du 3e Colloque international sur l' histoire de l'exégèse biblique au 16e siècle. Genève, 31 août - 2 Sept. 1988*, Etudes de philologie et d' histoire 43 (Geneva: Droz, 1990) 136-140.

'Homosexuality' and 'Trinity' in E. Ferguson (ed.), *Encyclopedia of Early Christianity* (New York: Garland Publishing, 1990) 435-436, 911-17.

'Reformation Studies in the 20th Century' in J.D. Douglas (ed.), *New 20th-Century Encyclopedia of Religious Knowledge* (2nd ed; Grand Rapids: Baker, 1991) 699-704.

'Robert Estienne's *Nova Glossa Ordinaria*. A Protestant Quest for a Standard Bible Commentary' in W. van 't Spijker (ed.), *Calvin Erbe und Auftrag. Festschrift für Wilhelm Heinrich Neuser zum 65. Geburtstag* (Kampen: Kok Pharos, 1991) 40-51.

'The Latin Fathers' in I. Hazlett (ed.), *Early Christianity. Origins and Evolution to AD 600* (In Honour of W.H.C. Frend) (London: SPCK, 1991) 148-162.

'The Watershed of Vatican II: Catholic Attitudes Towards Other Religions' in A.D. Clarke and B.W. Winter (eds.), *One God, One Lord in a World of Religious Pluralism* (Cambridge: Tyndale House, 1991) 153-171 (and 207-226 in enlarged edition, Carlisle: Paternoster Press and Grand Rapids: Baker, 1993).

'Martin Bucer (1491-1551) in England,' *Anvil* 9 (1992) 249-259.

'Martin Bucer and England—and Scotland' in C. Krieger and M. Lienhard (eds.) *Martin Bucer and Sixteenth Century Europe. Actes du colloque de Strasbourg (28-31 août 1991)* vol. 2 (Leiden: E.J. Brill, 1993) 523-532.

'George Cassander and the Appeal to the Fathers in Sixteenth-Century Debates about Infant Baptism' in L. Grane, A. Schindler and M. Wriedt (eds.), *Auctoritas Patrum. Contributions on the Reception of the Church Fathers in the 15th and 16th Century*, Veröffentlichungen des Instituts für Europäische Geschichte Mainz, Abteilung Religionsgeschichte 37 (Mainz: Philipp von Zabern, 1993) 259-269.

'Constantine and the "Mother of God:" *Oratio Ad Sanctorum Coetum* 11:9' in E.A. Livingstone (ed.), *Studia Patristica* 24 (Leuven: Peeters, 1993) 355-359.

'Accommodation and Barbarity in John Calvin's Old Testament Commentaries' in A.G. Auld (ed.), *Understanding Poets and Prophets. Essays in Honour of George Wishart Anderson* (Sheffield: Sheffield Academic Press, 1993) 413-427.

'Homosexuality' and 'Sexuality, Sexual Ethics' in G.F. Hawthorne and R.P. Martin (eds.), *Dictionary of Paul and His Letters* (Downers Grove and Leicester: Inter-Varsity Press, 1993) 413-15, 871-75.

'Family' and 'Fornication' in B.M. Metzger and M.D. Coogan (eds.), *The Oxford Companion to the Bible* (New York: Oxford University Press, 1993) 223-24, 232.

'Infant Baptism and the Christian Community in Bucer' in Wright (ed.), *Martin Bucer: Reforming Church and Com-munity*, 95-106.

Introduction: 'William Tyndale and the Tyndale Fellowship for Biblical and Theological Research' and 'Scripture and Evangelical Diversity with Special Reference to the Baptismal Divide' in Satterthwaire & Wright (eds), *A Pathway into the Holy Scripture*, 1-9, 257-275.

'Ambrose,' 'Gregory the Great,' 'Patristic Ethics,' etc. in D.J. Atkinson and D.H. Field (eds.), *The New Dictionary of Christian Ethics and Pastoral Theology* (Leicester: Inter-Varsity Press, 1995).

Introduction and 'Elsewhere in Edinburgh: Colleges Newer and Older' in Wright & Badcock (eds), *Disruption to Diversity*, pp.vii-xxxi, 239-258.

'Sixteenth-Century Reformed Perspectives on the Minority Church' in J.H. Leith (ed.), Calvin Studies VII (Colloquium...Davidson College, NC, January 28-29, 1994) (Davidson: Davidson College, 1994) 15-29, and in *Scottish Journal of Theology* 48 (1995) 469-488.

'Calvin's "Accommodation" Revisited' in Peter De Klerk (ed.), *Calvin as Exegete. Papers...Ninth Colloquium on Calvin and Calvin Studies...Princeton Theological Seminary...May 20, 21 and 22, 1993* (Grand Rapids: Calvin Studies Society, 1995) 171-190.

'Recovering Baptism for a New Age of Mission' in Donald Lewis and Alister McGrath (eds.), *Doing Theology for the People of God. Studies in Honor of J I Packer* (Downers Grove and Leicester, Inter-Varsity Press, 1996) 51-66.

'Augustine: His Exegesis and Hermeneutics' in Magne Saebo (ed.), *Hebrew Bible/Old Testament. The History of Its Interpretation* I/1 (Göttingen: Vandenhoeck & Ruprecht, 1996) 701-730.

'Baptism at the Westminster Assembly' in J.H. Leith (ed.), *The Westminster Confession in Current Thought*, Calvin Studies VIII (Davidson: Davidson College, 1996) 76-90.

'Andrew Hunter of Barjarg (1744-1809): Evangelical Divine in an Age of Improvement' in *Records of the Scottish Church History Society* 26 (1996) 135-168.

Forthcoming

'Calvin's Accommodating God' in W.H. Neuser & B.G. Armstrong (eds.), *Calvinus Sincerioris Religionis Vindex* (Kirksville: Sixteenth Century Journal Publishers, 1997) [Papers of the Sixth International Congress on Calvin Research].

'At What Ages were People Baptized in the Early Centuries? A Quest for Statistics' in E.A. Livingstone (ed.), *Studia Patristica* (Louvain: Peeters) [Papers of Twelfth International Conference on Patristic Studies].

'The Donatists in the Sixteenth Century' in L Grane, A Schindler, M Wriedt (eds.), *Auctoritas Patrum II. New Contributions on the Reception of the Church Fathers in the 15th and 16th Century*, Veröffentlichungen des Instituts für Europäische Geschichte Mainz, Abteilung Religions-geschichte (Mainz: Philipp von Zabern, 1997).

'Martin Bucer' in D.K. McKim (ed.), *Major Biblical Interpreters* (Downers Grove: InterVarsity Press).

Editorships

Consulting Editor for early and medieval sections in T. Dowley (ed.), *The History of Christianity* (Berkhamsted: Lion, 1977; revised edition, Oxford: Lion, 1990). Editions also in Afrikaans, Dutch, French, German, Italian, Japanese, Korean, Norwegian and Swedish.

Editor, *Essays in Evangelical Social Ethics* [papers of National Evangelical Conference on Social Ethics, 1978] (Exeter: Paternoster, 1979).

Joint Editor (with S.B. Ferguson), *New Dictionary of Theology* (Leicester: Inter-Varsity Press, 1988).

Editor (assisted by I.M. Campbell and J.C.L. Gibson), *The Bible in Scottish Life and Literature* (Edinburgh: St. Andrew Press, 1988).

Editor, *Chosen by God: Mary in Evangelical Perspective* (London: Marshall Pickering, 1989).

Consulting Editor in D.K. McKim (ed.), *Encyclopedia of the Reformed Faith* (Louisville: Westminster John Knox Press, and Edinburgh: St. Andrew Press, 1992).

Member of Editorial Commission of *Ioannis Calvini Opera Omnia* (Geneva: Droz, 1992ff.)

Chief General Editor of new English translation of Calvin's Old Testament commentaries (Grand Rapids: Eerdmans, and Carlisle: Paternoster, 1993ff.).

Chief General Editor in N.M.deS. Cameron (organiz. ed.), *Dictionary of Scottish Church History and Theology* (Edinburgh: T. & T. Clark, and Downers Grove: Inter-Varsity Press, 1993).

Editor, *Martin Bucer, Reforming Church and Community* (Cambridge: Cambridge University Press, 1994).

Joint Editor (with P.E. Satterthwaite), *A Pathway into the Holy Scripture* (Grand Rapids: Eerdmans, 1994).

Joint Editor (with G.D. Badcock), *Disruption to Diversity: Edinburgh Divinity 1846-1996* (Edinburgh: T. & T. Clark, 1996).

Editor, *Scottish Bulletin of Evangelical Theology*.

Assistant Editor, *Tyndale Bulletin*.

Editorial Advisory Board, *Christian History*.

Editorial Board, *Reformation and Renaissance Review*.

Editorial Advisory Board, *Bibliotheca Calviniana*.

Also numberous other articles in dictionaries and encyclopaedias.

Chapter 1

GREGORY NAZIANZEN'S BIBLICAL CHRISTOLOGY

T.A. Noble

Introduction

Of the three Cappadocian Fathers, Gregory of Nazianzus is often regarded as the least original and creative theologian. His dominant friend, Basil, the Metropolitan Archbishop of Caesarea, became the leading figure in the Nicene party following the death of Athanasius in AD 373, and is credited with advocating (yet not devising!) what was to become the orthodox formula for the doctrine of the Trinity in the Eastern Empire, μία οὐσία, τρεῖς ὑπόστασεις. Basil's younger brother, Gregory of Nyssa, had the most creative philosophical mind of the three, and has received considerable attention from scholars in the twentieth century.

Yet it was not Basil nor Gregory of Nyssa who was accorded the accolade of 'The Theologian' (or 'The Divine'), a title then shared only with St. John. It was the Nazianzen who was regarded as 'Gregory the Theologian'. Perhaps this was precisely because his lack of originality (of the wrong kind), combined with his high standing as an orator and a poet, fitted him to express most faithfully the commonly accepted faith of the Church at a turning point in its history. It was the sensitive and nervous Gregory who was called to re-establish a Nicene congregation in Constantinople, the Eastern capital, just as the orthodox emperor, Theodosius, was succeeding Valens, the Arian. By that time the Arian controversy (or better, controversies) had been splitting the Church into factions for over sixty years, in fact, virtually since the Council of Nicea had formulated the Creed of Nicea supposedly to settle the matter.

By 379, Athanasius had been dead for six years and news of Basil's death on 1st January had just reached Gregory who himself had retired in poor health to the monastery of St Thecla near the coast in Seleucia four years earlier. He had thankfully handed over his duties as auxiliary bishop of his late father's see of Nazianzus to the presbyter, Cledonius. At long last he could enjoy seclusion, withdrawal from the world to read and pray and think and write. It was a sense of duty rather than vanity which made him leave his seclusion at the call to enter the battle once again. Perhaps it would be best to say that he was unavoidably aware that he was the outstanding orator in the Church and that, being free to go and his health being restored, and knowing of the death of Basil, the great champion of orthodoxy, he felt compelled to answer the call to action.[1]

Theologia: The Doctrine of God

The Arians had possession of all the churches in the capital, and so in the little chapel attached to a house in the city and suitably named the Anastasia, that Gregory was to preach the five sermons known as The Five Theological Orations which were to gain him his recognition as 'The Theologian'.[2]

---

[1]For Gregory's famous ambivalence between public service (the bishop's throne) and monastic retreat (the mountain of encounter with God), see Brooks Otis, 'The Throne and the Mountain. An Essay on St. Gregory Nazianzus [sic],' *Classical Journal* 56 (1961) 146-165. The standard biography remains Paul Gallay, *La Vie de S. Grégoire de Nazianze* (Paris and Lyons: Emmanuel Vitte, 1943).

[2]In addition to the text in Migne's *Patrologia Graeca* 36, there are several critical editions of the Theological Orations now available. A.J. Mason

Arianism is usually regarded as a christological heresy, but such is the interconnection between christology and the Christian doctrine of God, that the doctrine of the Trinity became the central issue in the later stages of the controversy. It is the deity of Christ, after all, which implies the doctrine of the Trinity. R.P.C. Hanson was therefore accurate when he entitled his final *magnum opus* on the Arian controversy *The Search for the Christian Doctrine of God*.[3] Gregory's Theological Orations are therefore in the strict sense *theologia*. He was the one who expressed for the Church at this crucial turning point in its history its definitive doctrine of the Triune God. Yet at the heart of this *theologia* is christology.

The First and Second Theological Orations, 380

After an opening discourse deploring the way in which the mystery of God had been profaned and cheapened by godless and thoughtless disputes and chatter in the capital,

---

(ed.), *The Five Theological Orations of Gregory of Nazianzus* (Cambridge: CUP, 1899), Greek text with annotations, is still useful. J. Barbel (ed.), *Gregor von Nazianz: Die fünf theologische Reden* (Düsseldorf: Patmos-Verlag, 1963) gives Greek text and German translation. Paul Gallay (ed.), *Grégoire de Nazianze. Discours 27-31* (Paris: Cerf, 1978), the *Sources chrétiennes* edition, gives Greek text and French translation. The English translation of the Five Theological Orations included among the twenty-four orations translated by C.G. Browne and J.E. Swallow, in *Nicene and Post-Nicene Fathers*, Series II, vol. 7 (Oxford: Parker, 1894) 185-498, was re-published in E.R. Hardy and C.C. Richardson, *Christology of the Later Fathers* (London: SCM, 1954), which is Vol. 3 of the *Library of Christian Classics*. The latest English translation, by Lionel Wickham and Frederick Williams is in Frederick W. Norris, *Faith Gives Fullness to Reasoning. The Five Theological Orations of Gregory Nazianzen* (Leiden: Brill, 1991) 217-299. Frederick W. Norris supplies a full Introduction and Commentary. Wickham and Williams is used here for the Theological Orations except where otherwise noted. The older translation of Browne and Swallow is used (but frequently amended) for the other orations and the epistles. A fresh more exact translation of some passages will occasionally be given since loose translation (or 'dynamic equivalence') is useless when what is at issue is terminology.

[3] R.P.C. Hanson, *The Search for the Christian Doctrine of God* (Edinburgh: T. & T. Clark, 1988).

together with an insistence that the would-be theologian
must be purified before, like Moses, he approached the
mountain, Gregory then devoted his second discourse to the
incomprehensibility of the divine mystery. Our observation
of the world around us should lead us to posit the existence
of a God, but such an instinctive conclusion cannot bring us
to understand or conceive what or who God is. Comprehen-
sion is a form of circumscription, and the infinite God cannot
be circumscribed. The attempt to conceive deity is what
produces idolatry, for:

> No one has yet discovered or ever shall discover what God
> is in his nature (τὴν φύσιν) and essence (τῆς οὐσίαν)... But
> for the present what reaches us is a scant emanation, as it
> were a beam from a great light—which means that anyone
> who has "known" God or whose "knowledge" of him has
> been attested in the Bible, had a manifestly more brilliant
> knowledge than others not equally illuminated.[4]

Gregory surveys the knowledge of God of the saints of
Scripture from Enoch to Paul: they all 'knew in part'. Indeed
if our knowledge of the natural world—of fish and birds,
bees and spiders, earth, sea and air, the stars of heaven and
the spiritual world of purely intellectual angelic creatures—
is so incomplete, if knowledge of the nature of such 'secondary ones' (ἡ τῶν δευτέρων φύσις) is so imperfect, then how
much more imperfect is our knowledge of that which is the
first and unique one (τῆς πρώτης καὶ μόνης).

In the context in which these sermons were
preached, this insistence on the incomprehensibility of God
and on a proper and reverent apophaticism, was levelled
against the rationalism of the extreme Arians, the Neo-
Arians or Eunomians, who thought that they could define
the essence and nature of God.[5] According to them, God was
by definition τὸ ἀγέννητον, The Unbegotten, a term which
they equated with The Unbegun (τὸ ἀγένητον), the one with-

---

[4]*Orat.* 28:17 (PG 36:48C).
[5]Thomas A. Kopecek, *A History of Neo-Arianism*, Vols 1 & 2 (Cambridge, Mass.: The Philadelphia Patristic Foundation, 1979). Kopecek's
term, 'Neo-Arianism' is useful to replace the misnomer 'Anomoians.'
On the latter, cf. R.P.C. Hanson, 'A Note on "Like According to the
Scriptures,"' *Zeitschrift für Kirchengeschichte* 98 (1987) 230-232.

out beginning. With such a definition of the nature and essence of God as their premise, they then deduced that τὸ γεννητόν, The Begotten, was of a different essence (ἑτεροούσιος), and so was not God.

The Third Theological Oration, 380

Gregory takes up the dispute with the Eunomians more directly in the Third and Fourth Theological Orations, where he comes to christology, the heart of the argument. The Third Theological Oration begins with a brief statement of the doctrine of the Trinity. The options for opinions about deity are anarchy, polyarchy or monarchy.[6] Christians hold to monarchy, but a monarchy which is not limited to one person (πρόσωπον).

> Therefore Unity (μονὰς) 'from the beginning', moved into Duality (δυάδα), and came to rest in Trinity (τριάδος). And this is to us the Father, the Son and the Holy Spirit, the first being the Begetter (γεννήτωρ) and Emitter (προβολεύς), though impassibly, eternally and incorporeally, and of the others, the one the Begotten (τὸ μὲν γέννημα) and the other the Emission (τὸ δὲ πρόβλημα).[7]

Gregory defends the eternity, the impassibility, and the incorporeality of the generation of the Son (and by extension the emission of the Holy Spirit) against the Eunomians. He deals with a series of objections, easily showing the absurdity of some conundrums posed by their logic-chopping. He refutes the notion that unbegottenness is a definition of the essence or being of God. He admits that it may be said that the Father is greater than the Son in the sense that he is the cause (τῷ αἰτίῳ) of the Son, but that this does not justify the Eunomian conclusion that he is greater by nature (μεῖζων τῇ φύσει). He refuses to be intimidated by the dilemma they posed that 'Father' must be the name of either an essence (οὐσίας) or an action (ἐνεργείας), both of which they believed

---

[6]Wickham and Williams translate these as 'atheism, polytheism and monotheism' (Norris, *Faith Gives Fullness*, 245).
[7]*Orat.* 29:2 (PG 36:76B).

would lead to denying the deity of the Son, and introduces the term later explored by Augustine and Anselm: 'It is the name of the *relationship* (σχέσεως) in which the Father stands to the Son and the Son to the Father'.

This is a relationship which implies an identity of nature (ὁμοφυΐαν), as with us. And even if 'Father' *does* name the essence (οὐσία) of God, the common use of the term does not imply a different essence for a son. And even if 'Father' is the name of an action, the result of this action would still be the ὁμοούσιον.

It is at this point that Gregory, having dealt with the arguments of the Eunomians, turns to the positive statement of his christology from the Scriptures, the 'divine words' (τῶν θείων λογίων), for, he says, 'We have learned to understand and preach the deity of the Son from their great and uplifting voices'.[8] Although Gregory defends the deity of the Son from the Scriptures in the rest of the Third Theological Oration, and examines the interpretation of texts used to support the Arian position in the Fourth, the contours of his own biblical christology are best seen in his earlier sermons.

We shall therefore review Gregory's christology from the beginning, starting with passages from his first sermons, Orations 1 and 2, preached in 362, then from two of the Constantinople sermons, Oration 38, On the Theophany or Birthday of Christ, preached in the Anastasia at Christmas 379, and Oration 40, On Holy Baptism, preached on 6th January 380. Rather than summarizing, paraphrasing and collating, our method is to quote Gregory extensively, looking at each significant passage in chronological order and in context in order to hear the orator speaking for himself.

The Christological Parabola

First Oration on Easter, 362

Gregory's first brief sermon was preached in Nazianzus on Easter Day, 362, after his father the bishop, the elder Greg-

---

[8] *Orat.* 29:17 (PG 36:96B).

ory, had insisted on ordaining him a presbyter against his will. At the heart of the sermon is the New Testament theme of dying and rising with Christ. Gregory proclaims that he comes

> that he who today rose again from the dead may renew me also by his Spirit, and, clothing me with the new Man, may give me to his new creation, to those who are begotten after God, as a good modeller (πλάστην) and teacher for Christ, willingly both dying with him and rising again with him.[9]

The Pauline echoes (Rom. 6:4-11, 8:11, 2 Cor. 5:17 and Col. 3:9f.) are unmistakable. Another Pauline passage (1 Cor. 5:8), provides the basis for Old Testament allusions to the Passover which (as in the Passover liturgy) are made contemporary and put dramatically into the first person:

> Yesterday the Lamb was slain and the door-posts were anointed, and Egypt bewailed her first-born, and the destroyer passed us over, and the seal was dreadful and reverend, and we were walled in with the precious blood. Today we have escaped clean from Egypt and from Pharaoh, and from the burdens laid upon us, and we have been freed from the clay and the brickmaking; and there is none to hinder us from keeping a feast to the Lord our God, the feast of our departure, or from celebrating that feast, not in the old leaven of malice and wickedness, but in the unleavened bread of sincerity and truth, carrying with us nothing of ungodly and Egyptian leaven.[10]

These allusions to the Exodus Passover lead to the dying and rising theme once again:

> Yesterday I was crucified with him: today I am glorified with him. Yesterday I died with him: today I am quickened with him. Yesterday I was buried with him: today I rise with him.[11]

He exhorts his congregation (in an echo of Romans 12:1) to offer to God not gold or silver but 'ourselves, the possession

---

[9]*Orat.* 1:2 (PG 35:397A).
[10]*Orat.* 1:3 (PG 35:397A).
[11]*Orat.* 1:4 (PG 35:397B).

most precious to God'. His succeeding sentences ground this spiritual experience of the Christian in a thoroughly Pauline way in the dying and rising of Christ:

> Let us give back to the Image (τῇ εἰκόνι) what is made after the Image. Let us recognize our Dignity (τὸ ἀξίωμα); let us honour our Archetype (τὸ ἀρχέτυπον); let us know the power of the Mystery (τοῦ μυστηρίου), and for what Christ died. Let us become like Christ, since Christ became like us. Let us become gods (γενώμεθα θεοὶ) for his sake, since he became man for ours. He assumed the worse that he might give us the better; he became poor that we through his poverty might become rich; he took upon himself the form of a servant that we might receive back our liberty; he came down that we might be exalted; he was tempted that we might conquer; he was dishonoured that he might glorify us; he died that he might save us; he ascended that he might draw to himself us who were lying low in the fall of sin. Let us give all, offer all to him who gave himself a ransom and a reconciliation for us. But one can give nothing like oneself, understanding the mystery, and becoming for his sake all that he became for us.[12]

It is scarcely possible to overestimate the significance of these paragraphs in the first oration for Gregory's Christology. Clearly the orator is glorying in the great rhetorical antitheses, and is reflecting the 'wonderful exchange' of Irenaeus: 'Our Lord Jesus Christ, the Word of God, of his boundless love became what we are that he might make us what he himself is'.[13] But behind all of that, the fundamental motif is a thoroughly New Testament one: that Christ came down to die in identification with us in order that we might rise to eternal life in identification with him. In other words: Christ took our place that we might take his.

F.W. Norris draws attention to the importance of the motif expressed here for Nazianzen's whole theology:

---

[12]*Orat.* 1:4-5 (PG 35:397B-400A).
[13]*Adv. Haer.* 5:*praef.* Cf. James L. Kugel and Rowan A. Greer, *Early Biblical Interpretation* (Philadelphia: Westminster, 1986) esp. chapter 3, 'A Framework for Interpreting the Christian Bible,' for the significance of Irenaeus here. Cf. also Thomas F. Torrance, *Divine Meaning: Studies in Patristic Hermeneutics* (Edinburgh: T. & T. Clark, 1995) 106ff.

It could almost be said that in Gregory's view, all of theology could be included under the *kenōsis-theōsis* pattern. *Theōsis* is linked to nearly every facet of the Christian life while *kenōsis* is the corollary in Biblical terms which makes the latter possible.[14]

The two most notable biblical texts behind the motif are, according to Norris, Philippians 2:6-11 and 2 Corinthians 8:9, 'Though he was rich, yet for your sakes he became poor, so that by his poverty you might become rich'. While the *kenōsis* theme is explicitly there in Philippians 2 (Norris comments), the idea of *theōsis* has no such support.

As far as it goes, this comment is strictly accurate. Undoubtedly, *deification* is a Patristic and not a New Testament term, and it sounds particularly strange and even suspect to Western Christian ears. But it would be unfortunate if the presence of this particular concept were to distract us from seeing that the pattern as a whole is a thoroughly New Testament one. It is the parabola of the Philippians hymn, and therefore, by implication, of the other christological hymns of the New Testament. It is the descent-ascent theme of John, where the whole Gospel is most clearly in this parabolic pattern from the incarnational descent of the prologue to the (implied) ascension. It is the dying and rising theme in Paul, a theme in which christology, soteriology and Christian experience are inextricably one. It is the fundamental bi-polarity of the Christian gospel, the two-in-one pattern of the cross and the resurrection. It is this kerygmatic, parabolic pattern which is embedded in the second article of the creed.[15]

It is because this pattern incorporates the theme of the 'wonderful exchange', the substitutionary theme that Christ takes our place so that we might take his, that it implies the concept of *deification* for the Greek Fathers. The logic is clear: if God himself did not become genuinely

---

[14]F.W. Norris, 'Gregory Nazianzen's Doctrine of Jesus Christ' (thesis, Yale, 1970), 62.

[15]Kugel & Greer, *Early Biblical Interpretation*, 159ff., continue to refer to this as 'the redeemer myth' even though they recognize that the older view of Bultmann, that it originated in a pre-Christian Gnostic redeemer myth, is without foundation.

human, if someone less than God stooped (as the Arians claimed), then the whole christological-soteriological parabola is compromised. If it really was God *himself* who came, and he was genuinely incarnate, really became a human being, and was exalted to heaven thus taking our glorified humanity with him, and if human nature was *deified* in him, that is to say, became the very humanity of God, then, for the Fathers, it is legitimate to say by figurative extension that we who share the same human nature are 'deified' in him.

According to Brooks Otis, this is a point where Gregory goes beyond Basil. Neo-Arianism had reduced the Father to a 'bare philosophical theorem' whereas (according to Otis) 'the anti-philosophical piety of the East (especially of Egypt) was steadily tending towards a more and more physicalist and even crassly materialist concept of Christ and salvation'. The Cappadocians therefore had to show that salvation was neither simply physical on the one hand nor philosophical on the other, but was essentially *deification*, 'the finite's pursuit of the infinite'. Gregory was the first to develop this, drawing on Clement of Alexandria, especially for his image of Moses in the mountain-cloud. *Deification* is thus the core of Gregory's theology, according to Otis, and his great theological significance lies in that he was the one who first used the Clementine theology and Clementine metaphors in the new Nicene context.[16]

D.F. Winslow similarly gives deification a central place in Gregory's theology:

> Gregory's characteristic term for describing that union which is both the origin and goal of the theological-soteriological process was *theōsis*, a term he used perhaps more freely than any of the Greek Fathers.[17]

But if deification is a central concept for Gregory, he makes it clear in his second oration (reassuringly for Western Christ-

---

[16]Otis, 'The Throne and the Mountain,' 162f.

[17]D.F. Winslow, *The Dynamics of Salvation. A Study in Gregory of Nazianzus* (Cambridge, Massachusetts: Philadelphia Patristic Foundation, 1979) vi. The book is a revised version of Winslow's thesis, 'The Concept of Salvation in the Writings of Gregory of Nazianzus' (Harvard, 1967).

ians) that the term is employed figuratively to express a thoroughly biblical idea. To deify is 'to make Christ dwell in the heart by the Spirit'.[18] It is, in other words, a way of expressing the Pauline theme which is more familiar in Western theology (particularly in Calvin), union with Christ. Elsewhere, Gregory is even more clear that the word is not to be taken literally (κυρίως).[19]

Second Oration: In defence of his flight to Pontus, 362
The second oration is a defence of Gregory's flight to Pontus (to the seclusion of Basil's monastic community) after his enforced ordination. The whole oration is a seminal essay in pastoral theology on which John Chrysostom and Gregory the Great were later to be dependent. At its heart is the passage where, having made clear that 'deification' is used figuratively, he goes on to show that it is a synonym for 'salvation', and that soteriological concerns are central to his whole theology.

Deification, he proclaims in this significant passage, is the purpose of the law and the prophets...

> ...of the emptied Godhead, of the assumed flesh, of the novel union (ἡ καινὴ μίξις) between God and man, one consisting of two, and both in one. This is why God was united to the flesh by means of the soul, and the divergent things (τὰ διεστῶτα) so separate were knit together by the affinity to each of the element which mediated between them. So all became one for the sake of one, our progenitor, the soul because of the soul which was disobedient, the flesh because of the flesh which co-operated with it and shared its condemnation, Christ, who was superior to and beyond the reach of sin, because of Adam, who became subject to sin.[20]

Winslow sees already here in the insistence on the human soul of Christ a response to Apollinarianism, citing Gregory's letter to Cledonius twenty years later to show that he was aware of the problem of Apollinarianism as early as this

---

[18]*Orat*. 2:22, with reference to Eph. 3:17.
[19]*Cf.*, *Orat*. 42:17 (PG 36:477C).
[20]*Orat*. 2:23 (PG 35:432C-433A).

oration.[21] This clear insistence on the human soul of Christ comes from Nazianzen's Origenist heritage, as does the idea that the human soul, being an intellectual or spiritual reality rather than a material one, is somehow fitted by that to be the mediating element between deity (which is intellectual, spiritual reality) and the material flesh. This is all consistent with Nazianzen's understanding of creation, and therefore of humanity, as twofold, material and spiritual.[22]

But for our purposes, what is significant is the way this coheres with the fundamental pattern of his biblical christology, the descent-ascent, humiliation-exaltation, dying and rising, crucifixion-resurrection, two-in-one parabola incorporating the substitutionary exchange. For that pattern requires not only a full deity, but also a full and uncompromised humanity. Since Gregory's anthropology was that of a body-soul unity, then the incarnation had to mean that the Saviour was fully human, body *and* soul.

Nazianzen may leave undeveloped aspects of the Atonement which later Western theology was to consider central, but for him, soteriology is inseparable from the basic shape of New Testament christology. The cross cannot be abstracted from the christological parabola and the 'wonderful exchange'. His exposition of salvation therefore continues by expounding the Pauline contrast between Adam and Christ in Irenaean fashion. This 'deification' is the purpose not only of the nativity of Christ (as in the last passage quoted above), but also (as the same passage continues) of his life and ministry, and especially of his suffering and death. Our salvation, or deification, is the reason

> ...why tree is set over against tree, hands against hand, the one stretched out in self-indulgence, the others in generosity; the one unrestrained, the others fixed by nails, the one expelling Adam, the other reconciling the ends of the

---

[21]Winslow, *Dynamics of Salvation*, 79f., referring to J. Dräseke, 'Gregorios von Nazianz und sein Verhältnis zum Apollinarismus,' *Theologische Studien und Kritiken* 65 (1892) 473-512 and E. Mühlenberg, *Apollinaris von Laodicea* (Göttingen, 1969).
[22]*Cf.*, Anna-Stina Ellverson, *The Dual Nature of Man. A Study in the Theological Anthropology of Gregory of Nazianzus* (Uppsala thesis, Stockholm: Almquist & Wiksell, 1981).

earth. This is the reason for the 'lifting up' to atone for the fall, and of the gall for the tasting, and of the thorny crown for the dominion of evil, and of death for death, and of darkness for the sake of light, and of burial for the return to the ground, and of resurrection for the sake of resurrection.[23]

Winslow comments:

> The Cross of Jesus Christ is, for Gregory, the culmination and fulfilment of the *oikonomia* of the incarnation. It is the prime instrument of salvation. Gregory sees made manifest on the Cross of Calvary the deeper meaning of the condescension and self-emptying of the Son of God, and of his recapitulation of the whole created order.[24]

It is this same fundamental and soteriologically oriented biblical christology, evident in these early orations, which underlies Gregory's preaching in Constantinople seventeen years later.

Constantinople: Opposing Arianism

The Christmas and Epiphany Orations, 379-380

It was at Christmas, 379, that Gregory began a series of sermons significantly re-asserting the balance and bi-polarity of the christological parabola. Oration 38, On the Theophany or Birthday of Christ, begins with the nativity and the Virgin Birth:

> He that was without mother becomes without father (without mother of his former state, without father of his second). The laws of nature are upset: the world above must be filled.[25]

---

[23]*Orat.* 2:25: cf. also 2:98, where Gregory lists thirty-four Christological titles, 'both those more lofty ones which were originally his, and those more lowly ones which he later assumed for our sake.'
[24]Winslow, *Dynamics of Salvation*, 99.
[25]*Orat.* 38:2 (PG 36:313B).

But it quickly becomes evident that no point on the christological parabola can be understood in isolation. The birth and the death, Bethlehem and Calvary, Christmas and Easter, cannot be understood in isolation from each other, and Gregory cannot explain the significance of Christmas without looking forward to Good Friday and Easter:

> This is our present festival. It is this we are celebrating today, the coming of God to man, that we might go forth, or rather...that we might go back to God; that putting off the old man, we might put on the new; and that as we died in Adam, so we might live in Christ, being born with Christ and crucified with him and buried with him and rising with him... For where sin abounded grace did much more abound; and if a taste condemned us, how much more doth the passion of Christ justify us.[26]

It is this soteriological perspective which requires the full deity and humanity of the Saviour:

> The Word of God himself, who is before all worlds, the Invisible, the Incomprehensible, the Incorporeal, the Beginning of the beginning, the Light of light, the Source of life and immortality, the Image of the Archetypal Beauty, the immovable Seal, the unchangeable Image, the Father's Definition and Word, came to his own image and took on him flesh for the sake of our flesh, and mingled (μίγνυται) himself with an intelligent soul for my soul's sake, purifying like by like, and in all points except sin was made man... He came forth then as God with that which he had assumed, one from two opposites (ἓν ἐκ δύο τῶν ἐναντίων), flesh and Spirit, the latter deifying the former.[27]

Originally, man was a union, a commingling of the spiritual and material creation. But this is a new conjoining and union,[28] and its purpose is our salvation:

> He who gives riches becomes poor, for he assumes the poverty of my flesh, that I may assume the riches of his

---

[26]*Orat.* 38:4 (PG 36:316A).

[27]*Orat.* 38:13 (PG 36:325B).

[28]*Cf.*, Norris, *Gregory Nazianzen's Doctrine*, 85f., for Nazianzen's use of the Stoic terms μῖξις and κρᾶσις but not of παράθεσις or σύγχυσις.

Godhead. He that is full empties himself, for he empties himself of his glory for a short while that I may have a share in his fullness.... He partakes of my flesh that he may both save the image and make the flesh immortal.[29]

But once again, it is not incarnation in isolation from the whole parabola, reaching its nadir in the cross. Gregory remonstrates with 'those unthankful creatures', the Arians, 'for whom Christ died in vain':

Will you deem him little on this account, that he humbled himself for you; because the Good Shepherd, he who lays down his life for the sheep, came to seek for that which had strayed upon the mountains and hills...and having found it, took it upon his shoulders, on which he also took the wood [of the cross], and having taken it, brought it back to the higher life...?[30]

A little later on [in the Church year]...you shall see him... being betrayed and crucified, and crucifying with himself my sin; offered as a Lamb, and offering as a Priest; as a man buried in the grave, and as God rising again...[31]

Orations 39 and 40 followed soon after, probably on 5th and 6th January, 380. In the latter, On Holy Baptism, Gregory gives 'a short compendium of salvation'. Once again, after the doctrine of the Trinity (the one name of Father, Son and Holy Spirit into whom the catechumens are about to be baptized) and the doctrine of creation *ex nihilo*, Gregory proceeds to expound the christological parabola:

Believe that the Son of God, the Eternal Word, who was begotten of the Father before all time and without body, was in these latter days for your sake also made Son of Man, born of the Virgin Mary ineffably and stainlessly...in his own Person at once entire man (ὅλον ἄνθρωπον) and perfect God, for the sake of the entire (ὅλου) sufferer, that he may bestow salvation on your whole being (ὅλῳ σοι)

---

[29]*Orat.* 38:13 (PG 36:325C).
[30]*Orat.* 38:14 (PG 36:328A).
[31]*Orat.* 38:16 (PG 36:329BC).

having destroyed the whole condemnation (ὅλον τὸ κατάκριμα) of your sins; impassible in his Godhead, passible in that which he assumed, as much man for your sake as you are made God (γίνη θεός) for his.[32]

The integration of christology and soteriology is evident. If the *whole* human person is to be saved, the Saviour must be *wholly* God and *wholly* man. Both Arianism and Apollinarianism destroy the pattern. But because the incarnation cannot be divorced from the cross, Gregory continues:

> Believe that for us sinners he was led to death, was crucified and buried, so far as to taste death, and that he rose again, the third day, and ascended into heaven that he might take you who were lying low with him...

It was just a few months later that the Theological Orations followed.[33]

Third Theological Oration: Christological Hermeneutics
Having examined the christology of Nazianzen up to this point in his career, and having seen that its fundamental shape is the central bi-polar or parabolic New Testament christology of crucifixion–resurrection, humiliation-exaltation, descent-ascent, we return to the Theological Orations. The polemical stance of his christology in the Third and Fourth Theological Orations is now seen not to be definitive (as might so easily be assumed) but based upon this fundamental motif. A quick review of his use of Scripture in these Orations will show the polemical stance and the hermeneutical approach which are the results rather than the basis of his biblical christology. We need to remember that his polemic is directed here against the Arians, and therefore he

---

[32]*Orat*. 40:45 (PG 36:424B).
[33]The standard enumeration of Gregory's orations does not follow the chronological order in which, according to modern scholarship, they were delivered. Thus the Five Theological Orations, numbered as Orations 27 to 31, were given later in 380 than Orations 39 and 40. The accepted chronological order is that given by Gallay in his biography, based on the work of T. Sinko. J. Szmusiak has suggested the minor amendment that the first four Theological Orations were given during Lent 380, rather than in the summer and autumn.

is more concerned to safeguard the deity of Christ than to advance the understanding of his genuine humanity. Nevertheless, the humanity of Christ is an important part of the Nicene explanation for many of the Arian proof-texts.

Having dealt with the theological and logical quibbles of the Eunomians (1–6), and declared that it is from the 'divine words' he has 'learned to believe in and teach the deity of the Son', Gregory turns to Scripture. He lists eighteen christological titles implying deity, he contrasts these with twenty-two references which seem to imply that Christ is other than God, and he appeals to the standard Nicene hermeneutical rule, based on the bi-polar New Testament christology:

> In sum: you must predicate the more sublime expressions of the Godhead of the nature (φύσει) which transcends bodily experiences, and the lowlier ones of the compound (συνθέτῳ), of him who because of you was emptied, became incarnate and (to use equally valid language) was 'made man'.[34]

But even though the humanity is significant for the hermeneutical strategy, there is no thought here of human agency. The only subject is the divine Son. The incarnation is explained in Gregory's familiar Origenist terms:

> Through the medium of the mind he had dealing with the flesh, being made man, that god on earth. Man and God blended. They became a single whole, the stronger side predominating in order that I might be made God to the same extent that he was made man.[35]

Once again, the deity predominates. Gregory extends the rhetorical antitheses in detail through the earthly life, culminating in the climax of cross and resurrection:

> He is sold, and cheap was the price—thirty pieces of silver, yet he buys back the world at the mighty cost of his own blood. A sheep, he is led to the slaughter, yet he shepherds Israel and now the whole world as well. A lamb, he is

---

[34]*Orat.* 29:18 (PG 36:97C).
[35]*Orat.* 29:19 (PG 36:100A).

dumb, yet he is 'word', proclaimed by 'the voice of one
crying in the wilderness'. He is weakened, wounded, yet
he cures every disease and every weakness. He is brought
up to the tree and nailed to it, yet by the tree of life he
restores us... He surrenders his life, yet he has power to
take it again... He dies, but he vivifies, and by death
destroys death. He is buried, yet rises again. He goes down
to Hades, yet he leads souls up, ascends to heaven and will
come to judge the quick and the dead...[36]

The Fourth Theological Oration: Arian Proof Texts

In the Fourth Theological Oration, Gregory turns to deal in
more detail with scriptural texts which the Arians rely on
and which seem to present difficulties for his position. The
first is the old Arian proof-text, Proverbs 8:22, which Gregory tries to interpret (not at all convincingly to modern ears)
according to his hermeneutical rule: the 'begetting' refers to
his deity, the 'being created' to his humanity. He also deals
here with the identification of the Son with the 'servant' of
Isaiah (which to the Arians questioned his deity), employing
the 'wonderful exchange' as an explanation:

He was actually subject as a slave to flesh, to birth, and to
our human experiences; for our liberation, held captive as
we are by sin, he was subject to all that he saved.[37]

The second Arian proof-text is 1 Corinthians 15:25. Gregory
uses his logical training to show that this does not imply that
Christ's reign will end, only that salvation will be at one
point complete. Christ's subordination to the Father in this
passage is explained as a sharing in our subordination:

The one who releases me from the curse was called 'curse'
because of me. 'The one who takes away the world's sin'
was called 'sin' and is made a new Adam to replace the
old. In just this way too, as head of the whole body, he
appropriates my lack of submission. So long as I am an

---

[36]*Orat*. 29:20 (PG 36:101AB).
[37]*Orat*. 30:3 (PG 36:105C).

insubordinate rebel with passions which deny God, my lack of submission will be referred to Christ...[38]

Gregory continues to expound this further, clearly drawing on his christological theme of the substitutionary 'wondrous exchange'.

The third and fourth Arian proof-texts, taken together, are John 14:28, that the Father is 'greater' than the Son, and John 20:17, where Jesus refers to 'my God and your God'. Gregory's explanation is that 'greater' in John 14:28 must somehow be reconciled with 'equal' in Philippians 2:6, and argues according to his Trinitarian model that 'greater' refers to the Son's origination from the Father, but 'equal' refers to his sharing the same divine nature.[39] Once again, logic and his christological-trinitarian model are his weapons. 'My God' is spoken not by the Word in his deity, but by the *incarnate* Word, that is, in his humanity.

Fifthly, what the Word is said to receive in six different texts, he receives not as God, but in his humanity. Once again, the humanity of Christ explains texts which would otherwise call in question his deity. The sixth proof-text, John 5:19, 'The Son can do nothing of himself but only what he sees the Father doing', leads to a logical analysis of the meaning of 'can', that is, of different kinds of possibility and impossibility. Gregory selects the meaning of inconceivability: it is inconceivable that the Father and Son should not act in perfect concert.

The seventh is John 6:38, the Son's 'coming down from heaven not to do his own will, but the will of him who sent him'. Gregory links this with Matthew 26:39 (Luke 22:42), 'Father, if it be possible, let this cup pass from me; but not what I will—let thy will prevail'. He once again interprets the first text according to his Trinitarian doctrine: the Son who came down from heaven cannot be conceived to have a distinct will from the Father. But Gregory is also prepared to apply his christological rule here and to understand the second saying as the saying of the one who had genuinely become human. He carries through his

---

[38]*Orat.* 30:5 (PG 36:108C).
[39]*Cf., Orat.* 40:43 (PG 36:420B).

previously declared belief in the genuine human mind of Christ into a declaration of a genuine human will.[40]

The Arians' eighth argument is from John 17:3 in which it is said that God is 'the only true God' and Mark 10:18 (Luke 18:19) where God alone is said to be good. These do not pose serious difficulties, for if taken to exclude the Son, they would deny him even the status which the Arians attribute to him.

The ninth text, 'ever living to make intercession for us' (Heb. 7:25), is to be attributed to the continuing humanity of Christ. Gregory comments: 'Even at this moment he is, as man (ὡς ἄθρωπος), interceding for my salvation, until he makes me divine (ποιήσῃ θεὸν) by the power of his incarnate manhood'. Here is a clear attribution of human agency to the ascended Christ, still in the body, though no longer 'regarded according to the flesh'.

The tenth point is the ignorance of the Son indicated in Mark 13:32, 'No one except the Father knows the last day or hour, not even the Son himself'. Gregory's answer is strictly according to the rule, but heightens the paradox: 'He *does* know as God, but...as man, he does *not*'. Thirteen other texts are listed briefly, but present no problem to Gregory when the hermeneutical rule is applied: 'Expressions like these refer to the passible element and not the immutable nature transcending suffering'.

Having met these ten Arian proof-texts head on, Gregory now concludes his sermon with a more positive presentation of the deity and humanity of the Son from the christological titles. He begins with the names of God, reiterating the apophaticism of the Second Theological Oration. 'He Who Is' (ὁ ὤν) and 'God' (ὁ θεός) are 'in some special way names of his essence' (τῆς οὐσίας). Yet 'God' is 'a relational, not an absolute term' (τῶν πρός τι λεγωμένων ἐστί, καὶ οὐκ ἄφετος), as also is 'Lord'. God's other titles are put in two categories: those which belong to his power ('Almighty', 'King', 'Lord Sabaoth'), and those which belong to his providential ordering, such as 'God'. All of these titles of deity are shared by Father, Son, and Holy Spirit.

---

[40]Cf., Norris's Commentary in *Faith Gives Fullness to Reason*, 171f.

Gregory then turns finally to the Son's peculiar titles: 'Son', 'Only-begotten', 'Word', 'Wisdom', 'Power', 'Truth', 'Image', 'Light', 'Life', 'Righteousness', 'Sanctification', 'Redemption'. All of these he classifies as belonging to Christ 'on both levels, the transcendent and the human' (τοῦ τε ὑπὲρ ἡμᾶς καὶ δι' ἡμᾶς). He then lists those which belong to Christ as human: 'Man', 'Son of Man', 'Christ', 'the Way', 'the Door', 'Shepherd', 'Sheep', 'Lamb', 'High Priest' and 'Melchizedek'. Gregory restores some of the christological balance here by expanding a little on the humanity. He is called 'Man' not just because he became human that the invisible God might be visible to us,

but with the aim of hallowing Man through himself (ἵνα καὶ ἁγιάσῃ δι' ἑαυτοῦ τὸν ἄνθρωπον), by becoming a sort of yeast for the whole lump. He has united with himself all that lay under condemnation, in order to release it from condemnation. For all our sakes he became all that we are, sin apart—body, soul, mind, all that death pervades. The result is a man who, at the same time, is seen visibly, because spiritually discerned, as God.[41]

Here is the sanctifying assumption of sinful humanity so that in him it was sinless.

In connection with the title 'Christ', Gregory goes so far as to imply (in Antiochene fashion) that the Saviour is 'an anointed man', but quickly points out the difference. Unlike other men sanctified by the anointing of the Holy Spirit, we see here not simply the action (ἐνεργείᾳ), but the full abiding presence (παρουσίας) of the anointing deity in such a way that the Anointer is called 'Man' and that which is anointed (τὸ χριόμενον) is deified—made God (ποιῆσαι θεὸν).[42]

Gregory's peroration invokes the christological parabola, with its descent and ascent, its *kenōsis* and *theōsis*:

There you have the titles of the Son. Walk through them— those that are elevated, divinely, those that belong to the body, with a fellow feeling. Or rather, walk entirely divinely, that you may be deified (ἵνα γένῃ θεὸς), ascending from below on account of him who for our sakes descend-

---
[41]*Orat.* 30:21 (PG 36:132B).
[42]*Orat.* 30:21 (PG 36:132BC).

ed from on high. Above all and in everything, hold on to this and you will never go astray in either the loftier or lowlier names: 'Jesus Christ yesterday and today' in his incarnation and 'the same' spiritually for ever and ever. Amen.[43]

On the Words of the Gospel

On 24th November, 380, Theodosius arrived in the city. He evicted the Arians from the churches, and led Gregory in procession to the Church of the Holy Apostles. It was there some weeks later that he preached Oration 37, On the Words of the Gospel, 'When Jesus had Finished these Sayings', etc., an exposition of Matthew 19:1-12. The Oration begins with an extended passage on christology which includes this careful statement:

> What he was he laid aside: what he was not he assumed. Not that he became two, but he deigned to be one made out of the two. For both are God, that which assumed, and that which was assumed, two natures (δύο φύσεις) meeting in one, not two Sons.[44]

The condescension theme is strongly present in his comment on Matthew 19:2:

> If he had remained in his own eminence, if he had not condescended to infirmity, if he had remained what he was, keeping himself unapproachable and incomprehensible, a few perhaps would have followed—perhaps not even a few, possibly only Moses—and he only so far as with difficulty to see the back parts of God.... But inasmuch as he strips himself for us, inasmuch as he comes down (and I speak of an emptying, as it were, a laying aside and a diminution of his glory), he becomes by this comprehensible.[45]

---

[43]*Orat*. 30:21 (PG 36:133A).
[44]*Orat*. 37:2 (PG 36:284C-285A).
[45]*Orat*. 37:3 (PG 36:285B).

And once again, he goes on to make it clear that the passion of Christ is an inextricable part of the condescension.

Epilogue: Retirement

Gregory was recognized as Archbishop of Constantinople by the Ecumenical Council which met there in May 381 to re-establish the Nicene faith. His elevation went even further when he succeeded Meletius of Antioch as chairman of the council, but failing to reconcile the different factions, and having his position challenged by the newly arrived Egyptian delegation, he resigned from everything, preached a barn-storming sermon, Oration 42, The Last Farewell, to emperor, city and assembled bishops, and retired, free at last, to the family estates near Nazianzus.

Christology in the Later Orations and Poetry
One of his first acts on returning to Cappadocia was to preach an overdue panegyric on Basil which included a brief but striking statement of the humility and condescension shown in the passion of Christ. He is defending Basil, asking how it is possible to be filled with pride and yet,

> to know Christ, who condescended to the form of a slave, and ate with publicans, and washed the disciples' feet, and did not disdain the cross, in order to nail my sin to it; and more incredible still, to see God crucified (θεὸν σταυρούμενον).[46]

The final sermon in the collected *corpus*, Oration 45, The Second on Easter, repeats large sections of the Christmas Oration, and has some significant soteriological sentences rejecting the idea that the ransom of Christ's life was paid to Satan. Gregory is not sure either that it can be suitably said that God demanded a ransom, since he was not the one to whom we were in bondage. But he is prepared to say that the Father accepted Christ's sacrifice

---

[46]*Orat.* 43:64 (PG 36:581A).

on account of the Incarnation (τὴν οἰκονομίαν), and because
humanity must be sanctified by the humanity of God, that
he might deliver us himself and overcome the tyrant, and
draw us to himself by the mediation of his Son...[47]

The brazen serpent was not a type of Christ, he argues, but
of Death. So we say: 'O death, where is your sting? O grave,
where is your victory?' You are overthrown by the cross;
you are slain by him who is the Giver of Life. Later he adds:

> We needed an Incarnate God, a God put to death (θεοῦ
> σαρκουμένου καὶ νεκρουμένου), that we might live. We
> were put to death together with him, that we might be
> cleansed; we rose again because we were put to death with
> him; we were glorified with him because we rose again
> with him.[48]

Once again in this passage he speaks of 'God crucified (θεὸς
σταυρούμενος)'. Several of Gregory's poems, probably dating
from this final period of his life, are on christology,[49] but it
will be sufficient to turn to his Theological Letters in which
he takes up the problem of Apollinarianism.[50]

The Theological Letters

Three letters are grouped together as his 'Theological
Letters'. Two were written to Cledonius, the presbyter ad-
ministering the diocese of Nazianzus in his absence, and one
to Nectarius, his successor as Archbishop of Constantinople.
It is the second, Epistle 101, which is most valuable for its

---

[47]*Orat.* 45:22 (PG 36:653B).
[48]*Orat.* 45:28 (PG 36:661C).
[49]Translations of Carm. 1:1:2, On the Son (PG 37:401-408), and Carm.
1:1:11, On the Incarnation of Christ (PG 37:470-471) both appear in
John McGuckin, *St Gregory Nazianzen: Selected Poems* (Oxford: SLG
Press, 1986). A critical text of the former with a translation and commentary by D.A. Sykes appears in St Gregory of Nazianzus, *Poemata
Arcana*, ed. C. Moreschini (Oxford: Clarendon, 1997).
[50]*Cf.*, Paul Gallay (ed.), *Grégoire de Nazianze: Lettres Théologiques* (Paris:
Cerf, 1974) for Greek text and French translation. NPNF Vol. 7 includes
the English translation by C.G. Browne and J.E. Swallow, reproduced
in Hardy and Richardson.

constructive thought.[51] Whereas the Arian question had been raging for sixty years, and Gregory had done little more than express the standard Nicene arguments concisely and powerfully at the critical moment, the Apollinarian dispute was more recent and although Apollinarianism had been condemned, the arguments against it still had to be definitively formulated. In this significant and concise letter, Gregory did so, basing his new polemic once again on the christological parabola of the New Testament. Cledonius is not to allow the Apollinarians in Nazianzus to deceive themselves and to say that the Lord is 'without a human mind' (ἄνουν).

> For we do not sever the man from the deity, but we lay down as a dogma the unity and identity ἕνα καὶ τὸν αὐτὸν (ἕνα καὶ τὸν αὐτὸν) of the one who formerly was not man, who before all time was God and Son alone unmingled with body or anything corporeal, but who in these last days has also assumed humanity for our salvation…that the entire humanity (ὅλος ἄνθρωπος), fallen under sin, might be re-created by one who is fully human (ὅλῳ ἀνθρώπῳ) and at the same time God.

Gregory explains the christological implications carefully:

> If anyone introduce the notion of two Sons, the one from God as Father and the other from the mother, but not one and the same, may he lose his part in the sonship promised to those who truly believe! For God and man are two *natures* (φύσεις), just as there are simultaneously body and soul, but there are not two Sons or two Gods… For to speak concisely, the Saviour is of two 'whats' (ἄλλο μὲν καὶ ἄλλο), for the visible is not the same as the invisible nor the temporal as the timeless, but he is not two 'whos' (οὐκ ἄλλος δὲ καὶ ἄλλος). Never! For both are one by combina-

---

[51]Peter Bouteneff, in 'St Gregory Nazianzen and Two-Nature Christ-ology,' *St Vladimir's Theological Quarterly* 38 (1994) 255-270, calls it a Christological *tour de force*.

tion, the deity being humanized and the humanity being deified (or however one should express it).[52]

Here he has carefully accepted the increasingly favoured terminology of Antioch (the two 'natures') strongly opposed by the Alexandrians, while rejecting the dangerous Antiochene tendency to speak of 'two Sons'. He proceeds immediately to what D.F. Winslow describes as one of his most constructive and positive contributions, 'his application of what were Trinitarian categories to the formula of the twofold constitution of the God-man':[53]

> I say 'two "whats"' (ἄλλο καὶ ἄλλο) because this is the reverse of the case with the Trinity. For there we recognize different 'whos' (ἄλλος καὶ ἄλλος) in order to distinguish the *hypostases*. But we do not speak of different 'whats' (οὐκ ἄλλο δὲ καὶ ἄλλο), for the three are one and the same in deity.

A little later Gregory makes original use of another concept which was later to become important in Trinitarian theology. He writes of a *perichoresis* of the two natures (φύσεων), 'mingling and mutually indwelling each other (τῶν κλήσεων καὶ περιχωρουσῶν εἰς ἀλλήλας) according to the principle of their intimate union (συμφυΐας)'.[54]

This elaboration and refining of his christology brings him then to address the Apollinarian problem directly in the passage which includes his famous aphorism:

> If anyone has put his trust in him as a man without a human mind (ἄνουν), then he is himself really lacking a mind (ἀνόητος) and wholly unworthy of salvation. For the

---

[52]*Ep.* 101 (PG 37:177BC,180A). Elements of this translation are suggested by P. Bouteneff.

[53]Winslow, *Dynamics of Salvation*, 83

[54]*Ep.* 101 (PG 37:181C). Never in his orations does Gregory apply the term *perichôrêsis* to the hypostases of the Trinity. The idea, though not the word, is present however in the Fifth Theological Oration where he writes of 'one mingling of lights, as it were of three suns holding each other (ἐν ἡλίοις τρισὶν ἐχομένοις ἀλλήλων) (*Orat.* 31:14 (PG 36:149A)). Cf. V. Harrison, 'Perichoresis in the Greek Fathers,' *St Vladimir's Theological Quarterly* 35 (1991), 53-65.

unassumed is the unhealed (Τὸ γὰρ ἀπρόσληπτον, ἀθεράπ-ευτον), but that which is united to God, *that* is what is saved. If Adam only half fell, then only half is assumed and saved. But if the whole, then the whole must be united to the Begotten and so saved.[55]

For Gregory, the intellect is the most essential part of man, and if deity took the place of the human intellect in Christ, then we remain unaffected. The argument that two whole entities cannot be contained in the same space only applies to material entities. Moreover, by asserting that the Word could not assume a human mind, since the human mind was under condemnation, the Apollinarians are inconsistent. For by that reasoning, he could not assume our material, bodily existence either. If the purpose of the incarnation was only that humankind may come to know God through the veil of the physical flesh, such an incarnation devoid of human mind might suffice...

> But if it was that he might destroy the condemnation of sin by sanctifying like by like (τῷ ὁμοίῳ τὸ ὅμοιον ἁγιάσας) then as he needed flesh for the sake of the condemned flesh and soul for the sake of the condemned soul, so he also needed mind for the sake of mind which not only fell in Adam, but was the first to fall... For that which received the command was that which failed to keep the command, and that which failed to keep it was that which dared to transgress, and that which transgressed was that most in need of salvation, and that which needed salvation, *that* was what he took upon himself. Therefore he assumed the mind.[56]

It may well be asked: where exactly does this principle come from? The question is not so much an historical one: who was first to formulate it? Rather, it is a theological question about its basis and validity, for, after all, Gregory's famous aphorism (or Tertullian's) is not found in canonical script-

---

[55]*Ep.* 101 (PG 37:181C-184A).Winslow notes (*Dynamics of Salvation*, 81f.) that the dictum *quod assumptum non est non sanatum* appears in Tertullian, *De Carne Christi* 10, and Origen, *Dial. c. Heracl.* 6:20-7:5 and refers to A. Grillmeier, 'Quod non est assumptum,' *Lexicon für Theologie und Kirche*, 8:954-956.

[56]*Ep.* 101 (PG 37:188B).

ure. But then, neither is there an explicit statement of the
principle that the Saviour had to be fully God in order to
save us. Undoubtedly, the New Testament explicitly affirms
both the humanity and the deity of the Saviour. In addition,
it is asserted widely throughout Old and New Testaments,
that it is God himself who saves, while the christology of
Hebrews clearly asserts that Christ's humanity is *soteriologically necessary*—necessary in order to save us.[57]

Gregory's answer would undoubtedly be that in
addition both principles are inescapably *implied* in the New
Testament as a whole. He would point to the bi-polar motif
of cross and resurrection, dying and rising, sown in weakness—raised in power, humiliation and exaltation, descent
and ascent, Son of David according to the flesh, declared Son
of God according to the Spirit by his resurrection. He would
describe it as *kenōsis* and *theōsis*. This bi-polar or parabolic
pattern he would present as the very shape and movement
of the Christi-an gospel, a movement with which we must
identify in faith and experience if we are to share in the
salvation of Christ. He would see it as the substitutionary
'wondrous exchange', God the Son becoming what we are in
order that we might become what he is and share in his
unique relationship of sonship with the Father. He would
maintain, that in order to be the movement of reconciliation
between God and dying humanity, it had to begin precisely
with God. It had to be a movement of God *himself* from his
eternal glory. And he had to come all the way and identify
himself *fully* with dying humanity to the ultimate extent of
becoming himself a dying man. Unless he who was in the
form (or nature) of God genuinely took the form (or nature)
of enslaved humanity—*fully*—we are not saved.

To Gregory, the heretics were logic-chopping 'tech-
nicians' whose analytical way of thinking and hermeneutical
quibbling simply destroyed the faith. His opposition to
Arianism, the denial of the Lord's full deity, and his opposition to Apollinarianism, that brilliant and subtle hypothesis
which thought it secured the unity of his person by compromising his full humanity, were both based in his intuitive
grasp of the unity and coherence of biblical christology.

---

[57] See, for example, Hebrews 2:14-18 and 4:14-16.

Chapter 2

ATTITUDES TOWARDS JEWS IN PATRISTIC COMMENTARIES ON ROMANS

Gerald Bray

Introduction

It is now more or less accepted as a fact that most of the Fathers of the Church were anti-Jewish, if not anti-Semitic in the later, racist sense.[1] Polemical works directed against Jews and Jewish beliefs, as well as any number of isolated comments, can be cited to support this assertion, and the charge is often made that after the legalization of Christianity in the fourth century this hostile attitude hardened into open discrimination against the Jews as a nation, and not simply as a religious group. That this development had a theological and not a racial motivation is not denied, but from the standpoint of most modern scholars that scarcely improves matters. For them, if Christianity is supposed to be a religion grounded in love, it is hard to see how one of its results could have been persecution, particularly when the victims

---

[1]See *e.g.*, L.M. McDonald, 'Anti-Judaism in the Early Church Fathers' in C.A. Evans and D.A. Hagner (eds.), *Anti-Semitism and Early Christianity. Issues of Polemic and Faith* (Minneapolis: Fortress Press, 1993) 215-52.

were members of the parent faith. This apparent paradox has
troubled many modern Christians, who cannot forget the
horrors of the Holocaust, with the result that it is now very
difficult for us to read the writings of earlier times without
reacting to any and every sign of possible anti-Semitism. We
almost inevitably see any criticism of Judaism as at least
potentially 'anti-Semitic,' even if it seems obvious that if the
first Christians had not rejected their Jewish inheritance to
some degree, there would have been no Christianity (in the
sense that we understand it) at all. For whether we like it or
not, it was the relegation of the Mosaic law to a secondary
status, and the concomitant admission of Gentiles into the
Christian fellowship without forcing them to become Jews
first, which created the great caesura between the synagogue
and the Church, a process which we can see happening in
the pages of the New Testament.

Judging from the work which has already been done
on this subject, it seems that our appreciation of patristic
'anti-Judaism' may be seriously affected by the method we
adopt in investigating it. There is no shortage of patristic
material, but if we concentrate on tracts written against the
Jews, or take isolated anti-Jewish statements out of context, it
is obvious that we can build up a case for the predominance
of anti-Judaism among the early Christians, without really
determining whether this is a true reflection of patristic
opinion or not. What is required for a balanced approach to
the subject, is that we should examine material which is both
representative of patristic opinion and directed to the issue
concerned, without being obviously polemical. Perhaps the
best way of doing this is to look at how the Fathers read
what the New Testament has to say on this subject, and the
most obvious place to turn is to their commentaries on Paul's
epistle to the Romans. For a start, a large number of these
commentaries has survived, and they represent a wide range
of patristic opinion, even if some of the Fathers (and notably
Augustine) are only partially represented. Secondly, Romans
is clearly about Jewish-Gentile relations in the nascent
Church, and contains many passages which could be read in
an 'anti-Jewish' way if the commentator were so inclined.
Thirdly, Paul's remarks about Jews are balanced by his
approach towards Gentiles, all of whom must be regarded as

ex-pagans, and we can therefore compare what the Fathers had to say about them with what they wrote about Jews. For if it appears that they attacked pagans with as much (or more) vehemence than they attacked Jews, it will be difficult to sustain a charge of 'anti-Judaism,' and impossible to claim that they were 'anti-Semitic' in a racial sense. Lastly, a commentary on Romans has by its very nature to deal with the whole range of Jewish issues, including both their claim to be descended from Abraham (and therefore to be the inheritors of the promises God made to him) and the place and interpretation of the Mosaic law. Nowhere else do we find such an ideal background for assessing the Fathers' general attitudes and approach towards the Jews, and it is these that we propose to examine here.

The commentaries which have survived more or less intact are listed as follows. Pride of place must go to Origen (c. 185–c. 254), whose fifteen original books were abridged into a mere ten by Rufinus (c. 400) and translated into Latin.[2] From the evidence of the surviving Greek fragments it appears that although Rufinus occasionally added his own comments, he did not substantially alter Origen's views or approach. Next there is the massive Latin work of the unknown Ambrosiaster (c. 366–84) which remains a monument of careful biblical commentary and which can stand comparison with modern scholarship.[3] Then we have an anonymous Latin commentary from c. 400, which may have been composed by Constantius of Aquileia,[4] and which was used heavily by Pelagius, whose own commentary has also survived.[5] On the Greek side, we can point to commentaries by

---

[2]T. Heither (ed.), *Commentarii in epistulam ad Romanos*, 5 vols., (Freiburg im Breisgau: Herder, 1990-5).

[3]H.J. Vogels (ed.), *Ambrosiastri qui dicitur commentarius in epistulas Paulinas*, Corpus Scriptorum Ecclesiasticorum Latinorum 81.1 (Wien: Hoelder-Pichler-Tempsky, 1966).

[4]H.J. Frede (ed.), *Ein neuer Paulustext und Kommentar*, (Freiburg im Breisgau: Herder, 1974).

[5]A. Souter (ed.), *Pelagius' expositions of thirteen epistles of St Paul*, Texts and Studies 9.1–3 (Cambridge: University Press, 1922-31). The commentary has recently been translated into English by M. De Bruyn, *Pelagius' commentary on Romans*, (Oxford: University Press, 1993).

Cyril of Alexandria[6] and Theodoret of Cyrus (Cyrrhus),[7] which have survived in full, as well as the substantial fragments of Theodore of Mopsuestia,[8] which enable us to gain a reasonable impression of his views. Then there are the thirty-two homilies of John Chrysostom, which constitute a commentary of their own.[9] as well as the *Propositions* of Augustine, which stand in lieu of a proper commentary.[10] They have to be used with some caution, partly because of their fragmentary character and partly because they date from an early, pre-Pelagian phase of Augustine's career. Augustine did embark on an extended commentary of Romans, but he never got beyond the first seven verses, and so it must rank as one of the great unwritten books of antiquity. Nevertheless, what we do have is sufficiently rich and diverse, and comes from a broad enough range of sources, that we can safely say that we have access to what may fairly be called 'mainline' patristic opinion on this key question. The fact that they have never been systematically studied—many of them remain untranslated—merely serves to remind us of how urgent the task of reading and evaluating them is.

The covenant with Abraham and the Law of Moses

The best place to begin is with Ambrosiaster's prologue to the epistle as a whole. Most of the Fathers introduced their commentaries with a prologue, but only Ambrosiaster goes into this particular issue in any detail. He writes:

---

[6] PG 74:773-856.

[7] PG 82:43-226.

[8] K. Staab (ed.), *Pauluskommentare aus der griechischen Kirche: Aus Katenenhandschriften gesammelt und herausgegeben*, NT Abhandlungen 15, (Münster in Westfalen: Aschendorff, 1933) 113-72.

[9] PG 60:391-682. An English translation is available in P. Schaff (ed.), *A select library of the Nicene and post-Nicene fathers of the Christian church*, (Buffalo, NY: Christian Literature Company, 1886-90), Vol. 11, pp. 329-564.

[10] PL 35:2063-88. Edited and translated by P.F. Landes, *Augustine on Romans*, (Chico, CA: Scholars Press, 1982).

> '...because they [i.e. the Jews] rejected the Law which had been given to them, God preferred the Greeks to the Jews...when the Jews believed in Christ, they left the orbit of the Law and the prophets and became like the Gentiles, so that now both peoples depend on the mercy of God, hoping for their salvation not through the Law, but through faith in Jesus Christ'.

Ambrosiaster's argument has two aspects to it. On the one hand, the Jews have been rejected because of their own rejection of God's Law, and the 'Greeks' have been preferred instead. On the other hand, those Jews who believed in Christ have been united with the Gentiles, and both peoples now find their common salvation in him. The key to understanding Ambrosiaster lies in his use of the words 'Greek' and 'Gentile.' The former was essentially a religious term, referring primarily to a devotee of the Olympian gods but extendible in a more general sense to cover everyone whom we would normally call 'pagan' (a word which was not then used in this sense).[11] 'Gentile,' on the other hand, was an ethnic term, referring to all those who were not Jews by birth. Jewish Christians were not integrated with pagan 'Greeks' but with Christian Gentiles—a wholly different category. The bond of unity between different nations is faith in Christ, which has broken down the barriers which previously existed. Ambrosiaster uses the word 'Jew' in both senses because, then as now, Judaism was an ethnic religion, but it is clear that his negative remarks apply to the religion only. Once conversion occurred, purely ethnic differences ceased to amount to anything. This stands in sharp contrast to modern anti-Semitism, which has been easily extended to cover such figures as Benjamin Disraeli and Karl Marx, even though both men were descendants of Jewish converts to Christianity, and had never been practising Jews themselves.

---

[11]Ambrosiaster knew, however, that the apostle Paul used the word 'Greek' in this wider sense, and remarks on it in his commentary on Rom. 1:16. The use of 'Greek' to mean what we would call 'pagan' only became common after the legalization of Christianity in AD 313. Greek Christians were happy to call themselves 'Romans' but not 'Hellenes,' which to them had an inescapably religious connotation.

In Romans 2:9-10 that we come to a direct comparison between Jews and 'Greeks,' a word which is clearly used here as the equivalent of 'Gentiles,' (since they would all have been ex-pagans), and the Fathers were unanimous in concluding that Paul's reference applied primarily to the two peoples *before* the coming of Christ. Among both there were some who did what is right, either because (as Jews) they managed to obey the Law, or because (as Gentiles) they were a law unto them-selves and lived up to their own principles. Such people were certainly rare, but Chrysostom manages to name a few among the Gentiles—Melchizedek, Job, the repentant Ninevites and Cornelius the centurion, for example. Nevertheless, the Fathers did not dispute the priority which the apostle gave to the Jews, because they recognized the superiority of their position. To quote Ambrosiaster: 'Paul always puts the Jew first, whether he is to be praised or blamed, because of his privileged ancestry. If he believes he will be all the more honoured, because of Abraham, but if he doubts he will be treated all the worse, because he has rejected the gift promised to his forefathers'. This may be regarded as typical of the patristic approach. Far from being discriminated against, the Jews had a special place in the plan of God. But as always, much is required from those to whom much has been given. This is why the condemnation of the Jews is greater—it is not because they are inherently inferior, but the very opposite!

The real thrust of Paul's argument was summed up by Pelagius as follows: 'Paul puts Jews and Gentiles on the same level when he says that doers, rather than hearers, of the Law are righteous...'.[12] In the end there was no difference between the two, and the Jews were wrong to boast of their special heritage. God's primary concern was with obedience, and every human being would be judged according to the light given to him. In practice, this meant that Jews would have a harder time because they had been given a greater degree of light—a privilege with a catch to it, if ever there was one! The picture portrayed here is hardly flattering to the Jews, but neither can it be called discrimin-atory or hostile to them. The whole emphasis is put on Jewish-Gentile

---

[12]Commentary on Rom. 2:12.

equality, both as sinners and as believers. The spiritual emphasis of Christianity abolished the outward distinctions which the Law had introduced and perpetuated, so that all could compete on an equal basis.

When we get to Romans 2:17 a new note is sounded. The apostle Paul introduces the next phase of his argument with the words: '...if you call yourself a Jew...'. The Fathers were not slow to pick up on the meaning of this. Origen, for example, says:

> 'The first thing to notice here is that Paul does not say that the person he is rhetorically addressing is a Jew; only that he calls himself one, which is not at all the same thing. For Paul goes on to teach that the true Jew is the one who is circumcised in secret, i.e. in the heart, who keeps the Law in spirit and not according to the letter...the man who is circumcised visibly in the flesh, observing the Law in order to be seen by men, is not a real Jew; such a man only appears to be one.'

So those who observe the outward forms of Judaism, but do not live up to the spiritual principles which these outward forms represent, are not authentic Jews at all. This assertion immediately changes the parameters of 'anti-Judaism'. If Origen's statement is taken at face value, his condemnation is of hypocrites, not Jews. Obviously this distinction would have been easily lost on a Jew who lived after the time of Christ and had not been converted, but it should not be discounted for that reason. Origen was prepared to admit that there could be post-resurrection Jews who lived a righteous life without believing in Christ, because he wrote:

> 'It may happen that among those who are still under the Law, there will be someone who, because of pressure from his family and friends, has not believed in Christ, but nevertheless does what is good, upholds righteousness, loves mercy, preserves chastity and continence, guards modesty and meekness, and does every good work'.[13]

---

[13]Commentary on Rom. 2:10.

Such a person would not have enjoyed the gift of eternal life, which only Christ could bestow, but neither was he condemned out of hand. Origen, at least, was prepared to accept that God's judgement would continue to be based on the inner disposition of the heart, a criterion which might spare even the Jew who had apparently rejected Christ.

But it is in the final verses of Romans 2 that Paul lets fly at Jewish hypocrisy, and it is here that we would expect to discover the fathers, if they were so inclined, to add to the apostle's attacks by heaping up criticisms of their own. But what do we actually find? Almost invariably, the Fathers do no more than repeat what Paul said, and point out that the accusation originally came from the prophet Isaiah (52:5). Thus there is no way that it could be regarded as anti-Jewish or anti-Semitic, and the restraint of the Fathers in this respect is truly remarkable. The worst that is said about them is a comment of Ambrosiaster on Romans 2:22. He claims that: 'the Jew adulterates the Law by removing the truth of Christ from it and putting lies in his place.' Not a flattering comment, to be sure, but not a sign of deep-seated anti-Judaism. In any case, Ambrosiaster's remark was obviously an allegorization of what Paul was saying, and none of the other Fathers seems to have picked it up. Did they simply miss an opportunity to vent their anti-Semitism, or is it more likely that they had no such feelings, and were concerned to do no more than reflect what the apostle and the prophet before him so clearly said about their own people? The answer must surely be obvious—the Fathers were not anti-Jewish as such, and may even have felt a bit embarrassed by the trenchant criticisms levelled against the Jews by Paul and Isaiah, whose remarks they repeat, but with little or no embellishment.

This impression is confirmed when we look at what the Fathers had to say about the first part of chapter 3. Here Paul tells us why the Jews are a special people, and what the advantage is that they have. Just as the Fathers did no more than repeat the apostle's criticisms at the end of chapter 2, so now they do little more than echo his praises of the Jews. Pelagius, for example, writes simply, 'The Jews were at an advantage because the oracles of God were entrusted to them, while nothing was entrusted to the Gentiles'.[14] It is true that this did cause problems for some Christians, who could not understand why the Jews should have been entrusted with God's Word, but Chrysostom tackled them head on. As he wrote:

> 'What does "entrusted" mean? It means that the Jews had the Law put into their hands because God thought so highly of them that he entrusted them with oracles which came down from on high. I know that some people take the "entrusted" not of the Jews, but of the oracles, as if to say; "The Law was believed in." But the context does not allow this interpretation.'

Chrysostom then went on to add that the apostle said all this in order to accuse the Jews of ingratitude for the blessings they had received, but that is another matter. If there were people in the Church who thought that Jews were not suitable people to receive God's revelation to begin with, Chrysostom's remarks would certainly have put them in their place.

The patristic attitude is perhaps best summed up by Origen, when he wrote:

> '...it must be understood that these things are being said about Moses, the prophets and others like them, to whom the oracles of God were entrusted, because there can be no doubt that they were Jews, and that they had the circumcision. It would also apply to anyone who was wise, who was an intelligent listener, or who was a gifted counsellor—all of whom the Lord is said to have removed from Jerusalem because he was offended by the ungodliness of the people (cf. Isa. 3:1-3)... Even the apostles of Christ, and Paul himself, the vessel of election, came from the Jews and from the circumcision, and he had far more in every way than those whom he taught who were of the gentiles. For the oracles of God were entrusted to the Jews'.

The Jews missed out on God's promises because of their unbelief, not because of any racial or religious defect. Those

---

[14]Commentary on Rom. 3:2.

who did believe in Christ were fully accepted, and even honoured. As Ambrosiaster remarks:

> 'The Jews who did not believe excluded themselves from consideration, without doing the rest any harm. Paul commends Jewish believers, because it was not their fault that many of their kinsmen refused to believe'.[15]

It is true that by the fourth century, Jewish converts were a rarity, and therefore it would have been easy to assume that all Jews were automatically unbelievers, but even if there are indications that this identification was happening, it must not be pressed too far. The principle that belief in Christ was what mattered, not race or religious background, was clearly maintained by all the Fathers, and there is no indication that any of them regarded *unbelieving* Gentiles as superior to Jews—quite the reverse in fact! Later on in chapter 3, when Paul once again quotes the Old Testament in his denunciation of the Jews, the Fathers invariably universalized the context, to include the entire human race in the entail of original sin. As Chrysostom says:

> 'When Paul talks about every mouth being stopped, he does not mean that the purpose of the Jews' sinning was to shut them up, but that the reason they were rebuked was that they might not sin in ignorance. Furthermore, it was not just the Jews he was referring to, but the whole of mankind.'[16]

The whole emphasis is on demonstrating that Jews and Gentiles are equal in the sight of God, not that Jews are somehow inferior. Christ came as the Saviour of all men everywhere—to the Jews first, because of their special heritage, but to the Gentiles as well. The only difference is that the Jews should have believed but many of them did not, whereas the Gentiles had no reason to believe, although many of them did. It is to that extent, but no farther, that the Fathers might be regarded as 'anti-Jewish.' Pelagius summed it up perhaps best of all when he says:

---

[15]Commentary on Rom. 3:3.
[16]Commentary on Rom. 3:19.

'Did God create only the Jews, or is he exclusively concerned with them? For if the Gentiles sinned, so too did the Jews, and if the Jews repent, so too do the Gentiles. If Christ came to the Jews as promised by the Law, he came to the Gentiles also... Paul adds "also" so as not to appear to be excluding the Jews.'[17]

When, in chapter 4, Paul goes on to argue that Abraham was justified by faith, and not because he was circumcised, the Church Fathers obviously followed his logic, and accepted the premise that the true descendant of Abraham is the person who believes as Abraham believed, and not the one who can prove a physical descent through the sign of circumcision. It is certain that many Jews found this attitude offensive, but that it not the same thing as saying that the Fathers were being 'anti-Jewish' when they followed the apostle in this, for to them circumcision was neither here nor there. At no time did they discriminate against a man simply because he was circumcised, nor did they even suggest that it would be better for Jewish Christians to forgo the ritual altogether. As far as they were concerned, the whole issue was simply irrelevant, and they did not pursue it one way or the other. If it is true that they turned away from Judaism, it is also true that they did so because they believed that Christ had made the Law of Moses obsolete, not because they had any prejudice against Jews, whom they were fully prepared to acknowledge as the historically chosen people of God.

The unbelief and ultimate fate of the Jews

It is of course in Romans 9–11 that Paul turns his full attention to the Jewish people and their destiny, and it is in the patristic commentaries on these chapters that we are likely to find whatever evidence there may be of the Fathers' 'anti-Judaism'. Much of the earlier discussion was taken up with Abraham, Moses and the Law, and it is clear that the Fathers made a distinction between those Jews who lived before the coming of Christ and their own contemporaries. In these chapters however, the apostle turns his attention to Jews

---

[17]Commentary on Rom. 3:29.

after the coming of Christ, and examines what has happened to them as a consequence of their rejection of the Messiah. He begins by assuring his readers that he would wish to be cursed himself, if that would contribute to the salvation of the Jews. The Fathers all recognized that Paul was saying this in order to demonstrate the great love which he had for his people, though they were troubled by the extremes to which he took this. Pelagius even went so far as to say that Paul was referring to the zeal for the Jewish nation which he had shown before his conversion, but which he had since abandoned.[18] However, this interpretation is eccentric, and it was not followed by anyone else. Far more typical are the remarks of Ambrosiaster: '

> Paul lists so many indications of the nobility and dignity of the Jewish people and of the promises they received, in order to deepen his grief for all these things, because by not accepting the Saviour they lost the privilege of their fathers and the merit of the promises, and they became worse than the Gentiles... For it is a worse evil to lose a dignity than never to have had it.'[19]

In other words, Jews have sunk to the same level as Gentiles, which they should never have done because they knew better. Once again we see that they are not really being singled out for special condemnation—the end result is that they are in the same boat as the Gentiles, not worse off. Admittedly, it is not a pleasant place to be, but nobody can seriously maintain that Jews were being discriminated against, or that the Fathers had anything against them which did not apply equally well to unbelieving Gentiles.

The same principles are worked out in detail in the commentaries on the subsequent verses. The Fathers repeat what the apostle Paul has to say about the special character of the covenant promise made to Abraham. It was not given to all the patriarch's descendants, but only to those who had

---

[18]Commentary on Rom. 9:3: 'Paul wished this at one time, before he became a follower of Christ... But after he recognized the truth, he abandoned those whom he used to love in this way, yet still they do not repent.'
[19]Commentary on Rom. 9:5.

been chosen in Isaac, Abraham's faith child. The Christological implications of this were made clear by Ambrosiaster
when he commented: 'Abraham believed and received Isaac
on account of his faith, because he believed in God. By this
the mystery of the future faith was indicated, that they
would be brothers of Isaac who had the same faith by which
Isaac was born, because Isaac was born as a type of the
Saviour by the promise. Thus whoever believes that Christ
Jesus was promised to Abraham is a child of Abraham and a
brother of Isaac. Abraham was told that all the nations
would be blessed in his offspring. This did not happen in
Isaac, but in him who was promised to Abraham in Isaac,
that is Christ, in whom all the nations are blessed when they
believe. Therefore the other Jews [i.e., the unbelieving ones]
are children of the flesh because they are deprived of the
promise and cannot claim Abraham's merit, because they do
not follow the faith by which Abraham is counted worthy.'[20]
And as Pelagius put it: 'Not all Jews are children of Abraham, *but some still are...*,'[21] which is as clear an indication as
one could want that the Jews as a race had not been entirely
rejected, nor had Christians any reason to discriminate
against them on essentially racial grounds.

When we move on to the story of Esau and Jacob
things become more complicated, because here we see that it
was possible for God to reject one twin in favour of the
other, even when to the human eye there was no apparent
reason for doing so. The Fathers regarded Esau and Jacob as
types representing unbelievers and believers, and believed
that both were to be found in the same nation. This meant
that there were both unbelieving Jews and believing
Gentiles—an apparent contradiction which nevertheless had
ancient origins. As Ambrosiaster said; 'There is no doubt
that there are many unbelieving children of Jacob, for all the
Jews, whether they are believers or unbelievers, have their
origin in him. And that there are good and faithful children
of Esau is proved by the example of Job, who was a descendant of Esau, five generations away from Abraham, and there-

---

[20]Commentary on Rom. 9:7.
[21]Commentary on Rom. 9:7.

fore Esau's grandson.'[22] As always, it is faith (or the lack of
it) which is determinative, not any form of physical or racial
descent.

At this point Paul's argument takes a new turn, and
the Fathers follow him in it. Belief in Christ was not
ultimately a matter of personal choice. God had predestined
some for faith but not others, and the line between them was
drawn straight across what was really only a human (and
therefore a temporal, even an artificial) separation between
Jews and Gentiles. It is possible that the truth of who was
and who was not elect was more quickly perceived among
the Jews, since Christ had come to them, but the principle
remained valid for the entire human race. Ambrosiaster
expressed this well when he wrote:

> 'Paul restricts his grief to the fact that he discovered that it
> was long ago predicted that not all would believe, and he
> only grieves for them because they refused to believe out of
> jealousy. They had the opportunity however, as Paul
> demonstrates. At the same time, there was no point in
> grieving over those who were not predestined to eternal
> life, for God's foreknowledge had long ago decreed that
> they would not be saved. For who would cry over someone
> who is long dead? When the Gentiles appeared and
> accepted the salvation which the Jews had lost, Paul's grief
> was stirred, but this was mainly because the Jews were the
> cause of their own damnation.'[23]

But not all of the Fathers supposed that the rejection of the
Jews was meant to be permanent. Theodoret of Cyrus, commenting on Paul's quotation of Hosea 2:23, has this to say:

> 'This passage originally applied to Jews, not to Gentiles...
> It meant that God's people would lose their status and be
> called "Not my people" and "Not beloved." But then God
> promised that the rejected Jews would be called back

---

[22]Commentary on Rom. 9:10. Job's genealogy is somewhat fanciful, but
not entirely, since the land of Uz, where he came from, has been
identified with Edom, which is where Esau eventually went. In any
case, Ambrosiaster's point remains valid.
[23]Commentary on Rom. 9:13.

again. Thus, from having been God's people and then been rejected, they would return...'[24]

The same themes recur time and again in these chapters. Commenting on Romans 10:1, Ambrosiaster remarks: 'Since Paul wants to liberate the Jews from the Law, which is a veil over their faces, but does not want to appear to desire this out of any hatred for Judaism, he shows his love for them and says many good things about the Law.' Similarly, talking about the same passage, Chrysostom has this to say: 'Paul continues to demonstrate his deep-seated good will towards the Jews... He even does his best to find excuses for them, but in the end he is overcome by the facts and cannot do so.' And Augustine comments: 'Here Paul begins to speak of his hope for the Jews, lest the Gentiles in their turn become con-descending towards them. For just as the pride of the Jews had to be countered, because they gloried in their works, so also with the Gentiles, lest they become proud at having been preferred over the Jews.'[25] None of this excused the Jews from their failure to believe in Christ, and as Chrysostom goes on to say, Paul's apparent leniency towards them was leading to an even greater accusation against them.[26] But once again, the problem is unbelief, and it applies equally to the Gentiles, so that charges of anti-Judaism cannot really be sustained. As Ambrosiaster put it so clearly in his commentary on Romans 10:12:

> 'Neither the privileges of their ancestors nor the Law can do the Jews any good if they do not accept the merit and promise made to them. Neither do the Gentiles have anything to boast about in the flesh, if they do not believe in Christ.'

Coming to chapter 11 and the question of the final rejection of the Jews, the Fathers once again echoed the basically positive note sounded by the apostle Paul. Commenting on

---

[24]Commentary on Rom. 9:25.

[25]*Pr.* 66.

[26]Comment on Rom. 10:3: 'It was from small-mindedness and a desire for power that they erred, rather than from ignorance, and even their own righteousness was not based on keeping the Law.'

the first verse, Chrysostom says: 'God has not rejected his people, because Paul himself was one of them. If God had cast them off, he would not have chosen one of them as the one to whom he entrusted all his preaching, the affairs of the world, all the mysteries and the whole message of salvation.' Pelagius, commenting on the same verse, says; 'Because Paul had by this point humbled them far enough, he now encourages the Jews in the way a good teacher would, so as not to provoke them unduly. God has not rejected everyone, and not for ever, but only those who do not believe, as long as they do not believe. Paul reminds them that if God had rejected all the Jews, he too would have been rejected.'

A little further on, when commenting on Romans 11:11, Augustine has this to say:

> 'The Jews did not sin only to fall as a punishment, but so that their fall might serve the salvation of the Gentiles. Paul even begins to praise the Jewish people for this fall of unbelief, in order that the Gentiles should not become proud, seeing that the fall of the Jews was so important for their own salvation. On the contrary, the Gentiles ought to be all the more careful, lest they too should grow proud and fall also.'[27]

And Pelagius, commenting on the same verse, says:

> 'The Jews have not fallen away completely and beyond hope. God loved them so much that the Gentiles were called for their salvation, so that when the Jews saw that the Gentiles were being allowed into the kingdom of God, they might perhaps repent more easily.'

And Chrysostom, on the next verse, says: 'Paul is consoling the Jews in their distress, giving them reason to be confident of their salvation if they were to change.' And lastly, Ambrosiaster adds:

> 'However seriously the Jews may have sinned by rejecting the gift of God, and however worthy they may be of death, nevertheless, because they are the children of good people,

---

[27] Pr. 70.

whose privileges and many benefits from God they have received, they will be received with joy when they return to the faith, because God's love for them is stirred up by the memory of their ancestors.'

These remarks speak for themselves. The Fathers of the Church, like the apostle Paul before them, accused the Jews of having fallen through unbelief, and held out the hope that if they were to repent they would be saved, and restored to the honour and privileges which had been promised to their ancestors. This restoration would not leave Gentiles out in the cold—in the new dispensation of God's grace all the elect, both Jews and Gentiles, would share together in the inheritance of the kingdom of Christ.

Conclusion

Our survey of the major patristic commentaries on Romans has demonstrated a remarkably consistent approach to the question of Jews and Judaism. Like the apostle Paul, the Church Fathers saw the Jews primarily in terms of their belief or unbelief in Christ. They recognized that he had been sent to the Jewish people in fulfilment of the promises made to Abraham and his descendants, but that his coming had divided them. Jews who accepted Christ (a minority of the whole, but a not insubstantial one at the beginning) were saved by their faith in him, not by their Jewish ancestry or their obedience to the Law of Moses. In this respect, they were on exactly the same footing as the Gentiles and formed one new people with them. Jews who did not believe in Christ were guilty of rejecting the Messiah, and therefore they forfeited the promises which had been given to Abraham. The rejection of these Jews had a saving purpose however, because it opened the door to gentile converts. Eventually though, God would return to his people Israel and restore them to the place originally intended for them. That alone must surely prove that the Fathers were not 'anti-Semitic' in the modern sense of the term.

Whether they could be called 'anti-Jewish' though is more difficult. If that term is taken to mean that they were opposed to Judaism as a religion, then of course they were anti-Jewish. They believed, just as the apostles did, that the validity of Judaism as a religion had come to an end with the death and resurrection of Christ. This was not an 'anti-Jewish' stance in the historical sense, because Christ's mission and ministry was the fulfilment of Judaism and not a condemnation of it. Jews who refused to accept Christ were condemned for their blindness and their hardness of heart, which was particularly culpable because they should have known better. Once again, the Fathers would not have understood this as being anti-Jewish; they sincerely believed that the Jews had missed the boat by their rejection of Christ, and wanted them to see the error of their ways and repent. It is possible to interpret their attitude towards the Jews as one of rivalry for the right to Abraham's inheritance, and rivalry is known to produce a certain hostility, but even that is probably going too far. Their main concern seems to have been to demonstrate why it was not good enough for Jews to go on being Jews in the religious sense, and why it was not necessary for Gentiles to accept the religious claims of Judaism, even if those claims had once been the will of God.

Modern scholars who accuse the Fathers of anti-Judaism generally appear to do so because they believe that Christians should tolerate Jews and accept the idea that Judaism is a valid religion, even after the coming of Christ. In the light of events such as the Holocaust, such an attitude is comprehensible, but the Fathers of the Church would want to ask us whether it is really faithful to the teaching of the New Testament. Christianity would not have emerged as a distinct religion if it had found traditional Judaism satisfactory, and the mere existence of a Christian church is statement that somehow Judaism is not good enough. To any Christian, the centrality of Christ is so important that it is impossible to agree that those who reject him, even if they have some claim to be called God's people, have a faith of equal validity. It may be a hard pill to swallow, but the Fathers of the Church had a better understanding of the true nature of the Gospel than those who would regard Judaism as an acceptable alternative to it.

Chapter 3

THE SOURCES OF CALVIN'S CITATIONS IN HIS GENESIS COMMENTARY

Anthony N. S. Lane

Introduction

This is a very appropriate topic for an essay dedicated to David Wright. For many years he had an interest in the relation between the Reformers and the Fathers and we have participated together in the international symposia that have taken place to discuss this theme.[1] David also has a deep interest in Calvin's Old Testament commentaries, being Editor in Chief of the new Rutherford House Translation.[2] A

---

[1] L. Grane, A. Schindler, M. Wriedt(edd.), *Auctoritas Patrum. Contributions on the Reception of the Church Fathers in the 15th and 16th Century* (Veröffentlichungen des Instituts für Europäische Geschichte Mainz im Auftrag, Abteilung Religionsgeschichte (hrsg. R. Decot) Beiheft 37) (Mainz: Philipp von Zabern, 1993); L. Grane, A. Schindler, M. Wriedt (edd.), *Auctoritas Patrum II. New Contributions on the Reception of the Church Fathers in the 15th and 16th Century* (Veröffentlichungen des Instituts für Europäische Geschichte Mainz im Auftrag, Abteilung Religionsgeschichte (hrsg. R. Decot)) (Mainz: Philipp von Zabern, 1997).

[2] (Grand Rapids: Eerdmans & Carlisle: Paternoster. 1993ff.).

study, therefore, of the citations (patristic and otherwise) of Calvin's Genesis commentary is close to his interests.

This essay builds on two earlier studies. In a paper delivered at the International Congress on Calvin Research in 1994 I examined the sources of Calvin's 1543 response to Pighius.[3] That study showed how a wide range of patristic citations can be accounted for by the use of less than ten volumes. The present study will seek to do the same for the Genesis commentary. It also arises out of a recent article questioning whether Calvin used Lippoman's *Catena in Genesim*.[4] The attempt to answer that question necessitated tracing many of the sources of Calvin's citations and it seemed sensible to pursue this task to completion.

A word about the origin of the commentary.[5] Calvin lectured on Genesis from 1550 to 1552.[6] In the summer of 1550 he started work on his commentary, but it was delayed by the pressure of other work, appearing finally in 1554.[7] It

---

[3]'Calvin and the Fathers in his *Bondage and Liberation of the Will*,' in W.H. Neuser & B.G. Armstrong (eds.), *Calvinus Sincerioris Religionis Vindex* (Kirksville: Sixteenth Century Journal Publishers, 1997) 67-96.

[4]A.N.S. Lane, 'Did Calvin Use Lippoman's *Catena in Genesim*?' *Calvin Theological Journal* 31 (1996) 404-419. In a very few places text from this article has simply been repeated here. The results of the present chapter strengthen the conclusion that Calvin did not use Lippoman, but some of the details of the article have been revised.

[5]Cf. R. Peter & J-F. Gilmont, *Bibliotheca Calviniana. Les œuvres de Jean Calvin publiées au XVIe siècle* (Travaux d'Humanisme et Renaissance 255 & 281) (Geneva: Droz, 1991 & 1994) 1:519-523. Calvin also preached on Genesis, starting in 1559, but as these sermons come after the commentary they are of no interest for our present purposes.

[6]T. H. L. Parker, *Calvin's Old Testament Commentaries* (Edinburgh: T. & T. Clark, 1986) 29; CO 21:72,75.

[7]Parker, Calvin's *Old Testament Commentaries*, 25f. There Parker states, on the basis of the title page of the 1572 French edition, that this commentary was completed in collaboration with Nicholas des Gallars. He has subsequently (in personal conversation) revised this judgement, accepting the advice of Jean-François Gilmont that the later title page is unreliable. The Isaiah commentary certainly was produced by such collaboration (Peter & Gilmont, *Bibliotheca Calviniana* 1:404f.). It would not seriously affect our present inquiry if this should also have happened with the Genesis commentary as des Gallars' role was essentially scribal and Calvin checked the finished product. While the style might be des Gallars' and while he *may* have inadvertently mis-

should be noted how little time Calvin had for this work. During these years he published an average of over twelve volumes a year.[8] Assuming that the lectures on Genesis lasted approximately two years, Calvin had two weeks for each chapter—on top of all of his preaching, correspondence, pastoral and administrative work, in addition to all of his other publications. The indications are that he had an hour or less to prepare each lecture.[9] The revision of the lectures for publication would have been equally rushed. Whatever his natural inclinations might have been, Calvin did not have the leisure to study a wide range of authors. It should not surprise us to find that a number of his apparently wide-ranging citations can be traced to a small number of sources.

Does the time Calvin spent on Genesis mean that, for citations at the beginning of the volume, a source prior to 1550 must be sought? Not necessarily. Calvin includes on 3:6 a citation of Bernard which is probably derived from his reading of the 1552 Basel edition of Bernard's works.[10] This shows that, even at the beginning of the commentary, citations can be drawn from books published after 1550.

The Genesis commentary was reprinted as part of Calvin's 1563 Pentateuch commentary.[11] It is important to be clear what Calvin already knew in 1554 so all citations have been checked against the first edition itself, to the extent of verifying their presence there without necessarily checking

---

represented Calvin's view on occasions, he is unlikely to have taken it upon himself to add in his own citations.

[8]Cf. n.15, below.

[9]Jean Budé notes in his preface to Calvin's lectures on the Minor Prophets that he with difficulty found half an hour to prepare a lecture (cited by M. Engammare, 'Calvin connaissait-il la Bible?', *Bulletin de la Société de l'Histoire du Protestantisme Français* 141 (1995) 165, n.8); Colladon, in his *Vie de Calvin*, notes that Calvin usually had less than an hour to prepare his lectures (CO 21:109, cited by Parker, *Calvin's Old Testament Commentaries*, 21); Calvin, writing to Farel in 1554, comments that the hour for the lecture was approaching and that he had not yet been able to prepare (CO 15:148, cited by Engammare, *ibid.*).

[10]For evidence that Calvin was using the 1552 edition of Bernard, cf. A.N.S. Lane, 'Calvin's Sources of St. Bernard,' Archiv *für Reformationsgeschichte* 67 (1976) 258f., 263-265, 278.

[11]Peter & Gilmont, *Bibliotheca Calviniana*, 2:1013-1016.

for every textual variation. This has shown that the *Calvini Opera* edition must be used with caution.[12]

It is important to be clear about the question being tackled. The ultimate aim is to determine which sources Calvin used when preparing his Genesis commentary.[13] But how should one discover that? The obvious method, to compare Calvin's comments with those of his predecessors, is fraught with difficulties. First, to do this properly it is necessary to make the comparison for a substantial portion of the commentary, not just for isolated passages. Second, unless one does this for *all* of the commentaries available to Calvin one can easily be led astray. For obvious reasons, many commentators say similar things about the same passage. If one compares Calvin with just one or two of his predecessors one may be impressed with what at first sight appear to be impressive parallels, but, in fact, are mere commonplaces of the exegetical tradition. The time needed to make a suitably comprehensive study along these lines is very considerable, which is presumably why it has not so far been attempted.

The approach of this study is more modest. The aim is to determine, so far as is possible, the sources of Calvin's *citations*. We will be investigating his sources not by examining alleged parallels with other commentaries but by examining texts where Calvin openly refers to the views of others, whether by name (*e.g.*, Augustine) or more vaguely (*e.g.*, the Jews). When looking at Calvin's own views one can never be sure to what extent they are derived from others or are original to him; when looking at his citations of others, by contrast, one knows by definition that there is a source to be

---

[12]CO 23 contains the occasional textual note drawing attention to differences between the editions (*e.g.*, CO 23:13f.). This could easily lead the unwary reader into assuming that the 1554 edition conforms to CO except where indicated, which is far from true. This study has revealed a number of unnoted textual differences, most strikingly between CO 23:618:22-32 and p.332 of the 1554 edition.

[13]For an attempt at answering this question, *cf.* R.C. Gamble, 'The Sources of Calvin's Genesis Commentary: A Preliminary Report,' *Archiv für Reformationsgeschichte* 84 (1993) 206-221. Gamble has been working on a fuller study of this question, nearing completion. We have been working independently, without collaboration, on this issue.

found. If one can identify those sources one then knows at least some of the works that Calvin used while preparing his commentary. The present study will yield some very specific conclusions to provide a firm basis for the ongoing task of determining the sources of Calvin's exegetical views.

We will not, of course, presume that because Calvin *names* a particular source he has actually read or even set eyes upon the source himself. The study of his response to Pighius revealed that Calvin named and even exegeted texts that he did not actually have before him.[14] Calvin was hardly less busy by the time he came to prepare his Genesis commentary.[15] We must expect, therefore, that he will take short cuts in preparing his commentary. He did not have the leisure of the professional scholar to sit down for hours consulting every available source. Also, we must be realistic about the range of books available to Calvin at Geneva, which in intellectual terms was very different from Paris, Basel or Strassburg. Calvin's use of resources would have been curtailed by limitations of opportunity as well as by limitations of time. In this study, therefore, we will apply a hermeneutic of suspicion. For example, if Calvin once cites from a more obscure writer and the same citation is found in Luther's commentary which Calvin definitely used, the citation of the obscure writer is in itself no evidence that Calvin had read him. The aim will be to account for Calvin's citations by postulating the smallest necessary number of sources. This is not to deny that Calvin's reading *prior to* the preparation of the commentary was wide, but it is to question how many sources he had time and opportunity to use *whilst actually preparing* the commentary. Where, for example, Calvin cites a passage of Augustine which has no particular link to Genesis and for which no intermediate source has been found, the most natural explanation is that

---

[14]*Cf.* n.3, above.
[15]As a *very* crude indicator it may be noted that in 1542 and 1543, the relevant years for the response to Pighius, Calvin was responsible for 5 and 8 publications, respectively; for the years 1550-54, the relevant years for the Genesis commentary, he was responsible for an average of 12.6 publications per year (Peter & Gilmont, *Bibliotheca Calviniana* 1:104-143,332-543).

this is drawn from his memory of earlier reading of Augustine.[16]

We should not assume that Calvin's sources remain constant throughout the commentary. There are various reasons for doubting this. Some of Calvin's sources did not cover the whole of Genesis. A brief glance at the appendixes will show that Calvin's citations are not spread evenly throughout the commentary. When looking at sources that Calvin definitely did use we will also need to ask whether he used them for all of the commentary or for part only.

As wide as possible a range of commentaries available to Calvin[17] have been examined in the preparation of this article and these are listed at the end. The reader will be disappointed, but hardly surprised, to hear that I have not read every one of these from cover to cover. The method adopted has been to examine them as potential sources for Calvin's citations. In some instances it becomes quickly apparent that the commentary does not supply the right sort of material and a thorough reading has been unnecessary. Other sources, of which Calvin clearly made considerable use, have been examined thoroughly. But in no case is it claimed that a commentary has been examined absolutely exhaustively and that every last instance where it might be a source for Calvin's citations has been traced. While with Calvin's major sources the aim has been to find as many parallels as possible, the greater priority has been to find at least some plausible source for every citation.

One factor has been borne in mind when considering sources. The 1572 catalogue of the library of the Genevan

---

[16]For Calvin's ability to make later use of remembered earlier reading, cf. N. Colladon, *Vie de Calvin* (CO 21:109).

[17]Making use of the bibliography in A. Williams, *The Common Expositor. An Account of the Commentaries on Genesis 1527-1633* (Chapel Hill: University of North Carolina Press, 1948) 269-277. The colophon of Wolfgang Musculus's Genesis commentary (Basel: Hervagius, 1554) is dated September (Eee4a); the colophon of Calvin's commentary is dated July. We can assume, therefore, that Calvin did not use Musculus, a disappointing conclusion as Musculus could account for some of Calvin's more elusive citations. It is also assumed that Calvin used neither the German commentaries of Corvinus (1541) or Linck (1543), nor the Italian commentary of Brucioli (1540 & 1546).

Academy survives.[18] Some of Calvin's books ended up in this library. If a work is found there, it might be Calvin's copy or it might explain why the library did not take Calvin's copy, having one already. If, on the contrary, a work is not found there one must ask why the library chose not to take Calvin's copy. This is not an infallible guide, but it does affect the balance of probability that Calvin used a particular source. To avoid introducing an unwarranted bias, I have ignored this evidence until the very end. In other words, it has been used to confirm conclusions already reached but not to dictate conclusions in advance.

A variety of types of citations will be considered, in the following order. First will be the small number of Calvin's named references to contemporary authors. Second will be his references to different translations of Genesis. This will point to important sources of other types of citation. Next will come named references to patristic authors, which for the purposes of this study will include Josephus. Related to the patristic citations are the few references to ancient heresies, such as Arianism. The commentary is rich in Jewish citations and also contains a number of references to the pope or 'papists.' Finally there are two types of looser references. First there are unnamed references to a specific group such as the fathers or the Ana-baptists. Second there are numerous vague references to the views of others, described in loose terms simply as 'non-nulli' or 'alii'. This group is by far the largest and in order to contain the scope of the study such citations have been examined for the first eleven chapters only. All of Calvin's likely sources have been checked against these citations and where a source accounts for many of them this is a strong confirmation that Calvin was using it. While these citations have been used as confirmatory evidence it is not the goal of this paper to trace the source of every such vague reference. For each of these eight types of citation, details of each are listed in the appendixes at the end of the paper, with an indication of their probable source.

---

[18] A. Ganoczy, *La Bibliothèque de l'Académie de Calvin* (Geneva: Droz, 1969).

Apart from the last category of vague references the aim has been to consider every single citation fitting into each category,[19] but it would be rash to claim that no citations have been overlooked. The occasional minor lapse need not, however, be serious. The aim is to find clues which point to Calvin's sources and it is possible for the detective to catch the criminal without necessarily making use of every single clue.

Two other types of citation should also be mentioned. Calvin's Genesis commentary is rich in material from the classics, including proverbial sayings. Second, there are many discussions of the meanings of Hebrew words. When examining potential sources these, together with the classical citations, have been considered but there has been no systematic attempt to trace their source.[20]

It also needs to be stated that we must not assume that Calvin used only those writings which he cited. Calvin, unlike modern commentators, was under no obligation to document all of his sources. Where he does refer to the interpretation of others it is more often than not in vague terms such as 'some say'. Nor does he feel obliged to refer to all that he has read, as he himself indicates:

> It is not my intention to relate the ravings or the dreams of every writer, nor would I have the reader to expect this from me; here and there I allude to them, though sparingly, especially if there be any colour of deception; that readers, being often admonished, may learn to take heed unto themselves. Therefore, with respect to this passage, which has been variously tortured, I will not record what one or another may have delivered, but will content myself with a true exposition of it.[21]

---

[19]I am grateful to John Dawson, one of my students, for reading through Genesis 1–11 checking for citations that I might have missed.

[20]In a forthcoming study, in collaboration with Graham Davies, I hope to determine which Hebrew Bible(s) and grammar(s) Calvin used, as well as the sources of his Jewish citations, for all of his Old Testament commentaries, not just Genesis.

[21]J. Calvin, *Commentaries on the First Book of Moses called Genesis* 2 vols (Grand Rapids: Eerdmans, 1948 reprint) 1.221f. Apart from quotations,

This quotation also reminds us that Calvin, *in his comment-aries*, more often cites others in order to disagree with them. While in the *Institutes* and the polemical treatises Calvin is citing authorities as witnesses in his favour, in the comment-aries he is dialoguing with his fellow expositors.

So how should one select which potential sources to check? Clearly all works cited by Calvin must be checked as well as works by authors that he names, such as Augustinus Eugubinus Steuchus. Again, all of the significant sixteenth-century commentaries prior to 1554 have been checked, as have important medieval predecessors such as the *Glossa ordinaria*, Nicolaus of Lyra, Bede, Rabanus Maur, Hugo of St. Charo and Dionysius Carthusianus. Annotated Bibles such as Münster's are obvious potential sources. Finally, in 1562 Henricus Stephanus published at Geneva a volume which is generally attributed to Augustinus Marlorat: *Genesis cum catholica expositione ecclesiastica...sive, Bibliotheca expositionum Genesews*, a compilation of extracts from the works of eleven authors.[22] This obviously post-dates Calvin's commentary, but it does reveal which authors on Genesis a French Reformed pastor considered most useful and which Calvin was also not unlikely to have used.

Named Contemporary Citations[23]

A good place to start is with Calvin's own contemporaries, for the obvious reason that he had little or no opportunity to be acquainted with their writing through intermediary

---

this translation has often informed the English paraphrases of Calvin's text found in this paper.

[22](Geneva: H. Stephanus, 1562). Cf. P. Chaix, A. Dufour & G. Moeckli, *Les Livres Imprimés a Genève de 1550 a 1600* (Geneva: Droz, 1966 - revised edition) 54. There is a key indicating which *authors* are being used but, unfortunately, not which of their *works*. That is usually, but not always, obvious. Also, the indications in the text as to which author is being quoted are often reliable. Some Calvin quotations are attributed to others. The authors are: Vatablus, Luther, Musculus, Calvin, Fagius, Oecolampadius, Artopaeus, Pagninus, Münster, Steuchus and Marlorat.

[23]Named contemporary citations are listed in Appendix 1. #n = citation n in that list.

sources. A citation from Ambrose has had over a thousand years to be used by others, a citation from Luther's commentary is hot off the press.

Before considering those contemporaries explicitly cited, there is one contemporary author who is not named but may safely be considered a potential source for other, explicit, citations. That is John Calvin. If the Genesis commentary contains a citation which has earlier appeared in another work of Calvin's we need look no further for the source. The purpose of this study is to identify the sources used by Calvin *while preparing* his Genesis commentary, not the sources of his earlier works.

Calvin names four contemporary authors, three of them only once. Most significant is Luther, who is named no less than five times.[24] It is reasonably safe to assume that this is evidence for Calvin's use of Luther's commentary, something that would have been not unlikely even if there were no citations. This assumption is greatly strengthened by two facts. First, as we shall see, many of Calvin's other citations can be traced to the Luther commentary. Second, Calvin himself confirms this when he states, with reference to this commentary, that out of respect for Luther he had abstained more than a hundred times from naming him.[25] Calvin's first-hand knowledge of Luther is therefore certain.

This does not mean, however, that Calvin had access to *all* of Luther's lectures on Genesis. These were published in four volumes, from 1544–54.[26] The first predates Calvin's exegesis of Genesis; the last volume clearly appear-ed too late to be used. What of the other two? First, of Calvin's four references to Luther, three appear in the first volume, the fourth in the second volume, which ends at 25:10. Second, all of Calvin's citations after 25:10 have been sought in Luther. This search has yielded all but nothing.[27] This suggests that

---

[24]##3-7.
[25]CO 9:54.
[26]See details in section XI, below.
[27]Jews #60,61,63; Translations #113; Papists #27.

he had at least the first two volumes before him and therefore had access to Luther's exposition of chapters 1–25:10.[28]

Second, commenting on the first verse of Genesis, Calvin chides 'Steuchus' for maintaining the error that unformed matter has existed from eternity.[29] To what is Calvin referring here? Augustinus Eugubinus Steuchus taught, in his *Cosmopoeia*, that there are three heavens and that the most transcendent of these, the *coelum empyrium* is eternal.[30] But it is unlikely that Calvin could have so misunderstood this as to accuse Steuchus of teaching the eternity of unformed matter.[31] In fact Calvin is referring to another work of Steuchus, his *Recognitio Veteris Testamenti ad Hebraicam Veritatem*.[32] Commenting on Genesis 1:1 ('creavit'), Steuchus does not exactly teach the eternity of unformed matter, but he does allow that the Hebrew word 'bârâ' need not imply creation *ex nihilo*.[33] Calvin's opposition to the idea of eternal unformed matter immediately follows his own claim that 'bârâ' must mean creation out of nothing.[34] Thus it seems likely that Calvin is thinking of Steuchus' *Recognitio* at this point. Shortly afterwards there is further confirmation that this is correct. A few sentences after the critique of Steuchus

----

[28] Calvin's Luther citations have also been checked to confirm that he is not referring to Luther's *In Genesin, Mosi Librum Sanctissimum…* *Declamationes* (Hagenau: Ioan. Secerius, 1527) which is found in WA 24.

[29] #1.

[30] In his 1535 *Cosmopoeia*. Cf. T. Freudenberger, *Augustinus Steuchus aus Gubbio* (Münster i. W.: Aschendorff, 1935), 219-230.

[31] R. Stauffer, "L'exégèse de Genèse 1,1-3 chez Luther et Calvin," in *In Principio: interpretations des premiers versets de la Genèse* (Paris: Études Augustiniennes, 1973), 256-258, maintains that Calvin is referring to this teaching of Steuchus, while acknowledging that it is difficult to see why his attack was so imprecise. Stauffer points out that earlier M. Réveillaud had, incorrectly, given Steuchus's *De perenni philosophia* as the source.

[32] Venice, 1529. There was a 1531 edition published by Sebastian Gryphius at Lyon (*Augustini Steuchi Eugubini Veteris Testamenti ad veritatem Hebraicam Recognitio*) a copy of which was found in the library of the Genevan Academy in 1572 (Ganoczy, *Bibliothèque*, 231). Both editions have been consulted but references will be to the 1531 edition, since the copy in the Genevan Academy library might be the one which Calvin used.

[33] *Recognitio*, 25-28.

[34] CO 23:14f.

Calvin criticizes those who see a reference to the Trinity in
Genesis 1:1. The point criticised is found in Steuchus immediately after the discussion of 'creavit.'[35] Thus it is almost
certainly Steuchus again who is being criticized. Also, many
of Calvin's other citations can be traced to the *Recognitio*, as
will be seen.

Third, a few lines later, Calvin refers to Servetus,
criticizing him for the view that the first beginning of the
Word was when God commanded that there should be
light.[36] Calvin was already aware that Servetus held such
views, having attacked them in the 1539 edition of the
Institutio.[37] The current citation, therefore, should be seen as
a recollection of earlier reading rather than evidence that
Calvin read Servetus in his preparation for the Genesis commentary. Finally, Budé is cited for the statement that 1600
Attic drachmas are worth about 250 pounds of French
money.[38] This seems to be based upon Budé's *De asse*.[39]

Citations of Translations[40]

Citations of translations are the next to be traced. By examin-
ing these we will be able to ascertain some works which
Calvin clearly had before him while expounding Genesis.
These will be potential sources for other types of citation.

---

[35]*Recognitio*, 28-32.

[36]#2.

[37]*Inst.* 1:13:8. Calvin does not name Servetus in the 1539 *Institutio*, but
OS 3:118, n.1 identifies two passages from Servetus. Cf. also Stauffer, *In
Principio*, 264. The source appears to be Servetus, *De Trinitatis Erroribus
Libri Septem* (s.l., 1531) 47a; E.T.: E.M. Wilbur (transl.), *The Two Treatises
of Servetus on the Trinity* (Harvard Theological Studies 16) (Cambridge
(MA): Harvard University Press, & London: Humphrey Milford: 1932)
75.

[38]#8.

[39]G. Budaeus, *De asse & partibus eius* (Paris: M. Vascosanus with R.
Stephanus & J. Roigny, 1541) 44b appears to yield a different result, but
can perhaps give Calvin's answer. Maybe Calvin made a mistake in
haste. I am grateful to my colleague Peter Hicks for help with dis-
entangling Budé's Latin.

[40]Citations of translations are listed in Appendix 2. #n = citation n in
that list.

When is a translation not a translation? In English there are two words which are clearly distinct: 'translate' and 'interpret'. Latin is less straightforward and Calvin can use many different words to mean translate: 'vertit,' 'legit,' 'transferit,' 'transtulit,' 'fecit,' 'reddiderit,' 'habet,' 'exponit,' 'expressit,' 'interpretit,' and others.[41] Unfortunately all of these (even 'vertit') can be used in a looser sense than 'translate.' The situation is also complicated by the fact that Calvin is not always concerned to quote translations exactly.[42] For example, he states that Jerome's rendering of 2:18 is 'Quod sit illi simile' where the Vulgate reads 'similem sui' or 'similem sibi.' The key word is 'similem' and for the rest the sense suffices. Again, he cites the Vulgate translation of 3:1 as 'Cur dixit Deus?' when in fact it is 'Cur praecepit Deus.' It is the first word that Calvin is discussing and for the others the sense suffices. This means that in seeking the translation that Calvin is citing one has to realise that he may not be quoting it with total accuracy. Where there are significant differences between Calvin's quotation and his alleged source, that is indicated in Appendix 2, below, in a note. Readers are therefore in a position to judge for themselves whether sources are being alleged on adequate grounds.

Two criteria have been used to determine what are citations of translations. First, the context in Calvin. The aim has been to consider only those passages which are citing *someone else's* translation of the text, not those which are simply discussing Calvin's translation, nor those which concern the interpretation of the text rather than strictly its translation, nor those which discuss the meaning of a Hebrew word in general rather than its translation in this particular place.[43] Second, where it is not sufficiently clear

---

[41]See Appendix 2. Listed in order of first occurrence.

[42]For the (considerably worse) looseness of Calvin's biblical citations in his sermons on Genesis, cf. Engammare, 'Calvin connaissait-il la Bible?', 163-84.

[43]For an alternative approach, cf. H. F. van Rooy, 'Calvin's Genesis Commentary—Which Bible Text did he Use?' in B. J. van der Walt (pref.), *Our Reformational Tradition. A Rich Heritage and Lasting Vocation* (Potchefstroom: Potchefstroom University for Christian Higher Education, 1984) 203-216, where Calvin's translation (of the first three chapters only) is compared with the Vulgate, Pagninus and Münster

from the context in Calvin whether or not it is a translation that is being cited, the evidence of the actual translations available to Calvin has been allowed to influence the decision. Clearly this could have the effect of biasing the final list in favour of the translations examined, but this second criterion has only rarely been invoked and does not affect the overall picture.

Finally, two types of translation have been excluded from this section: citations of the 'Chaldaeus paraphrastes' and citations of the translations of Jewish interpreters. These will be considered below under Jewish citations. The citations of translations will be considered in three parts: the Septuagint, Jerome and the Vulgate and the remainder.

1. Septuagint

Calvin twelve times refers to the way in which 'Graeci' or 'Graeci interpretes' translate the text,[44] all of these referring to the Septuagint. This would appear to be a clear indication that Calvin consulted the Septuagint while expounding Genesis. It may be that he did, but the evidence is unclear. All twelve citations are also found in Steuchus's *Recognitio*.[45] where we find not just the text of the Septuagint but also Calvin's comment about it, such as the statement that they have missed Moses' sense,[46] or that they read the text incorrectly.[47] Thus while Calvin *may* have looked at the Septuagint, if he did so it did not lead him to refer to any passage nor to express any opinion which was not already to

---

translations. The advantage of this method is that there is plenty of material to consider. The drawback is that while Calvin's translation might be very similar to Pagninus's, for example, that does not prove that Calvin was actually dependent upon Pagninus. If, on the other hand, Calvin states that some have translated a passage in a certain way, he is explicitly declaring that he has seen such a translation. It is also perhaps suspicious that only three translations are considered and that the verdict is that Calvin was dependent upon these same three. In the final paragraph of the article the author acknowledges the need to look at more than just three chapters and to consider a wider range of potential sources than those available to him (in South Africa).

[44]##1,11,15,21,33,36,39,67,88,98,106,108.
[45]Full details will be found in Appendix 2.
[46]#33.
[47]#36.

be found in the *Recognitio*, which he was constantly using. Calvin betrays no knowledge of or judgement about the Septuagint which he would not have found in Steuchus.

2. Jerome and the Vulgate.

Calvin refers to the Vulgate in a variety of ways: 'vetus interpres,' 'Hieronymus,' 'vulgaris translatio' and 'Hieronymi versio.'[48] The picture is further complicated by the fact that Jerome also discusses the text of Genesis in his *Hebraicae quaestiones in Genesim*, a work which Calvin cites explicitly. Every reference to Jerome's translation has been checked in this work as well as in the Vulgate. There are four references to Jerome discussed in this section where it could be the *Hebraicae quaestiones* that Calvin has in mind, though in every instance the Vulgate is also a possible source.[49]

Clearly other commentators also discuss the Vulgate and it is theoretically possible that Calvin could have derived his knowledge of it indirectly. But this is *a priori* unlikely and also examination of the other citations of translations will point towards a particular edition that Calvin probably used.

3. The Remainder

A wide variety of contemporary translations have been examined as potential sources for Calvin's citations.[50] The great majority of his citations are accounted for by three volumes. A number are found in Steuchus's *Recognitio*. Many are found in the Zurich translation of 1543. Others are found in the notes of Francis Vatable. These notes are found, together with the Vulgate and Zurich translations, in Robert Stephanus's 1545 edition of the Latin Bible. This edition must be very likely as a source for Calvin. If he did not use it he must have gained access to its translations and notes from another source or sources. Finally, Calvin on occasions

---

[48]See Appendix 2. Listed in order of first occurrence. R.J. Mooi, *Het Kerk- en Dogmahistorisch Element in de Werken van Johannes Calvijn* (Wageningen: H. Veenman, 1965) 136, states that Calvin never names Jerome in connection with the Vulgate translation. This is not true inasmuch as references to Jerome sometimes refer to the Vulgate.
[49]##7,37,69,86.
[50]These are listed in section XI, below.

seems to be using either the Latin translation or the notes of
Sebastian Münster's Latin Bible. These three volumes are
sufficient to account for all but seven of Calvin's citations of
translations, including those of the Septuagint and Jerome.

What of the remaining seven? These will be
considered individually. One is a reference to Luther, whom
we know Calvin to be using.[51] Another is in Fagius's
Exegesis, a work which is a likely source of some of Calvin's
other (especially Jewish) citations.[52] Another is introduced
by 'vertunt,' but appears to be an account of the manner in
which the passage is interpreted rather than a verbal translation of it.[53] Another claims that 'communiter vertunt
interpretes' where the translations give the same sense in
different words. One translation does, however, come close
to Calvin's wording, Fagius's *Thargum*, a work which is a
likely source of some of Calvin's Jewish citations.[54] One has
been found only in the Pagninus translation.[55] Another is
found as a variant reading in Servetus's revision of the
Pagninus translation.[56] This points to the distinct, and intriguing, possibility that Calvin used the Servetus edition.
There are three other places where Servetus's variant readings are a possible source, the alternatives being Vatablus's
notes or the *Recognitio*.[57] Further support for this possibility
comes from the records of Servetus's trial where mention is
made of this edition both in the thirteenth interrogation (17th
August 1553) and in Calvin's refutation of Servetus published the following February.[58] Given the dating, the likeli-
hood that Calvin used the Servetus edition while preparing
this commentary, and that it has left its mark, is very great.
H. F. van Rooy argues that Calvin's own translation of

---

[51]#32.

[52]#28.

[53]#66.

[54]#87. Calvin's text is 'non sic fieri decet;' Fagius's is 'sic enim non
decebat fieri.'

[55]#55. According to Marlorat, *Genesis*, 120, however, Vatablus has a
similar reading, but this is not found in the Vatablus notes in the 1545
Stephanus Bible.

[56]#111.

[57]##54,68,70.

[58]CO 8:745f.,497f.

Genesis 1–3 'shows a strong influence by the Pagnini translation'. If his reading of the evidence is correct this would further substantiate the idea that Calvin used an edition of the Pagninus translation.[59]

This leaves just one citation which has not to date been traced.[60] A later author, however, attributes this translation to Vatablus, although it is not found in his notes as they appear in the 1545 Stephanus Bible.[61] Assuming that the ascription to Vatablus is not mistaken, this might suggest that Calvin had access to Vatablus's notes from some other source, either instead of, or as well as, the 1545 Bible. Such a slender piece of evidence does not warrant any firm conclusion, but it does remind us that Calvin's access to the Vulgate, the Zurich translation and Vatablus need not be through the 1545 Bible in which they appear together.

The study of the citations of translations has yielded the following conclusions. Calvin definitely used the *Recognitio*, Münster's Latin Bible[62] and the 1545 Stephanus Bible (or the same material in other edition(s). There is evidence, soon to be confirmed, that he used the two works of Fagius. It is probable that he used the Servetus revision of Pagninus's translation.

---

[59]van Rooy, 'Calvin's Genesis Commentary,' 215. (For reservations about his method, cf. n.43, above.) He suggests that Calvin used a Stephanus edition of Pagninus, but our evidence points rather to Calvin's use of the Servetus edition.

[60]#79.

[61]M. Poole, *Synopsis Criticorum aliorumque S. Scripturae Interpretum* vol.1 (London: J. Flesher & T. Roycroft, 1669) 79.

[62]M. Engammare, 'Le Paradis à Genève. Comment Calvin prêchait-il la chute aux Genevois?', *Études Théologiques et Religieuses* 69 (1994) 332f, suggests that Calvin for his Genesis sermons used Münster's 1546 *Biblia hebraica*. He gives no reason for favouring this particular edition over the 1534 or 1551 editions. For the present study all three editions have been examined. The 1546 is fuller than the 1534 edition, but does not thereby provide a source for any further citations. The 1551 edition is abridged and omits material which accounts for seven citations: Jews ##3,4,28,29,55,56. Vague #77. As the extra material in the 1546 edition covers no new citations and as the 1534 edition is in the Genevan library (Ganoczy, *Bibliothèque*, 160), this is the edition that Calvin is most likely to have used.

Named Patristic Citations[63]

1. Augustine

Augustine is cited twenty-two times in Calvin's Genesis commentary. Five of these citations are to his *Quaestiones in Heptateuchum*.[64] Given Calvin's regular use of Augustine, it is safe to assume that he was working with the original, unless the same citations are found in another work which Calvin was likely to have used. One of the citations is also found in Luther[65] and another had already appeared in Calvin's Romans commentary.[66] These parallels are not, however, sufficient to revise the judgement that Calvin was using Augustine for himself. Calvin does not cite the Genesis part of this work elsewhere, except once in the Romans commentary,[67] which would suggest that Calvin read it for the specific task of expounding Genesis.

Two other Augustinian expositions are also cited. In the Argument Calvin gives the *De Genesi contra Manichaeos* as one of two marginal references for Augustine's comment on the Manichees.[68] The same passage was cited, more briefly, both in the 1539 *Institutio*[69] and in the 1552 *De aeterna dei praedestinatione*.[70] The citation in the Genesis commentary is fuller, which suggests that Calvin possibly turned to the work again while preparing either the Genesis commentary or the *De aeterna dei praedestinatione*, having remembered the passage from the 1539 *Institutio*. Either way the citation is no evidence that Calvin made more general use of this work of Augustine's while preparing the commentary. This verdict is

---

[63]Named patristic citations are listed in Appendix 3. #n=citation n in that list.

[64]##21,34,36,41,43.

[65]#34.

[66]#41.

[67]L. Smits, *Saint Augustin dans l'oeuvre de Jean Calvin* (2 vols) (Assen: van Gorcum, 1956 & 1958), 2:237.

[68]#2.

[69]*Inst.* 3:23:2.

[70]CO 8:312f.

supported by the fact that there is no other citation of this work until later in the 1550s.[71]

Calvin also cites an opinion of Augustine and Eucherius on the tree of life, the former coming from the *De Genesi ad litteram*.[72] The Eucherius citation was already found in the 1539 *Institutio* and the reference to Augustine was added in 1550.[73] The *De Genesi ad litteram* is also cited explicitly three times in the 1539 *Institutio* and twice in the 1552 *De aeterna dei praedestinatione*.[74] Calvin is unlikely here to be depending upon his reading for the 1539 *Institutio* as he there mentioned Eucherius without Augustine. The new citations after 1550 probably reflect new reading. The 1550 *Institutio* was nearly complete in February 1550 and in April Beza was writing to Calvin conveying Melchior Wolmar's thanks for his copy.[75] It is probable that Calvin turned to this work with an eye to his imminent exposition of Genesis and that his reading also yielded citations for his revision of the *Institutio* and for his treatise on predestination. There are other passages where this work is a possible source.[76]

There are two other expositions of Genesis by Augustine: *De Genesi ad litteram imperfectus liber* and *Locutiones in Heptateuchum*. Calvin appears never to have cited these works[77] and no evidence of their use has been

---

[71]Smits, *Saint Augustin dans l'oeuvre de Jean Calvin*, 2:202. Some of the 'citations' mentioned by Smits are where this work is just one of a number of possible sources for a general comment of Calvin's. In one place (CO 5:202) Calvin refers to the entry on this work in Augustine's *Retractationes*, which is of course no evidence for Calvin's direct knowledge of this work.

[72]#10.

[73]*Inst.* 2:2:9. Smits, *Saint Augustin dans l'oeuvre de Jean Calvin*, 2:201 wrongly dates this citation as 1539.

[74]Smits, *Saint Augustin dans l'oeuvre de Jean Calvin*, 2:201f.

[75] Peter & Gilmont, *Bibliotheca Calviniana* 1:373.

[76]E.g. #13; Heresies #3; Vague ##1,3,4,21,26,28,35,36.

[77]Smits, *Saint Augustin dans l'oeuvre de Jean Calvin*, vol.2. The former work is a possible source for one 1539 citation (*Institutio* 2:1:11, OS 3:240) for which the alternative source is the *Opus imperfectum contra Iulianum*. Since there are many other places where Calvin is likely to be referring to the latter work (Smits, *Saint Augustin dans l'oeuvre de Jean Calvin*, 2:209f.) and no other places where Calvin is likely to be

found from comparing them with the citations in his Genesis commentary. The last three books of the *Confessiones* are also an exposition of the first chapter of Genesis and there are some parallels with Calvin's citations, but none that requires the use of this particular work.[78]

Calvin four times cites Augustine's *De civitate dei* by name and it is the likely source of two further citations.[79] This is a work which Calvin regularly cited throughout his career[80] and with which he was clearly familiar. With one exception, the passages cited here have not previously been cited by Calvin. But rather than postulate that Calvin chose to read through the entire *De civitate dei* while expounding Genesis, it is most likely that he is citing it from memory, perhaps sometimes with the aid of an index to trace a particular passage. The exceptional passage is Augustine's comment on the discrepancy between Genesis 46:8 and Acts 7:14, which was also cited in Calvin's earlier (1552) Acts commentary.[81] Since 46:8 comes at the end of Genesis it is most likely that Calvin turned to this passage while preparing his Acts commentary and simply repeated the reference when he came to the Genesis passage.

This leaves nine further Augustinian citations. Two concern his Trinitarian analogies in his *De trinitate*.[82] This is a work that Calvin cited throughout his career, though more especially in the late 1550s.[83] Augustine's analogies are well-known and Calvin's reference to them probably reflects memory of earlier reading, possibly brought to recollection by Luther's briefer mention of them.[84] Another citation is

---

referring to the former, the simplest explanation is that the latter is the source here too.

[78]See the Appendixes for details.

[79]##3,7,20,22; ##13,44. #13 could come from a variety of sources. Smits, *Saint Augustin dans l'oeuvre de Jean Calvin*, 2:131 suggests *Enarrationes in Psalmos* 18:2:15. Another possibility is *De natura et gratia* 29:33. More likely is *De Genesi ad litteram* 11:5:7 & 11:15:19.

[80]Smits, *Saint Augustin dans l'oeuvre de Jean Calvin*, 2:159-163.

[81]#44.

[82]##5,6.

[83]Smits, *Saint Augustin dans l'oeuvre de Jean Calvin*, 2:254-256.

[84]WA 42:45.

fully accounted for by Luther.[85] Augustine's famous prayer, 'Give what you command and command what you will' is often quoted by Calvin prior to this time,[86] as is also the statement that God crowns his own gifts.[87] Three other citations are loose enough that they cannot be tied to any one passage.[88] Given this vagueness, and the fact that they can be attributed to works Augustine that Calvin had at earlier stages cited,[89] there is no need to postulate fresh reading of Augustine nor indeed any intermediate source, unless a work which Calvin probably used should turn out to have the same citation. Finally, Calvin erroneously claims Augustine for the view that Adam and Eve fell after a mere six hours.[90] Calvin is either relying upon an inaccurate memory of Augustine or has been misled by an intermediate source.

This survey of the Augustine citations reveals one work which Calvin definitely seems to have been using while preparing his commentary, the *Quaestiones in Heptateuchum*. It is also highly likely that he made some use of the *De Genesi ad litteram*. He probably looked up in the *De Genesi contra Manichaeos* a passage that he had cited earlier. He may have checked some passages in the *De civitate dei*, being led to them either by memory or via the index.

2. Jerome

References to Jerome fall into three groups. First, there are citations of the Vulgate, which have already been considered under translations. Secondly, there are citations of Jerome's *Hebraicae quaestiones in Genesim*. This Calvin never names, but three times he refers to Jerome this work is in mind. [91] One of the translation citations also appears to refer to the

---

[85]#23 and WA 42:310.

[86]#17. E.g. in the 1536 *Institutio* (OS 1:55).

[87]#25. E.g. in the 1539 *Institutio* 2:5:2.

[88]#15,29,33. For suggested sources, cf. Smits, *Saint Augustin dans l'oeuvre de Jean Calvin*, 2:131.

[89]As can be seen from Smits, *Saint Augustin dans l'oeuvre de Jean Calvin*, vol.2.

[90]#14. Cf. Smits, *Saint Augustin dans l'oeuvre de Jean Calvin*, 2.295.

[91]##39,40,45. Four of the passages which have been treated as citations of the Vulgate might possibly refer to the *Hebraicae quaestiones*. See n.49, above.

Hebraicae quaestiones.[92] There are other passages where this work is a possible source, but only these four where it is the only source discovered. This evidence is limited, but given that Jerome is explicitly named, given Calvin's regular use of Jerome and given that no intermediate source has been found, it is safe to assume that he was working with the original.

This leaves just four citations of Jerome. With reference to Genesis 2:18 Calvin notes that this teaching refutes those with a negative view of marriage, as is found in Jerome's *Contra Iovinianum*. This is the first time that Calvin mentions Jerome's work against Jovinian in this context. But Calvin rebukes Jerome on this matter in the 1539 Institutio[93] and repeatedly makes the same point in his commentaries.[94] It is very likely that it was Jerome's work against Jovinian that provoked those comments and that the only new feature of the present passage is that Calvin now actually mentions the work. With reference to Mount Ararat, Calvin cites a passage from Jerome's *Liber de situ et nominibus locorum hebraicorum.*[95] This he may have read from Jerome himself, but it is noteworthy that there is no indication that Calvin made any other use of this work.[96] It is more likely, therefore, that Calvin's source is Steuchus's *Recognitio*, where all that Calvin mentions is to be found. Finally, with reference to Melchizedek, there is a double citation of Jerome's 'ad Evagrium,' in fact Jerome's *Epistola* 73 to Evangelus.[97] This letter would easily be found by looking up Melchizedek in the index of a contemporary collected edition of Jerome's works, where the recipient was called Evagrius. Calvin

---

[92]Translations #71. A further four references to Jerome might refer either to the Vulgate or (less likely) to this work. See n. 49 above.
[93]#12
[94]*Inst.* 4:12:28.*Comm.* I Cor, on 7:1,7,9,33,36 (1546); *Comm.* Heb. on 13:4(1549).
[95]#27.
[96]All the possible Hebrew names and places have been checked.
[97]##30,31.

probably knew of the letter already and either cited it from memory or looked it up.[98]

This survey of the Jerome citations reveals only one work which Calvin almost certainly was using while preparing his commentary, the *Hebraicae quaestiones in Genesim*. Calvin may also have consulted Jerome's *Epistola* 73.

3. The Remainder

There remain sixteen citations from other fathers. These fall into a number of distinct groups. Two are derived from other citations already considered.[99] Three are found in other works which we know Calvin to have been using.[100] One of these is, however not straightforward. In the Argument Calvin cites (Cassiodore's) *Historia Tripartita* on the question of what God was doing before he created the world.[101] Later, in the 1559 *Institutio* he attributes the same story to Augustine.[102] Luther in his Genesis commentary also cites it, attributing it to Augustine.[103] The most likely explanation is that Calvin read it in Luther, made a mistake in attributing it to the *Historia Tripartita* in his Genesis commentary and followed Luther more accurately in his 1559 *Institutio*.

A further seven citations are found in earlier works of Calvin and are presumably cited from memory.[104] Three of these are worthy of particular mention. First, on 14:18 Calvin attacks the ancient writers of the church, such as Tertullian, for seeing the parallel between Melchizedek and Christ in the fact that they offered bread and wine, a parallel which is never drawn in Hebrews.[105] The same point is

---

[98]The reason for assuming prior knowledge is that he would have to have had some reason for looking for a letter by Jerome on Melchizedek.

[99]#19 is found in the passages of Augustine cited immediately after (##20,21); #26 is found in the passage of Jerome cited immediately after (#27). #26, like #27, is fully covered by Steuchus's *Recognitio*, which is the probable source.

[100]##1,9,18.

[101]#1.

[102]*Inst*. 1:14:1.

[103]WA 42:8f.

[104]##4,8,11,32,35,37,42.

[105]#32.

made by Luther, who mentions Lyra but not the fathers.[106] Calvin's source for the *fathers* would seem to be the 1548 Augsburg *Interim*, which he printed in full in his attack on it. The *Interim* cites passages from Cyprian, Arnobius and John of Damascus, then mentions Jerome, Augustine, Ambrose, Chrysostom and Theophylact.[107] But what of Tertullian? Not only is he not mentioned in the *Interim* but he does not seem even to have made the point concerned. The simplest explanation is that Calvin was working from memory. In his reply to the *Interim* he adds Athanasius to the above list.[108] But in fact the reference to Athanasius in the *Interim* does not relate to Melchizedek.[109] Thus even when answering a document which he is publishing in full in his own reply, Calvin can make mistakes of detail, almost certainly because of the time pressure under which he worked. It is not surprising then that he should, a few years later, draw on his (inaccurate) memory of that work without taking time to check the details.

Second, Calvin approves Ambrose's allegory of 27:27,[110] presumably because his approval of its message of justification by faith outweighed his disapproval of allegory! This passage was not new to Calvin, having been cited already in the 1539 *Institutio*. Significantly, one of the very few additions that Calvin made in the 1553 edition of that work comes at this point, where he adds a quotation of Ambrose's own words.[111] The picture is clear. When preparing his Genesis commentary Calvin remembered and looked up the passage cited in 1539. He decided not only to cite it in the commentary but also to add a further quotation to the next edition of the *Institutio*. Both of Calvin's explicit Ambrose citations are recycled from the *Institutio*.[112] A brief examination of Ambrose's exegetical works on Genesis will show why this should be so. Ambrose's homiletic and allegorical approach makes his works of theological interest

---

[106]WA 42:536-538.
[107]CO 7:579f.
[108]CO 7:644.
[109]CO 7:579.
[110]#42.
[111]*Inst*. 3:11:23 (OS 4:207).
[112]##37,42.

(hence the citations in the *Institutio*) but of little value for a careful exegete like Calvin. Any other Ambrose influence is likely to reflect past reading, not fresh study for the exegesis of Genesis.

Third, there appears to be incontrovertible evidence that Calvin used Chrysostom's homilies while preparing his commentary. Chrysostom was, together with Augustine and Jerome, one of the three fathers whom Calvin most often cited in his commentaries.[113] He cites Chrysostom's understanding of the image of God in terms of dominion.[114] This comment has not be found elsewhere, except in Steuchus's *Cosmopoeia*, which Calvin does not appear to have been using.[115] Furthermore, Calvin's copy of Chrysostom's works survives, together with his extensive underlinings, which include the homilies from which this comment is drawn.[116]

Despite this apparently impressive evidence, it seems that Calvin almost certainly did *not* use Chrysostom's homilies while preparing his Genesis commentary. It is noteworthy that Chrysostom is mentioned only once in this commentary and it is almost exclusively in his *New* Testament commentaries that Calvin cites him.[117] In his *Preface to Chrysostom's Homilies* Calvin states that his praise of Chrysostom's exegesis applies especially to his New Testament homilies.[118] A check has revealed that very few of Calvin's citations are found in Chrysostom's homilies.[119] A look at the nature of Chrysostom's Genesis homilies, which are more moralistic and homiletic than exegetical, will indicate why

---

[113]Mooi, *Het Kerk- en Dogmahistorisch Element*, 371,377,380-81,393f.
[114]#8.
[115]*Cosmopoeia* 106. This is one of the very few citations that have been found in the *Cosmopoeia*. The evidence suggests that Calvin is very unlikely to have been using it.
[116]A. Ganoczy & K. Müller, *Calvins Handschriftliche Annotationen zu Chrysostomus* (Wiesbaden: Franz Steiner, 1981) esp. 58-66.
[117]Mooi's figures (cf. n.113, above) are 3 citations in the OT commentaries; 126 citations in the NT commentaries.
[118]CO 9:834.
[119]A careful, but not exhaustive, check revealed just three parallels apart from the explicit citation: Chrysostom is, together with other more likely sources, a possible source for two statements about the views of the ancients (Specific References, ##10,11); one vague reference is found in Chrysostom (#46).

Calvin may not have bothered to consult them. But what of the one citation and the underlining? The question is *when* Calvin read and underlined the volume. The answer appears to be clear. The volume was published in 1536 and Calvin cites the Genesis homilies seven times in the 1539 *Institutio*, explicitly naming them five times.[120] Calvin also in that edition refers to Chrysostom's interpret-ation of the image of God, though without naming him.[121] Lest there be any doubt that Chrysostom is in mind, he is explicitly named for this same point in the *Psychopannychia*.[122] Thus Calvin's citation of him here reflects his memory of his reading of the homilies in the late 1530s and of his two earlier citations of this particular point. The paucity of citations that it is even possible to trace to Chrysostom's homilies suggests that Calvin is most unlikely to have used them for the prepar-ation of his commentary. Calvin *did* read Chrysostom's Genesis homilies, but in the late 1530s, not in the early 1550s.

This leaves four remaining citations. On 3:6 Calvin cites Bernard's warning about the potential for sin in fallen human nature.[123] A previous study has shown that this is probably evidence of Calvin's renewed reading of Bernard following his acquisition of the 1552 Basel edition of the *Opera Omnia*.[124] This is not reading for the Genesis comment-ary in particular but general reading of Bernard which gives rise to a number of new citations from 1554.

Calvin cites Origen four times in his Genesis com-mentary. Three of these are already accounted for, Calvin's sources being Luther, Augustine and the earlier Galatians commentary.[125] That leaves just one citation, to the effect that (with reference to the Ark) Origen boldly sports with allegories.[126] This general knowledge of Origen requires no new reading of him, beyond the knowledge earlier shown. Given the allegorical character of Origen's *Homiliae in Genesim*, there would be little incentive for Calvin to devote

---

[120]*Inst*. 2:2:4 (3x), 2:5:3, 3:4:38, 3:15:2, 3:16:3.
[121]*Inst*. 1:15:4 (OS 3:181, n.a).
[122]CO 5:181.
[123]#16.
[124]See n.10, above.
[125]##9,19,35.
[126]#24.

his precious time to rereading them while preparing his own exposition.

On 9:4 Calvin criticised Tertullian for banning Christians from tasting the blood of cattle.[127] To the best of my knowledge, Calvin had not previously mentioned Tertullian's teaching on this point. The reference is to Tertullian's *Apology*, which Calvin had already cited in 1543 and 1548.[128] Unless one of the works used by Calvin also mentions Tertullian, we should assume that Calvin remembered this detail from his earlier reading of Tertullian and chose to mention it at the appropriate point.

On 23:11 Calvin cites Josephus for the judgement that a sanctuary shekel was worth four Attic drachmas.[129] Here will either have been working from memory or will have checked up the relevant passage from Josephus.

The study of Calvin's sixteen citations from the 'remaining fathers' has produced very little evidence of direct reading of them by Calvin. There appears to be contemporary reading of Bernard (but not for the preparation of this commentary) and probably memory of earlier reading of Tertullian and Origen. There is a reference to Josephus which may have required Calvin to check the passage concerned. None of this suggests that Calvin read any of the fathers in his preparation for this commentary, other than Augustine and Jerome. It may be that some other father was a source for the commentary, but evidence for this is not be found in Calvin's citations.

Citations of Ancient Heresies[130]

There are seven explicit references to ancient heresies in Calvin's Genesis commentary. On the first verse, Calvin notes how some in seeking to oppose Arianism have fallen

---

[127]#28.

[128]*Apologia* 9:13. Calvin cites this work in his 1543 *Supplex exhortatio* (CO 6:531) and his 1548 commentary on Phil. 1:7 (CO 52:11).

[129]#38.

[130]Citations of ancient heresies are listed in Appendix 4. #n = citation n in that list.

into Sabellianism.[131] This is a citation not so much of the ancient heresy as of those who are accused of it, whose identity is discussed below.[132] In his comment on 1:26 Calvin refers to the Anthropomorphites who locate the likeness to God in the human body.[133] In the 1539 *Institutio* Calvin already refers to them in general terms[134] and in the *Psychopannychia* he mentions their belief with reference to Genesis 1:26.[135] The Anthropomorphites are mentioned in Augustine's *De haeresibus*,[136] with which Calvin was familiar by 1543 even if he had not known it in 1539.[137] In commenting on 3:6 Calvin notes that Pelagius denied original sin and again that he taught that Adam's sin is passed on by imitation.[138] Apart from the fact that such information was well-known, Calvin already states as much in the 1539 *Institutio*.[139]

There are two references to the Manichees. First, Calvin states that they deduced the existence of two principles or Gods from the fact of Adam's temptation.[140] This much could be deduced from Augustine's account of Manichaeism in his *De haeresibus*,[141] a work which Calvin seems to have read (especially the chapter on the Manichees) in order to respond to Pighius in 1543.[142] The present

---

[131]#1.

[132]#2 under Vague References.

[133]#2

[134]*Inst.* 1:13:1.

[135]CO 5:180.

[136]*De haeresibus* 50 (PL 42:39).

[137]Lane, 'Calvin and the Fathers in his *Bondage and Liberation of the Will*,' 73.

[138]##4,5.

[139]*Inst.* 2:1:5f. In the 1539 edition this is a statement about the 'Pelagiani,' but it suffices to show what will come as no surprise: that Calvin by this time was familiar with the teaching of Pelagius. The same is shown by the many references to Pelagius in the 1543 response to Pighius (e.g. CO 6:293,299,301,331,360). Calvin refers in his Romans commentary to the Pelagian view that sin is transmitted from Adam by imitation, but this comment is not added until the 1556 edition (T.H.L. Parker (ed.), *Iohannis Calvini Commentarius in Epistolam Pauli ad Romanos* (Leiden: Brill, 1981) 110).

[140]#3.

[141] *De haeresibus* 46. Another possible source is Augustine's *De Genesi ad litteram* 11:13:17 (a work cited by Calvin).

[142]Cf. n.137, above.

comment is, therefore, no evidence of further reading on Manichaeism. The other reference is simply the accusation that a certain Jewish opinion smacks of Manichaeism.[143] Calvin learned about the Jewish opinion from Luther, who immediately before mentions the Manichees in connection with another Jewish view.[144] Luther may have given Calvin the idea of mentioning the Manichees and his existing knowledge of their teaching (through Augustine's *De haeresibus* among other works) would have sufficed.

Towards the end of the commentary Calvin states that Reuben's forgiveness in Genesis 35:22-27 refutes the error of Novatus (whom he has confused with Novatian?) and the Novatianists.[145] Calvin was already aware of their teaching by the time of the 1539 *Institutio*[146] and betrays no further knowledge here.

Calvin's citations of ancient heresies betray no new knowledge of them. Calvin simply inserts references to them where he deems it appropriate, making use of his earlier reading.

Jewish Citations[147]

Tracing Calvin's Jewish citations is no easy task. He rarely names sources, referring instead to 'rabbini', 'Hebraei' and 'Iudaei'. Also, this topic has in the past received almost no attention.[148] The present study will take a tentative first step towards tracing Calvin's sources, to be extended at a later date.[149]

Many of Calvin's Jewish citations can be accounted for on the basis of works which we already know Calvin to

---

[143]#6.

[144]WA 42:271f.

[145]#7.

[146]*Inst.* 4:1:23.

[147]Jewish citations are listed in Appendix 5. #n = citation n in that list.

[148]D.L. Puckett, *John Calvin's Exegesis of the Old Testament* (Louisville: Westminster John Knox, 1995) 78, n.64, which surveys the question, reveals how little is known. W. McKane, *A Late Harvest. Reflections on the Old Testament* (Edinburgh: T. & T. Clark, 1995) 46f. presents a similar picture.

[149]See n.20, above.

be using: Luther's commentary, Steuchus's *Recognitio*, Münster's *Hebraica Biblia Latina* and Vatablus's notes. Of the sixty-five Jewish citations, at least forty-two are covered by these works.[150] Where a citation is accounted for by works which we already know Calvin to be using there is no need to postulate further sources. This has one interesting implication. At least eleven of Calvin's citations are found in Lyra's *Postilla*. Most of these are also found in Luther,[151] and the remainder are all found in other works used by Calvin. This would suggest that Calvin was not himself using the *Postilla*, a conclusion that is strengthened by the fact that hardly any of Calvin's citations are found in the *Glossa ordinaria*.

What of the twenty-three citations not covered by works which we already know Calvin to be using? Five of these are observations about the Jews rather than references to specific Jewish exegesis.[152] A further seven can be accounted for by the use of two other works. Three of these citations are found in Fagius's *Exegesis*, which also accounts for one translation citation.[153] Four others are found in another work of Fagius, his *Thargum*.[154] Calvin four times refers to the 'Chaldaeus paraphrastes' and while two of these citations are found in another source (such as Vatablus's notes) the other two are not. In addition to accounting for these two citations, Fagius's work also accounts for some others in other categories. It is likely, therefore, that Calvin used these two works of Fagius, a judgement that would be

---

[150]See Appendix 5 for details.

[151]For further information about ##3,10,13,14,21,22,25,30,31,33,37,42-45,47, cf. [C.] Siegfried, 'Raschi's Einfluss auf Nicolaus von Lira und Luther in der Auslegung der Genesis,' *Archiv für wissenschaftliche Erforschung des Alten Testamentes* 1 (1867-69) 435f., 438-40, 444, 448, 450f., 455f. and 2 (1871-72) 44-47. This list was compiled by checking *all* of Calvin's Jewish citations against Siegfried, not just those which have been found in Luther or Lyra. The fact that the parallels dry out at ch.24 reinforces the conclusion that Calvin used only the first two volumes of Luther and that his access to Lyra was not direct but via Luther.

[152]##39,50,52,53,57. The only one that requires any *specific* knowledge of Jewish claims is #39 and this is unlikely to refer to this passage in particular.

[153]##6,9,12. Cf. Translation #28.

[154]##23,41,48,49.

reversed only by the discovery of some other source that covers the same citations.

This leaves eleven citations unaccounted for. Two of these are found in other works, but not specifically with reference to the Jews.[155] Three others are found partly, but not wholly, in other works.[156] With one other it is possible that, while the sources do not contain all that Calvin reports, he deduced the rest.[157] One citation may reflect a knowledge of Jewish polemics in general rather than of the exegesis of Genesis in particular.[158] Finally, four citations have not been traced at all.[159]

What conclusions may be drawn? A high proportion of Calvin's Jewish citations, including all of those which name specific Jewish authors, have been traced in works which we have reason to believe Calvin to be using. What of the recalcitrant eleven? There are various possibilities. In his lectures on Daniel Calvin twice refers to the teaching of his colleague Antoine Chevallier, once acknowledging the latter as his source for a Jewish citation.[160] Chevallier was not in Geneva while Calvin was preparing his Genesis comment- ary, but the possibility that Calvin derived some of his citations from oral tradition cannot be discounted. Also possible is that Calvin derived the missing citations from intermediate sources that I have not traced: either that I have failed to discover them in works that I have examined or that they are in other works that I have not examined. Finally, there is the possibility that Calvin read Rabbinic sources for himself: either the writings of individual rabbis or one of the editions of the *Rabbinic Bible*. This last possibility cannot be discounted and will be examined more thoroughly in the future.[161] It is too early to reach a conclusion on the basis of the evidence so far examined.

---

[155]##19,27. See the notes on these citations in Appendix 5.
[156]##21,22,33. See the notes on these citations in Appendix 5.
[157]#45. See the note on this citation in Appendix 5.
[158]#35.
[159]##38,51,58.
[160]CO 40:557,604 on Dan 2:1,44f.
[161]See n.20, above.

Citations of 'Pope' and 'Papists'[162]

There are thirty-six places where Calvin refers to the pope or
to the 'papists,' but only in a minority of these does one need
to seek a source. In most of the instances Calvin moves from
the text to make a point against the papists, without implying any knowledge of their exegesis of the passage concerned. There are just eight, or maybe ten, instances where
Calvin is actually commenting on the Roman Catholic exegesis of the passage.[163] With the remaining citations there is
no need to trace a source in order to account for them, but
where they are paralleled in an earlier work this strengthens
the case for Calvin having used that work. In fact we find
five such passages where Calvin is following Luther,[164]
further confirmation for his use of the latter.

   Of the ten citations, five are straightforwardly found
in confirmed sources.[165] Of the others, one is in Cajetan's
commentary.[166] One is found in Luther's commentary, but in
a volume which Calvin was probably not using.[167] This is
one of those citations where it is not certainly necessary for
Calvin to have a knowledge of Roman Catholic exegesis.
Finally there are three citations for which no source has been
found, one of these being the other citation for which it is not
certainly necessary for Calvin to have a knowledge of
Roman Catholic exegesis.[168]

   What can we conclude from this? Calvin's use of
Luther is confirmed. Some of Calvin's citations can be traced
to the 1548 Augsburg *Interim*, to which Calvin had earlier
responded. This suggests that the as yet untraced sources for
the other citations may be found not in Roman Catholic
exegetical works but in dogmatic and polemical works.
These have not been searched systematically as the present
concern is to trace sources that Calvin used for the actual

---

[162]Citations of 'Pope' and 'Papists' are listed in Appendix 6. #n =
citation n in that list.
[163]##1,6,9,14,18,19,26,35 and, less certainly, ##27,36.
[164]##2,4,10,16,21.
[165]##1,9,18,19,35.
[166]#26.
[167]#27.
[168]##6,14,36.

writing of the commentary. But a casual glance at the English translation of Eck's *Enchiridion* reveals it to be a potential source of no less than five of the ten citations, including three of those for which no definite source had been found.[169] It does not necessarily follow, of course, that Calvin used Eck's *Enchiridion*. There may be dozens of other polemical works appealing to the same passages of Genesis. But it does strongly suggest that the five problem citations originate not from sources like Cajetan's commentary but from Calvin's earlier reading of Roman Catholic polemical works. Another possible source is Calvin's experience of face-to-face discussion with Roman Catholics, as at the colloquies of Hagenau, Worms and Regensburg.

It should also be noted that Calvin's citation of 'papist' views goes beyond the explicit citations considered here. In one place he criticises those who seek to justify idolatory by childishly differentiating between 'dulia' and 'latria,' a clear reference to Roman Catholic thought.[170] To start considering non-explicit citations would make the task endless and also introduce an element of subjectivity, but it should be remembered that there are unnamed as well as explicit citations of papists, Jews, etc.[171]

Specific Unnamed References[172]

There are twenty-three places where Calvin's citation is precise enough to specify a particular group but does not fit into the categories so far considered. These fall into a number of different categories. Five are already in earlier writings of Calvin.[173] Another five are found in Luther,

---

[169]J. Eck, *Enchiridion of Commonplaces* (Grand Rapids: Baker, 1979) 94a (#6), 111 (#35), 131 (#9), 134 (#27), 244 (#26).

[170]CO 23:325:6-9 on 23:7.

[171]A glance at the sources traced in Appendix 8 will reveal some further Jewish influence.

[172]Specific unnamed references are listed in Appendix 7. #n = citation n in that list.

[173]##6,9,15,16,21.

Steuchus's *Recognitio* or Jerome's *Hebraicae quaestiones*.[174] Of these, one is especially significant. Calvin, commenting on Genesis 35:22, refers to a painting of the sacrifice of Iphigenia.[175] This allusion is found in Luther—in his comment on 4:9. Here is a dependence that would never have been traced by searching commentaries under 35:22. It may well be that other citations whose sources have not been traced are also to be found in the known sources, but in unexpected places.

Most of the other citations reflect general knowledge rather than knowledge of the exegesis of Genesis. Calvin draws upon his knowledge of contemporary science[176] and of contemporary theology.[177] He draws upon his knowledge of the Libertines and the Anabaptists, groups against which he had written.[178] He refers to a philosophical commonplace (possibly prompted by Luther)[179] and makes a general comment about the fathers.[180]

This leaves just four citations. A reference to the canonists is found in the *Decretum Gratiani*, a work with which Calvin was certainly familiar.[181] In commenting on 1:26 Calvin notes that some of the Fathers sought to defeat Arianism by stating that Christ alone is God's image.[182] This probably originates from Calvin's reading about Arianism rather than his reading for the Genesis commentary. Calvin states that some of the ancients say Adam and Eve were allured by intemperance of appetite.[183] This also may originate from Calvin's reading about the Pelagian controversy rather than his reading for the Genesis commentary. Finally, his comment almost all ancient authors agree that

---

[174]##10,11,18,20,22. Other possible sources for #10 are Chrysostom, *Homily* 22 and Augustine, *Quaestiones in Heptateuchum* 1:3.

[175]#22.

[176]##1-3.

[177]##13,23.

[178]##7,14.

[179]#4, later incorporated into the *Institutio* (1:5:3).

[180]#17.

[181]#19. Mooi, *Het Kerk- en Dogmahistorisch Element*, 306-12.

[182]#5.

[183]#8, later incorporated into the *Institutio* (2:1:4).

the mountains of Armenia are the highest could be a misreading of Luther.[184]

Examining Calvin's specific unnamed references has pointed to no new sources but has provided further evidence for sources already found.

Vague References[185]

In Calvin's Genesis commentary there are many hundreds of vague references to 'nonnulli,' 'alii,' etc. To attempt to trace these for the whole commentary would be a huge undertaking, yet such citations can provide useful confirmatory evidence. As a compromise, only citations from the first eleven chapters have been considered. Also, the aim has been not so much to trace every one as to check all potential sources against them. This limited study yields some interesting results.[186]

Of the one hundred and twenty-nine citations examined, no less than seventy are accounted for by Luther. With almost fifty of these Luther is the only source found. Here is overwhelming confirmation of Calvin's extensive use of Luther. Many others are accounted for by sources so far identified. These are listed below with, after each source, two numbers: the number of citations accounted for and the number of these not accounted for by any other established source. Steuchus, *Recognitio* (10, 5); Augustine, *De Genesi ad litteram* (9, 2); Fagius, *Exegesis* (9, 2); Vatablus's notes (5, 2); Münster, *Hebraica Biblia Latina* (4, 1); Fagius, *Thargum* (3, 2); Augustine, *De civitate dei* (2, 2); Augustine, *Quaestiones in Heptateuchum* (1, 1).

This leaves thirty-two so far unaccounted for. Three of these are comments general enough not to require a specific source. A further five are comments about sceptical views that are unlikely to be part of the exegetical tradition. Of the remaining twenty-four, six have been traced to other sources: two to Cajetan's commentary and one each to

---

[184]#12.

[185]Vague references from chapters 1-11 are listed in Appendix 8. #n = citation n in that list.

[186]All of the figures given below can be verified from Appendix 8.

Josephus's *Contra Apionem*, Chrysostom's homilies, Augustine's *De Genesi contra Manichaeos* and Eck's *Enchiridion*. None
of these should be regarded as conclusive as the citations
themselves could well have other sources. It is possible that
a more thorough search could trace some more to Luther, for
example. This leaves just fourteen citations with no source
and four with inadequate sources suggested.

The study of the vague references confirms the
sources already traced, especially Luther. There is insuffi-
cient evidence to propose any new sources.

Conclusions

This study has traced sources for the overwhelming majority
of Calvin's citations. A fairly clear picture has emerged.
Calvin reused material from earlier works (especially the
Institutio, also polemical works and commentaries) and also
cited works that he had earlier read (such as Augustine's *De
civitate dei* and the *Decretum Gratiani*). He also consulted
works for specific questions, such as Budé's *De asse* and
Ambrose's *De Iacob et vita beata*. He was reading Bernard's
works at the time and reveals this by inserting an apt saying
when it suits him.

But which works did Calvin actually use in the
preparation of the commentary? Which works were on his
desk and guiding Calvin in his exegesis? This study has
revealed a small number of such works. Calvin clearly made
extensive use of the first two volumes of Luther, for the first
twenty-four and a half chapters. He also relied heavily upon
Steuchus's *Recognitio* throughout his commentary. This surprising reliance upon a Roman Catholic bishop might have
gone undetected were it not for the one solitary reference in
the first chapter. This disparaging remark gives a totally
false impression of the actual nature of Calvin's relationship
to Steuchus. These two works have pride of place. Also
important are three translations with notes that Calvin used
throughout: the 1545 Stephanus Bible with the Vulgate and
Zurich translations and the Vatablus notes (or some other
edition(s) with this material), Münster's *Hebraica Biblia Latina*
and Fagius's *Thargum*. Calvin may also have used the

Pagninus/Servetus translation for some or all of the time. For the opening chapters he used Augustine's *De Genesi ad litteram* (ch.1–3) and Fagius's *Exegesis* (ch.1–4). From chapter four he used Augustine's *Quaestiones in Heptateuchum* and for the whole commentary he consulted Jerome's *Hebraicae quaestiones*.

This is a modest bibliography. That is what makes it plausible. Calvin did not have the leisure to read dozens of commentaries. These works he could have used in the odd hours that he had to prepare the lectures and then write up the commentary.

Calvin is rightly regarded as one of the great commentators of all time. This is all the more remarkable when we consider how little time he had and how little he read. Not the least of his skills was the ability to read little and then to make the maximum use of this material in producing a commentary of lucid brevity.

Works Checked

Where a work is found in the 1572 library catalogue of the Genevan Academy, its reference there is given. Gn = item n in Ganoczy, *La Bibliothèque de l'Academie de Calvin*.

Bible editions
Hebraica Biblia Latina planeque Nova Sebast. Munsteri Tralatione vol.1, (Basel: M. Isengrinus & H. Petrus, 1534) [G3]

Libri Moysi quinque (Paris: R. Stephanus, 1541)

Biblia...Interprete Xante Pagnino Lucense (Köln: M. Novesianus, 1541)

Biblia Sacra ex Santis Pagnini Tralatione (Lyons: Hugo à Porta, 1542) [G42] [Servetus' revision]

Biblia Sacrosancta Testamenti Veteris & Noui (Zurich: C. Froschouer, 1543)

Biblia Sacra cum Glossis, Interlineari & Ordinaria, Nicolai Lyrani Postilla & Moralitatibus, Burgensis Additionibus, & Thoringi Replicis, vol.1 (Lyons: G. Treschel, 1545) [G73]

Biblia (Paris: R. Stephanus, 1545) [G50]

Hebraica Biblia Latina planeque Nova Sebast. Munsteri Tralatione vol.1.1, (Basel: M. Isengrinus & H.Petrus, 1546)

Moses Latinus ex Hebraeo factus ... per Sebastianum Castalionem (Basel: J. Oporinus, 1546) [G43 = 1554 edition]

Biblia, Interprete Sebastiano Castalione (Basel: J. Oporinus, 1551) [G43 = 1554 edition]

Hebraicus Pentateuchus... [Sebastian Münster] (Venice: Justinianes, 1551)

Other Works

Ambrosius, *Hexaemeron* (PL 14:133-288) [G69=1555 edition]

Ambrosius, *De Paradiso* (PL 14:291-332) [G69=1555 edition]

Ambrosius, *De Cain et Abel* (PL 14:333-80) [G69=1555 edition]

Ambrosius, *De Noe et Arca* (PL 14:381–438) [G69=1555 edition]

Ambrosius, *De Abraham* (PL 14:441-524) [G69=1555 edition]

Ambrosius, *De Isaac et Anima* (PL 14:527-60) [G69=1555 edition]

Ambrosius, *De Iacob et Vita Beata* (PL 14:627-70) [G69=1555 edition]

Ambrosius, *De Ioseph Patriarcha* (PL 14:673-704) [G69=1555 edition]

Ambrosius, *De Benedictionibus Patriarcharum* (PL 14:707-28) [G69=1555 edition]

P Artopoeus, *ΑΦΟΡΙΣΜΟΙ. De Prima Rerum Origine ... breves Aphorismi* (Basel: H. Petrus, 1546)

Augustinus, *De Genesi ad litteram* (PL 34:245-486) (in vol. 3 of Erasmus edition) [G72]

Augustinus, *De Genesi ad litteram imperfectus liber*(PL 34:219-246) (in vol. 3 of Erasmus edition) [G72]

Augustinus, *De Genesi contra Manichaeos* (PL 34:173-220) (in vol. 3 of Erasmus edition) [G72]

Augustinus, *Locutiones in Heptateuchum* (PL 34:485-546; CCSL 33:381-465) (in vol. 3 of Erasmus edition) [G72]

Augustinus, *Quaestiones in Heptateuchum* (PL 34:547-824; CCSL 33:1-377) (in vol. 4 of Erasmus edition) [G72]

Basil, *Homiliae in Hexaemeron* (PG 29:93-208) [G28,65]

Bede, *In Pentateuchum Commentarii* (PL 91:189–394)

Cajetan, *Commentarii...in quinque Mosaicos libros* (Paris: J. Parvus, 1539) [G77.I]

W. Capito, *Hexemeron Dei Opus* (Strassburg: W. Rihel, 1539) [G97.I]

Ambrosius Catharinus, *Enarrationes in Quinque Priora Capita Libri Geneseos* (Rome: A. Bladus, 1552) [G76.I]

Chrysostomus, *Homiliae in Genesim* (PG 53f.:21-580) [G70]

Dionysius the Carthusian, *Enarratio in Genesim* (*Opera Omnia* vol.1 (Monstrolii: S. M. de Pratis, 1896)) [cf. G88]

(Pseudo-)Eucherius, *Lucubrationes in Genesim* (Basel: Froben, 1531) (PL 50:893-1048) [G63.I]

P. Fagius, *Exegesis sive Expositio Dictionum Hebraicum* (Isen, 1542)

P Fagius, *Thargum, hoc est, Paraphrasis Onkeli Chaldaica in Sacra Biblia* (Strassburg: G. Machaeropoeus, 1546) [G20.I]

Gregory of Nyssa, *De opificio hominis* (PG 44: 125-256)

Gregory of Nyssa, *Explicatio apologetica in Hexaemeron* (PG 44:61-124)

Hieronymus, *Hebraicae quaestiones in libro Geneseos* (PL 23:935-1010; CCSL 72:1-56) [G61]

Hieronymus, *Liber de situ et nominibus locorum hebraicorum* (PL 23:859-928) [G61]

Hieronymus, *Liber interpretationis hebraicorum nominum* (PL 23:771-858; CCSL 72:59-161) [G61]

Hugo of St. Charo, *Textus biblie cum postilla*, vol.1 (Basel: J. Amerbach, 1504)

A. Lippomanus, *Catena in Genesim* (Paris: C. Guillard, 1546)

M Luther, *In Primum Librum Mose Enarrationes* (Wittenberg: P. Seitz, 1544) [ch.1–11:26] (WA 42) [cf. G93]

M. Luther, *In Genesin Enarrationum...Tomus Secundus* (Nürnberg: J. Montanus & U. Neuber, 1550) [ch.11:27–25:10] (WA 42-43) [cf. G93]

M. Luther, *In Genesin Enarrationum ...Tomus Tertius* (Nürnberg: J. Montanus & U. Neuber, 1552) [ch.25:11-36] (WA 43-44) [cf. G93]

M. Luther, *In Genesin Enarrationum...Tomus Quartus* (Nürnberg: J. Montanus & U. Neuber, 1554) [ch.37–50] (WA 44) [cf. G93]

P Melanchthon, *In obscuria aliquot capita Geneseos annotationes* (Hagenau: J. Secerius, 1523) (CR 13:761-792) [cf. G92]

J. Oecolampadius, *In Genesim Enarratio* (Basel: J. Bebel, 1536)

Origen, *Homiliae in Genesim* (PG 12:45-262) [G47]

Rabanus Maur, *Commentarius in Genesim* (PL 107:439-670)

C. Pellican, *Commentaria Bibliorum, id est XXIII. Canonicorum Veteris Testamenti Librorum*, vol.1 (Zurich: C. Froschauer, 1536) [G105]

G. Pepin, *Expositio in Genesim* (Paris: J. Parvus, 1528)

A E Steuchus, *Recognitio Veteris Testamenti ad Hebraicam Veritatem* (Lyons: S. Gryphius, 1531) [G210]

A. E. Steuchus, *Cosmopoeia...Expositio trium capitum Genesis* (Lyons: S. Gryphius, 1535)

Thomas Aquinas, *Postilla seu Expositio Aurea...in Librum Geneseos* (Antwerp: J. Stelsius, 1563)

J. Ziegler, *In Genesim Mundi...Commentarii* (Basel: J. Oporinus, 1548)

U. Zwingli, *Farrago annotationum in Genesim* (Zurich: C. Froschouer, 1527) [cf. G107]

Appendixes

Abbreviations used for sources:

Cajetan: Cajetan, *Commentarii … in quinque Mosaicos libros*
Cast: Castellio, *Moses Latina* and *Biblia*
CD: Augustine, *De civitate dei*
Comm.: Calvin's commentary on
Eck: J. Eck, *Enchiridion of Commonplaces* (Grand Rapids: Baker, 1979)
Fag: Paul Fagius, *Exegesis*
Gen Lit: Augustine, *De Genesi ad litteram*
Heb Qu: Jerome, *Hebraicae quaestiones in Genesim*
Inst(39/50) x:y:z: Calvin, *Institutio* (1539/1550) at x:y:z in 1559 edition
LXX: Septuagint
Mün: Sebastien Münster, *Hebraica Biblia Latina* (1534)
Origen: Origen, *Homiliae in Genesim*
Pagn: Pagninus, *Biblia*
Post: Nicolaus de Lyra, *Postilla*
Qu Hept: Augustine, *Quaestiones in Heptateuchum*
Rec: Augustinus Eugubinus Steuchus, *Recognitio* (1531)
Tharg: Paul Fagius, *Thargum*
Serv: Servetus's 1542 revision of the Pagninus Bible
Vat: Vatablus notes in 1545 Stephanus *Biblia*
WA: *D. Martin Luthers Werke* (Weimar: Böhlau, 1883ff.)
Zur: Zurich Latin Bible

It is Calvin's practice in commenting on a passage to give the number of the first verse only rather than the extent of the passage (*e.g.*, 1:16 rather than 1:16-19) and this has been followed here. To claim a work as a source for an opinion is, of course, only to state that the opinion is there *described*, not that it is necessarily approved.

For many citations more details on sources will be found above in the main body of text and notes. Where a source is relevant, but not sufficient to account for Calvin's citation, the source is listed in brackets and a footnote explains the situation.

Appendix 1: Named Contemporary Citations

Listed below are all named citations of contemporary authors in Calvin's Genesis commentary which indicate some knowledge of their writings.

#	CO 23:	Genesis	Author	Content	Source
1	15:3-13	1:1	Steuchus	eternity of unformed matter	Rec 25-28
2	16:39-49	1:3	Servetus	Word not eternal	Inst(39) 1:13:8
3	113:30-36	6:3	Luther	Hebrew דוך refers to external ministry	WA 42:273
4	113:50-53	6:3	Luther	ditto	ditto
5	169:12-13	11:10	Luther	patriarchs' suffering like martyrdom	WA 42:428
6	170:4-7	11:27	Luther	Terah's missing sixty years	WA 42:431f
7	193:40-42	13:14	Luther	God spoke through a prophet	WA 42:518
8	325:52-326:1	23:11	Budaeus	value of Attic drachma in French pounds	*De asse* lib.2

Listed below are all explicit citations of translations of the Book of Genesis found in Calvin's Genesis commentary. Where there is a question mark after a source it means that the translation is not quite what Calvin says and may or may not be in Calvin's mind. Calvin's word for 'translate' is given.

Where the reading is found in a translation, no further information is given beyond the name of the translator/translation; where the reading is found in the notes the page or folio number is also given; where the reading concerned is a variant reading found in the margin, this is signified by 'v.l.'

#	CO 23:	Genesis	Citation[1]	Source
1	18:27-29	1:6	Greeks placuerit vertere: στερέωμα	Rec 46; LXX
2	18:27-29	1:6	Latins follow Greeks with 'firmamentum'	Vulg; Mün; Pagn; Fag 14 Rec 46
3	24:7-10	1:21	vulgo legunt 'cetos'	Mün; Pagn; Zur
4	24:7-10	1:21	vulgo legunt 'cete'	Vulg; Cast
5	34:44	2:5	alii transferunt 'virgultum'	Vulg; Pagn; Zur; Rec 77
6	36:32-33	2:8	vetus interpres transtulit 'paradisum'	Vulg
7	36:39-40	2:8	Hieronymus verterit 'a principio'	Vulg; Heb Qu 2:8
8	37:49-50	2:8	vetus interpres fecit 'voluptatem'	Vulg
9	39:49	2:10	no one doubts חידקל = Tigris (14)	e.g. Vulg; Cast; Mün 3a; Rec 100; Vat 2b
10	43:53-55	2:10	omnes interpretes vertunt 'Aethiopiam' (13)	Vulg; Cast; Mün; Pagn; Tharg; Vat 2b
11	47:52-53	2:18	Graeci interpretes reddiderunt: Κατ' αὐτὸν	Rec 110; LXX
12	47:53-54	2:18	Hieronymus: 'Quod sit illi simile'	Vulg[2]
13	50:28-29	2:23	interpres forced reddere 'viraginem'	Vulg; Heb Qu 2:23; Mün; Tharg; Zur; Fag 68
14	50:55-56	2:24	vetus interpres transtulerit 'in carne una'	Vulg
15	50:56-51:2	2:24	Graeci interpretes habent 'erunt duo in carnem unam'	Rec 114; LXX
16	57:39-40	3:1	vetus interpres transtulit 'Cur dixit deus?'	Vulg[3]
17	59:25	3:5	quidam vertunt 'similes *angelis*'	Fag 76; Rec 117; Tharg a5a; Vat 3a
18	60:1-3	3:6	להשכיל exponi potest 'ad videndum'	Vulg; Vat 3a[4]
19	60:1-3	3:6	להשכיל exponi potest 'ad prudentiam'	Mün; Tharg; WA 42:121; Vat 3a
20	65:16-17	3:8	Hieronymus vertit 'ad auram post meridiem'	Vulg
21	65:18-19	3:8	Graeci, omitting word 'wind,' posuerunt 'ad vesperam'	Rec 120; LXX
22	67:6-8	3:11	vulgaris translatio habet 'nisi quod de arbore'	Vulg[5]
23	67:53-54	3:13	vertunt interpretes 'Quare hoc fecisti?'	Vulg
24	70:13-16	3:15	Hieronymus vertit 'conteres caput' + 'insidiaberis calcaneo'	Vulg
25	71:12-21	3:15	Papists translate 'she' shall bruise	Vulg; WA143; Rec 123
26	72:50	3:17	vetus interpres transtulit 'in opere tuo'	Vulg
27	73:31-35	3:17	עצבון vertunt 'dolorem'	Mün; Zur; Fag 98; Rec 127
28	74:26-27	3:19	alii vertunt 'laborem' in place of sudorem	Fag 100
29	82:42-46	4:1	quidam exponunt 'cum Domino'	Zur; Fag 118
30	82:46-47	4:1	altera interpretatio 'possedi *a Domino*'	Mün; Pagn; Tharg; Fag 118 Rec 131[6]
31	82:47-48	4:1	Hieronymus vertit 'per Dominum'	Vulg (v.l.);[7] Fag 118
32	82:52	4:1	alii subtilius 'possedi virum Dei'	WA 42:179f[8]
33	88:22-32	4:7	Graeci interpretes miss Moses' sense	Rec 134; LXX

[1] Numbers in brackets are those of the verse being translated, where this is different.

[2] Vulg readings are 'similem sui' and 'similem sibi,' the latter in the 1545 Stephanus Bible.

[3] Vulg reads 'Cur praecepit ... Deus?'

[4] Vulg reads 'aspectuque delectabile;' Vat 3a reads 'ad contemplandum.'

[5] Vulg reads 'Nisi quod ex ligno.'

[6] Rec 131 reads 'possedi a Deo.' Mün, Tharg and Pagn read 'acquisivi ... a domino.'

[7] In the Stephanus Bibles the text reads 'per Deum' with 'per Dominum' as a variant reading. In Heb Qu the reading is 'per Deum.' Fag cites Vulg as 'per Dominum.'

[8] Luther gives the text as 'Aquisivi virum Domini' and proceeds to cite it as 'Aquisivi virum Dei.'

#	CO 23:	Genesis	Citation	Source
34	89:1-3	4:7	Hieronymus vertit 'recipies'	Vulg
35	91:4-5	4:8	Hieronymus expressit 'Veni, egrediamur foras'	Vulg[9]
36	114:4-7	6:3	Graeci legerunt wrongly 'Non permanebit'	Rec 157; LXX
37	115:40-44	6:4	Hieronymus reddidit badly	Heb Qu 6:4; Vulg
38	119:46-47	6:9	vetus interpres solet reddere תמים as 'perfectum'	Vulg
39	137:18-21	8:6	negative has crept into Graecam versionem (7)	Rec 181; LXX
40	137:18-21	8:6	negative has crept into Latinam versionem (7)	Vulg;[10] Heb Qu 8:6f; Rec 181
41	137:35-36	8:6	Hieronymi versio habet 'ramum [fuisse] virentibus foliis' (11)	Vulg
42	140:21-23	8:21	adulterina illa versio: 'cogitatio prona ad malum'	Vulg
43	146:11-12	9:5	Hieronymus reddidit אך as 'enim'	Vulg
44	146:11-15	9:5	others legunt particle אך 'adversative' as 'alioqui sanguinem vestrum'	Mün
45	146:11-15	9:5	optime sic vertere licet 'et sane sanguinem vestrum'	Vat 6b
46	154:52-53	9:27	most interpretes accipiunt יפח as 'dilatare' Vulg; Mün; Pagn; Tharg; Zur; Rec 193	
47	159:34-36	10:8	Hieronymi versio placet: paraphrase follows (9)	Vulg
48	165:31-32	11:4	quidam interpretes vertunt: 'Antequam dispergamur'	Vulg; Cast; Rec 209[11]
49	180:3-8	12:6	'Elon' quidam vertunt 'quercetum'	Zur
50	180:3-8	12:6	'Elon' alii vertunt 'convallem'	Vulg
51	180:3-8	12:6	'Elon' alii vertunt as place name	Rec 218f; Vat 8a
52	197:16-17	14:1	vetus interpres Arioch ex 'Ponto' accersit	Vulg
53	199:35-37	14:14	cur vetus interpres verterit 'numeravit Abram expeditos suos vernaculos'	Vulg
54	216:1-3	15:9	alii pro 'trienni' [heifers, etc.] vertunt: 'triplicatam'	Mün 13a; Serv (v.l.)
55	220:52-54	15:16	quidam accipiunt עון pro 'poena'	Pagn; Vatablus?[12]
56	229:48-50	16:12	quidam exponunt פרא to mean 'sylvestrem'	Mün; Pagn; Tharg c2b; Vat 10a[13]
57	230:49-50	16:13	quidam vertunt 'Annon vidi post visionem meam?'	Zur[14]
58	231:1-3	16:13	alii sic accipiunt 'An ego vidi post visionem meam?' i.e. so late	Mün 14a
59	231:10-11	16:13	Hieronymus vertit 'posteriora videntis me'	Vulg
60	236:4-7	17:4	some transferunt 'Ecce, ego ferio tecum foedus'	Zur
61	236:4-7	17:4	others transferunt 'Ecce, ego et foedus meum tecum'	Mün
62	246:9-11	17:19	quidam accipiunt אבל pro 'vere'	Mün; Pagn; Tharg
63	253:19-21	18:10	Hieronymus vertit 'vita comite revertar'	Vulg
64	255:4-5	18:13	quidam vertunt פלא as 'occultum' (14)	Tharg; Vat 11a
65	261:10-11	18:21	Hieronymus vertit 'si opere compleverint'	Vulg
66	261:20-22	18:21	alii vertunt 'si ita fecerint, iam adest ultimus…'	interpretation, not translation[15]
67	268:47-48	19:5	Graeci interpretes verterunt 'cognoscere' in sense of 'rem habere'	Rec 259; LXX
68	309:1-2	21:32	alii vertunt 'puteum septem'	Serv (v.l.); Vat 13a
69	315:11-12	22:2	Hieronymus exposuit 'terram visionis'	Vulg; Heb Qu 22:2
70	315:14-15	22:2	quidam interpretantur 'myrrham Dei'	Serv (v.l.); Vat 13a
71	318:26-30	22:14	some activum verbum 'videbit' in passivum transtulerunt	Heb Qu 22:14[16]
72	334:40-41	24:12	Hieronymus vertit 'occurre' instead of 'occurrere'	Vulg
73	336:40-41	24:22	Hieronymus pro 'dimidio' posuit: 'duos siclos'	Vulg
74	340:18-20	24:63	שוח exponi potest 'egressum esse meditandi'	Vulg; Serv (v.l.); Zur; Mün 22b
75	340:18-20	24:63	שוח exponi potest 'egressum esse orandi'	Mün; Pagn; Tharg; Rec 281; Vat 5b
76	347:45-46	25:21	some vertunt 'praesente uxore'	Tharg d4b; Vat 15b

9 Vulg reads 'egrediamur foras,' without the 'Veni.'

10 'non revertebatur' is a variant Vulgate reading which is found in the text of the Stephanus Bibles.

11 Vulg reads 'antequam dividamur;' Rec 209 has the Vulgate reading but also mentions the Zurich reading 'ne forte dispergamur;' Cast reads 'antequam…dispergerentur.'

12 Pagn reads 'punitio.' According to Marlorat, Genesis, 120, Vatablus notes 'nondum venit tempus quo puniantur.' This is not found in the Vatablus notes in Stephanus's 1545 Bible.

13 Calvin adds 'et venandis feris addictum,' which is not found in the translations and may indicate his use of a Hebrew dictionary.

14 Zur reads 'Annon etiam hic vidi post videntem me?'

15 This citation has been retained because Calvin uses the word 'vertunt,' but here he is paraphrasing rather than giving a verbal translation.

16 Rec 272 makes the point of passive versus active, but it is only Heb Qu that draws from the translation the moral mentioned by Calvin.

#	CO 23:	Genesis	Citation	Source
77	391:45-46	28:12	some vertunt particulam עַל 'prope' (13)	Mün; Pagn[17]
78	410:1-4	30:8	alii vertunt 'coniunctionibus Dei coniuncti sum'	Mün 29a; Vat 18b[18]
79	410:4-5	30:8	alii vertunt 'duplicata sum duplicationibus Dei'	Vatablus?[19]
80	410:11-13	30:8	ab aliis affertur 'luctata sit divinis aut praeclaris luctationibus'	Mün 29a; Vat 18b[20]
81	411:49-50	30:14	omnes vertunt 'mandragoras'	e.g. Vulg; Cast; Mün; Pagn; Tharg; Zur; Rec 295
82	415:12-13	30:29	Hieronymus transtulit 'antequam venirem' (30)	Vulg
83	416:7-8	30:33	quidam legunt 'quando *tu venies* ad mercedem meam'	Vat 19a
84	416:8-10	30:33	alii vertentes in tertia persona 'ad mercedem *ventura sit*'	Mün; Tharg; Zur[21]
85	428:1-2	31:29	quidam exponunt 'manus mea est ad Deum'	Mün 31a
86	445:31-32	32:28	Hieronymus faithfully renders sense	Vulg; Heb Qu 32:28f
87	458:25-26	34:7	communiter vertunt interpretes 'non sic fieri decet'	Tharg[22]
88	491:28-30	37:38[23]	Graeci exponunt 'lanionum praefectum'	Tharg f6a; Vat 24a; Rec 333; LXX[24]
89	493:43	38:2	quidam vertunt 'negotiatorem'	Zur; Vat 24a
90	511:33-34	40:1	quidam intelligunt 'annum integrum' (4)	Pagn;[25] Mün 40a; Tharg g2b; Vat 25a
91	524:47-48	41:40	alii legere malunt 'armabitur'	Mün; Pagn; Vat 26a
92	524:48-49	41:40	alii [legere malunt] 'cibabitur ad nutum vel mandatum'	Tharg; Zur; Mün 42a[26]
93	525:5-9	41:40	אברך: some exponunt 'patrem tenerum' (43)	Heb Qu 41:43; Pagn; Mün 42a; Vat 26a
94	525:9-11	41:40	אברך: some vertunt 'patrem regis' (43)	Tharg; Mün 42a; Vat 26a
95	525:11-13	41:40	אברך: alii afferunt 'genu flecte' (43)	Vulg; Heb Qu 41:43; Cast; Mün; Vat 26a
96	525:16-19	41:40	by some vertitur 'mundi redemptor' (45)	Vulg; Heb Qu 41:45; Rec 349[27]
97	525:16-19	41:40	by others [vertitur] 'mysterio-expositor' (45)	Heb Qu 41:45; Cast; Pagn; Tharg; Mün 42a; Rec 350; Vat 26a[28]
98	525:19-21	41:40	Graeci leave words untranslated (45)	Rec 349; LXX
99	525:23-24	41:40	quum כוהן significet 'principem' (45)	Pagn; Tharg; Mün 42a; Vat 26a
100	548:33-34	44:5	alii vertunt 'in quo tentando tentavit vos, vel rimando rimatur'	Vat 28a
101	550:51-52	44:18	quidam vertunt 'peccavero in patrem meum' (32)	Mün; Zur
102	550:51-52	44:18	[quidam vertunt] 'reus ero peccati' (32)	Vulg; Tharg
103	550:52-54	44:18	alii [vertunt] 'obnoxius ero: propterea …' (32)	Pagn; Vat 28b
104	556:41-43	45:22	Hieronymus transtulit 'binas stolas'	Vulg
105	556:41-44	45:22	alii interpretes eum sequuti exponunt 'dissimiles vestes'	Vat 29a
106	562:3-6	46:8	numerical error once only apud graecos interpretes	Heb Qu 46:26f; Rec 356f; LXX
107	570:28	47:12	alii vertunt 'pubem'	Zur
108	577:48-49	47:31	Graeci verterunt 'ad summitatem virgae'	Rec 359; LXX
109	581:30-32	48:3	עולם accipitur by some as 'diuturno tempore' (4)	Mün 49a; Tharg h5b; Vat 30b[29]
110	581:30-32	48:3	accipitur by others as 'aeternitate' (4)	Vulg; Cast; Pagn; Zur; Mün 49a; Tharg h5b[30]
111	592:44-46	49:3	quidam vertunt 'tu virtus mea et principium *seminis*'	Serv (v.l.)[31]

---

[17] These both read 'iuxta eam.'

[18] These both read 'coniuncta sum per Deum.'

[19] According to Poole, *Synopsis* 1:79, this is Vatablus' reading. It is not found in the Vatablus notes in Stephanus's 1545 Bible.

[20] Neither of these gives the text precisely as Calvin has it. With Mün, the text is 'luctationibus divinis luctata sum' and the notes give the alternative meaning 'magnificis.'

[21] These versions bring out Calvin's point without having the exact wording.

[22] Tharg reads 'sic enim non decebat fieri;' the other translations all have the same sense in different words.

[23] The 1554 edition and CO both have v.38, in error for v.36.

[24] Tharg f6a and Rec 333 read 'coquorum principem,' Vat 24a reads 'magistro coquorum.'

[25] Pagn reads 'per annum;' the other works all have the word 'integrum' as well.

[26] These all give the sense mentioned by Calvin, not the exact words.

[27] These all read 'salvator mundi.'

[28] These all give the sense of 'mysterio-expositor,' but not the exact wording.

[29] These all give the sense mentioned by Calvin, not the exact words.

[30] These all give the sense mentioned by Calvin, not the exact words.

[31] The Servetus variant reading is 'tu fortitudo mea et principium seminis.'

#	CO 23:	Genesis	Citation	Source
112	592:44-46	49:3	alii vertunt 'tu virtus mea et principium *doloris'*	Vulg; Zur; Mün 50a[32]
113	595:20-21	49:5	מכרות quidam accipiunt pro 'gladiis'	Zur; Mün 50a[33]
114	595:23	49:5	מכרות: others vertunt 'habitationes'	Rec 363f
115	595:35	49:5	שור quidam vertunt 'taurum' (6)	Heb Qu 49:5f; Mün 50a; Rec 365; Vat 31a
116	599:5-6	49:10	Hieronymus vertit 'qui mittendus est'	Vulg
117	599:18-19	49:10	alii interpretes exponunt 'filium eius'	Tharg; Mün 50a; Vat 31a
118	602:37-43	49:10	scio 'aggregatio' exponi by some interpretibus 'debilitatio'	Mün 50a
119	602:37-43	49:10	by other interpretibus 'obedientia'	Mün 50a; Rec 370; Vat 31a[34]
120	606:33-34	49:22	alii vertunt 'filium decoris'	Mün 50b
121	607:31-34	49:22	quidam vertunt 'inde pastor lapis Israel' (24)	Vulg; Mün
122	607:34-36	49:22	alii legunt 'pastor lapidis,' in genitivo casu (24)	Mün 50b

Appendix 3: Named Patristic Citations

Listed below are all named citations of the Fathers and of Josephus in Calvin's Genesis commentary, excluding instances where 'Jerome' means 'the Vulgate.' As CO is not fully reliable for Calvin's marginal references these have all been checked in the 1554 original.

#	CO 23:	Genesis	Author & Source {Text + (margin) + [actual]}: Content	Source
1	7f.:38-40	Argument [Cassiodore] *Historia Tripartita*		WA 42:9; Augustine, *Confessiones* 11:12:14
2	9f.:2-4	Argument Augustinus, (*De Genesi contra Manich.*) [1:2:4]		Inst(39) 3:23:2
3	9f.:2-4	Argument (Lib. II *de Civit. Dei*)		CD 2:11:5, 2:12:12
4	18:45-48	1:6	Gregorius [*Epp*. 9:105, 11:13]: books of unlearned	CO 7:26 (1544); Inst(50) 1:11:5
5	25:55-26:7	1:26	Augustinus, Librum 10 *de Trinit.* [10:11:17-12:19]	(WA 42:45)[35]
6	25:55-26:7	1:26	et 14	(WA 42:45)
7	25:55-26:7	1:26	item *de Civit. Dei* libro 11	CD 11:24-40
8	26:35-38	1:26	Chrysostomus [*Homiliae in Genesim* 8:3f,9:2-4,10:3f]	*Psychopannychia* (CO 5:181)
9	37:9-13	2:8	Origenes: allegorises Garden of Eden	WA 42:68,74; Rec 91f
10	38:51-54	2:9	Augustinus: tree of life figure of Christ	Gen Lit 8:4:8; Inst(50) 2:2:9
11	38:51-54	2:9	Eucherius: ditto [*Lucubrationes in Genesim* lib.1 in c.2 , v.9]	Inst(39) 2:2:9
12	46:30-34	2:18	Hieronymus, *Contra Iovinianum* prior liber	Inst(39) 4:12:28 & Comm. various
13	60:35-38	3:6	Augustinus: pride = beginning of all evils	Gen Lit 11:5:7, 11:15:19; CD 14:13:1
14	63:1-2	3:6	Augustinus: Adam & Eve stood for 6 hours only	not Augustine
15	63:15-17	3:6	Augustinus: wretched freewill which so unstable	*Enchiridion* 106:28?
16	63:18-21	3:6	Bernardus: potential for evil since fall	*Epistola* 1:3
17	90:53-54	4:7	Augustinus: give what you command …	e.g. Inst(36) (OS 1:55)
18	114:44-47	6:3	Lactantius [*Divinae institutiones* 2:14]: 120 years = limit of human life	Rec 160
19	123:8-10	6:14	Origenes [*Homiliae in Genesim* 2:2]: geometrical cubits	##20,21
20	123:10-12	6:14	Augustinus lib. *de Civitate Dei* 15: agrees with Origen	CD 15:27:3
21	123:10-12	6:14	et lib. 1 *Quaestionum in Genesin*: ditto	Qu Hept 1:4
22	123:44-48	6:14	Augustinus, lib. 15 *de Civitate Dei*: allegorises Ark	CD 15:26
23	123:44-48	6:14	[lib.] 12 *adversus Faustum* [12:14,16]: ditto	WA 42:310
24	123:48f.	6:14	Origenes: allegorises Ark	Origen 2:3-6
25	129:13-14	7:1	Augustinus: God crowns his own gifts	e.g. Inst(39) 2:5:2
26	136:55-137:1	8:3	Josephus [*Antiquitates* 1:93-95]: fragments of Ark remain	#27; Rec 179
27	137:1-2	8:3	Hieronymus [*Liber de situ et nominibus locorum hebraicorum* (PL 23.859)]	Rec 179

---

[32] These all give the sense mentioned by Calvin, not the exact words.

[33] Mün and Zur read 'machaerae eorum.'

[34] Mün has the noun 'obedientia;' the others use the verb.

[35] Luther refers to Augustine's *De trinitate*, but without specifying which books.

#	CO 23:	Genesis	Author & Source {Text + (margin) + [actual]}: Content	Source
28	145:55-146:1	9:4	Tertullianus: Christians not to taste blood [*Apologia* 9:13]	memory
29	189:12-15	13:1	Augustinus: rich & poor together heirs of life	*Enarrationes in Psalmos* 85:3?
30	201:20-22	14:18	Hieronymus *ad Evagrium*: heaps together absurdities	*Ep.* 73:2-10 ad Evangelum
31	201:26-29	14:18	Hieronymus: vestiges of Melchizedek's palace	*Ep.* 73:7
32	202:41-45	14:18	Tertullianus et similes: type of Eucharist	*Interim* (CO 7:579f,644)
33	241:56-242:2	17:12	Augustinus: 8th day signifies resurrection	CD 16:26?
34	299:42-45	21:8	Augustinus: significance of Isaac's weaning	Qu Hept 1:50; WA 43:145
35	302:25-29	21:10[36]	Origenes [*Homiliae in Genesim* 7:2-6, esp. 7:2]: allegorises	Comm. Gal. 4:22f.
36	317:41-42	22:12	Augustinus: forced exegesis	Qu Hept 1:58
37	322:46-49	23:2	Ambrosius: too much mourning wrong	*De Abraham* 1:9:80; Inst(36) (OS 3:19)
38	325:52-53	23:11	Josephus: shekel worth 4 Attic drachmas [*Antiquitates* 3:195]	memory/checked
39	326:10-15	23:16	Hieronymus: letter removed from Ephron's name	Heb Qu 23:16
40	326:26-29	23:16	Hieronymus: ditto	Heb Qu 23:16
41	343:35-38	25:1	Augustinus: source of Abraham's vigour	Qu Hept 1:35,70 ; Comm. Rom. 4:19
42	378:4-13	27:27	Ambrosius: allegorises	*De Iacob et vita beata* 2:2:9; Inst(39) 3:11:23
43	470:43-46	35:10	Augustinus: Jacob/Israel w.r.t. present/future life	Qu Hept 1:114
44	561:47-49	46:8	Augustinus: Stephen adds three born in Egypt	CD 16:40 ; Comm. Acts 7:14
45	588:32-34	48:22	Hieronymus: allegorises money	Heb Qu 48:22

Appendix 4: Citations of Ancient Heresies

Listed below are all explicit references to ancient heresies in Calvin's Genesis commentary.

#	CO 23:	Genesis	Heresy	Content	Source
1	15:25-30	1:1	Arriani; Sabellius	others' relation to them	general
2	26:28-30	1:26	Anthropomorphitae	likeness in body	*Psychopannychia* (CO 5:180); Inst(39) 1:13:1
3	55:15-23	3:1	Manichaei	temptation implies two Gods	Gen Lit 11:13:17, *De haeresibus* 46
4	61:53-56	3:6	Pelagius	denied original sin	Inst(39) 2:1:5f.
5	62:15-17	3:6	Pelagius	sin transmitted by imitation	Inst(39) 2:1:5f.
6	113:19-22	6:3	Manichaei	some Jews accused of	Augustine, *De haeresibus* 46
7	474:35-44	35:22	Novatus; Novatiani	refuted by this passage	Inst(39) 4:1:23

Appendix 5: Jewish Citations

Listed below are references to post-biblical Jews in Calvin's Genesis commentary. Excluded are Calvin's references to 'Hebraei' where he he is thinking of the Hebrew language rather than views of Jewish exegetes or theologians.

#	CO 23:	Genesis	Content	Source
1	21:36-37	1:14	Rabbis say מועדים refers to Jewish festivals	Fag 20; Rec 52
2	24:47-50	1:24	Some Hebrews distinguish iumentum & bestias	WA 42:41; Fag 25; Mün 2a
3	25:28-30	1:26	Jews say 'us' = earth or angels	WA 42:43; Fag 26; Mün 2a
4	34:3-7	2:3	Jews say fauns, etc. = imperfect animals	Mün 3a

---

[36] In CO 23:302 the verse number (12) is given; in the 1554 edition no such number is given so this comment is listed under 21:10.

#	CO 23:	Genesis	Content	Source
5	34:35-37	2:4	Some Hebrews: Yahweh first used when world complete	Fag 37; Mün 3a; Rec 78f
6	47:46-47	2:18	Some of rabbis say כנגדו here is affirmative	Fag 60f
7	57:15-21	3:1	Kimhi: אף כי means quanto magis	Fag 74f; Mün 4a
8	57:23-25	3:1	better Chaldaeus paraphrastes: verumne	Tharg; Vat 3a
9	86:32-35	4:5	Jews say Cain defrauded God	Fag 122f
10	86:43-48	4:5	Hebrews: Abel's sacrifice consumed by fire	Fag 125; Post 45a; Heb Qu 4:4f; Rec 132[37]
11	88:39-42	4:7	some Hebrew doctors refer נשא to Cain's countenance	WA 42:199; Fag 127f
12	88:42-44	4:7	other Hebrews apply it to remission of sins	Fag 127; Tharg
13	96:56-97:8	4:15	Jewish interpretation of this verse	WA 42:223; Post 46a
14	100:49-55	4:23	Jewish fable about Lamech	WA 42:235 & 223
15	105:49-51	5:2	Jewish writers say only married people called Adam	WA 42:248
16	111:50-53	6:1	Chaldean paraphrast: promiscuous marriages condemned	Rec 156; Tharg b2b; Vat 4b
17	113:14-19	6:3	some Hebrews derive word from נדן	WA 42:272
18	113:22-24	6:3	other Jews derive word from דון	Rec 158
19	115:2-3	6:3	Jews say years cut off because human wickedness	(Heb Qu 6:3)[38]
20	122:39-42	6:14	Jews not agreed about type of wood: cedar, fir-tree or pine	Mün 6b; Rec 169f[39]
21	122:42-48	6:14	Jews not agreed about number of stories	(WA 42:309; Post 51a-b)[40]
22	122:48-54	6:14	Jews not agreed about window: number & purpose	(WA 42:310f; Post 51a)[41]
23	136:53-55	8:3	Chaldaeus paraphrastes designat quod montes Cardu	Tharg b3b[42]
24	136:53-55	8:3	quos alii Carduenos vocant	Rec 180; Tharg b3b
25	141:32	8:22	Jews divide year into six parts	WA 42:353; Post 55a
26	146:22-23	9:5	Jews distinguish four types of homicide	WA 42:359; Tharg b4b
27	153:16-19	9:25	Jews say Ham not cursed because special favour	(WA 42:384)[43]
28	163:20-24	11:1	Jews commonly reckon 340 years between Flood & Babel	Mün 10b
29	163:46-47	11:1	common opinion of Jews [= previous item]	Mün 10b
30	166:54-56	11:7	Jews say God addressing angels	WA 42:422; Rec 210
31	170:38-44	11:28	Jews say Haran burnt because shunned idolatry	Post 59b; Heb Qu 11:28; Rec 214f
32	176:30-32	12:1	noun גוי detestable to Jews but here term of honour	WA 42:445
33	177:55-178:3	12:3	Jews say bless/curse in s.o. means after their pattern	(Mün 11a; Post 60b; Vat 8a)[44]
34	192:18-19	13:10	Hebrews call anything excellent 'divine'	WA 42:506f
35	193:44-50	13:14	Jews contend over word עולם (v.15)	general?
36	211:27-28	15:6	Jews, whose blindness is well known, miss the point of the verse	WA 42:563
37	230:52-54	16:13	Hebrews: why Hagar surprised	WA 42:599; Mün 14a; Post 67b; Tharg c2b[45]
38	232:18-22	16:14	some Hebrews say name of well is testimony to double favour	?
39	242:49-50	17:13	Jews object that Christ violates circumcision law	general
40	243:15-24	17:13	wrong to say that circumcision is still in force for Jews	WA 42:651
41	267:3-6	19:1	Jews say one angel to destroy Sodom, other to preserve Lot	Tharg c4a
42	298:56-299:4	21:7	Jews say Sarah suckled local infants to prove motherhood	WA 43:144; Post 75b
43	318:4-6	22:13	Jews say ram created on sixth day	WA 43:233; Post 78a
44	321:18-22	23:1	Jews say why word 'years' repeated	WA 43:270; Post 79b

[37] Heb Qu & Post quote the Theodotian translation; Rec & Fag cite other sources.

[38] Heb Qu has it, but without mentioning the Jews. It is cited by WA 42:279, Rec 162, Post 50b.

[39] Mün & Rec between them have the necessary information.

[40] Post is not clearly about the Jews; Luther has some of the information, but mostly not explicitly referring to the Jews.

[41] Post contains most, but not all, of what Calvin says of the Jewish view; Luther has most of it, but some not explicitly referring to the Jews.

[42] The text of Tharg has 'super montes [Cordu]' and the notes give this as 'Cardu' (b3b).

[43] Luther has the information, but without mentioning the Jews.

[44] Mün, Post and Vat all have the same material, which refers to blessing only, not to cursing, and which doesn't mention any biblical proofs.

[45] Luther and Post both say thought *angels* seen only in A's house; while Calvin says *God*. Mün has 'dei nuncium,' while Tharg has 'per angelos suos se conspiciendum praebuit dominus,' which best explains Calvin's reference to 'God' rather than to 'angels.'

#	CO 23:	Genesis	Content	Source
45	330:44-48	24:2	most Jews say implies circumcision & Abraham author of such a way of swearing WA 43:300f?; Mün 22a?; Rec 277?; Tharg d3b[46]	
46	330:51-53	24:2	some Jews say it was token of subjection	Mün 22a; Rec 277; Tharg d3b
47	333:30-34	24:10	some Hebrews: servant took document WA 43:321; Mün 22a; Post 80b; Tharg d3b	
48	338:29-31	24:33	some Hebrews say right/left hand = Lot/Ishmael (v.49)	Tharg d3b
49	346:42-45	25:18	Chaldean paraphrast supplies word 'lot'	Tharg d4b
50	353:14-18	25:28	Jews wrong to glory in flesh in light of Isaac's behaviour	general
51	391:1-5	28:12	Hebrews say Jacob's ladder is figure of Providence	(Tharg e1b; Vat 17b)[47]
52	411:36-46	30:14	Jews wrong to glory in their origins	general
53	461:36-40	34:25	Jews wrong to glory in their origins	general
54	483:38-41	37:9	certain Hebrews interpret it of Bilhah	Mün 37b
55	491:27-29	37:38[48]	some Hebrews say Potiphar was lanionum praefectum	Mün 37b; Tharg f6a
56	491:30-31	37:38	other Hebrews say Potiphar was praefectum militum Mün 37b; Tharg f6a; Vat 24a	
57	493:31-33	38:1	Moses does not glorify Jewish ancestors	general
58	495:48-49	38:10	The Jews prate insufficiently modestly about this shameful matter	?
59	511:20-22	40:1	Gerundensis: Pharaoh made them eunuchs because enraged	Mün 40a
60	562:41-43	46:8	Hebrews say Jochebed, mother of Moses, also included	Mün 47a
61	598:13-599:2	49:10	Jews obscure interpretation of this verse	Mün 50a-b; Rec 368-70; Tharg i2a-4a
62	599:9-12	49:10	some Jews say שילוה denotes place Shiloh	Mün 50a; Rec 368f; Tharg i2b
63	599:22-23	49:10	Jews refer this to David	Mün 50a; Tharg a2a-3b
64	599:41-600:4	49:10	Jews haughtily object that events convicts us of error	Mün 50a-b
65	601:52-602:3	49:10	some Jews say Judah given *right* (vs. glory) of government	?

Appendix 6: Citations of 'Pope' and 'Papists'

Listed below are the explicit references to the pope or to 'papists' in Calvin's Genesis commentary.

#	CO 23:	Genesis Content		Source
1	71:12-21	3:15	papists translate 'she' shall bruise	Vulg; WA 42:143; Rec 123
2	120:45-48	6:9	shows papists foolish to urge following fathers	WA 42:300
3	124:8-10	6:18	papists foolish to say doctrine of faith distracts from good works	general
4	134:2f	7:17	papists ridiculous to fabricate ark without word	WA 42:334
5	148:54-56	9:11	papists enchant bread etc. with magical whisperings	general
6	152:18-20	9:23	papists seek cover from cloak of Shem & Japeth	Eck 94a
7	154:28-33	9:25	pope claims to prophesy, but he is servant of servants as Canaan was	general
8	181:51-55	12:7	papists claim to worship God but trifle with foolish pageantry	general
9	203:5-15	14:18	papists find sacrifice of mass here *Interim* (CO 7:579f,644); WA 42:537-40; Eck 131	
10	236:20-27	17:4	religion of papists is fictions of men	WA 42:625f
11	240:19-27	17:9	papists have abolished sacraments because word of God missing	ditto
12	255:33-35	18:13	papists plunge into labyrinth with talk of absolute power of God	Comm. Is 23:9
13	270:54-271:3	19:9	papists criticise us for paucity of numbers and novelty	general
14	290:10f	20:7	papists base patronage of dead intercessors on this	?
15	298:19-27	21:4	papists boast of seven sacraments	general; cf. WA 43:141

---

[46] Mün, Rec and Tharg note that the Jews relate this method of swearing to circumcision as the sign of the covenant. Luther (following Lyra) mentions circumcision only. He also, unlike the others, discusses whether the practice originated with Abraham, but without stating the Jewish view. It might be that Calvin would have deduced from the reference to circumcision and the covenant that the Jews thought the practice originated with Abraham.

[47] Tharg and Vat say that for Hebrews Jacob's ladder means that inferiors depend upon superiors.

[48] The 1554 edition and CO both have v.38, in error for v.36.

#	CO 23:	Genesis	Content	Source
16	303:26-30	21:10[49]	papists boast of their succession	WA 43:155
17	306:14-18	21:20	pope denies rights of parents in marriage	*Interim* (CO 7:574,640)
18	318:49-51	22:15	papists find merits of works here	WA 43:256
19	319:16-20	22:15	what God meant as encouragement papists interpret as merit	ditto
20	326:29-33	23:16	papal sacrificers sell burial rights	general
21	331:50-52	24:3	pope denies rights of parents in marriage	*Interim* (CO 7:574,640); WA 43:296-8
22	377:12-15	27:21	papists make force of sacrament depend on intention of priest	general
23	384:23-26	27:41	papists commend confession as deterrent against sin	*De scandalis* (OS 2:226)
24	389:19-34	28:6	corruptions of popery make thorough reformation necessary	general
25	392:17-20	28:13	sacraments of papacy frivolous because no word	general
26	394:45-47	28:17	papists misapply this to their temples	Cajetan 120; Eck 244
27	396:45-397:2	28:20	papists take this as precedent for their vows[50]	WA 43:606; Eck 134
28	404:44-49	29:30	papists make practices of fathers laws and have unworthy fathers	general
29	428:50-55	31:30	papists think to escape idolatry because don't call idols gods	general
30	457:19-22	34:4	pope breaks bond of nature: parental rights re marriage	*Interim* (CO 7:574,640)
31	467:15-19	35:2	papacy full of superstitions because earlier generations tolerated it	general
32	469:9-11	35:7	papists have an affected humility which is degrading	general
33	469:31-34	35:7	in papacy ceremonies are empty because word missing	general
34	559:54-560:5	46:2	without the word, sacraments of papacy are lifeless	general
35	585:31-40	48:16	papists find prayers to dead here Inst(39) 3:20:25; *Interim* (CO 7:583,653); Eck 111	
36	594:14-19	49:5	Papists say punishment remains while guilt remitted	general?

Appendix 7: Specific Unnamed References

Listed below are those references in Calvin's Genesis commentary, where he is explicitly citing the views of a particular group, without naming individuals.

#	CO 23:	Genesis	Content	Source
1	22:10-12	1:15	'astrologi' rightly say moon opaque	general
2	22:22-25	1:16	'astrologi' distinguish between spheres	general
3	22:26-28	1:16	'astrologi' prove Saturn larger than moon	general
4	25:25-26	1:26	man called μικρόκοσμος by ancients	commonplace; cf. WA 42:51
5	27:20-23	1:26	some fathers say Christ alone is God's image	?
6	35:38-42	2:7	'animali vita' meant, against most ancients	*Psychopannychia* (CO 5:181); Tharg a3b
7	39:32-35	2:9	libertines say pure lust is innocency	general
8	60:32-33	3:6	some of the ancients say Adam & Eve allured by intemperance of appetite	?
9	62:45-47	3:6	ancient figment of traducianism	Inst(39) 2:1:7
10	111:47-50	6:1	ancient figment of intercourse of angels & women	Heb Qu 6:2; Rec 153; Tharg b2b
11	114:44-47	6:3	some ancient writers say 120 year lifespan	Heb Qu 6:3; Rec 160
12	136:51-53	8:3	Armenia's mountains highest claimed by ancient writers	WA 42:338?[51]
13	141:6-8	8:21	philosophers transfer [original sin] from nature to habit	general
14	148:33-35	9:9	ignorant Anabaptists exclude infants from covenant	general
15	202:29-45	14:18	ancient church writers say bread & wine typical	*Interim* (CO 7:579f,644)
16	202:52-53	14:18	falsehood of the ancients thus refuted	ditto
17	228:52-55	16:10	most of ancients say that Christ present in all the oracles	general
18	251:30-35	18:2	some of ancient writers say Abraham perceived Trinity	WA 43:11-14; Rec 252
19	326:26-29	23:16	canonists say sacrilege to sell sepulchre	*Decretum Gratiani* II, c.13, q.2, c.13
20	330:48-51	24:2	Christian writers say it is in honour of seed	WA 43:301; Heb Qu 24:9; Rec 277

---

49 In CO 23:302 the verse number (12) is given; in the 1554 edition no such number is given so this comment is listed under 21:10.

50 CO 23:396:45 erroneously reads 'iustitia' where p.206 of the 1554 edition has 'stultitia.'

51 If Calvin is dependent upon Luther, he has misread him.

#	CO 23:	Genesis	Content	Source
21	428:56-429:2	31:30	metonymy is ancient idolaters' excuse	Inst(36-43) 1:11:9
22	474:6-9	35:22	Moses acts like painter of sacrifice of Iphigenia	WA 42:206f
23	522:11-20	41:17	philosophers prefer Plato to God's word	general

Appendix 8: Vague References

Listed below are vaguer references in Calvin's Genesis commentary, as far as chapter 11, where he is explicitly citing someone's views, without being precise about whose. The following list is not totally exhaustive. A reference, for example, to the view held by the great majority of commentators (CO 23:25, lines 49f., on 1:26) is of little interest in seeking to trace Calvin's sources. Where the point concerned is found in a wide range of sources only those are listed that we know Calvin to be using.

#	CO 23:	Genesis	Content	Source
1	14:34-35	1:1	frivolous to expound 'beginning' as Christ	WA 42:8f; Heb Qu 1:1; Gen Lit 1.4.9-6:12
2	15:20-33	1:1	inferred from plural Elohim that Trinity implied	WA 42:10; Rec 28-32
3	17:54-56	1:5	error that world was made in one moment	WA 42:4,52,91; Gen Lit 4:33
4	18:11-16	1:5	this falsehood supported from Ecclus 18:1	Gen Lit 4:33:52
5	18:39-41	1:6	some allegorise waters as angels	CD 11:34
6	21:19-21	1:14	abused to justify astrological predictions	WA 42:33f
7	22:2-5	1:15	some dishonestly reproach Moses for inexactitude	sceptics
8	23:27-30	1:20	birds could not come from water	Augustine, *De Genesi contra Manichaeos* 1:15:24
9	23:50-52	1:21	some say fishes created because waters insufficient	?
10	25:36-38	1:26	others say plural we	WA 42:43
11	27:12-15	1:26	some say particles indicate image eschatological	?
12	29:34-36	1:28	some infer that people were then vegetarian	WA 42:54f; Origen 1:17 (69)
13	29:49-51	1:28	prudent judgement that earth marred by Flood	WA 42:74f
14	31:35-37	2:1	error that world formed in a moment	as #3
15	34:10-13	2:3	some say 'creavit ut faceret' means God didn't withhold preservation	Tharg a3a
16	34:14-17	2:3	others say 'faceret' refers to *man* making works by his industry	?
17	34:24-27	2:4	'ingrati' & 'maligni' say world eternal or remove memory of creation	sceptics
18	36:47-49	2:8	some say Eden covered whole world	WA 42:55,74
19	37:44-47	2:8	some locate Eden in region of Mesopotamia	Rec 84f
20	39:12-14	2:9	some restrict tree of life to corporeal life	WA 42:70f
21	39:50-51	2:10	many say Pison/Gihon are Ganges/Nile	WA 42:74 ; Mün 3a; Rec 100-3; Gen Lit 8:7:13
22	39:53	2:10	others say Danube	Rec 103
23	39:55-40:2	2:10	others say names of two of the rivers now obsolete	Rec 105
24	40:6-11	2:10	some get round this by saying surface of globe changed by Flood	WA 42:74f
25	46:40-42	2:18	some say singular 'faciam' because woman inferior	?
26	47:55-48:2	2:18	some say woman made/'good' only for procreation	WA 42:87-89; Gen Lit 9:5:9;
27	48:8-10	2:18	others say means woman ready for obedience	Vat 2b
28	48:43-45 + 49:2-10	2:21	profane & perverse are sceptical about method of making woman	WA 42:92,97; Gen Lit 9:16:30
29	50:5-6	2:23	it is demanded how Adam knew this	sceptics
30	50:32-35	2:24	it is doubted whether God, Adam or Moses is speaking	WA 42:101
31	53:14-16	3:1	some say more acuteness found in other animals	Cajetan 27
32	53:33-37	3:1	opinion that Spirit purposely used obscure figures	WA 42:109
33	54:19-21	3:1	some foolishly allegorise snake	i.e. = Satan: Fag 72; Cajetan 27
34	54:21-25	3:1	many surprised no mention of tempter's own fall	Inst(43) 1:14:16
35	54:25-27	3:1	'fanatici' say Satan created evil	Gen Lit 11:20:27; cf. Inst(43) 1:14:16

#	CO 23:	Genesis	Content	Source
36	55:3-6	3:1	some ask why God allowed temptation	Inst(39) 3:23:2-9; Gen Lit 11:4:6
37	55:30-35	3:1	many suppose God not cause of sin but left Adam to freewill	Inst(39) 3:23:6
38	55:44-45	3:1	some offended to hear that God willed the Fall	Inst(39) 3:23:6
39	55:56:56:2	3:1	unskilled infer from this that fall not free	Inst(39) 3:23:6
40	56:7-12	3:1	impious doubt whether snake could speak	Cajetan 27
41	56:46-49	3:1	curious sophists say Satan tempted because jealous of incarnation	?
42	57:25-26	3:1	some say snake's question is *simple* interrogation	?
43	57:25-26	3:1	others say *ironical* interrogation	WA 42:112
44	57:35-37	3:1	some say Satan openly denying God's word	cf. WA 42:112
45	57:37-39	3:1	others say weakening confidence by inquiring about cause	WA 42:115
46	58:1-4	3:1	some say Satan implies all trees forbidden	Chrysostom, *Homiliae in Genesim* 16:3
47	58:4-5	3:1	others that he implies that all trees are permitted	WA 42:115
48	58:30-33	3:1	some suppose added 'touch' charges God with excessive severity	?
49	59:8-13	3:5	some say Satan craftily praises God	WA 42:119
50	59:13-15	3:5	others say Satan charges God with envy	WA 42:119
51	60:6-8	3:6	some deduce Adam present when Eve fell	Fag 78; Rec 119
52	60:13	3:6	some refer particle עמה to conjugal bond	?
53	61:31-33	3:6	'perversi rhetores' say Eve/Adam allured by beauty/Eve	?
54	63:2-4	3:6	others say Satan delayed temptation till sabbath	WA 42:62,108
55	65:29-30	3:8	others understand [word] as 'plaga vel regione australi'	WA 42:127
56	65:31-37	3:8	others say means time of clear daylight	WA 42:127
57	68:40-42	3:14	many interpret this passage allegorically and subtly	WA 42:138
58	69:24-27	3:14	some learned & able say serpent previously walked upright	WA 42:140
59	72:22-25	3:15	others say 'seed' refers to Christ	WA 42:144f; Rec 123
60	73:55-74:1	3:18	some say earth is exhausted by long time	cf. WA 42:155f
61	74:2-4	3:18	others that God's blessing impaired by increasing wickedness	WA 42:161
62	74:6-10	3:18	some say Adam deprived of all former fruits	WA 42:156f
63	74:31-33	3:19	some ignorant persons say all to do manual labour	WA 42:157f
64	75:53-76:4	3:19	some say God remits guilt (v.15) but retains punishment (v.19)	Eck 77
65	77:5-8	3:19	some understand 'you shall die' (2:17) in spiritual sense: physical death anyway	?
66	77:34-37	3:20	Some say Adam called Eve mother of living because of future hope	WA 42:164f
67	78:51-54	3:22	some say plural 'us' refers to angels	WA 42:166
68	78:56-79:6	3:22	some Christians read Trinity in here	WA 42:167
69	79:12-15	3:22	those who think it is ironical are mistaken	WA 42:166
70	80:12-18	3:23	some say turning sword points to chance for repentance	WA 42:172
71	82:52-83:4	4:1	others say Eve thought Cain = deliverer	WA 42:144; Fag 118f;
72	83:16-18	4:2	some think Abel so called out of contempt	WA 42:180f; Fag 120
73	83:31-34	4:2	some censure Eve's judgement about sons	WA 42:182; Fag 120
74	85:54-86:2	4:4	vain philosophy that talks of faith, ignoring God's grace	general
75	86:2-4	4:4	faith purifies only because of gift of regeneration	Inst(39) 3:11:15
76	87:41-49	4:6	good men, pious and learned, say Adam speaking	WA 42:194
77	88:46:51	4:7	third exposition: exaltation refers to honour	Mün 4b; Vat 3b
78	88:52-55	4:7	others say Cain needed purity of heart through faith	Tharg a6b; cf. WA 42:196-8
79	90:13-21	4:7	nearly all commentators refer this to sin …	WA 42:199; Fag 129
80	90:45-46	4:7	childish trifle to say this proves free choice	Inst(39) 2:5:16; WA 42:199
81	91:2-4	4:8	some think Cain hid anger	WA 42:200; Fag 131
82	91:35-37	4:9	some say Adam speaking here	WA 42:202
83	94:3-6	4:11	some say cruelty ascribed to earth—like wild beast	Fag 136
84	94:16-20	4:11	some say Adam cursed less than Cain to spare human race	WA 42:214
85	94:22-27	4:11	others say Cain receives temporal punishment only	WA 42:215
86	94:55-95:3	4:12	some distinguish נע = no settled abode & נד = know not where to turn	WA 42:216f
87	96:52-56	4:15	some say Cain wanted one immediate death	WA 42:222
88	97:38-40	4:15	commentators say Cain's body became tremulous	WA 42:226; Fag 143
89	99:10-13	4:17	mockers ask where Cain found builders & citizens	Qu Hept 1:1; cf. CD 15:8
90	102:27-30	4:24	some infer Adam & Eve left childless by loss of Abel & Cain	WA 42:239
91	106:12-13	5:3	some object that Seth & family unfallen because elected by grace	Inst(39) 2:1:7
92	109:23-24	5:29	some suppose Lamech thought Noah was the Christ	WA 42:259
93	109:44-47	5:32	they err who say Noah chaste because remained single 500 years	WA 42:261

#	CO 23:	Genesis	Content	Source
94	113:26-30	6:3	some interpret it: God will no longer govern by his Spirit	Rec 158
95	114:20-21	6:3	those wrong who restrict 'flesh' to lower part of soul	general
96	115:40-44	6:4	other interpreters blunder after Jerome WA 42:285; Mün 6b; Qu Hept 1:3; Vat 5a	
97	116:5-7	6:4	some expound עולם ('a saeculo') as 'coram mundo'	WA 42:288
98	116:7-9	6:4	some think this spoken proverbially	Mün 6b
99	117:31-33	6:5	some expound particle 'continuously' to mean from infancy	?
100	119:25-28	6:8	some unlearned deduce subtly that we merit grace	general
101	127:54-128:4	7:1	year begins at autumnal equinox OR in March	WA 42:327
102	131:23-29	7:8	ditto for Hebrews: political versus sacred year	ditto
103	136:24-28	8:3	some think 150 days = whole time since beginning of Flood	WA 42:337
104	136:51-53	8:3	some deny view of ancient authors that Ararat is Armenia	WA 42:338
105	137:21-25	8:6	textual error → fable about raven → futile allegories	WA 42:339,372-5
106	137:28-30	8:6	some philosophise about olive branch	WA 42:376
107	137:35-38	8:6	some say Vulg confirms idea Flood began in September	WA 42:327
108	137:46-49	8:15	Profane say that Noah stayed in because timid	sceptics
109	145:32-34	9:4	some say not eat member cut off from living animal	WA 42:359; Rec 187
110	146:40	9:6	some say 'in man' means before witnesses	Tharg; Vat 6b
111	146:40-42	9:6	others say 'in man' means by man blood to be shed	WA 42:360
112	146:46-48	9:6	some say merely political law for punishment of homicide	WA 42:360f
113	149:21-23	9:13	certain eminent theologians say no rainbow before Flood	WA 42:365f
114	157:39-158:1	10:1	mockers doubt rapidity of population growth	sceptics
115	159:51-53	10:10	Semiramis built Babylon OR he only adorned it Josephus, Contra Apionem 1.142	
116	160:3-7	10:10	some say not in chronological order: 10:10 after 11:1ff	WA 42:403
117	160:33-39	10:11	opinion that Asshur here is a country not a person	Vat 7a
118	162:45-49	11:1	some conjecture tower built against further flood	WA 42:410;
				Josephus, Antiquitates 1.114
119	163:16-24	11:1	some prefer Berosus (130 years) to Jews	(WA 42:414 ; Cajetan 64)[52]
120	163:24-29	11:1	others say Babel built because population already dispersing	?
121	165:39-46	11:4	some say Noah warned of future dispersion	WA 42:416f
122	165:46-48	11:4	others say they prophesied against themselves	WA 42:415
123	166:19-27	11:6	some interpret v.6 as God vigilant against wickedness (Ps 34:16)	WA 42:420?
124	166:27-31	11:6	others say comparison between less & greater size of population	?
125	168:4-6	11:9	error of those deriving Babylon from Jupiter Belus	Rec 211
126	169:38-40	11:10	others say not absurd that third son born after two years	WA 42:426
127	170:8-10	11:27	others say lived with father 60 years in Charran	CD 16:14f
128	170:33-35	11:27	some object that Sarah step-daughter of or adopted by Nahor	WA 42:431
129	170:51-53	11:28	others say Ur so called because in valley (Hebrew אורים)	?

---

52 Luther doesn't mention Berosus and says about 100 years; Cajetan mentions Berosus but has 151 years.

Chapter 4

CALVIN THE HEBRAISER?

Influence and Independence in Calvin's Old Testament lectures, with special reference to the 'commentary' on Jeremiah

Mark W. Elliott

In an age where the 'anxiety of influence' has been detected as a psychological and linguistic factor operating on authors, the current interest in the reception of authorities by the Reformers is also explained by a wish to see the hand of God and his divine inspiration as providing a continuity of ideas from age to age.[1] In Calvin's own case, the influence of Bernard, Augustine, and even Gregory Nazianzen has been noticed. These are more used as authorities in the *Institutes* and in polemical writings. When it comes to the New Testament commentaries, the influence of Chrysostom and a few others is apparent. Yet there seem to be few such authorities salient in the text of his comments on the Old

---

[1]I refer principally to the immense work, edited by Irena Backus, *The reception of the Church Fathers in the West* (Leiden: Brill, 1996); see also some of Jaroslav Pelikan's *The Reformation of the Bible/ The Bible in the Reformation* (New Haven & London: Yale University Press, 1996).

Testament. Calvin's debt to Jerome is obvious as the author
of the Vulgate, especially when it comes to matters of Middle
Eastern geography where respect is shown to someone who
had made that land his home.[2] Nevertheless, Ganoczy and
Scheld have argued that where biblical hermeneutics was
concerned, Jerome's authority was significantly lower than
that of Augustine: thus Peter and Paul really did have a fall
out as Galatians 2 suggests and it was not the ceremonial law
but the whole law which was abrogated or superseded
according to Paul.[3]

   One can perhaps speak of Calvin and Jerome as
'kindred spirits.' William McKane has noted the similarity of
the two men, in that they both sought the *Hebraica veritas*,
and both deliberately by-passed the Septuagint to get there.
In Calvin's case, however, the Septuagint was not so much
compared as ignored, although McKane's estimation of
Jerome as holding the Septuagint to be a worthy contributor
to interpretation of the true text overemphasizes the practical
amount of use the LXX offered him.[4] In any case, Calvin was
a professor of theology, not the Old Testament specialist at
the fledgling Genevan Academy.[5] This suggests that the

---

[2]Alexandre Ganoczy und Stefan Scheld, *Die Hermeneutik Calvins:
Geistesgeschichtliche Vorausetzungen und Grundzüge* (Wiesbaden: Franz
Steiner Verlag, 1983) 147: ...eine Vielzahl der Calvinischen Verweise
auf die Vulgata bezieht sich ja auf ihn—spielt Hieronymus bei den
Erläuterungen zur Geographie des Heiligen Landes eine wichtige
Rolle. Offensichtlich vertraut Calvin dem Kirchenlehrer, weil dieser
längere Zeit in Palästina lebte und die Verhältnisse dort aus eigener
Erfahrung kannte.'
[3]*Ibid*, 147f.
[4]W. McKane, 'Calvin as an Old Testament Commentator,' *Nederduitse
Gereformierde Teologiese Tydskrif* 25 (1984) 250-59, at p.256. See also his
Select Christian Hebraists (Cambridge: CUP, 1988) *Appendix* 3 and p.118:
'Jerome had espoused *Hebraica Veritas*, and yet on occasions he accuses
the Jews of having corrupted their text. He replies to Rufinus, and
others who complain, that they ignore the laws of dialectic: in a
dispute one speaks now in one way, now in another.' McKane admits
(283, n.47) that it is Richard Simon who asserts that such a defence
against allegations of inconsistency is found in Jerome's *Apologia
adversus Rufinum*, and that he, McKane, cannot locate it in P. Lardet's
Source Chretiennes edition (Paris: Cerf, 1983).
[5]See A.J. Baumgartner, *Calvin Hébraïsant et Interprete de L'Ancien
Testament* (Paris: Fischbacher, 1889) 24 on the *Leges academiae genevensis*

Academy would not permit students to dogmatics before a grounding in biblical theology, and to biblical theology before a grounding in the biblical language. Calvin was more of a team-player than is often communicated by studies of this doughty individual. David Steinmetz is thus only half right when he comments: 'Calvin appears to have held the chair on Old Testament and to have lectured on the Hebrew text of the Bible...Calvin's principal occupation was the interpretation of Scripture,'[6]—as if Calvin needed to do everything. In Geneva around 1560 there was then a (possibly humanist, even 'modern') re-casting of the idea of theology as sacred *science.*

Calvin's biblical commentaries are notable for the paucity of names of other writers. This has been explained and defended on the grounds of Calvin's disdain for the prolix and his *Tendenz*, at least after the Seneca *De Clementia* commentary, to eschew lengthy debate with secondary authorities. Many of the commentaries so-called are actually notes from lectures, and Parker has noted that these are less polished, and have even fewer references to other authors than the commentaries which were created in Calvin's study. The lecture format, the fact that it is engagement with the text of Scripture and not a debate with diverse theological opinions, the rush to get through while time and health permitted,[7]—these factors hide the salient fact that in his commentaries Calvin is trying more to defend Old Testament Scripture from bogus interpretations of it than to find doctrine in it.[8] This reluctance at times to tie the Old to

---

(1559). Antoine Chevalier had the honour of being the first Professor of Hebrew. Yet Calvin lectured on the Old Testament during his few years at the Academy. T.H.L. Parker notes (*John Calvin* (London: J.M. Dent, 1975) 154) that the work of 'dogmatics' was left for the *Institutes*.

[6]*Calvin in Context* (New York: OUP, 1995) 19. Cf. Parker, *John Calvin*, 153f.

[7]'[Jean] Budé confirms the fearful pressure of work that forces him to "leave home after having had usually hardly half an hour to meditate on these lectures"' (T.H.L. Parker, 'Calvin the Biblical Expositor,' *Churchman* 78 (1984) 23-31, at p.29).

[8]David L. Puckett, *John Calvin's Exegesis of the Old Testament* (Louisville: Westminster John Knox, 1995) 16: 'It has been argued that the two parties Calvin consciously opposed in the theological arena—Roman Catholics and Anabaptists—were also his principal rivals as he

the New is the occasion of the slander by Hunnius of Calvin as *Calvinus Judaizans* —with which David Puckett introduces his recent book. The meanings of many prophecies are neither to be found in the exile (without remainder) nor in Christ (without remainder), but remain in the future for the people of God. It is thus a concern with Lutheranism that pervades the commentaries. As is well known, Calvin did not lecture on Systematic Theology. Steinmetz is overbold in asserting that much in Calvin's commentaries is of the order of commonplaces. Summing up Calvin's use of the Church Fathers in his commentaries on the *New* Testament: 'In every case, explicit and anonymous, in which Calvin has referred to Patristic exegesis, he has quarreled with it'.[9] Yet perhaps we can allow that *sub*consciously he was indebted to sacred exegesis as his *Institutes* often reveal more clearly. For example, his hermeneutic of *accommodatio* can be linked to a *Patristic* dislike of speculation and the Fathers' insistence that God reveals himself as he is, so that to speak of God having an absolute power which we do not yet know is speculation.[10] Nevertheless, the Calvin of the late commentaries seems often uncomfortable with theological overlaying wherein the Doctrines of the Trinity and of Christ's Incarnation upstage the valid historical meanings. Scripture was too important a foundation for it to be itself golden and ornate. The drive towards popularising in Calvin's understanding coincided with a disillusionment with the idea that Councils and doctrinal statements might prove to be of any spiritual use to believers.[11]

---

exegeted the Old Testament [citing Anthony Baxter, *John Calvin's Use and Hermeneutics of the Old Testament* (Ph.D., Sheffield, 1987) 330]... Much more common are his criticisms of interpretations that he believes represent Jewish and Christian exegetical traditions.'

[9]Steinmetz, *Context*, 136.

[10]See E.P. Meijering, *Calvin wider die Neugierde. Ein Beitrag zum Vergleich zwischen reformatorischem und patristischem Denken* (Nieuwkoop: de Graaf, 1980) 59f.

[11]See Olivier Millet, *Calvin et la dynamique de la parole: étude de rhétorique réformée* (Paris: Honoré Champion, 1992) 773f. It seems that the mature Calvin was quite relieved that no doctrinal agreed statement came from any 'ecumenical' colloquies such as Poissy in 1561, especially after the *debâcle* of the Worms Colloquy in 1557.

Calvin's Old Testament hermeneutics

Augustine tended to favour the New Testament message in his interpretation of the Old and sometimes this was abetted by his trust in the wording of the Septuagint. Even though this was a criticism that could be levelled at the Gospel writers and Paul, Calvin was quick to defend the New Testament writers whose divergences from the Old Testament text were only 'apparent.' However he did not spare Augustine.[12] The 'objective' verifiability of interpretations mattered; a lack of it would not invalidate the Christian message, but it might lose the battle over the powerfulness of a particular text. This can be explained as the gift of Calvin's humanism; but as an 'early modern,' he would not, as Bouwsma has suggested, be happy with loose ends and any amount of 'cognitive dissonance.' Where Calvin allowed allegory it was really only typology on the grounds that the meaning could not be at least fully accounted for in the events and characters of the Old Testament. What added to his confidence in finding the right interpretation was his 'allowing' the object to determine his understanding of it.[13]

Calvin's Hebrew and his Old Testament

At the end of the last century, Antoine Baumgartner contested Richard Simon's low estimation of the quality of Calvin's Hebrew.[14] It should be noted that Simon had scant regard for most of the scholars of the Reformation: Sebastian

---

[12]See Ganoczy-Scheld, *Die Hermeneutik Calvins*, 179f. Also, Puckett, *Exegesis*, 54 and n.15 for references to Calvin's commentaries where Augustine is accused of over-speculating. Generally, L. Smits, *Saint Augustin dans l'oeuvre de Jean Calvin*, 2 Vols., (Assen: Van Gorcum, 1956-58).

[13]Ganoczy-Scheld, *Die Hermeneutik Calvins*, 182: 'Vergleicht man Calvins Ideal der Schriftauslegung mit seinem Verständnis der Schrift, lassen sich mehrere Entsprechungen feststellen die bezeugen, daß der Reformator die Prinzipien seiner Interpretation dem zu interpretierenden Objekt angleicht.'

[14]Baumgartner, *Calvin Hébraïsant*.

Münster, for instance, was treated with sneering sarcasm.[15] Yet he reserves his strongest barbs for Calvin,[16] criticising him for having the gall to correct Olivetan's translation of the Scriptures into French (1535) after writing a glowing preface for it. The Geneva-corrected French Bible was in fact dragged back closer to the Vulgate in places and displays some of Calvin's own prejudices. He did not have the grammatical tools to make a better job of it.

So much, then, for Simon's account. Baumgartner does not answer him line for line but simply contends that, as to Simon's low estimation and allegation that Calvin often got the meanings of words wrong, one should expect that opinion from a work vitiated by the spirit of *parti pris*. For a man of his time Calvin was up there with the best, and he should not be criticised for not knowing what has only been learned in the succeeding centuries. Baumgartner makes much of the fact that the attempt in Western Christendom to make Hebrew studies a reality came to little, and that after 1311 when Clement V realised the need for Christian 'oriental studies' little happened before 1480, and that it was only with Reuchlin and, more significantly for Calvin, Vatable at the Collège de France that Hebrew studies began in earnest. Calvin is worthy of our admiration as a pioneer. There is, Baumgartner admits, no hard evidence that he studied under Vatable, but they shared a common place of origin and 'esprit'. Olivetan *could* have helped him, but their relationship was, it would seem, wholly epistolary. Baumgartner concludes that on Calvin's return to Paris, Gérard Roussel would have got him started on Hebrew, and have followed this up when in Basle at the end of 1534 where Oecolampadius had been 'interpreter of Scripture' until his

---

[15]R. Simon, *Historia critica veteris testamenti* (Amsterdam: Blaviana, 1685) 116: 'Qua in re censet se Hieronymum imitatum esse qui quotidie Judaeos tanquam oracula consulebat... Rabbinicam eruditionem affectat.'

[16]*Ibid.*, 135: 'Calvinus, qui primae quidem Olivetani editioni praefationem praefixerat, ac illam exactam et fidelem dixerat, haud diu illam ferre potuit. verum illam castigare voluit propter multos errores et ut Olivetani rudis et dura atque inintelligibilis dictio mollietur. id vero facinus supra Calvini qui vix Hebraice legere poterat, et nil ferme Graeci sciebat, vires erat.'

death in 1531, and where Münster was about to produce his Hebrew Bible. The reason Calvin does not mention what he learned in Basle is that he preferred silence where his teachers were concerned. The argument overall is a little weak.

A more specific piece of evidence comes from Theodore Beza who claimed Grynaeus and Capito had given Calvin instruction in Hebrew, yet the reference is confusing because it locates this education in Basle.[17] Baumgartner seems to think this 'mistake' of location invalidates it as evidence, not that Grynaeus and Capito were in Basle in 1535, but that Calvin was helped while in Strasbourg between 1538 and 1541, despite his many other duties. Yet Strasbourg and Basle were hardly far apart. Ganoczy aids the cumulative case: 'I follow the opinion of the OC editors on the date and place of the composition of the two prefaces [to Olivetan's French Bible]: "We believe that they were written...at the same time that he was considering his first *Institutes* at Basle and concentrating on his biblical studies" (9, lxii)'.[18] Baumgartner admits that Calvin never regarded himself as a Hebrew specialist and was largely self-taught.[19] Simon may well have been right to suspect that Calvin lacked the grammatical skills. The first Hebrew grammar to be published in Geneva was Chevallier's in 1567, four years after the Reformer's death.[20] Eventually Baumgartner admits that Calvin never knew Hebrew well enough to teach it, but knew his Hebrew roots and the importance of literal ('mot à mot') translation.[21]

---

[17]*CO* 21:124.

[18]Alexandre Ganoczy, *The Young Calvin*, (Philadelphia, Westminster Press, 1987) (=ET of *Le jeune Calvin: Genèse et évolution de sa vocation réformatrice* (Wiesbaden: Franz Steiner, 1966)) 334, n.19.

[19]Baumgartner, *Calvin Hébraïsant*, 25: 'Calvin n'a donc jamais enseigné la langue historique à Genève. Il avait dû en acquérir par lui-même une connaissance vraiment sérieuse et détaillée, ses commentaires le montrent assez clairement.'

[20]*Rudimenta hebraicae linguae...* (Geneva: H.Fuggeri, 1567).

[21]Baumgartner, *Calvin Hébraïsant*, 45-52; also p.61: 'Il n'a pas été un hébraïsant spécialiste, mais il a su grouper les résultats de la science de son époque. Pourtant il ne s'est pas servi d'une science de second main, qu'il ne s'est pas arrogé un droit qui ne lui revenait point, mais qu'il a su mettre à profit ses propres études et parler en connaissance de cause.'

Calvin could have been expected to be familiar with his Old
Testament to some degree of detail, given that, twenty years
previously he had read through Olivetan's translation to
correct it and make it more intelligible. The importance of
this has perhaps been underestimated, although it has recently been reviewed carefully by Francophone scholars
associated with Bernard Roussel.[22] It might be thought that
the glosses of Sebastian Münster and Robert Estienne would
be reflected in his lectures, since the former's own Latin
translation[23] and the latter's edition of a recent Latin translation[24]—both with copious marginal commentary—would
have been available in Geneva. However, an overview of
both these potential sources shows little similarity with
Calvin's exegesis.[25] It seems likely that the influence worked
more from Calvin to Estienne.

---

[22]The obvious starting-place is B. Roussel (ed.), *Olivetan, traducteur de la
Bible (Actes du colloque de Noyon, de mai 1985)* (Paris: Cerf, 1987); also G.
Bedouelle & B. Roussel (eds.), *Le temps des Réformes et la Bible*, La Bible
de tous les temps 5 (Paris: Beauchesne, 1989). A more detailed and
thorough examination, such as was called for by Baumgartner one
hundred years ago is a *desideratum*.

[23]This folio (Basle, 1535) was stylistically an improvement on Sancti
Pagnini's 1528 translation: see Basil Hall, 'Biblical Scholarship: Editions
and Commentaries' in S.L. Greenslade (ed.), *The Cambridge History of
the Bible: from the Reformation to the Present Day* (Cambridge: CUP, 1963)
vol.3, 38-93, at pp.70f.

[24]The 1557 folio edition (1st octavo edition, 1544-46) with the Vulgate
and Pagnini's translation side by side and his own comments, much
influenced by Vatable, was gifted to Geneva for the Academy by
Estienne. Cf. D.F. Wright, 'Robert Estienne's *Nova Glossa Ordinaria*. A
Protestant Quest for a Standard Bible Commentary,' in W. van't Spijker
(ed.), *Calvin: Erbe und Auftrag: Festschrift für W. Neuser* (Kampen: Kok
Pharos, 1991)40-51, at p.45, n. 29: 'In November 1550 Calvin wrote to
Farel of Estienne as "now wholly ours" (*CO* XIII, 657).' See also Hall,
'Biblical Scholarship,' 65-67.

[25]Without going into detail, Estienne's annotations in 1557 were even
more reliant on Pagnini's comments than in 1540 and 1546, although
he has illuminated places where the Dominican's translation seemed
obscure. Towards Vatable, a 'Nicodemite' he is a bit more guarded
('nunquam tamen sine optima et manifestissima ratione'). But he
admits that one needs many words to translate a few Hebrew words
and there is much polysemy due, amongst other things, to the pointing
of the Hebrew.

Calvin and Jeremiah

My examples come from Calvin's commentary on Jeremiah. Part of the problem with recent studies, along with a large degree of generalisation, has been an agnosticism about the occasion and background of this commentary, originally delivered as lectures. Not least in importance is the fact that these 193 lectures were given during the onset of Calvin's physical decline.[26] They began on April 15th, 1560 and were finished on September 9th, 1563.[27] Before the summer of 1563 when he became seriously incapacitated by nephritis, his worries were as much political as physical. For instance, there was the wooing of Navarre by Lutherans and their persistence at the colloquies, the absence of Beza, the persecution and insurgency of Huguenots in different places —all of which is reflected in anxious correspondence. Oberman has commented that, in Calvin's theology as well as the christological extra dimension of a glorified man alongside the Word, there were 'extras' of God's sovereignty exercised providentially outwith the Church (as well as over the Eucharist 'within' it).[28] It must also be noted that the idea of a local Christ—exalted, not universal, fitted with a Jewish/Messianic idea of christology which Luther would have played down too much. The dedication to the Elector Palatine Friedrich who did not always want to be known as a 'Calvinist' was an attempt to encourage him to keep faith with the Reformed cause.[29] In the Preface, Calvin excused

---

[26]This is clear from a reading of the correspondence. See *CO* 19:*passim*. As Bruce Gordon notes, Calvin was as scared of a Lutheran France as much as a Romanist France, which explains his orientation towards Zurich in those times of turbulence and personal pain ('Calvin and the Swiss Reformed Churches,' in A. Pettegree, A. Duke, G.Lewis (eds.), *Calvinism in Europe:1540-1620* (Cambridge: CUP, 1994) 64-81).

[27]See T.H.L. Parker, *Calvin's Old Testament Commentaries* (Edinburgh: T.& T. Clark, 1986) 29.

[28]'Der "Extra"-Dimension in der Theologie Calvins' in his *Die Reformation: von Wittenberg nach Genf* (Göttingen: Vanderhoeck & Ruprecht, 1986) 253-282.

[29]There was also a Frech translation with some additional comments of an informal nature. See Adolph Zahn, *Die beiden letzten Lebensjahre von Johannes Calvin* (Leipzig: E. Ungleich, 1895) 52, who adds: 'Wir [= Wie] sehr ihm Jeremiä Zeit ein Bild seiner eigenen war, lässt sich begreifen.'

the style of the written-down lectures which were delivered 'extempore,' especially the first volume which had gone to press without his permission. Within the preface is a riposte to the Lutheran doctrine of the ubiquity of Christ. He did not hesitate to attack renegades such as Francis Baldwin in the Dedication to Friedrich, in case the latter might think the French Reformed to be all like the former and thus look less kindly on the Reformed scholars at Heidelberg.

It seems that the school run by Oecolampadius and Münster at Basle, with its distinction between teachers of the biblical languages and professors of theology, served as one model for the Genevan Academy (there was also influence from those at Lausanne and Strasbourg). The commentary by Bullinger on Jeremiah would have appeared too late to be influential, and Ganoczy's evidence is such that the Academy's library received its copy (1557–59) through Peter Martyr's collection. Can we know that Calvin had it let alone read it? It seems unlikely. However, it cannot be altogether excluded as a possibility.[30] More hopeful is the case of the lectures/commentary of Oecolampadius. Again, Ganoczy's research is helpful in ascertaining that Oecolampadius alone among the Reformers may have been the one who went ahead of Calvin in giving lectures.[31] We know of lectures published in Strasbourg by Apianus in 1533, and also of their republication in Geneva in 1558.[32] It is more *possible* that Calvin would have had access to these.

Did Calvin have sources? Three examples from Calvin's lectures on the early part of Jeremiah

In his linguistic work on the Hebrew text, Calvin, while independent of the glosses of Münster and Estienne, was not totally without help. His comments on Hebrew words appear to owe much to Münster's edition of Rabbi David Kimchi's *Sepher ha-shorim*, a dictionary with Latin words

---

[30]I am indebted to Mr. A.N.S. Lane for this point.

[31]No. 116 in the catalogue in A. Ganoczy, *La Bibliothèque de l'Académie de Calvin* (Geneva: Droz, 1969).

[32]*Ioannis Oecolampadii commentarii omnes in libros prophetarum* (Geneva: J. Crispin, 1558).

down the margins. These one-word entries are exactly the
meanings given by Calvin of Hebrew words at Jer. 1:16 (r#)
with Calvin's preferred *quia*; the dictionary offers *quemad-
modum*), 2:8 (#pt with *tenere/comprehendere*), 2:21(qr# with
vitis optima), 2:25 (Pxy with *discalcere*), and 2:35 (K) with
modo). Apart from this lexical guidance, can we be sure that
Calvin was otherwise unaided when it came to his
interpretations?

It seems unlikely that Calvin had direct access to
Jerome's commentary on Jeremiah. There is a mention of the
Erasmian edition of his works in the library of the Genevan
Academy, but with annotations by Peter Martyr (which
means there is no such proof that Calvin had them).[33] By
'Jerome' it is more likely that Calvin meant the Vulgate. Very
early on Calvin attacks Jerome for imagining that, at the time
of his calling, Jeremiah was a boy rather than a young man.[34]
Calvin does not specify but he may have been annoyed at
Jerome's association of fitness for the prophetic role with
pre-pubescent sexual purity.[35] Calvin adds that God would

---

[33]Ganoczy, *Bibliothèque*, 179: item 61. *Hieronymi Opera ... per Des.
Erasmum* (Basel: Froben, 1553): 'annotations de la main de P. Martyr.'
From a brief review of Bullinger's commentary, the Zurich Reformer
likely did use a copy of Erasmus's edition.

[34]*Iohannes Calvinus in Ieremiam* (Geneva: J. Crispin, 1563) 2: 'Suspicio
etiam Hieronymi valde frivola est, quia ex voce r)n , quam paulo post
subiiciet Propheta, colligit fuisse puerum, cum coepit prophetare: quasi
vero non se puerum metaphorice appellet. Quoto aetatis suae anno
vocatus fuerit ad munus propheticum, nescitur: tamen credibile est,
tunc fuisse stata, vel media aetate, quoniam opus fuit authoritate non
vulgari: deinde si fuisset puer, certe non tacuisset de tanto, aetam
insigni miraculo, quod scilicet fuisset creatus Propheta ante iustam, et
maturam aetatem.'

[35]The use of 'puer' in the Vulgate is enough. It is interesting to see
Jerome compare Jeremiah for the genuineness of his youthful
innocence compared with Moses's reasons for modesty. Cf. Jerome:
Hieronymus in Hieremiam 1:1; CSEL 59 (ed. S Reiter) (Vienna & Leipzig:
F. Tempsky & E. Freytag, 1913) 5-7: 'Hieremias cum esset adhuc puer,
prophetare coepit...Detestatur officium, quod pro aetate non potest
sustinere, eadem verecundia, qua et Moses tenuis et gracilis vocis esse
se dicit. sed ille quasi magnae robustaeque aetatis corripitur, huic
pueritiae datur venia, quae verecundia et pudore decoratur.' Virginity
was on his mind as he wrote this commentary at a time when he was

not have called him so early, and anyway one would have
expected Jeremiah to have mentioned it more often if he had
had that responsibility on his shoulders before maturity. (Yet
Jerome may have been right in supposing that the calling
came before Jeremiah was a priest.) Here we see in operation
Calvin's criterion that that which is more likely is to be
preferred. For the same reason he immediately scorns the
interpretation of 'the Jews' that Hilkiah, Jeremiah's father,
was not just from the priests of Anathoth, but was the high
priest of that name in 2 Chron. 34:15, the person who found
the book of the law during Josiah's reign. Kimchi alleged
that his father, Joseph was the first to make this connection.[36]
Calvin's caution regarding the rabbis seems judicious—it
was the Anathoth, not the Jerusalem priesthood that Hilkiah
came from.

It appears then that there was no patristic guide for
him through the Old Testament as Chrysostom had been for
the New Testament.[37] However, Oecolampadius, with his
kindred 'sensible' spirit, may have been a help.[38]

Calvin does not refer to any other writer again until
he reaches Jer. 2:20 at the start of his seventh lecture. Here
Jerome is actually the translator he follows, preferring 'I will
not serve' to 'I will not transgress' rendered by the other
interpreters in reliance on the eleventh-century *Qere* variant
of rwb() for db(). The identity of these *interpretes* is not
altogether clear.[39] He adds that there is no need to think that
the verb needs to have the object 'idols' supplied, as if by

---

contending with Pelagius's obstinacy about marriage and sexuality, as
the preface shows (p. 4).

[36]See W.L. Holladay, *Jeremiah* I (Philadelphia: Fortress, 1986) 16.

[37]Puckett asserts (*Exegesis*, 74, n.13), paraphrasing John Walchenbach
(*John Calvin as a Biblical commentator: An Investigation into Calvin's use of
John Chrysostom as an Exegetical Tutor*'(Ph.D., University of Pittsburgh,
1974)), that Chrysostom knew no Hebrew, and 'Calvin apparently
found no suitable replacement for Chrysostom among Christian
exegetes of the Old Testament.'

[38]*Oecolampadius in Ieremiam*, 4: 'videtur autem etiam fuisse adolescens,
quamvis r)n ministrum exponere potes: nam Iosua r)n dicitur natus
annos quinquaginta.'

[39]*Iohannes Calvinus in Ieremiam*, 13v: 'Sed interea repudio quod
adducunt interpretes: nec dubito quin locus hic corruptus fuerit:
quoniam inualuerat illa expositio, Non serviam idolis.'

this route Israel's intentions at least were good. Calvin is trying to show that from the start Israel refused to serve God in her heart. Oecolampadius makes no comment. Bullinger, however, is helpful[40] as one who shared some common sources with Calvin. As Bullinger points out, Jerome's Vulgate is better than the common 'I will not transgress' or the alternative 'I will not deviate,' although Bullinger does not note the *Qere* reading. He simply says that it makes better sense than the sense based on the reading in the Hebrew text used by German translations: it is possible that he has in mind specifically Zwingli's translation and interpretation of 1531 (Zurich Bible and commentaries on Jeremiah in the same year).

On Jer. 3:18 one question that arises is : who were the Jews both in the sense of his sources and those he felt might justifiably criticise fanciful Christian exegesis? It is my contention that they were not, as Puckett thinks actual Jews. Calvin was afraid, as Puckett states of ridicule at the expense of the Christian interpretation of Jer. 31:22[41] and admires that which most Christians have missed about Jer. 3:17-18, that it, a prophecy of all the nations gathering at the temple, refers to the Messianic age.[42] It would not be too far off the

---

[40]H. Bullinger, *Ieremias propheta expositus, concionibus CLXX* (Zurich: Froschover, 1575 (first edition: 1557)) fol.15v: 'Sequitur quam gratiam benefico Deo populus retulerit. Et dixisti, Non transibo, *Darhinder tum ich nit. Daryn lassen ich mit nit füren. Daryin gon ich nit.* Nostri aiunt, *In das bockshorn laß ich mit zwingen.* Alii minus perspicue verterunt, Non pravaricabor. Sed alii, sicuti et vulgaris interpres, sensum reddiderunt non male, Non servam. Significat enim Deus se veluti connubio sibi devinxisse populum istum, neque gravibus oppressisse aut onerasse oneribus.'

[41]*CO* 38:680.

[42]*CO* 37:563=*Iohannes Calvinus in Ieremiam*, fol.26r: 'Sed quia reditus ille, ac restitutio populi quoddam fuit regni Christi praecludium, ideo semper incipere convenit a tempore illo, quoties vaticinantur de nova Ecclesia. Verum quidem est, reparationem totius mundi quarendam esse in Christi adventu: sed iam tunc coepit Deus Ecclesiam suam restituere, cum Iudaeis manum porrexit, ut urbem extruerent, et templum, donec prodiret Christus. Quantum ad praesentem locum spectat, sive per Gentes intelligere libeat decem Tribus, vel utrumque regnum: sive promiscue omnes orbis populos, sensus Prophetae perinde clarus esset: ampliorem scilicet fore Ecclesiam, ubi Deus

mark to call Calvin an 'Antiochene' here, in that he actually seems to by-pass the Incarnation as the focus of the Scriptures. It operates as a pivot, but is itself not the centre of attention. That is reserved for God's redemption of the Church, and through the Church. Oecolampadius had denied any validity to the interpretation that this spoke of the 'historical' return and reunification of Israel and Judah, preferring a spiritual, christological explanation.[43]

Conclusion

It can be said that the cases of Oecolampadius and Bullinger serve notice that we should not accord Calvin the honour of having been the first great Reformation Old Testament exegete. However, Calvin seems to have remained independent in the practice of his exegesis. The most important forerunner for him was Olivetan's bible and, more specifically, the process of his own revision of it. Just as Calvin's Latin was self-consciously classical, as if he felt he were renewing the language, and cleansing it from scholastic accretions, so his interpretation takes us back through the true symbols, the Hebrew words, to the truer realities of God's will and ways. Those words were closer to the original manifestations, and therefore were grounded on objective history and less on reflection and interpretation of the post-apostolic Church.[44]

---

populum reduxerit, quam prius fuisset: postea Deum facturum, ut floreat vera pietas.'

[43]*Oecolampadius in Ieremiam*, 18: 'non enim congruit, neque primae neque secundae captivitatis. In primam non rediit Israel. In secunda non rediit Iuda: nam per totum mundum dispersi sunt. Ideo simpliciter accipiandum, ab Aquilone, id est, a captivitate. Aquilonares enim sunt gentium typus generalis. Proinde hic non opus est intelligere terrenum transitum. A terra enim Aquilonis, hoc est, a peccato, ad terram cognitionis Iesu Christi, quod in illo liberatio a tenebris, salus et iustitia est.'

[44]Compare Calvin's evading discussion at any length about the precise nature of the Trinity. He preferred to do theology as exegesis of Scripture: see Serena Jones, *Calvin and the Rhetoric of Piety* (Louisville: Westminster John Knox Press, 1995).

Chapter 5

CALVIN AND THE POWER OF THE ELDER: A CASE OF THE ROGUE HERMENEUTIC?

Roy Kearsley

Few topics for discussion are more appropriate for a tribute to David Wright than John Calvin, of whom he has such a formidable knowledge. The revival of interest in the theology of Calvin continues unabated towards the 21st century. Attention for many has now turned to Calvin's hermeneutics, and the last twenty years has seen some impressive and helpful studies on the subject. I want to use this supply of tools to explore critically Calvin's understanding of the role of the elder.

One of the lingering deficiencies in some approaches to Calvin's hermeneutics is that they concern themselves more with establishing a scientific history of exegesis than with setting Calvin's exegetical work in the context of his mission and calling. Calvin's awareness of the living character of the biblical texts needs to be mirrored in ours of *his* writings, even if this contextual character is often deceptively overshadowed by the sheer depth and timeless wisdom of his words. Calvin can sometimes today receive attention as if he were mainly an exegetical brain programmed by principles in the broad catholic tradition or the 16th century humanist revolution. Much of the time this approach will suffice. But we need sometimes to ask if such a methodology ever breaks down under the scrutiny of more contextual questions. William J. Bouwsma has rightly called into question the tendency to treat Calvin 'as a dispassionate systematiser,' more a mind than a personality.[1]

So could Calvin's exegetical purity sometimes be influenced, even skewed, by the struggle in Geneva, or even by the broader context of the reformation in Europe? This paper will briefly explore in Calvin's description of the elder's role, a strain which *is* conditioned by the Genevan context and which departs from his more sure-footed general biblical hermeneutic on the Christian ministry.

Of course, it is true that Calvin must emerge against the background of the preceding and contemporary scholarly tradition. Elsie Ann McKee has helpfully specialised with great care here.[2] She laments the dominance of the 1559 edition of the *Institutes* and consequent neglect of development in Calvin's thought.[3] Calvin's impression of novelty, she claims, arises from his organisation of exegesis rather than his content. Her case-study in Calvin's treatment of texts relating to the plurality in ministry certainly shows that in some respects Calvin followed in a long tradition of both method and substance, and stood influentially at the head of subsequent post-reformation trends.[4] There is no point in denying this continuity. T.F. Torrance comes to a skilfully crafted parallel conclusion to McKee concerning Calvin's relationship to scholasticism. Ockham, Scotus and Major all played their part in the shaping of Calvin's principles and method.[5] But even so, the choices did not always necessarily flow effortlessly without external pressure. McKee herself argues that Calvin's advance on Bucer's exegesis of

---

[1] William J. Bouwsma, *John Calvin. A Sixteenth-Century Portrait* (Oxford: OUP, 1988) 2. The last few words he cites from the work of W. Monter.
[2] Elsie Ann McKee, 'Exegesis, Theology & Development in Calvin's *Institutio*: A Methodological Suggestion,' in E.A. McKee & B.G. Armstrong (eds.), *Probing the Reformed Tradition* (Kentucky: Westminster/John Knox, 1989) 154-172.
[3] *Ibid.*, 156.
[4] Elsie Ann McKee, *Elders and the Plural Ministry. The role of Exegetical History in Illuminating John Calvin's Theology* (Geneva: Droz, 1988).
[5] T.F. Torrance, *The Hermeneutics of John Calvin* (Edinburgh: Scottish Academic Press, 1988) 70-95.

Ephesians 4:11-12, for instance, is to address the still untackled task of application.[6] Torrance for his part too, sees in Calvin's hermeneutic a bias against intellectualism and speculation. Knowledge of God is practical.[7]

Hans-Joachim Kraus had earlier offered a summary of the principles of exegesis held to undergird Calvin's hermeneutical method.[8] Kraus concluded that, whilst Calvin was unwilling to give up the consensus of interpretation, the basic principle of all his exegetical work was 'the edification of the church'.[9] Kraus is confident that in Calvin the contemporary applications were not artificially brought in,[10] but does that mean that his exegesis always ignored the near horizon and that his interpretation was always context-free? Like it or not, we cannot ignore the possible impact of the historical context upon Calvin's exegetical conclusions. We may wish only with caution to endorse Van Ginkel's view of Calvin as 'busy giving a biblical foundation to offices which he himself created in his church order'.[11] All the same, we surely have to entertain the possibility that Calvin's exegesis, besides honouring tradition and contemporary humanism, bowed also before contingency and political necessity.

The pressures of the historical circumstances are well-known. The Geneva in which Calvin worked was a tiny republic arising from a social revolution which created new classes, including a new clerical class and a social elite.[12] Tensions were rife between clerical and secular powers, citizens and non-citizens, native Genevans and incomers. The tension between clerics and civil leaders went far back to even before the Reformation.[13] The reasons had much to do

---

[6]McKee, *Elders and the Plural Ministry*, 154.

[7]Torrance, *Hermeneutics of John Calvin*, 70-73.

[8]H. Kraus, 'Calvin's Exegetical Principles,' *Interpretation* 31 (1977) 8–18.

[9]Kraus, 'Calvin's Exegetical Principles,' 11.

[10]*Ibid.*

[11]P. Coertzen, 'Presbyterial Church Government. Ius Divinum, Ius Ecclesiasticum or Ius Humanum?' in W. van 't Spijker (ed.), *Calvin. Erbe und Auftrag. Festschrift für Wilhelm Heinrich Neuser* (Kampen: Kok Pharos, 1991) 329-342, at p.337.

[12]Coertzen, 'Presbyterial Church Government,' 331.

[13]William G. Naphy, *Calvin and the Consolidation of the Genevan Reformation* (Manchester: University Press, 1994) 19.

with economic factors, local politics and the broader politics
of struggle for power or freedom between one Swiss city and
another, and between alliances of them and the duchy of
Savoy.[14] The Roman Church's alignment with Savoy and its
wealth-driven power had long since soured the relationship
between religious and civic leadership in Geneva.[15] Coertzen
goes so far as to say that Geneva's church order sprang not
from the New Testament but from the need for a church
body in this situation concerned with community spirit and
responsibility.[16] In addition to the context of Geneva, Calvin
had stayed at Strasbourg during the reforming work of
Bucer. In recent years Bucer's Strasbourg has played a larger
part in reassessing Calvin's originality in Geneva.[17] Bucer
strongly emphasised the notion of moral discipline through
the ecclesiastical offices. He retained the idea of penitential
discipline, though as a means of improvement rather than
absolution.[18] His influence on Calvin is likely in the whole
field of church discipline and the adoption of the fourfold
offices.[19] Even Bucer was not original in his adoption of
church discipline, being influenced by Oecolampadius and,
by reaction, some Anabaptists.[20]

Given that a variety of influences have played upon
Calvin's understanding of the New Testament ministry, I
propose an approach here that may look unusual. Rather
than beginning with Calvin's comments on the main biblical
texts, I want instead to close with these. This is because
Calvin's actual handling of the texts is best seen not in
vacuum, but against the background of (a) the careful standards and assumptions that usually dominated Calvin's
thinking on the Church and its offices and (b) the living
context in which the editions of the *Institutes* developed.

---

[14]One particularly lucid account among many treatments is Alister
McGrath's excellent *A Life of John Calvin, A Study in the Shaping of
Western Culture* (Oxford: Blackwell, 1990).
[15]Naphy, *Calvin and the Consolidation*, 19.
[16]*Ibid.*, 331-2.
[17]The chief authority here is Willem van 't Spijker, *The Ecclesiastical
Offices in the Thought of Martin Bucer* (ET; Leiden: E J Brill, 1996).
[18]*Ibid.*, 81-82.
[19]*Ibid.*, 340.
[20]*Ibid.*, 213-233.

Two main themes dominate the greater part of Calvin's approach to the biblical teaching on ministry. The first of these is a faith in Scripture as the Word of God which powerfully transforms people's lives and the life of the Church. Confidence does not seem to rest, for the greater part, on canon law and human regulations or discipline. R.S. Wallace cites a pointed account from Calvin's comments on Isaiah 49:2 and Hosea 1:11:

> By the preaching of the Word...Christ...exercises his rule over the hearts and minds of his people. Whereas David ruled over his earthly kingdom by a golden sceptre, Christ's heavenly kingdom is presided over by the sceptre of the preached Gospel. When Christ gave Peter and the apostles the promises that they would be given the keys of the kingdom of heaven and would be able to 'bind or loose' people on earth, he was referring to the effect their preaching of the Word of Christ was to have on its hearers.[21]

A true church for Calvin is one seeking to be ruled by the Word of God itself.[22] Significantly, it is the *doctrine*, or *teaching*, of the pastors and teachers that has power,[23] and the rule associated with the bishop is not so much governing as 'feeding' of the flock.[24] No-one is so wise that they do not need to be taught by the Word of God,[25] and 'those who rule' (in the crucial Hebrews 13:17) must be obeyed not because of some special dignity in their office, but because 'the Spirit commands us to receive obediently the teaching of holy and faithful bishops and to obey their wise counsels'.[26]

---

[21]R.S. Wallace, *Calvin, Geneva and the Reformation* (Edinburgh: Scottish Academic Press, 1988) 132-133. This is typical of the Reformers generally. See Paul Avis, *The Church in the Theology of the Reformers* (London: Marshall, Morgan & Scott, 1981).

[22]Wallace, *Calvin, Geneva and the Reformation*, 133.

[23]J.W. Fraser (tr.), *Calvin's Commentaries: The Acts of the Apostles 14-28* (Edinburgh: St Andrews Press, 1966) 174-175.

[24]*Ibid.*, 184.

[25]W.B. Johnston (tr.), *Calvin's Commentaries: The Epistle of Paul the Apostle to the Hebrews, and the First and Second Epistles of St Peter* (Grand Rapids: Eerdmans, 1980) 113.

[26]*Ibid.*, 212.

Even church government itself rests upon the main function of the teaching of the Word, as Calvin's understanding of 2 Tim 3:3 insists: 'The spiritual government of the church (which) can no more be separated from teaching than a man can from his soul'.[27] Statements like these make the occasional dividing of teaching and ruling into two separate roles secondary and uncharacteristic in Calvin. B.G. Armstrong is surely right to say that Calvin's job definition for the pastoral ministry is primarily the communication of the message in line with the Old Testament provision of proclaimers of promise.[28] The *Institutes* reinforces the teaching of the commentaries. 4:3:1. leaves us in no doubt:

> Now we must speak of the order by which the Lord willed his church to be governed. He alone should rule and reign in the church as well as have authority and pre-eminence in it, and this authority should be exercised and administered by his Word alone.[29]

Teaching and preaching as an external aid to birthing and strengthening faith in the believer, flowed from pastors and teachers, 'through whose lips he would teach his own; he furnished them with authority' (4:1:1). Moreover, the teaching office does not indicate superiority either of character or of office. The listeners should be humbled that the teaching comes through other human beings as 'puny' as themselves and even of lower worth (4:3:1). Even in the courts of the bishops the only authority is that of the Word of God (4:11:7-9). They do not touch the power of the sword, and to include coercive authority in their role leads remorselessly to corruption and evils. According to H. Höpfl, ecclesiastical *potestas* is distinguished by Calvin from force, coercion and

---

27 T.F. Smail (tr.), *Calvin's Commentaries: The Second Epistle of Paul the Apostle to the Corinthians, Timothy, Titus and Philemon* (Edinburgh: Oliver & Boyd, 1964) 223.

28B.G. Armstrong, 'The Pastoral Office in Calvin and Pierre du Moulin,' in van 't Spijker (ed.), *Calvin. Erbe und Auftrag*, 157-167, at p.160.

29J.T. McNeill and F.L. Battles (eds.), *Calvin: the Institutes of Christian Religion* (Philadelphia: Westminster, 1967) 1053. All quotations from the *Institutes* will be from this edition.

domination.[30] There could be only one Lord in the Christian Church. Accordingly the *potestas* of the Church is that of '*gubernatio, regimen* or *politia* and by the force of these terms, which Calvin had selected with care, such power extends to the issuing, interpreting and enforcing of laws and commands'.[31] Once more, it is not laws devised by the Church itself. Even in the sphere of church discipline (binding and loosing), 'that promise made to Peter...ought to be referred solely to the ministry of the Word...' (4:11:1).

The second main theme dominating Calvin's approach to ministry is that of service. Of course, one could sceptically conclude that he blazes away at abuse of power for ecclesiastical reasons rather than the humbling of his own ministers. His handling of 1 Peter 5:1-5 could superficially be taken to be a case in point.[32] The passage urges ministers to feed the flock and then goes on to warn them against lording it over those entrusted to their care. There is explicit reference to the pope at the beginning but Calvin berates him, not for abusing power, but for neglecting the feeding of the flock. His sideswipe at the use of the term 'clergy' to describe 'those entrusted to their care' is only a means to an end. He wants to underline the fact that no-one owns the Church. Every ministerial activity is held on trust from the one Chief Shepherd. An excellent opportunity now present-ed itself to list the abuses of the medieval church or the excessive powers used to subdue dissent, but Calvin passes up this chance to score points off the pope's men. This can only be, because he believes that the maxim calling to service rather than lordship strikes all ministers, including the reformed pastors. The grounds for his position are not polemical but theological. According to his comments on v.5, all believers are to be in mutual subjection and this does not exclude the elder. These words were written in 1549 when Calvin's highly developed system of ministry in Geneva might have had much to gain from striking a different note.[33]

---

[30]Harro Höpfl, *The Christian Polity of John Calvin* (Cambridge: CUP, 1982) 113-115.

[31]*Ibid.*, 113.

[32]Johnston (tr.), *Calvin's Commentaries*, 315-7.

[33]See also Armstrong, 'Pastoral Office,' 160-163.

Calvin's handling of the key passage, Hebrews 13:17, points in the same direction.[34] The ground for honour does *not* lie in the office itself. It is earned, and so the greater burden the ministers bear, the more honour they should receive because of 'the more trouble they take for our sakes'. Honour does not rest in arbitrary power but springs from the 'greatest labours' and 'utmost dangers'. Thoughts like these permeate Calvin's writings on the work of the min-istry. On Matthew 20:24-28 he comments that primacy 'has no place in his kingdom...Christ appoints pastors of his Church, not to rule but to serve'.[35] His sermon on 1 Timothy 3:6-7, points out that all offices of the Church are called 'diakonies,' that is to say, services.[36] Surprisingly, Calvin even says that when God calls ministers he does not charge them with the government of the Church, but calls them to be subject to the rule of Christ, 'to be ministers, not lords'.[37] In his commentary on the same text, he states it yet more clearly: 'Pastors are not ordained to dominate. Why then? For the service of the faithful...servants of Jesus Christ, and of his people and flock'.[38] Again, only God has authority, and so the authority of the overseer is really nothing more than service.[39] The authority of the pastor stems from being bound by the spirit and in slavery to the Spirit in contrast to those who are slaves to Satan.[40] The minister governs the Church through administration of the Word and only insofar as the servant role is followed, 'restraining every desire to domineer', and regarding 'the service of the people of God, the highest honour to which he may aspire'.[41] Calvin observes that even

---

[34]*Ibid.*, 213-214.
[35]So cited in J.K.S. Reid, '*Diakonia* in the Thought of Calvin,' in James I. McCord and T.H.L. Parker (eds.), *Service in Christ* (London: Epworth, 1966) 101.
[36]*Ibid.*, 105.
[37]*Ibid.*, 103, from Calvin's commentary on 1 Corinthians 4:1.
[38]*Ibid.*
[39]Fraser (tr.), *Calvin's Commentaries*, 182-183.
[40]*Ibid.*, 174-175.
[41]On 2 Cor. 4:5, cited in this way by Armstrong, 'Pastoral Office,' 162.

an apostle, Paul, speaks of his voluntary submission to the church that he founded.[42]

The pervasiveness in Calvin of eldership as service, establishes beyond all doubt that, for him, ministry really means ministry. We are therefore justified in using this axiom from the essential Calvin as a kind of control-hermeneutic by which we can test the soundness of his hermeneutic in other texts. Where appropriate, we may even use Calvin against Calvin if it goes some way towards explaining his reputation for authoritarian clericalism. For in some of his comments on biblical texts he shows an unhealthy eagerness to secure disciplinary functions for the ministry. By way of parenthesis, three factors generating this inconsistency in Calvin are worthy of special comment.

First, whilst Calvin could clearly distinguish be-tween the separate *spheres* and *sanctions* of the civil and spiritual powers,[43] he still made much of their parallel purpose, namely to ensure order.[44] By this route the ways of political government cast their shadow on ecclesiastical life. Höpfl observes that Calvin had imported philosophical concepts of order, harmony, law and punishment into his politics and understood these as biblical.[45]

When universal harmony and order becomes the main thrust in ecclesiology, lines of responsibility and power become blurred.[46] McGrath's observation on Calvin is, there-fore, not so surprising: 'The two powers, religious and secular, are to be regarded as theoretically complementary.

---

[42]R. Mackenzie, tr., *Calvin's Commentaries: The Epistles of Paul the Apostle to the Romans and to the Thessalonians* (Edinburgh: Oliver & Boyd, 1961) 343, on 1 Thess. 2:7.

[43]The Church may only use the Word of God whilst the civil powers may use coercion and force when necessary: *Institutes* 4:11:3-5, 8. See Höpfl, *Christian Polity*, 95. The claim of K. Rendell, *John Calvin and the Later Reformation* (London: Hodder, 1990) 17-18 that Calvin intended to do away with the rigid distinction between the civil power and the spiritual agency seems to be a misleading statement if intended to mean, as Rendell says, that he saw 'government as being indivisible'.

[44]*Institutes* 4:11:1 and 4:12:1 especially.

[45]Höpfl, *Christian Polity*, 52-55.

[46]So Höpfl, *Christian Polity*, 122-127. He believes that Calvin this way gets himself into difficulties on the relationship between church and civil power (122).

In practice, however, their relationship was somewhat more turbulent'.[47]

Second, Calvin had collected the core of his ideas from Bucer's Strasbourg where Bucer had already fought battles which were to replicate themselves in Geneva. To Bucer, we can attribute an emphasis on penitential discipline the danger of the secular power of the clergy, which can erode true discipline[48] and the fourfold office.[49]

Third, the interaction of powers in Calvin's thinking was surely not unaffected by the tempestuous relationships between clergy and political powers in Geneva itself. The more wealthy and influential citizens who inhabited the hierarchy of ruling councils in Geneva ruled the city tightly and took as their first canon, a wholehearted suspicion of everything foreign. The city's freedom was fragile and the earlier role of the Roman clergy in undermining Genevan autonomy meant that every possible device for controlling city life fell under the acquisitive gaze of the magistrates. Calvin was convinced that only the penetration of biblical teaching and discipline could, in fact, ensure that the community lived in peace and moral social order. It may have been, as Torrance suggests, that with the revival of interest in the early church fathers, Calvin and others revived the office of *seniores* of the North African church who were civil functionaries helping to maintain public and moral order and who become associated with the clergy.[50]

Calvin did not see any hope in the moral example of an elite class which took every opportunity to exploit the poor and weak.[51] His battles against what he saw as moral laxity were more often than not with the powerful rich in

---

[47]McGrath, *Life of John Calvin*, 171. This candid view should balance the rather sanguine view that Calvin 'viewed both church and state as unified by the overarching purpose of arresting evil but separated by a porous membrane...' (G J Gatis, 'The Political Theory of John Calvin,' *Bibliotheca Sacra* 153 (1996) 449-467, at p.453). It is not taking enough account of the muddy waters of Geneva.

[48]Van 't Spijker, *Ecclesiastical Offices*, 180-186.

[49]*Ibid.*, 340.

[50]T.F. Torrance, 'The Eldership in the Reformed Church,' *Scottish Journal of Theology* 37 (1984) 503-518, at p.504.

[51]Naphy, *Calvin and the Consolidation*, 157.

Geneva. Clearly, he succumbed to the temptation to think that the real officers of social discipline would be members of the ecclesiastical establishment. William Naphy thinks that Calvin could not have been expected to understand the external pressures on Geneva, the causes of factions and the distrust of clerics and foreigners.[52] This perhaps does not do justice to Calvin's astuteness in general, nor to the shared consciousness of such a small community as Geneva's. Even if he understood the situation, Calvin did not necessarily appreciate the appropriate moves to handle it. His approach lay in establishing a strong church leadership with a tight order of discipline. Only this could guarantee the moral oversight of society. The evidence has been strong enough to suggest that Geneva's church order is not due so much to the New Testament, as to the need of the church for a body concerned with discipline, sanctification, community spirit and responsibility.[53]

To achieve his intentions in this area, Calvin first developed his understanding of the ministry. Unfortunately, ambiguity afflicted his views even as late as the last edition of the *Institutes*. He believed the presbyterian order to be given in Scripture.[54] Yet it is difficult to harmonise *Institutes* 4:3:4 where teaching and pastoral offices in Ephesians 4:11 are distinct (though, admittedly, the pastor teaches), with *Institutes* 4:4:1. where, using the same text, the two seem identical. Equally, whilst his commentary on 1 Timothy 5:17 teaches that elders are presbyters, they were not ordained in Geneva nor admitted to the Venerable Company of Pastors, which Torrance describes as a presbytery.[55]

More important, Calvin's move to distinguish the role of elders from that of pastors looks very much like a reaction to the pressure of the political councils against the intervention of the 'clergy' in the affairs of its people. One way to deal with this was to have the church exercise its discipline partly through those who were themselves not

---

[52]*Ibid.*, 27.
[53]Coertzen, 'Presbyterial Church Government', 331-332.
[54]*Institutes*, 4:3:1; 4:4:1; 4:10:8; 4:10:30. Van Ginkel, thinks Calvin saw presbyterianism as a divine institution, according to Coertzen, 'Presbyterial Church Government', 339.
[55]Torrance, 'The Eldership', 506-507.

employed clergy but magistrates, men from within the councils. This left the professional clergy to exercise influence mainly through their preaching. In Calvin's case it was a bonus, because his preaching influence was considerable.[56] The solution lay, therefore, in the 'consistory,' a disciplinary body in which the lay magistrate-elders at first outnumbered the clergy. The main revolution in Calvin, then, is not simply the twofold presbyter but the lay presbyter with disciplinary powers.[57]

The discipline exercised by the consistory certainly went beyond serious doctrinal error and touched upon morals, and whilst Calvin rejected a monarchy of the church, Höpfl believes he still opted for an aristocracy of merit, though carefully monitored.[58] To achieve this at all on a biblical basis, Calvin has to identify the gift of 'governing' in 1 Corinthians 12:28 with the elder's office of moral discipline. The success of this venture is assessed below, but meantime it is clear enough that it would be very unwise to consider Calvin's exegesis of such key passages in isolation from the political pressures which constituted the living context of his theology.

The consistory is both the focus and justification for Calvin's view of the eldership, but Walther Köhler has argued that far from drawing a line between the spiritual and civil courts, it seems very similar to Zwingli's marriage court.[59] Moreover, it had the power to report misdemeanours to the civil magistrates for trial and punishment...and it

---

[56]Naphy, *Calvin and the Consolidation*, 144-166, though in fact we have no evidence that Calvin was 'ordained' to the preaching office.

[57]McKee, *Elders*, 100-103. The strength of this case rests on McKee's claim to find a duality of roles within the office of presbyter even in medieval and early 16th-century exegesis.

[58]Höpfl, *Christian Polity*, 97-98. For Calvin's rejection of the rule of an hereditary caste see J.T. McNeil, 'Calvin and Civil Government,' in D. McKim (ed.), *Readings in Calvin's Theology* (Grand Rapids: Baker, 1984) 273.

[59]Quoted in McKee, *Elders*, 16 and also received sympathetically by McGrath, *Life of John Calvin*, 112. Naphy, *Calvin and the Consolidation*, comments that the elders on the consistory were there for their skill as civil magistrates not for being of spotless character. His view of Calvin is unduly negative, but he may still not be wide of the mark.

did. The consistory was thus not at all outside civil penal processes. It is almost universally agreed that the elders' role in all this was the moral oversight of the church members (which in Geneva meant everyone who valued their citizenship) and the exercise of discipline. Höpfl pulls no punches on the comprehensiveness of this activity. Although the elders had no personal coercive authority they were provided with offices to ensure that offenders attend the consistory.[60] Höpfl believes that a new lay clericalism was taking shape.[61] Nor did the power of admonition and reporting to the magistrates exhaust the powers of the group. They could also excommunicate, which in Geneva meant inevitable expulsion, and it has been suggested that the progressive emphasis on the sacrament in Calvin was due to its increased importance in discipline.[62] The moral and credal testing of members under pain of excommunication has sometimes been seen as an elitist rigour compared to the more relaxed Roman approach.[63] As it happens, in practice excommunication was not so quickly invoked, but perhaps that was partly because the threat of it was so effective. At any rate, a number of things become very clear. First, one cannot separate the programme of Calvin from the experiments of Bucer and his colleagues under political and religious pressure in Strasbourg. Second, one cannot separate Calvin's laicising and empowerment of the eldership from the claustrophobic and xenophobic atmosphere of a city which lived only on the knife-edge of freedom. If Calvin had lived in the atmosphere of post-reformation religious freedom and in a large cosmopolitan city, would he have thought of the consistory, or gleaned it from the biblical 'proof' passages? To answer this question fairly, we have, at last, to review his use of the key texts.

Höpfl is incisive and almost acid here. He sees Calvin's view of church order as justifiable simply on the basis that it was *compatible with* the (non-prescriptive) biblical statements. In other words it fitted Calvin's own

---

[60]Höpfl, *Christian Polity*, 94.

[61]*Ibid.*, 97, 102. See also Bouwsma, *John Calvin*, 219-22.

[62]Höpfl, *Christian Polity*, 98.

[63]M Mullett, *Calvin* (London: Routledge, 1989) 27.

occasional willingness to justify extra-biblical practical arrangements in the *adiaphora* (non-essentials). But Calvin wanted to command more justification than this. He unnecessarily wished to make a doctrinal stand and was induced into 'strained exegesis'.[64] It is precisely Calvin's handling of the texts germane to the idea of the consistory, amongst others, which Höpfl finds to be strained. These include: 2 Corinthians 4:6 where ministers do *not*, (*pace* Calvin), enjoy an office of 'governing'; 1 Corinthian 12:28ff and Romans 12:8 which again do *not* provide proof for a New Testament senate of elders or primitive consistory; Matthew 18:15-18 which does *not* provide a prescriptive mechanism for disciplining in the church.[65]

Höpfl seems to be on the right lines. However, is he being stern enough with Calvin when excusing the consistory on the basis of practical necessity? The consistory contradicted everything that Calvin himself had said about the function of the ministry. The ministry was mainly service not authority; it was pastoral not political; its power was the power of the Word not of the sword. Only a prior commitment to the consistory, probably dreamed of at Strasbourg with such towns as Geneva in mind, can explain its introduction against the greater flow of Calvin's biblical exegesis.

When we look more closely at the texts involved we find that Höpfl judges Calvin correctly otherwise. On Matthew 18:18, Calvin interpreted the 'church' which presides, as representative of the assembly of Israel. Apparently, precedents existed for this in earlier commentators but not for the move to a mirror image of this 'sanhedrin' in the New Testament church.[66] Nor does the text show that the New Testament 'representatives' of the church mainly occupied themselves with matters of domestic moral discipline. It is interesting that originally, Calvin himself had settled for seeing in the text the whole church acting in discipline. It looks as though the situation in Geneva later exerted a

---

[64]Höpfl, *Christian Polity*, 107-8.
[65]Höpfl, *Christian Polity*, 260, n.16.
[66]Well spotted by McKee, *Elders*, 34-43.

pressure on Calvin to adopt the alternative reading of it as a council for discipline.[67]

Calvin's treatment of Romans 12.8 from 1539 onwards, fares even worse. He interprets *proistamenous* as 'those who rule'. This meant that there were elders (*seniores*) who ruled over the other members and exercised discipline. They were similar to secular rulers who watch over people day and night.[68] The image of the watchtower is a favourite one with Calvin, but here it lets him down since usually he is at pains to put some distance between civil ruling and the serving and teaching ministry of the church. He can have deserted such a salient faith only with the consistory in mind. Moreover the verb does not mean rule at all. It is a gift of administration rather than of rule, though it has to be admitted that the translation 'ruling' had been entertained long before Calvin.[69] What is more, it is not even described as an office just as the other gifts listed are not. Even if he is not the first to make such an interpretation, choosing it cannot be excused as a pre-critical mistake in one of his stature.[70] His other move with this text is to link it in the 1543 edition of the *Institutes* with 1 Corinthians 12:28 and to modify 1 Timothy 5:17 to identify the office there with a presbyter who rules.[71] Much rests here on the term *gubernationes* in 1 Corinthians 12:28. McKee can find precedents for Calvin's way of seeing in it ecclesiastical powers of ruling.[72] However Calvin rejects Zwingli's application of it to the secular ruler and opts for the tradition that applies it to church leaders.[73] The choice, far from necessary, is significant. The character of political government, which in previous readings of the text characterised merely the civil powers, is now imported into the life of the Church, the very thing that Calvin denounces in the *Institutes*. In some ways such power is more dangerous and less justifiable in the church than in the civil courts where Zwingli put it,

---

[67]So understood by McKee, 'Exegesis,' 160-161, 164.
[68]Mackenzie (tr.), *Calvin's Commentaries*, 270-271.
[69]McKee, *Elders*, 44-50.
[70]McKee, 'Exegesis,' 164.
[71]McKee, 'Exegesis,' 160-161.
[72]McKee, *Elders*, 68.
[73]McKee, 'Exegesis,' 165-166.

admittedly with even less *exegetical* justification than Calvin
had. In fact, modern translators have dissolved the question
of whether Romans 12:8 or 1 Corinthians 12:28 refer to civil
or ecclesiastical rulers by rendering *gubernationes*, 'adminis-
trations'. It has nothing to do with ruling at all.

It is here that one wishes to be less excusing to
Calvin than is Elsie Ann McKee. She cautions us against too
quickly accusing Calvin of reading his views into a text with
regard to church order. It is coherent application that dominates his work in such texts, it is argued, and this means that
some choice from the various, equally respectable, strands of
tradition was unavoidable. The 'historical legitimacy of
Calvin's interpretation' is not, however, the only concern in
Calvin's use of these texts. Nor is it merely a question of
Calvin's making choices just because he *has* to choose. He is
quite happy to sit on the fence on other practical issues, for
example the permanence and nature of some gifts and
offices in the Church. The choice stems, in fact, from the
context of the struggle in Geneva which drives Calvin's
selections from, and blending of, the interpretations available to him from the traditions. It is this too which helps to
explain the development of his thinking through successive
editions of the *Institutes*.

But all such considerations only drive the question
further back. Why did Calvin swim so contrary to the tide of
his own more usual way of understanding the function of
church offices? A number of possibilities come to mind.

First, churches often exert greater pressure in moral
matters when there is a new moral culture to nurture.
Leaders of fledgling Christian churches in hostile conditions
tend to nurture more keenly the unfamiliar biblical standards in such communities. Calvin saw himself and other
reformers precisely in that light in the struggle for European
Christendom. He believed prevailing standards to be pre-
Christian, and only radical application of Scripture could
ensure social sanctification.

Second, whilst it may, perhaps, be true of Calvin that
'one of the ruling passions of his life was a hatred of public

mess',[74] he was even more concerned about the latent threat to the reformation movement of antinomianism, a danger which he perceived, along with Bucer, to be illustrated amongst some of the 'Anabaptists'. If the cities of the reformation used their newly found freedom to plunge into libertarianism, they simply played into the hands of their enemies. The deep legalistic prejudices to salvation through 'faith alone' waited hopefully for confirmation that such a doctrine led to lawlessness. Calvin's Geneva was not going to fall victim.

Third, Calvin's politico-social analysis was quite unformed. He failed to realise what would become of a consistory invested with such powers. Although the intention may have been to give greater prominence to the Word that transforms, in fact the move excessively empowered *human* pressure, social, external and coercive. He did not adequately realise how human dynamics and the interplay of power works, a strange failing in one whose theology recognised so clearly human frailty.

It is agreed by most modern commentators that the consistory could not claim to be an obvious application of the relevant biblical texts. Elsewhere in Calvin, appropriate hermeneutical influences, such as choices from the exegetical tradition, historico-grammatical analysis and organised application all played their part in the development of his more impressive general approach to ministry, one unduly neglected by many of his modern devotees. But Geneva and its unruly cross-winds gave birth to a rogue hermeneutic, with profound results upon theologies of church order in some streams of reformed theology. These results, I suggest, remain with us to this day. But that is another story.

---

[74]Owen Chadwick, quoted by Wallace, *Calvin, Geneva and the Reformation*, 31.

Chapter 6

ARMINIUS'S USE OF RAMISM IN HIS INTERPRETATION OF ROMANS 7 AND 9

F. Stuart Clarke

'After a short time [at the University of Geneva, Arminius] was compelled to repair to the University of Basle, because he could not secure the favour and regard of some of the principal men in Geneva...He removed solely on account of his invincible attachment to the philosophy of Petrus Ramus, which he publicly defended in the warmest manner, and which he taught in private to...admirers of that logical system.'[1]

Thus Bertius, a quarter of a century afterwards, described Arminius's attachment to Ramism in his funeral oration of 1609. Ramus was a humanist reactionary against mediaeval orthodoxy, not at first in theology; it was only in his late forties, around 1562, that he abandoned his previous Roman Catholicism for the Reformed faith. But since the time of Thomas Aquinas the western Church had embraced Aristotelianism as its philosophy, and Ramus was a severe critic of Aristotle.

---

[1] *The Works of Arminius*, translated by James Nichols, vol. 1 (London: Longman, Hurst, Rees, Orme, Brown and Green, 1825; reprinted with Introduction by Carl Bangs, Grand Rapids: Baker, 1986) 23.

Two doubtful assumptions have been made about Bertius's statements. The first is that Arminius had fallen foul of, among others, the principal man in Geneva, Theodore Beza, Calvin's successor as head of the (theological) Academy founded by Calvin in 1559. Breward states that Beza was hostile to Ramus,[2] and certainly he was suspicious of him. When in 1570 Ramus sought a teaching position in Geneva, Beza replied acknowledging Ramus's 'superior qualities' and 'genius', but giving two reasons why he could not agree; first, there was neither vacancy nor money to pay an extra professor; second, that frankly they had at Geneva a 'determination to follow the position of Aristotle, without deviating a line, in logic or in the rest of our studies'.[3] But while Beza himself was consistent in his own philosophical or theological opinions, he was more tolerant than most contemporaries of differing views among his students. According to Arminius's friend Uitenbogaert, the man whom Arminius offended was the new Spanish Professor of Philosophy, Petrus Galesius, a strict Aristotelian.

The second assumption is that because, after about a year at Basle, Arminius was allowed to return to Geneva in 1584 and remained there till 1586, he must have been 'cured' of his Ramism. This may derive from another report from Uitenbogaert that after his return, Arminius 'did not dispute so much, conducted himself in a milder manner, and was not so enamored with the Ramist philosophy as formerly'.[4] The last sentence can at once be disproved by a study of Arminius's own writings. Bertius was more correct in speaking of his 'invincible attachment' to Ramism. On his return, Arminius may have given an undertaking not to bring up

---

[2] *The Works of William Perkins*, introduced and edited by Ian Breward, Courtenay Library of Reformation Classics 3 (Appleford, Abingdon: Sutton Courtenay Press, 1970) 171f..

[3] Charles Waddington, *Ramus, sa Vie, ses Ecrits et ses Opinions* (Paris: Ch. Meyruels, 1855) 229f., quoted and translated in Carl Bangs, *Arminius: A Study in the Dutch Reformation* (Nashville and New York: Abingdon Press, 1970; 2nd ed. 1986) 61. It will be clear how much this article is indebted to the exhaustive studies of Dr. Bangs, especially in establishing the biographical details of Arminius's career; though at certain points I have ventured to interpret the evidence differently.

[4] *De Kerckelicke Historie* Part 3, 102, quoted in Bangs, *Arminius*, 73.

the issue of Ramism, but there is no evidence. More likely he himself judged it prudent, in view of his earlier experience, to refrain from contentious issues.

During his time at Basle, Arminius had publicly presented expositions of several chapters of the Epistle to the Romans under Johannes Jacobus Grynaeus, Professor of Sacred Literature and Dean of the Theological Faculty, who remained a friend, correspondent and possible influence upon his theological opinions. Ever since Luther's epoch-making *Lectures on Romans* of 1515-16, the Epistle had remained a first choice for any Protestant theologian who wished to comment on the Bible, but there may have been another reason for Arminius's choice, both at this stage and later. Of all biblical writers Paul is the one who approaches his material in a way which most resembles later logical analysis, and of all his letters Romans is the one in which he uses this approach most fully. When at length Arminius began his ministry at Amsterdam, he preached a series of sermons on Romans, alternating with the prophecy of Malachi.[5] The series on Romans was very long, November 6, 1588 to September 30, 1601, about 85% of Arminius's Amsterdam ministry.

As Bangs says, none of the sermons are extant, nor any others from this period of his ministry.[6] But early in 1592 objections were raised to the doctrinal content of the sermons on Romans 7:14-25. Whereas Calvin and Beza had applied this passage to a regenerate man, Arminius interpreted it of an unregenerate man, which his main critic, Petrus Plancius, called Pelagianism and the heresy of teaching the perfectibility of man in this life. Arminius agreed that he interpreted the passage in a different way from some Reformed theologians, but argued that the doctrinal standards of the time, the *Belgic Confession* and the *Heidelberg Catechism*, allowed freedom on this point, a view accepted both by the Burgomasters, the secular government, and the Consistory, the court of presbyters corresponding to the Scottish kirk-session. A little over a year later complaints

---

[5] A book which has influenced Romans, notably of course Mal. 1:2-3 in Rom 9:13.

[6] Bangs, *Arminius*, 186.

again reached the Consistory over Arminius's interpretation of Romans 9. Arminius acknowledged that he interpreted 9:18, 'So then [God] has mercy on whomever he chooses and hardens whomever he chooses' in a different way from the margin (not text) of the *Confession*, but claimed that other ministers also took similar liberties. At a later meeting he expressed concern over his opponents' interpretation of Article 16 of the *Confession*, on Eternal Election, which states that God delivers and preserves 'all whom he, in his eternal and unchangeable counsel, of mere goodness hath elected in Jesus Christ our Lord.' His opponents understood that such election was the result of God's arbitrary decree to bestow faith. Arminius argued that the election was of all *believers*. The Consistory found this an acceptable interpretation, closed the meeting and Arminius's teaching was never again challenged in the Amsterdam Consistory.

Arminius also produced two writings, the *Dissertation on the True and Genuine Sense of the Seventh Chapter of St. Paul's Epistle to the Romans*, hereinafter called the *Dissertation*, and the *Analysis of the Ninth Chapter of the Epistle to the Romans*, hereinafter called the *Analysis*. He made later use of both works, but neither was published in his lifetime, and it is doubtful whether he intended to publish. The *Dissertation* and *Analysis* were both published in 1612–13, the latter as an appendix to the *Examination of Dr. Perkins's Pamphlet on Predestination*, with long dedicatory prefaces from the nine orphan children of Arminius, who doubtless needed the money from successful publications. The Dedication to the *Dissertation* claims that Arminius began the commentary in response to the controversy, had finished and was in the process of correction when 'he was prevented by death and thus rendered incapable of giving it a final polish'[7]—presumably for publication. That is as may be, but it seems likely that the original versions of both works were prepared by Arminius for his own use as ammunition for the controversies, as the subject-matter exactly coincides.

A modern reader who approaches either work hoping to find a full commentary on the chapter, will be disappointed. One would not expect a commentary written

---

[7] *Works*, 2:485.

in the 1590s to include all that is contained in one written in the 1990s, but many sixteenth century commentaries, *e.g.*, those of Luther and Calvin, are far more adequate by present-day standards. Strictly speaking the *Dissertation* and *Analysis* are not biblical commentaries, but treatises of Ramist logic which use the Scriptures to prove one theological point each; in the *Dissertation*, that Paul has an unregenerate and not a regenerate man in mind in Romans 7:14-25; in the *Analysis*, that those whom God loves and chooses are not beneficiaries of a hidden, apparently arbitrary, divine will, but are identifiable as believers.

With its Dedicatory Preface, the *Dissertation* is Arminius's longest work. Only his collected *Public Disputations* occupy more pages in the *Writings*.[8] When Gomarus, Professor at the University of Leiden since 1594, was opposing the appointment of Arminius at a specially convened conference in 1603, he based his objections largely on Arminius's exposition of Romans 7, perhaps more so than on his views on predestination. Plancius, Gomarus's fellow Belgian Calvinist émigré who had led opposition to Arminius in Amsterdam over both chapters, had encouraged, if not instigated, Gomarus's opposition. In reply, Arminius took his manuscript of Romans 7 (the *Dissertation* or an earlier version of it) from his pocket and offered it to anyone to read. No one, not even Gomarus, accepted the invitation when they saw the size of it! Gomarus grudgingly admitted that Arminius's views were passable, and he was unanimously appointed.

The manuscript of the *Dissertation* and the first edition of 1613 included a large fold-out chart containing the argument in the form of a Ramist diagram, unfortunately dropped from subsequent editions, the collected *Opera Theologica* of 1631 and Nichols's English translation, also used by Bagnall. Ramus, of course, did not invent the idea of putting a philosophical or theological concept in diagrammatic form. In the text of the *Dissertation*, under Romans

---

[8] This comparison is made from the *Writings* in the 1956 photographic reprint by Baker Book House, Grand Rapids, of the American 1853 Nichols/Bagnall edition of the *Works* (Auburn and Buffalo: Derby, Miller and Orton, 1853), used here in preference to the edition mentioned in n.1 because it is of uniform pagination throughout.

7:25, the Ramist Arminius introduces a diagram showing the links and the direct and indirect oppositions between the Law of God, the Law of the Mind, the Law of Sin and the Law of the Members, which Bangs finds 'curiously like an *Aristotelian* Square of Opposition'.[9] Walter J. Ong, in his *Ramus: Method and the Decay of Dialogue* (the sub-title is significant), argues that the invention of printing facilitated the reproduction and hence the making of charts and diagrams, and that before Ramus, Agricola in *De Inventione Dialectica* of 1529 had produced similar charts.[10] But Ramus, with his math-ematical approach to logic and his use of a binary system, gave a great boost to the diagrammatical representation of concepts. The binary system method was later used success-fully, for example in biology, in the Linnean classification of plant and animal species. Its value for theological analysis remains more debatable. Ramus made a series of binary distinctions within the general until the number of species was exhausted. Bangs describes a Ramist chart, with its binary distinctions, as 'curiously like a computer program,'[11] and mentions one of his students who reduced Arminius's exposition of Romans 7 to such a programme—before 1970, when the computer was much less dominant than it is today. Ramist philosophy was the computer of the sixteenth century and excited both the same enthusiasm from young students, and the same hesitation, opposition and downright fear from some of their elders, as the computer does today. The style and presentation of a theological work influenced by Ramus is therefore diagrammatic, whether expressed in words or diagram. Ramism will also influence its content.

One might not expect to find Ramist influence in modern sport, but one should look at the concept of the 'knock-out' competition. In a present-day football annual, for instance, containing records for the last season, one will find a Ramist chart in reverse showing how, out of all entrants for the cup, the number is narrowed down in perfect binary form until at last we reach the final winning team. The chart

---

[9] Bangs, *Arminius*, 190.
[10] As quoted in Bangs, *Arminius*, 58.
[11] Bangs, *Arminius*, 59.

shows who they beat on the way, at what stage and by what score. The illustration is not quite so far-fetched as it might seem. Where it is a question of truth and falsehood, Ramism will see the issue in terms of a protracted argument, at each stage of which there will be choice of two answers, one right and the other wrong. The effect is to insist on clear definitions whether or not the evidence is strong enough. Disagreements would be resolved by confrontation rather than consensus; opinions would be polarised, things would be seen in black and white rather than shades of grey, football-type passions could be aroused. The later sixteenth century would be for many reasons an age of controversy, but Ramism contributed to this.

Bangs speaks of the 'distinctions and clarity' of the *Dissertation*,[12] but it is not an easy book to read. The effective beginning is the distinction in the 'First Part'[13] between an unregenerate man under the law, and a regenerate man under grace. According to Arminius an unregenerate man can show a good deal of the workings of the Holy Spirit; he refers to Matthew 7:22, 11:28; Romans 2:13-18; 1 Corinthians 13:2; Galatians 2:16; Hebrews 6:4f.; 2 Peter 20:2f.; Revelation 3:17f., all of which could truly be said of some who are still unregenerate. He appeals to Beza's 'beautiful distinction' between 'the things which precede regeneration' and 'regeneration itself,' which even more significantly is taken from Beza's *Refutation of the Calumnies of Tilman Heshusius*.[14] He also appeals to Calvin's description of 'initial fear' in those who are still unregenerate, as described in the *Institutes*. One might suspect this was a man who knew he was under attack for alleged unorthodoxy, and wanted to display his agreement with recognised pillars of orthodoxy; but independent evidence from about this time shows that Arminius still in general identified himself with the Calvinists, in his letter of March 1591 to his old friend and teacher at Basle, Grynaeus, with whom he had no reason or need to dissemble: 'Our opponents, who are numerous here,

---

[12] Bangs, *Arminius*, 187.

[13] *Works*, 2:491-498.

[14] 1527-88; the orthodox Lutheran whose book published in 1560 marks the split between later Lutheranism and Calvinism on the subject of predestination.

deny [original sin] altogether'.[15] Such opponents could never
have been Calvinists. They might well have been followers
of Coornhert, who, some have imagined, led Arminius
astray. Arminius's conscious rejection of Calvinism may
have come later than has usually been supposed. Later, in
discussing Romans 7:14 he quotes Calvin's ambiguous
observation 'The apostle now begins to bring the law and the
nature of man a little more closely into hostile contact,' while
conceding that by 7:15 Paul according to Calvin 'now
descends to the particular example of a man already regenerate;' and that Beza against Castellio concedes that Paul is
'considering himself not within the boundaries of grace'
when he says 'But I am carnal, sold under sin.'[16] Arminius
takes the definition of a regenerate man from various Pauline texts. The significant ones for his argument are Romans
6:2,6f.,11: 'he is dead to sin; his old man is crucified with
Christ, that the body of sin might be destroyed, that hence-
forth he should not serve sin; he is freed from sin and is alive
to God through Jesus Christ our Lord,' and Colossians 2:11:
'In Christ Jesus the Lord, he is also circumcised by the
circumcision made without hands, in putting off the body of
the sins of the flesh by the circumcision of Christ.' So a
regenerate man is one who is under grace and over whom
sin has no dominion.

Arminius then goes back to the connection between
the seventh chapter and the sixth.[17] He describes 6:13-14, in
which Paul makes important binary distinctions, as the
'proposition of the apostle':

Do not yield your members as instruments of
unrighteousness to sin ...

But yield them as instruments of righteousness to God,
from which Paul drawn an 'enthymeme'[18]

Antecedent: For sin shall not have dominion over you,
(the Consequent, the enthymeme's unstated premise,
being identical with the Proposition)

---

[15] J.H. Maronier, *Jacobus Arminius: een Biographie* (Amsterdam: Y.
Rogge, 1905) 60-61, quoted Bangs, *Arminius*, 139.
[16] *Works*, 2:517.
[17] *Works*, 2:498-502.
[18] A late sixteenth-century word of logic, not occurring in English till
1588, only a few years before the date of the *Dissertation*.

Proof: For you are under grace.

From this and the following verses he draws four Enunciations:

1. Christians are not under the law.
2. Christians are under grace.
3. Sin shall have dominion over those under the law.
4. Sin shall not have dominion over those under grace.

With only cursory mention of the rest of chapter 6 as 'persevering in the same exhortation,' Arminius turns to chapter 7. He finds the first two enunciations illustrated in the marriage 'simile' of 7:2-4, and the latter two enunciations illustrated in 7:5-6, arguing that "wste should be given what he calls its 'normal sense,' introducing not the *purpose* but the *result* of the preceding action, noting also that 7:5 begins 'When we *were* (imperfect) in the flesh...' Arminius interprets 7:5 as tantamount in meaning to his third enunciation, and finds 7:7-13 a fuller explanation of it.[19]

This is followed by 'the rendering of the cause' from verse 14 to the end of the chapter, and he gives a detailed verse by verse commentary, which, with excursuses to consider other Pauline texts, and opinions of other theologians ancient and modern, occupies the middle third of the work. He finds that the opening participle gár indicates its connection with what precedes; as the former part of the chapter was concerned with a man under the law, who was denoted from 7:7 onwards by the pronoun 'I,' a man under that law is still the subject. There is no room here, or need, to consider the commentary on every verse in detail. He has already argued that there are two different kinds of unregenerate men:

'An unregenerate man is—not only he who is entirely blind, ignorant of the will of God, knowingly and willingly contaminating himself by sins without any remorse of conscience, affected with no sense of the wrath of God, terrified with no compunctious visits of conscience, not oppressed with the burden of sin, and inflamed with no desire of deliverance—but it is also he who knows the will of God but does it not...'[20] and it is this second kind of

---

[19] *Works*, 2:503ff.
[20] *Works*, 2:497f.

unregenerate man whom Arminius finds described in 7:14-15; one of whom many good things can be said, but all held in tension with the sinful, carnal urges which continue to have dominion. Not until we come to chapter 8 does Paul begin again to speak of the regenerate man. This passage is the culmination of Arminius's argument, and is pressed through as relentlessly by the following of one line and the rejection of the alternative, as for example the distinction between the elect and the reprobate in the argument and opening chart of Perkins's *Armilla Aurea*.

Arminius continued to preach through Romans 8, with its mention in verses 29 and 30 of the predestination which was to cause so much trouble during his later ministry at the University of Leiden. But his preaching on Romans 8 raised no controversy in 1592-93, although Plancius had charged him with incorrect views on this subject, among others, at the Amsterdam Classis of January 1592. Arminius had then refused to discuss it on the grounds that the issue was his interpretation of Romans 7 which said nothing about predestination. He put nothing in writing about Romans 8; the next controversy arose over his interpretation of Romans 9, which since the time of Origen's attack on Gnostic theories, has been regarded as a classic formulation of the doctrine. It should however be noted that the word predestination itself is not used in Romans 9. We need to approach the controversy without preconceptions as to what it was about.

Arminius had probably taken up too much valuable time in preparing the *Dissertation*. The *Analysis* is much shorter; 39 pages in the Bagnall edition as compared with 235 for the *Dissertation*. Again we may assume that its original purpose was to supply Arminius himself with the arguments he needed when challenged in the Consistory, which in his absence on April 22, 1593 required him to 'declare distinctly and without any circumlocution his opinion on all the articles of the faith.'[21] He learned of this at the Consistory meeting on May 6 and asked for reasonable time to prepare his reply. Presumably the first draft of the

---

[21] *Protocollen der Kerkeraad Amsterdam*, II/108, quoted Bangs, *Arminius*, 148.

Analysis was produced during the following fortnight and was used at the meetings on May 20 and 27. The latter meeting accepted Arminius's statement and declared the matter closed. The *Analysis* may have been revised for sending in 1596 to Snecanus, who had himself published his own *Introduction to the Ninth Chapter of Romans*.

Ramist influence is less noticeable in the *Analysis*. Arminius no longer feels the need to display his philosophical position so much. But there is a strong logical framework. Arminius argues that the scope (message) of the whole Epistle is:'that the Gospel, not the law, is the power of God to salvation, not to him that worketh but to him that believeth,'and that Romans 9–11 is not an excursus or a separate sermon on the salvation of the Jews added at this point, as has later been suggested, but an integral part of the argu-ment making its own distinctive contribution.

After the Proem, 'I could wish to be anathema from Christ for my brethren', comes the Antecedent, 'Most of the Jews were rejected,' and a denial of the Consequent, 'But it does not follow from this that God's word has failed'.[22]

Arminius gives the full question as 'Whether the word of God is not made of none effect, if those of the Jews who seek righteousness, not from faith, but from the law, are rejected by God'; or alternatively, whether God's covenant with the Jews is not made null and void if God's message is accepted. The Jews say Yes; Paul and later Christians say No. But there are two ways of saying No from the Christian side: First, God indeed, by the word of promise, invites all the Jews...to participation in the covenant, but...by his eternal decree and purpose He has determined to make only some... actually partakers, the rest being passed by and left in their former state. (The decree of predestination according to Beza and others.)

Second, God...signified that he would reckon as his sons those only of the Jews who should strive to obtain righteousness and salvation from faith, but that he would hold as strangers those who would seek ... the same from the law. (Snecanus and Arminius.)[23]

---

22 *Works*, 3:486.
23 *Works*, 3:487-88.

Romans 9:6-13 has obvious attractions for a Ramist, being an argument based on binary distinctions. In 9:6f.,[24] Arminius finds a division among the physical descendants of Abraham. Those descended through Ishmael are children of the flesh; only those descended through Isaac are children of promise, and Romans 4:9f. and Galatians 3 and 4 passim, show that the children of promise are those who have faith.[25] The first type, Isaac and Ishmael, is found in verses 7 and 9. But not all descended through Isaac are children of promise either, so we have the second type of Jacob and Esau.[26] Esau signifies those Jews who sought righteousness and life through the law; Jacob signifies those who seek it through faith in Christ, and he does so because as the younger son he needed the grace of calling to receive the promise.[27] The question why some believe and others do not is not handled by the Apostle here and has nothing to do with his scope.[28] But why the question of 9:14? The nature of the accusation depends on the answer chosen from the Christian side. If we put it Beza's way, God is accused of purely arbitrary love and hatred of individuals; if we put it Snecanus's way, God is accused of arbitrary choice of believers as a class, rather than of those who seek merit by obeying the law. Either way, God displays his freedom; the justification of his action is that he acts from mercy and compassion.[29] Romans 9:19 introduces a further Jewish objection. Why doth (God) then find fault? or, as Arminius analyses it:

> Antecedent: God hardens whom he will.
> Consequent: Therefore he cannot with good cause find fault with those who are hardened.
> Ratio (reason): Because no one can resist his will.[30]
> To this he asks the question, For what cause can God rightly find fault/be angry? Answer: Sin.

Arminius rejects the concept of a twofold will of God, hidden and revealed. The will of God is one and the same in

---

[24] *Works*, 3:489.
[25] *Works*, 3:490.
[26] *Works*, 3:492.
[27] *Works*, 3:496.
[28] *Works*, 3:498.
[29] *Works*, 3:500.
[30] *Works*, 3:503.

itself, distinct only in its objects. God may not always reveal to us what he wills to do, only sometimes, according as he judges it to conduce to his glory and our salvation. Instead, Arminius understands Paul to make a twofold re-sponse to 9:19, of reproof and refutation:

1. Reproof
    (i) Chiding, verse 20.
    (ii) Reason; the comparison of God and man.
    (iii) Confirmation of the reason from the potter and clay illustration; the work of God.

This work of God is further analysed[31]
    (a) That man should be made and be a vessel,
    (b) That he become a vessel of sin,
    (c) That he then become a vessel of either wrath or money.

God originally made men vessels for illustrating his right-eous goodness and anger.[32] Man by transgressing the commandment made himself a bad vessel, or sinner. God decrees to make man, according to conditions pleasing to Himself, a vessel of either wrath or mercy, when the condition is either rejected or fulfilled.

2. Refutation[33]
    (i) God does not harden any except those who have already become vessels of the most just divine wrath, by their own fault.
    (ii) 9:22b, 'endured with much long-suffering,' shows that the mode of hardening is by patience and gentleness, not by the omnipotent action of irresistible will.
    (iii) Is it not just for God sometimes to display His will and power against such persons? If not, he will never be free to do so.

The predictable conclusion is 'that this passage...does not serve to confirm that opinion which many suppose.'[34]

The *Analysis* is the last piece of biblical commentary that we have from Arminius. He may have felt that while he had more than adequate gifts to expound the Bible to a

---

31 *Works*, 3:511.
32 *Works*, 3:512.
33 *Works*, 3:515f.
34 *Works*, 3:519.

congregation like that of Amsterdam, his gifts as a scholar were rather for dogmatic theology. This is a view with which later generations have concurred, whether or not they agree with the Synod of Dort, that Arminius misused those gifts.

Two general points may be made in conclusion: the first more general, the second particularly concerned with Arminius himself.

The first point is that the younger Arminius overestimated the help to be gained from logical analysis in general, and Ramism in particular, for the solution of theological problems; rather as in the present century, P.N. Harrison's work on the Pastoral Epistles, and A.Q. Morton's analysis of sentence length in the Pauline corpus as a whole, overestimated the help that mathematical counting could give in finally solving vexed questions of authorship. As one tool among others in the right hands, Ramism in the sixteenth century or the computer in the twentieth, have their place and use. Neither tool should supersede and replace, or even dominate, all others. In particular they do not replace the judgement of the mature scholar with the Spirit and the mind of Christ. With logical analysis as with the computer, one gets out what one puts in. Arminius never gave up his Ramism completely. He used it, for example, with charts, in an important letter of 1598 to Uitenbogaert about predestination, but it was never quite so dominant in his later works.[35] It has been speculated that Arminius's reply to Perkins's short work on predestination of 1598 was prompted by ad-

---

[35]Recent studies of Arminius have stressed his medieval scholastic background and minimised the Ramist influence. Richard E. Muller, *God, Creation and Providence in the Thought of Jacob Arminius* (Grand Rapids: Baker, 1991) 277 says, 'As this study has shown, the impact of Ramism on Arminius's thought was minimal…compared with…mediaeval scholastic philosophy and theology, and specifically Thomism. The Aristotelian philosophy that Arminius is thought to have shunned looms large in his teaching.' Evert Dekker, in *Rijker dan Midas: Vrijheid, genade en predestinatie in de theologie van Jacobus Arminius* (Zoetermeer: Boekencentrum, 1993) only once considers Ramism at any length (22f.) and quotes van Berkel's comment on Ramus's 'banal and simplistic' logic compared with Aristotelianism. While agreeing that Ramism had only limited influence on the details of Arminius's theology, the present study would protest that Ramist influence upon his method is too clear to be so summarily dismissed.

miration for Perkins as a fellow-Ramist, along with disappointment that Perkins had taken a different line on
predestination. As Ian Breward has shown, while Perkins
was prepared to make use of Ramism and had begun his
Armilla Aurea with a Ramist chart illustrating his thesis, he
was not in fact all that committed to Ramism and considered
himself an Aristotelian.[36] If Arminius had read *Armilla Aurea*
he must have known what to expect from Perkins on predestination. More likely he was looking for someone with
whom to discuss the question, someone who might reply, as
Junius had not done, and who would argue with him more
than either the mild-mannered Junius, or than Uitenbogaert
who agreed with Arminius anyway. Arminius's introduction[37] was a polite invitation to Perkins to argue, and
Perkins's alleged Ramism probably played little part. When
Arminius was called to Leiden as Professor in 1602-03, he
did not expect Gomarus, who was as much a Ramist as he
was, to show him any Ramist solidarity, nor did he get it.
Gomarus was determined to give Arminius a rough ride,
and did so till the latter's death in 1609.

The second point is that his family's publication of
the *Dissertation* and the *Analysis* have done nothing for
Arminius's posthumous reputation, except perhaps negat-
ively. Both books were originally published in English by the
Nichols, father and son, and by Bagnall, in the middle part of
the 19th century. The extremely influential ICC Commentary
on *Romans* by Sanday and Headlam, published in 1895, after
giving a short but tolerably fair summary of the *Analysis*
says: 'It was quite clear (by the nineteenth century) that, as
against Arminius, Calvin's interpretation of chapter 9 was
correct,' though the authors then turn on Calvin and say that
it was equally clear that *his* interpretation was inconsistent
with chapter 10 and the language which Paul habitually uses
elsewhere.[38] Even more tart is their description of Arminius's 'tracts' as admirably illustrating Hallam's statement
that 'everyone who had to defend a cause, found no course

---

[36] Breward, *Works of Perkins*, 3f, 51, 86 and 171f.
[37] *Works*, 3:266f.
[38] William Sanday & Arthur C. Headlam, *A Critical and Exegetical Commentary on the Epistle to the Romans*, (The International Critical Commentary) (Edinburgh: T. and T. Clark, 1895), 274.

so ready as to explain the Scriptures consistently with his own tenets.'[39] This dismissive summary has meant that in the twentieth century many have ignored Arminius's other work as unworthy of consideration. Arminius was a very late maturer in some respects. For all his great intelligence and wide knowledge, he was still producing juvenilia like the *Dissertation* and the *Analysis* in his thirties, when he was already an ordained Reformed pastor and a married man beginning a family, at an age when Calvin had already produced the earlier versions of the *Institutes*. Arminius did not have a long career, for he died around the age of fifty; but controversy made him mature quickly, as is shown in his later works and particularly in the *Declaration of Sentiments*.

A case can still be made, I believe, for the positions Arminius defends in both works. The question is how well does he make it. In the *Dissertation* both Arminius and his opponents were convinced that Paul must have *either* a regenerate *or* an unregenerate man in mind. We may now think it possible that Paul was thinking rather of man as sarx, flesh, the mere man in contrast with God.[40] In discussing Romans 9 neither Arminius nor his opponents, nor most commentators, have recognised the real difficulty; that while Romans 9–11 begins and ends with the problem of the salvation of the Jews and remains on that subject most of the time, in 9:17 Paul introduces the Gentile Pharaoh who is not a child of Abraham either of the flesh or of the promise.

The *Dissertation*, for all the industry and learning that produced it, is now little more than a theological curiosity. The *Analysis* remains perhaps more important, but as a stage in the author's theological development rather than as a work of theology in its own right. Arminius's later work, particularly on predestination, is a very different matter.

---

[39] Sanday and Headlam, *Romans*, Introduction, civ.
[40] A point made in the lectures on Romans 1-8 delivered at the University of Cambridge in the Easter term of 1954 by Prof. C.F.D. Moule, unfortunately unpublished so far as I have been able to discover.

Chapter 7

FAITH SEEKING UNDERSTANDING:

Some Neglected Aspects of John Owen's Understanding of Scriptural Interpretation

Carl Trueman

Introduction

One of the great mixed blessings of the theological revolution inaugurated by Karl Barth earlier this century has been the re-newed interest in the theology of the Reformation and the subsequent period of Reformed Orthodoxy.[1] The blessing is mixed because, on the one hand, it has brought to the attention of the theological world the significant contribution of the great theologians of the sixteenth and seventeenth centuries to the on-going Western tradition;

---

[1] Almost every page of Barth's own *Church Dogmatics* bears witness to the importance of Orthodoxy for his thinking. Indeed, Barth himself confesses that the works of the Reformed Heppe and the Lutheran Schmid were crucial to the development of his understanding of the dogmatic task: see E. Busch, *Karl Barth: His Life from Letters and Autobiographical Texts* (ET; Grand Rapids: Eerdmans, 1994), 153-54.

while, on the other hand, it has led to the development of models of historical interpretation based upon contemporary theological agendas rather than upon properly historical criteria. As a result, the last half century has witnessed a steady growth in works about the era of Reformed Orthodoxy, and watched the development of distinct dialogues between modern systematicians and the great theologians of the seventeenth century;[2] but it has also seen the imposition on these theologians of questions and criteria with which they themselves would have been unfamiliar.[3]

As theologians of the twentieth century have sought historical justification for their own distinctive positions, one of the areas upon which they have focused has been the doctrine of scripture. Here, many have claimed to find a fundamental shift within Reformed theology from the 'dynamic' position of such as Calvin, to the more rigid and static formulations of the High Orthodox, such as Francis Turretin.[4] That such findings comport very well with certain contemporary ecclesiastical agendas is scarcely surprising— and nor, it should be added, can subsequent responses to such interpretations be separated from agendas that are equally determined by modern pre-suppositions.[5] The

[2]In addition to the monumental *Church Dogmatics* of Barth himself, other such examples of note include G.C. Berkouwer, *Studies in Dogmatics*, 14 vols. (ET; Grand Rapids: Eerdmans, 1952-75); Otto Weber, *Foundations of Dogmatics*, 2 vols. (ET; Grand Rapids: Eerdmans, 1981).
[3]An excellent discussion of the way in which modern theological agendas have shaped the way in which Reformed Orthodoxy has been investigated and evaluated is found in R. A. Muller's discussion of the Calvin against the Calvinists question: 'Calvin and the "Calvinists": Assessing Continuities and Discontinuities between the Reformation and Orthodoxy,' *Calvin Theological Journal* 30 (1995) 345-75; and 31 (1996) 125-60.
[4]The classic statement of this argument is found in Jack B Rogers and Donald K McKim, *The Authority and Interpretation of the Bible: an Historical Approach* (San Francisco: Harper and Row, 1979); cf. Weber, *Foundations* 1, 118-21; also Berkouwer, *Holy Scripture* (ET; Grand Rapids: Eerdmans, 1975), 30-32.
[5]For critiques of the Rogers-McKim proposal which yet operate within the narrow terms of debate set by their book, see J.D. Woodbridge *Biblical Authority: A Critique of the Rogers/McKim Proposal* (Grand Rapids: Zondervan, 1982); J.D. Hannah, *Inerrancy and the Church* (Chicago: Moody Press, 1984).

problem with such a debate is obvious: it narrows the field of scholarly investigation to those areas which are perceived to be directly relevant to the present and thus prevents a broader investigation of the wider theological and historical context of the primary texts.

An example of this is John Owen. Owen's doctrine of scripture has been the focus of a number of studies over the years—indeed, as a 'transitional' figure between Calvin and High Orthodoxy, he has proved a crucial point of conflict in the debate surrounding the so-called Rogers-McKim proposal.[6] Nevertheless, the attention this debate generated for Owen's theology was narrowly focused upon the issue of the nature of inspiration and of the authentication of scripture as truth—questions which reflect the debates about the nature of biblical authority and inerrancy which have so plagued the evangelical world of the twentieth century. The results have consequently failed to engage significantly way a whole range of issues which were of concern to Owen himself and which, for a historian of doctrine, are worthy of investigation in their own right.

One example of a concern which runs throughout Owen's own discussions of scripture but which is absent from those modern treatments of his writings which are preoccupied with questions concerning inspiration and inerrancy, is his emphasis upon the positive relationship between personal piety and biblical interpretation. That this has been neglected in the secondary literature is most unfortunate: as will become clear, it is the connection which Owen makes between piety and biblical interpretation which allows him to overcome a number of significant problems which had arisen for Reformed theology in his own day; indeed, failure to see this connection will inevitably lead to fundamental misunderstanding of his thought.

---

[6]See Rogers and McKim, *Authority and Interpretation*, 218-23; and the response by Stan N. Gundry, 'John Owen on Authority and Scripture' in Hannah, *Inerrancy and the Church*, 189-221.

The Problem of the Interpretation of Scripture

One scholar has recently made the following observation concerning Owen's approach to scriptural interpretation:

> In keeping with this [scholastic] mentality, John Owen despised those who appealed to the 'bare word' of Scripture, and whose only hermeneutic was 'away with the gloss and interpretation; give us leave to believe what the word expressly saith'. His impatience was understandable, for, as Wesley himself was to point out, there were no texts in which it is said in 'express terms' that Christ did not die for all'.[7]

Leaving aside the particular doctrinal point which forms the context of Owen's statement, that of so-called 'limited atonement', it is clear that the author of the above comment regards Owen's theological method as undermining, at the very least, the whole notion of the perspicuity of scripture.[8] In fact, however, such a specious argument fails to set Owen's own position within its historical context and thus misses the specific significance of Owen's attack on those who appeal to the bare word of scripture.

From the time of the Reformation up until the latter part of the sixteenth century, it had been enough for theologians to appeal to the bare text of scripture as a basis for delimiting the powers of human reason and guaranteeing correct interpretation.[9] By the time of Owen, however, the situation was not quite as straightforward. The basic problem was that significant groups, such as the heterodox Arminians and the heretical Socinians, had arisen who also claimed the Protestant scripture principle and yet whose theology was clearly at odds with that of the Reformed

---

[7]A.C. Clifford, *Atonement and Justification: English Evangelical Theology 1640-1790—An Evaluation* (Oxford: Clarendon Press, 1990), 142, quoting from Owen, *Works*, 16 vols. (Edinburgh: Banner of Truth, 1965-68), 10, 303.

[8]See how the discussion continues, *Atonement and Justification*, 142 ff.

[9]See J.P. Donnelly, 'Italian Influences on Calvinist Scholasticism,' *Sixteenth Century Journal* 7 (1976) 81-101, esp. 92; R. A. Muller, *Post-Reformation Reformed Dogmatics* vol. 2 (Grand Rapids: Baker, 1993), 340-42.

Orthodox.[10] For Owen this problem became particularly acute in his clash with the English Socinian, John Biddle,[11] whose *A Twofold Catechism* (London, 1654), was composed of a series of leading questions followed by lists of proof-texts: the underlying ideology was plain—the bare text of Scripture, taken at face value, is the truth. The problem, of course, was that the context into which these texts were placed by Biddle—that of highly tendentious questions—itself presupposed a particular framework of interpretation. Throughout the *Catechism*, Socinian theology is clearly pre-supposed in the type and manner of questions asked, for example in the question on God's immutability:

> Are there not, according to the perpetual tenour of the Scripture, affections or passions in God, as anger, fury, zeal, wrath, love, hatred, mercy, grace, jealousie, repentance, grief, joy, fear?[12]

The question is about as neutral as the old chestnut, 'When did you stop beating your wife?' and clearly assumes the validity of a doctrine of divine mutability. What is significant, in light of the adherence of both Orthodox and Socinian to the principle of scripture alone, and the catena of proof-texts used to answer each of Biddle's questions, is that the *Catechism* cannot be refuted by a simple reiteration of the Protestant position on the sufficiency and perspicuity of the Bible, a point of which Owen himself was only too aware.[13]

It is in this context that Owen's criticism of those who appeal to the bare text of scripture must be understood. Seen in this light, his statement does not necessarily mark a fundamental point of discontinuity with his Reformed forebears, nor an attempt to bring biblical interpretation under

---

[10]See *The Works of James Arminius*, 3 vols. (ET; Grand Rapids: Baker, 1986), 2, 80-92; *The Racovian Catechism* (ET; London: Longman, 1818) 1-19.

[11]On Biddle, see H.J. McLachlan, *Socinianism in Seventeenth-Century England* (Oxford: Oxford University Press, 1951), 163-217.

[12]*Twofold Catechism*, 11.

[13]For Biddle's statement of the Scripture principle, see *Twofold Catechism*, 1-6; cf., Owen's discussion of this in Biddle, where he grudgingly ac-knowledges that he can find no fault in Biddle's position, *Works* 12, 85-86.

the control of an incipient rationalism—nor, for that matter, a statement about specifically scholastic methodology; it represents, rather, an appeal for scriptural interpretation to be conducted in terms of specific theological principles within a particular theological context. This is clear in the sentences subsequent to the passage quoted by Clifford, where Owen speaks of 'the gift of interpretation agreeable to the proportion of faith'.[14] What Owen is doing is implicitly acknowledging that the fact that scripture is perspicuous does not guarantee correct interpretation and doctrinal formulation. Given the Socinian insistence that theology is to be based firmly on Scripture, but Scripture interpreted according to the standards of human rationality, the point at issue is not the authority of scripture, nor even its perspicuity, but the manner and criteria of correct interpretation. For Owen, this can only take place when two factors are taken into account: the subjective context of interpretation, *i.e.*, the believer's faith; and the objective principle of interpretation, *i.e.*, the analogy of faith.

The Subjective Context: The Believer's Faith

It is Owen's adherence to the principle of scripture's perspicuity which points clearly towards the vital connection between a true understanding of the biblical text and the believer's personal faith. In Book 6.2 of his massive work on the Holy Spirit, Owen states that anyone using their rational faculties and equipped with the necessary linguistic skills can understand the grammatical meaning of scriptural propositions.[15] However, this does not constitute true understanding of the Bible or of any specific passage in it. True understanding involves a personal, committed belief that what the Bible says is true and that it reflects the will of God, and this kind of existential involvement with, and understanding of, the biblical text is not open to human beings via their unaided natural faculties.[16] Thus, what one might call the grammatical perspicuity of scripture gives no real insight

---

[14]*Works* 10, 303.
[15]*Works* 4, 156.
[16]*Works* 4, 156-58.

into the personal, transforming implications of the Bible's meaning for the individual reading the text.

The reason that human beings cannot, by their own effort, translate their grammatical understanding of the words of Scripture into the understanding of true faith is twofold: first, humans are sinful, with minds morally corrupted and darkened in such a way that they are blind to the real truth of scripture;[17] and, second, their minds are natural and finite and thus incapable of grasping the supernatural truth which scripture expresses.[18] These two factors prevent any simplistic connection being made between the *objective* perspicuity of the scriptures and their *subjective* perspicuity. This tension can only be resolved for Owen via the work of the Holy Spirit. Commenting on Ephesians 1:17-19, he makes the following statement:

> It is a *revelation* that the apostle prays for, or a *Spirit of revelation* to be given unto them. This greatly offends some at first hearing, but wholly without cause; for he understands not a new *immediate external revelation from God.* Believers are not directed to look after such revelations for their guide....But there is an *internal subjective revelation*, whereby no *new things* are revealed unto our minds, or are not outwardly revealed *anew*, but our minds are enabled to discern the things that are revealed already.[19]

In this statement is the key to understanding why Scripture, although objectively perspicuous, is not perspicuous to everyone: the objective scriptures and the subjective human faculty of knowing need to be brought together by the work of the Holy Spirit. The believer does not enjoy the advantage over the unbeliever of new objective revelation, but rather knows the same revelation through faith—a new, supernatural mode of knowing. The Holy Spirit removes the blindness caused by sin and exalts human reason to a level beyond that which it could achieve through its own, finite nature.[20] The result is that the interpretation of the Bible, and

---

[17]*Works* 4, 176.

[18]*Works* 4, 193-94.

[19]*Works* 4, 134 (his emphasis); *cf.*, *Works* 4, 156-57.

[20]*Works* 4, 126; cf. *Works* 3, 125. For detailed discussion of Owen's understanding of the relationship of faith and reason, see Carl R.

the subsequent dogmatic theological task, are neither purely rational nor irrational but rather suprarational—grace perfects and exalts nature.

This basic insight into the relationship between the objective givenness and subjective appropriation of revelation stands behind Owen's thinking on a number of closely related issues. First, it serves radically to delimit the usefulness of so-called external proofs for the reliability, truth, etc. of scripture. The radical qualitative distinction between mere natural, rational knowledge of the scriptures and that which exists in the context of faith, pointing as it does to the basic discontinuity between natural modes of knowing and the believer's mode of knowing, prevents the external proofs from enjoying any real apologetic value with reference to unbelievers; they function, rather, as helps to confirm the faith of those who already believe.[21]

Second, this approach to the subjective appropriation of revelation points to the close connection that exists in Owen's theology between biblical interpretation and personal piety. Given the way in which Owen develops his position in terms of the categories of Aristotelian psychology, this may come as a surprise to those convinced that piety and those theologies which use Aristotle are mutually exclusive, but it is quite clear that the language, logic, and even physics of Aristotle serve merely to underline the radical discontinuity between natural reason and faith and to point towards the need for the action of the Holy Spirit in both exalting and sanctifying human faculties.[22] It thus clarifies the foundation upon which Owen is then able to build his understanding of the piety involved in biblical interpretation.

The crucial role of personal piety in the task of interpretation is nowhere shown more clearly than in the discussion of the means of understanding the Bible contained in *Causes, Ways, and Means of Understanding the Mind of God*. Here, he defines the interpretative task in terms of three

---

Trueman, *The Claims of Truth: John Owen's Trinitarian Theology* (Carlisle: Paternoster, 1997), ch. 2.

[21]*Works* 4, 20 ff.

[22]E.g., the Aristotelian presupposition that no effect can exceed its cause is fundamental to Owen's argument regarding external evidences for scripture's truth, *Works* 4, 50.

areas: spiritual; disciplinarian, or technical; and ecclesiastic-al.[23] Of these, the first is most important as this consists of those areas relating to the personal spiritual life of the believer which relate directly to faith and which are there-fore the essential presuppositions of the correct use of skills from the other two categories. Foremost in the area of spiritual discipline is prayer, a point which serves both to emphasise the delimitation of reason in Owen's thinking, and to underscore the anti-Pelagian thrust of his theology:

> The first thing required as a *spiritual means* is *prayer*. I intend *fervent and earnest prayer* for the assistance of the Spirit of God revealing the mind of God.... And this also, by the way, invincibly proves that the due investigation of the mind of God in the Scripture is a work above the utmost improvement of natural reason...for were we sufficient of ourselves, without immediate divine aid and assistance, for this work, why do we pray for them? with which argument the ancient church perpetually urged the *Pelagians* as to the necessity of saving grace.[24]

It is, therefore, because the truths of Scripture, and the mode in which they must be grasped, far surpass human powers that prayer, and thus the piety of the individual believer, stand at the heart of the task of interpretation. What is significant about this, and what is highlighted in the passage by the close correlation of prayer, revelation, and anti-Pelagianism, is the way in which it places human respons-ibility within the overall context of divine sovereignty in the task of biblical interpretation and thus points towards the objectivity of the whole in God himself. Indeed, so confident is Owen of the objective reliability of true prayer and piety in achieving sound results in terms of biblical interpretation and subsequent doctrinal belief that he is certain that no-one who prays in such a fashion could ultimately remain con-vinced of any error concerning a fundamental truth.[25] Thus, given the right attitude of prayerfulness, the believer would

---

[23]See *Works* 4, 199 ff.
[24]*Works* 4, 201-02.
[25]*Works* 4, 203.

eventually come to a sound understanding of all the most basic—and essential—doctrines of the faith.

In his reference to fundamental truths, Owen's thought touches on an issue which was of great importance within Reformed Orthodoxy in the latter part of the seventeenth century: that of fundamental articles.[26] While the development of fundamental articles was rooted in the catechetical practices of the Reformation churches, it also came increasingly to serve the polemical purpose of maintaining a stable doctrinal core for Christianity while allowing for the Protestant principle of scripture alone. As such, the close connection which the Orthodox made between the Bible and the articles served to counter Counter-Reformation claims about the obscurity of the Bible and the need for the church as an institution to define what was and was not essential to the faith.[27]

For Owen, the situation was complicated by the existence of the Socinians. He had to be able to stress the Protestant notion of scripture alone as the basis for the rejection of Catholic additions to the faith but he had to do so at the same time as countering both the heterodox ideas of the Arminians and the heretical reductionism of the Socinians, the latter of which especially sought to evacuate the faith of much of its historic content. This is why the emphasis on personal piety and prayer is so important: the conflict with the Arminians and the Socinians was ultimately about how scripture should be interpreted, not about its status as the sole cognitive and perspicuous basis for theology; it is therefore the method or process of interpretation which was at issue; and thus the role of the human subject was as much a point of concern as the objective nature of the task. Were his statements on the issue to end

---

[26]On fundamental articles, see Richard A. Muller, *Post-Reformation Reformed Dogmatics* vol.1 (Grand Rapids: Baker, 1987), 287-95; Martin I. Klauber, 'Between Protestant Orthodoxy and Rationalism: Fundamental Articles in the Early Career of Jean LeClerc,' *Journal of the History of Ideas* 54 (1993), 611-36; idem, *Between Reformed Scholasticism and Pan-Protestantism: Jean-Alphonse Turretin (1671-1737) and Enlightened Orthodoxy at the Academy of Geneva* (Selinsgrove: Susquehanna University Press, 1994), 170 ff.

[27]See Klauber, *Between Reformed Scholasticism*, 171.

with a discussion of personal piety, however, Owen's resolution of the problem would smack of a naive positivism rooted in a purely subjective notion of interpretation; but such is not the case, as the emphasis upon subjective piety is balanced by his understanding of the objective dimension of biblical interpretation in the analogy of faith.

The Objective Principle of Interpretation

As the very existence of Arminians and Socinians demonstrated, a simple appeal to the bare text of scripture was in the seventeenth century no longer a sufficient defence against heterodoxy and heresy—a distinct change from the early years of the Reformation.[28] As noted above, Owen faced this problem in a particularly acute form in his controversy with John Biddle. Confronted by the blunt literalism of Biddle's approach, Owen not only stressed the central importance of personal faith and piety as focused upon the act of prayer and the subjective work of the Holy Spirit, but also stressed the importance of sound principles of biblical interpretation. Bible passages were not to be taken in isolation, but were to be understood in the theological context:

> [W]hat sense soever any man supposeth or judgeth this or that particular place of Scripture to yield and give out the best of his rational intelligence is immediately to give place unto the *analogy of faith*—that is, the Scripture's own

---

[28]See Donnelly, 'Italian Influences on Calvinist Scholasticism,' 92. The Reformers also faced attacks on their doctrine from those holding to radical scriptural principles: *e.g.*, Calvin in his conflict with the anti-trinitarians. Nevertheless, the rise and growth of Arminianism and Socinianism in the latter part of the sixteenth century meant that the threat posed by such biblicists to orthodoxy was much greater in the seventeenth than in the mid-sixteenth century. The theological focus was now placed less upon matters relating to scriptural sufficiency, the role of the church and tradition in interpretation, etc., and more upon issues relating directly to perspicuity and related questions of interpretation and theological context. A quantitative change in the threat posed by groups holding to a radical Scripture principle was thus one of the major factors which led Reformed theologians to make significant changes to the way in which theology was pursued in the post-Reformation context.

declaration of its sense in other places to another purpose,
or contrary there-unto.[29]

This statement is, as far as it goes, merely a reaffirmation of
the classic Protestant principle that obscure passages of
Scripture are to be interpreted in the light of those which are
clear. As such it stands in basic continuity with the exegetical
principles of the Reformation, but also stands vulnerable to
the same weaknesses so dramatically evident in, for example, the clash at Marburg between Luther and Zwingli,
where the problem was, from one angle, how to decide
which passages were clear and thus foundational for understanding biblical teaching on the eucharist. Such a baldly
stated principle scarcely provided a base from which to
refute the theological results of Biddle's radical biblicism.[30]

Nevertheless, there is evidence in Owen's writings
that this basic problem of interpretation was to be overcome
by paying careful attention to the specifically trinitarian
nature of theology. In an important passage in his work, *Of
the Divine Original of the Scripture* (1659), Owen argued in
strong terms that rejection of, or failure to grasp, the doctrine
of the trinity effectively prevented any true understanding of
theology at all.[31] Such a position radically delimits the role of
autonomous reason in matters of theology while at the same
time pointing towards the fundamentally salvific function of
the Scriptures.[32] The whole of God's conversation with humanity, according to Owen, consists in the communication
of God's love to men and women.[33] Therefore, the problem

---

[29]*Works* 4, 224.

[30]Owen effectively conceded precisely this point by admitting that he
found nothing to criticise in Biddle's statement of scriptural sufficiency
in his *Twofold Catechism*: see *Works* 12, 85.

[31] *Works* 16, 340-42.

[32] 'Here [on the doctrine of the trinity] is reason entangled; yet after a
while finds evidently, that unless this be embraced, all other things
where-in it hath to do with God will not be of value to the soul....Now
when the mind of man is exercised about these things [of salvation], he
finds at last that they are so wrapped up in the doctrine of the Trinity,
that without the belief, receiving, and acceptance of it, it is utterly
impossible that any interest in them should be obtained or preserved.'
Works 16, 340-41.

[33] *Works* 16, 341.

with Socinian biblicism was not (self-evidently) its commitment to the principle of Scripture alone but that its failure to understand the Bible in a true and edifying manner; it does this because it failed to set the Bible within the proper interpretative context, *i.e.*, the trinitarian framework of salvation.

The centrality of the trinity to Scripture, and thus to its interpretation, is made quite explicit by Owen in a passage which epitomises his whole theological scheme:

> [T]he Scripture speaks not of any thing *between God and us* but what is founded on this account. The Father worketh, the Son worketh, and the Holy Ghost worketh. The Father worketh not but by the Son and his Spirit; the Son and Spirit work not but from the Father. The Father glorifieth the Son, the Son glorifieth the Father, and the Holy Ghost glorifieth them both. Before the foundation of the world the Son was with the Father, and rejoiced in his peculiar work for the redemption of mankind. At the creation, the Father made all things but by the Son and the power of the Spirit. In redemption, the Father sends the Son; the Son, by his own condescension, undertakes the work, and is incarnate by the Holy Ghost. The Father, as was said, communicates his love and all the fruits of it unto us by the Son, as the Holy Ghost doth the merits and fruits of the mediation of the Son. The Father is not known nor worshipped, but by and in the Son; nor the Father nor Son, but by the Holy Ghost.[34]

Within Owen's overall theological scheme, there are sound reasons for the importance of the trinitarian basis of biblical interpretation. Owen makes it quite clear in his massive work, *Theologoumena Pantodapa* (1661), when he describes the history of theology from Adam to the apostles, that natural theology/general revelation are inadequate to point towards God as gracious and merciful because they can only speak of God as Creator.[35] God is only revealed as Redeemer through Christ: the union of the Word with human flesh provides the basis for a theology of union and for Christ's subsequent

---

[34]*Works* 16, 342.
[35]*Works* 17 (Edinburgh: Johnstone and Hunter, 1854), 51.

prophetic office;[36] and the Scriptures are authoritative because they focus upon Christ and speak of him who is the
foundation of all truth.[37] The scriptures, then, have a christo-
centric focus, but this, in turn, points to a deeper trinitarian
focus: the incarnation of Christ depends upon his appointment as Mediator, and that appointment is itself rooted in
the eternal covenant of redemption between the persons of
the Godhead.[38] It is only because of this trinitarian covenant
that Christ is appointed Redeemer, the theology of union
and the prophetic office are made possible, that God is
revealed as a merciful Redeemer, and the Holy Spirit is sent
forth to bring men and women to salvation. The covenant
thus stands both as the causal foundation and as the content
of the revelation of salvation.

This points clearly to the way in which the subjective
and objective poles of biblical interpretation are brought together in Owen's theology. To borrow terminology favoured
by Anthony Thiselton,[39] for interpretation to take place, the
two horizons of text and interpreter must be brought together in some way; for Owen, this takes place through the
action of the Holy Spirit exalting the faculties of the believer
through faith and piety and thus enabling the mind to grasp
the profundities of the trinitarian covenant underlying the
scriptural revelation of God's grace, especially as it is revealed in, and focused upon, the historical person of Jesus
Christ. That this activity of the Spirit is itself rooted in the
eternal covenant relations of the trinity serves to give the
whole structure a remarkable theological unity.

Conclusion

As yet there are no significant studies of the exegetical and
interpretative strategies of the Reformed Orthodox of the

---

[36]*Works* 1, 65-69; *Works* 17, 38; for a full discussion of Owen's christology and his understanding of the communication of properties, see
Trueman, *The Claims of Truth*, chs. 2, 4.

[37]*Works* 1, 82ff.

[38]*Works* 10, 163-79.

[39]See his *The Two Horizons: New Testament Hermeneutics and Philosophical Description* (Carlisle: Paternoster, 1980).

seventeenth century—a state of affairs which has allowed the kind of claims about proof-texting and dogmatic *apriorism*, epitomised in the quotation from Alan Clifford's study of Owen, to go almost unchallenged. Of course, while one must beware of over-generalising from the example of one specimen theologian, it is clear from Owen's writings that while the challenges raised by Arminianism and Socinianism prevented him from building his theology upon a straightforward reiteration of the Reformers' scriptural principle, his response was not characterised by a blunt, positivistic emphasis upon proof-texts but by a plea for interpretation to take place within both the subjective and objective context of salvation. Subjectively, this requires an acknowledgement of human sin and finitude coupled with an emphasis upon godly and faithful prayer—an activity rooted within the saving and sovereign work of the Holy Spirit. Objectively, it means understanding the material dependence of scripture upon Christ and thus upon the intra-trinitarian covenant of redemption. For the believer, the subjective and objective horizons of interpretation are brought together by the Holy Spirit in an act itself determined by the covenant of the trinitarian God.

Critics may argue that Owen has still not met and refuted the Socinian objections, that his presupposition of the doctrine of the trinity assumes *a priori* the fundamental point at issue in the debate. There is some truth in this, but this is not the result of an overly-rational or deductive mentality but the consequence of his understanding of theology: faith, in terms of both its content and its mode, is supernatural and thus discontinuous with the merely natural. As his emphasis upon godly, 'faithfull,' prayer demonstrates, the act of interpretation is not ultimately something which can be done in the public sphere according to universal rational criteria; it is rather an act of faith conducted according to the suprarational criteria of faith. The two tasks, then, of theologian and exegete are intimately related—and neither can be divorced from the life of faith.

At the beginning of this essay, I argued that the way to approach the past was to set aside the concerns of the present, as failure to do so had led to instances of herm-eneutical anachronism and to the production of distorted and imbalanced readings of history. Nevertheless, the results of *church* history and historical *theology* should not stop at the level of mere antiquarianism but should try to speak in some way to the church of today. Therefore, in conclusion, I would like to suggest that a careful reading of Owen points to an understanding of the theological task which receives its unity from the fact that it is an act of faith, not only in terms of its mode of knowing but also in terms of its content. The price Owen pays for this is that the apologetic potential of his approach, specifically in terms of his battle with the Socinians, is severely limited; the advantage he gains, however, is that the task of doctrinal formulation and statement and that of biblical interpretation are brought into close relation, so that one cannot be pursued effectively without the other. Now, while it is true that we cannot return to the pre-Enlightenment, pre-critical world in which Owen was able to work, this need not prevent us learning from him. In the seventeenth century, theologians were faced by the massive task of systematising and consolidating the theology of their Reformer forebears; to do so, they looked back to the patterns and models hammered out in the Middle Ages by the giants of scholastic theology. Positive appropriation of these models enabled them to achieve their self-imposed task and yet did not involve a rejection of the Reformation or a return to the content of medieval systems. Academic theology today is in a state of fragmentation, with its various subdisciplines now so specialised that they are pursued in basic isolation from each other, even within a single department or faculty. If the problem in the seventeenth century was the restatement of Reformation theology in a new polemical and pedagogical context, the problem today is one of recapturing the essential unity of the discipline as a basis for restating theology in a critical yet coherent and cohesive manner. To do so, however, the very dynamics of the discipline as currently pursued need to be carefully rethought. In our so-called post-modern world, it is here that careful reflection upon the formal relationship between personal commitment, doctrine, and biblical exegesis which we find in the writings of John Owen may yet prove to bear fruit.

Chapter 8

PERSPECTIVES ON JUDAS: BARTH'S IMPLICIT HERMENEUTIC

John E. Colwell

The mere fact that, whether successfully or otherwise, a comparative study of Karl Barth and Jacques Derrida can be attempted evidences a biblical hermeneutic underlying the *Church Dogmatics* which, while implicit rather than explicit, anticipates a contemporary debate and therefore may be suggestive of possibilities from which that contemporary debate could benefit.[1]

I say 'implicit rather than explicit' since Barth has surprisingly little to say explicitly on the theme of biblical interpretation. While it may be valid to observe that 'Barth's exegesis…displays a great variety of hermeneutical skills and principles,'[2] his underlying and all-pervading concern is 'that the biblical texts must be investigated for their own

---

[1] Graham Ward, *Barth, Derrida and the Language of Theology* (Cambridge: CUP, 1995). For a discussion of this comparison see the 'Article Review' by Bruce Lindley McCormack in *SJT* 49 (1996) 97-109.

[2] D.F. Ford, 'Barth's Interpretation of the Bible' in S.W. Sykes (ed.), *Karl Barth: Studies of his Theological Method* (Oxford: Clarendon, 1979) 56; *cf.*, David Kelsey's comment '…one of the fascinating things about Barth's *Dogmatics* is the inventiveness and variety of the ways he uses the Bible' (D.H. Kelsey, *The Uses of Scripture in Recent Theology* (London: SCM, 1975) 39).

sake to the extent that the revelation which they attest does not stand or occur, and is not to be sought, behind or above them but in them'.[3] Simply stated, Barth's concern is with the text itself rather than with that which might or might not underlie it. As Francis Watson has commented, 'Barth ...postulates an "intra-textual realism" in which one regards the text in its final form as the irreducible witness to a divine-human history which occurs prior to and beyond the text, but which can only be known in its textual mediation'.[4] This is not to deny that revelatory events have occurred in the past, nor is it to deny that Scripture bears witness to these revelatory events, but it is to recognize that the text of Scripture is given to us with the promise that 'the word of God is living' (Heb. 4:12) that through this text revelatory events will occur afresh in the present and the future.[5] For Barth, this focus on the text itself need not involve an 'annulling of the results of biblical scholarship in the last centuries,' nor need it imply a 'neglect of efforts in this direction,' but it does necessitate 'a radical re-orientation concerning the goal to be pursued'.[6] At best, the fruits of historical-critical research may fulfil the rôle accorded by Calvin to the *adminicula*, testimonies which act as secondary aids to our 'feebleness,' but which should not distract our attention from the *testimonium*, the inner witness of the Spirit through which God attests the text itself.[7] David Kelsey comments that, in authorizing

---

[3]K. Barth, *Church Dogmatics* (hereafter referred to as *CD*), eds. G.W. Bromiley and T.F. Torrance (ET; Edinburgh: T. & T. Clark, 1956–75) I/2:494.

[4]Francis Watson, *Text, Church and World: Biblical Interpretation in Theological Perspective* (Edinburgh: T. & T. Clark, 1994) 230.

[5]For a general discussion of Barth's approach to hermeneutics see Werner G. Jeanrond, 'Karl Barth's Hermeneutics' in Nigel Biggar (ed.), *Reckoning with Barth: Essays in Commemoration of the Centenary of Karl Barth's Birth* (London & Oxford: Mowbray, 1988) 80-97.

[6]*ibid.* Note the comment of C.A. Baxter, 'Barth—A Truly Biblical Theologian?' *Tyn.B.* 38 (1987), 14, that Barth's theological position precludes his use of the 'historical critical methods in order to establish historical events in which God had revealed himself would be wasted energy'.

[7]John Calvin, *Institutes* 1:8:13.

his theological proposals by appeal to the New Testament narratives just as they stand in the received texts,' Barth 'takes them as the expressions of a tradition having a particular point of view and not as the sources for historical reconstruction either of earlier traditions out of which the final tradition may have been fashioned or of "what really happened".[8]

Indeed, towards the end of his life Barth displayed a degree of impatience with the advocates of historical-critical method, speaking of a 'struggle' which could only now 'get on my nerves'.[9]

Clearly it is this concern to engage with the text in its 'final form,' together with the reappraisal of an appropriate rôle for historical-critical method, that invites comparisons between Barth and more recent approaches to biblical interpretation. But, while Barth outlines this concern explicitly within his *Prolegomena*, it is within the text of the *Dogmatics* as a whole, and especially within the small print sections, that the outworkings of this concern are most clearly (albeit implicitly) demonstrated. Arguably no Christian theologian has ever evidenced a greater concern to interact with the text of Scripture and to develop a coherent account of theology in response to that which is heard.[10] The text of the *Church Dogmatics* is interspersed with sections in small print within which Barth converses with the text of Scripture, with the Christian tradition, and with the arguments of other theological writers. While it may be possible and (given the length of the volumes) tempting to 'skip over' these small print sections this should be discouraged. Barth's theological enterprise is seriously misunderstood if the text of the *Dogmatics* is ever perceived as replacing or displacing

---

[8]Kelsey, *Uses of Scripture*, 45.

[9]'...daß mir die Äußerungen ihrer späteren und heutigen Nachfolger nicht mehr unter die Haut oder gar zu Herzen, sondern, als nur zu bekant, nur noch auf die Nerven gehen konnten.' K. Barth, 'Nachwort' in *Schleiermacher-Auswahl mit einem Nachwort von Karl Barth* (München u. Hamburg: Siebenstern Taschenbuch Verlag, 1968), 290-312, at p. 291.

[10]Note Barth's comment: 'If I understand what I am trying to do in the *Church Dogmatics*, it is to listen to what Scripture is saying and tell you what I hear.' R. C. Johnson, 'The Legacy of Karl Barth,' *Reflection* 66:4 (1969) 4, quoted in Ford, 'Barth's Interpretation,' 55.

the biblical narratives or theological traditions to which it is a response. For Barth the text of Scripture is irreducible and irreplaceable.[11] Herein lies the root of Barth's impatience with the demythologizing programme of his friend Rudolf Bultmann: we simply are not in a position to reinterpret, and thereby to replace, the narratives of Scripture and the form in which they are given to us; to do so is a falsification rather than a translation.[12]

The small print section in which Barth interacts with the narratives concerning Judas occurs at the conclusion of his discussion of the doctrine of election. As Colin Gunton has noted, perhaps the most significant feature of Barth's innovative treatment of the doctrine is that he places it where he does, as part of the doctrine of God.[13] The doctrine of election can be recognized as the

> sum of the Gospel' because it identifies the nature of God, it identifies him as the One who for us too is the 'One who loves in freedom, it identifies him as the One who in Jesus Christ elects us and is for us.[14]

Barth previously confesses that he would have preferred 'to follow Calvin's doctrine of predestination much more closely' but that he 'could not and cannot do so': 'As I let the Bible itself speak to me on these matters, as I meditated upon what I seemed to hear, I was driven irresistibly to reconstruction'.[15]

---

[11]Cf., W.C. Placher's comment, *Narratives of a Vulnerable God: Christ, Theology, and Scripture* (Louisville: Westminster John Knox Press, 1994) 40 that 'Christians do not figure out the "real meaning" of the biblical narratives in some doctrinal formulation and then discard the stories, but doctrines serve as aids for reflection on the biblical narratives'.

[12]'It cannot be a question of translating the saga or legend into verifiable history, but of repeating (in whatever language) the saga or legend as such, of a renewal of the form commensurate with the history envisaged in these accounts. On the pretext of a translation from antiquated to more modern language we cannot put another history in the place of this history. Otherwise the translation is a falsification.' (*CD* III/3:375.)

[13]C.E. Gunton, 'Karl Barth's Doctrine of Election as part of his Doctrine of God,' *Journal of Theological Studies* 25 (1974) 381-392.

[14]*CD* II/2:3.

[15]*CD* II/2:x.

This reconstruction leads Barth not only to locate his treatment of the doctrine within the doctrine of God, nor just to identify Jesus Christ as both the electing God and the elected man, nor even to recognize that just as he alone is the true elected one he alone at the Cross is the true rejected one,[16] it also leads him to order his treatment in the manner that he does, beginning with the election of Jesus Christ and only turning to consider the election of the individual when he has first considered the election of the community. Even in his consideration of the election of the individual Barth only addresses the question of the determination of the rejected once he has first discussed the determination of the elect and, since his consideration of the story of Judas concludes this discussion of the determination of the rejected, it is this small print section that forms the conclusion of his treatment of the doctrine of election.

Barth begins his reflections on the narratives concerning Judas with the observation that he appears as '(t)he character in which the problem of the rejected is concentrated and developed in the New Testament',[17] that despite his undoubted identity as 'a disciple and apostle', 'no more so, but also no less so, than Peter and John,' and despite the 'remarkable calm with which the New Testament speaks of Judas Iscariot',[18] he is also undoubtedly identified as '*the* great sinner of the New Testament'.[19] Barth considers the nature of the uncleanness of Judas to be evident in the incident of the anointing of Jesus in Bethany and 'in the contrast there drawn between Judas and Mary': for Judas 'it is too little a thing that the death of Jesus should be glorified' by Mary's offering; he 'is not opposed to the surrender of Mary's costly ointment', but 'he wants something for it—namely 300 denarii—not for himself...but to give to the poor'.[20] The Synoptic Gospels seem to understand the sin of Judas similarly: he hands Jesus over 'for a payment of

---

[16]'...similarly–since no one outside or alongside Him is elected as the bearer of divine rejection–no one outside or alongside Him is rejected' (*CD* II/2:421).
[17]*CD* II/2:458.
[18]*CD* II/2:459.
[19]*CD* II/2:461.
[20]*CD* II/2:462, referring to John 12:1-8.

money'; for Judas 'Jesus was for sale'; he could be surrend-
ered 'for something else which appeared better'.[21]

It is at this point that Barth considers the problematic
reference in Matthew to the narrative of Zechariah 11:4-17
(although Matthew attributes the reference to Jeremiah).
Within the Zechariah narrative (itself enigmatic) it is the
prophet, 'as the embodiment of Yahweh Himself,' who
receives thirty pieces of silver and throws them into the
treasury. In the narrative in Matthew, Judas appears to be
taking the place of the prophet but then, 'in fact, the whole
situation is reversed': rather than himself tending the sheep
prepared for slaughter he hands over 'the Good Shepherd
Himself for slaughter—a feature which is quite alien to the
original context'. In and through Judas, Israel rejects 'the
protection of the Good Shepherd' and all that is left to it is
'the modicum of religion with which it tried to buy off its
God,' a 'contribution towards repairing over and over again
the dilapidated temple,' an action comparable to that of
Esau, a selling of 'their birthright for a mess of pottage'.[22]

Before proceeding we might pause to consider the
implications of the manner in which Barth handles this reference. It is not at all unusual for New Testament commentators to show some degree of embarrassment concerning the
use of Old Testament passages by New Testament writers,
especially within Matthew. Barth, though admitting that the
application given 'is quite alien to the original context',
displays no such embarrassment. Even when referring to the
apparent confusion between Zechariah and Jeremiah in
Matthew's account Barth is content to observe that '(w)e
have here another example how even in its misunder-
standings and confusions the Bible is usually more instruct-
ive that other books in their accuracy'.[23] All texts are
inevitably creative rather than merely repetitive or imitative;
every decoding is a fresh encoding.[24] The original intentions
of an author are simply not available to a reader behind or

---

[21]CD II/2:463.

[22]CD II/2:463ff.

[23]CD II/2:468.

[24]This is especially pertinent if, as Mason comments, the text of
Zechariah itself represents a living tradition. R. Mason, *Cambridge Bible
Commentary: Haggai, Zechariah, Malachi* (Cambridge: CUP, 1977) 6ff.

beyond the text. But even though the author's intention, behind the text, is unavailable, this need not imply that a text can mean just anything. Once committed to writing, a text bears its own intentionality in relation to the other texts with which it is juxtaposed. The meaning of a text, in terms of its reference, is to be heard in relation to its co-text and, in particular, in relation to the focus of that co-text. In this respect Barth anticipates so-called 'canonical criticism' both by recognizing the givenness of the juxtaposition of the texts of Scripture and, more significantly, by affirming their christological focus.

Moreover, inasmuch as the context of the reader of the text is a living and changing context, the meaning of the text is continually being given to be heard afresh. If, on the one hand, Barth affirms the christological focus of Scripture he also, on the other hand, affirms its pneumatological dynamic: it is through the Spirit that this word is heard afresh as the Word of God.[25] As Mark Wallace has argued in response to Anthony Thiselton, this is not an emphasis which '...separates human understanding from divine revelation and thereby scuttles hermeneutics as a legitimate theological task';[26] it rather affirms that, if the theological task is to be 'legitimate,' it must be recognized as pneumatological.[27] To separate the pneumatological from the christological would certainly be illegitimate: the reference of the text is not arbitrary; for Barth, as for Calvin, the Spirit is the Spirit of the Word. For this reason it is more appropriate to speak of a Trinitarian hermeneutic than a christological or pneumatological hermeneutic: the Spirit causes the text to be heard afresh in terms of its christological reference.[28] Once

---

[25]Cf. CD IV/1:227: 'He speaks for Himself whenever He is spoken of and His story is told and heard.'

[26]Mark I. Wallace, 'The World of the Text: Theological Hermeneutics in the Thought of Karl Barth and Paul Ricoeur,' Union Seminary Quarterly Review 41 (1986) 1-15, at p.1, referring to A.C. Thiselton, The Two Horizons: New Testament Hermeneutics and Philosophical Description (Grand Rapids: Eerdmans, 1980) 87-92.

[27]It is this sense of the present dynamic of what Scripture does that seems to be missing from D Kelsey's study and, in particular, from his discussion of Scripture's inspiration.

this dynamic is recognized Matthew's use of the text of
Zechariah ceases to be a source of such embarrassment.

Barth next turns to consider the reference to the
repentance of Judas in Matthew 27:3. While '(t)here is no
reason not to take seriously this repentance' we must also
recognize its 'incompleteness' and therefore its 'unreality'.
The incompleteness of Judas' repentance corresponds to the
'incompleteness of his surrender': in 'contrast to Mary' he
continues to stand in dependence upon his own work and,
consequently, it is 'impossible for him to make restitution for
this deed': '(h)ow can there be grace for him when he will
not live wholly by grace, when he has completely rejected
grace?'. Barth suspects that it is for this reason that the
account of the end of Judas in Acts appears to know nothing
of his repentance or of his suicide. What both accounts
affirm, albeit in differing ways, is that both Judas and his
apostleship came to an end.[29]

But, without in any degree diminishing the gravity
of this 'end' it must simultaneously be affirmed that Judas is
identified as 'one of the twelve', what he does 'affects them
also'. All ask the question 'Lord, is it I?' when Jesus declares
that one of their number will betray him. Whereas John
identifies Judas as the one who objects to Mary's offering,
Mark simply states that the objection was raised by 'some of
those present' and Matthew identifies the objection as coming from 'the disciples':

> (t)he literary process which we see here may consist in the
> interaction of different traditions, but it may also consist in
> the fact that Matthew's statement is a conscious clar-
> ification of Mark's (or Mark's a conscious blurring of
> Matthew's?), while John's is a conscious concentration into
> one person.... Or could it be that John's statement is the
> original, and that it has been generalised by Matthew and
> Mark?[30]

[28]It is in this respect that the criticism of C.E. Gunton, *A Brief Theology
of Revelation* (Edinburgh: T. & T. Clark, 1995) 16ff. & 66ff on the
'immediacy' of revelation in Barth may be an overstatement.
[29]*CD* II/2:465ff.
[30]*CD* II/2:471f.

Whichever may be the case, and we have no assured means of resolving this, the effect of these literary variations is to clarify that all the disciples are implicated in this sin of Judas.

In his discussion of these literary variations Barth does not appear overly to be concerned with the precise correspondence (or in this case, non-correspondence) between the narratives and the events to which they refer. There is no attempt here to harmonize literary variations—a process that verges on the farcical in some inerrantist responses to such apparent differences—rather the variations themselves are exploited for their theological utility. For Barth, as Francis Watson observes, '...the assertion that the gospel texts refer us to historical–theological reality, and that these texts are the irreducible means of access to this reality, should not be understood as necessitating a precise, detailed correspondence between the narratives and the course of historical events'.[31] But this lack of concern for detailed correspondence ought not to be misconstrued: it is not that Barth is denying the referential function of the narratives or the historical actuality of the events to which they refer. It is rather that he is denying that we have any valid access to these events other than in the manner in which they are narrated. It is for this reason that Barth rejects the category of myth and, while retaining categories of saga and legend, insists that such literary forms, though not capable of historical verification, do not deprive biblical narrative of its character as history.[32] For Barth the historical actuality of the central events referred to in the biblical

---

[31]Watson, *Text*, 229

[32]'Whether it can be verified historically or is saga or legend does not affect its credibility in this respect. If we believe it, it is because we see that it has happened as the revelation and work of divine grace, and this is the gift of our enlightenment by the Holy Spirit. If this recognition and gift be presupposed only for a moment, the fact that a biblical history cannot be verified historically but has only the form of saga or legend cannot deprive it of this character or make it incredible as real history. Thus, although we must regard the relevant sphere as saga or legend, we must accept it as true and not false legend in the relevant sense, and therefore treat this history too as credible in its distinctive form' (*CD* III 3:374).

narrative is crucial: referring to the Cross and Resurrection he affirms that

> (e)verything depends upon the fact that this turning as it comes from God for us men is not simply imagined and presented as a true teaching of pious and thoughtful people, but that it happened in this way, in the space and time which are those of all men.[33]

For Francis Watson and others, it is at this point that Hans Frei and those who interpret Barth similarly have seriously misrepresented him by downplaying the referential function of the biblical narratives.[34] Only if the narrated story is true can it be proclaimed confidently in the world as the truth that defines and interprets all truth. Frei's view of the text as 'self-contained' privatizes revelation and thereby jeopardizes proclamation.[35]

The identification of Judas with the other apostles implicit in these literary comparisons is similarly demonstrated in John's account of the washing of the disciples' feet. It is not merely Judas whose feet need washing; it is not Judas but Peter who objects to the process, being 'inclined to

---

[33]CD IV/1:247f.

[34]Compare the following comment quoted by Vanhoozer: 'Frei simply abandons the whole issue of the text's inspiration and historicity instead of "retaining them as institutional premises (features, coordinates) of the discourse..."' Kevin J. Vanhoozer, *Biblical narrative in the philosophy of Paul Ricoeur: A Study in hermeneutics and theology* (Cambridge: CUP, 1990) 177, referring to Sternberg, *The Poetics of Biblical Narrative: Ideological Literature and the Drama of Reading,* (Bloomington: Indiana University Press, 1987) 81.

[35]'Frei's self-contained text is a privileged space in which one unsubstitutable individual (the reader) encounters another (Jesus). In its largely justified emphasis on the important tautology that narrative is narrative, this hermeneutic of self-containment proves unable to achieve an adequate correlation of the text with the church and the world. Indeed, the perceived need to protect the text from the world may stem from the failure adequately to address the church's proper concern with the fundamental truth of the biblical story of salvation: for if, and only if, this story is true, then all worldly reality must be understood in the light of it. The claim that the text is fundamentally true liberates it from self-containment and enables it to shed its light on worldly realities—now, and not just at the parousia.' Watson, *Text,* 29

be independent in face of Jesus' (and thereby anticipating his denial).[36] The inclusion of Judas in the Lord's Supper and in the washing of the disciples' feet raises the question 'whether and how far this took place effectively for Judas as well'. Barth suggests that, in the light of the Gospel accounts, 'it would be both hasty and illegitimate to give a final answer one way or the other'.[37] It is this unanswerable question that underlies the parallel Barth traces between Judas and Paul. Surely it is Paul, rather than Matthias, who replaces Judas *de facto*, Paul who describes himself as 'the εκτρωμα...as the least of the apostles...as the first of the sinners to save whom Jesus came into the world'.[38]

The remaining half of Barth's discussion of Judas focuses on the use within the New Testament of the term παραδοῦναι, 'handing-over'. Barth has already noted that Paul, who initially persecutes the Church by 'handing-over' men and women to the Jewish authorities, is turned by grace from being the 'ghost of Judas' to fulfil Israel's destiny as a 'light to the Gentiles', fulfilling 'the handing-over of Jesus to the Gentiles: not this time in unfaithfulness, but in faithfulness to Israel's calling and mission'.[39] The sin of Judas is similarly described as a 'handing-over' of Jesus. Barth considers it no 'mere semantic accident' that this word with a 'purely negative meaning when applied to the act of Judas' is also used 'positively to define and describe the apostolic ministry': the message of Jesus is that which is 'handed-over'.[40] This parallel alone causes Barth to ponder whether or not the act of Judas, for all its 'faithlessness' may foreshadow 'the act of the faithful apostolic tradition'.[41]

But, with far greater significance, the same word is used of a divine 'handing-over'. The 'handing-over' to Satan referred to by Paul in the context of some form of excommunication[42] can only be an 'earthly counterpart' to the 'handing-over' of men and women by God that is the

---

[36]*CD* II/2:472ff.
[37]*CD* II/2:475f.
[38]*CD* II/2:478f.
[39]*CD* II/2:478.
[40]*CD* II/2:482.
[41]*CD* II/2:483.
[42]1 Cor. 5:1ff.; 1 Tim. 1:19f.

recurring theme of Romans 1:24ff.; a 'wrathful delivery in which God abandons man and leaves him to himself'.[43] But, in turn, this 'wrathful' handing-over cannot be considered other than in the light of the handing-over of the Son by the Father and the corresponding handing-over of the Son of himself:[44]

> We cannot understand the positive divine παραδου'ναι, which is the basis of all others and in the light of which even that of Judas ultimately stands, unless we hold to the original and authentic παραδου'ναι. And to know this we cannot begin at a lower level than that of the decree of God's eternal love, in which the Father sent the Son and the Son obeyed the Father, by which the will of God turned towards man even before he was created–his creation itself being dependent upon this decree–with the inconceivably merciful intention of enabling him, and all creation through him and in him, to participate in fellowship with Him and eternal life, by giving Himself to be his Covenant-partner.[45]

The handing-over of Jesus, therefore, cannot be said to occur as an outcome of 'human tragedy' or 'by chance'; it is identified as the eternal will of God; it is God's will and not the outcome of impersonal fate.[46] It is the great divine 'Yes' that includes, encompasses and overwhelms every conceivable 'No'. In the light of the handing-over of Jesus the handing-over of men and women under divine wrath can 'only be like the sighing of creation'. It is for this reason, Barth supposes, that 'this handing-over of wrath is never mentioned without direct or indirect reference to the eschatological possibility of a saving aim and meaning'.[47] Similarly, the apostolic 'handing-over' of the message of Jesus must be identified as having its origin in this eternal

---

[43]*CD* II/2:488. Note the manner in which, in a later volume, Barth defines the divine wrath of judgment: 'If the fire of His wrath scorches us, it is because it is the fire of His wrathful love and not His wrathful hate.' *C.D.* III/2:609.

[44]*CD* II/2:488; *cf.* Rom. 4:25, 8:32; Gal. 2:20; Eph. 5:2 & 25.

[45]*CD* II/2:491.

[46]*CD* II/2:493.

[47]*CD* II/2:495.

decision and handing-over: the apostolic παραδοῦναι is an echo of this divine and eternal παραδοῦναι.[48]

But finally and most pertinently, the more profoundly one considers the 'will and deed' of Judas in handing-over Jesus the more exactly it appears to correspond to what God actually 'willed and did in this matter'. In this sense Judas, 'alone of all the apostles, was actively at work in this decisive situation, in the accomplishment of what was God's will and what became the content of the Gospel'. The action of Judas, for all its sinfulness, is nonetheless the action through which the divine handing-over is accomplished.[49] Judas, the 'sinner without equal,' fulfils the will of God 'not in spite of his unparalleled sin, but in it'.[50] And in this sense at least, in the very act of his sinful handing-over, Judas, as one of the twelve, fulfils an apostolic ministry in correspondence to the divine handing-over. And in this sense at least, even as one 'who is wholly rejected,' Judas is elect.

Barth's literary reading of the text, and in particular his juxtaposition of the Father's παραδοῦναι of the Son and the παραδου'ναι of Jesus by Judas, only reiterates the distinctive understanding of the relatedness of divine and human action that characterizes his account of election and providence and underlies the entirety of the *Church Dogmatics*. The foundation for this distinctive understanding is laid in Barth's exposition of God's eternity: the divine eternity is not God's otherness to time, nor merely his everlastingness as the possession of infinite time, it is rather his presence within time as the One he is, as the Lord of time, as 'the One who loves in freedom'.[51] Divine and human action, therefore, are never to be related dualistically: God's freedom in time constitutes rather than jeopardizes our human freedom and, since his freedom is as the One who loves, our actions can be pressed into the service of his

---

[48]*CD* II/2:498.
[49]*CD* II/2:501f.
[50]*CD* II/2:503.
[51]*CD* II/1:608ff. For a fuller account of the implications of the relatedness of the concepts of eternity and election in Barth's thinking see my discussion in John E. Colwell, *Actuality and Provisionality: Eternity and Election in the Theology of Karl Barth* (Edinburgh: Rutherford House, 1989).

actions without the forfeiture of their integrity as our actions.
The divine handing-over occurs through the human
handing-over rather than despite it, and it does so without
the freedom of either being abolished. Consequently, as
David Ford seems to acknowledge, Barth's literary analysis
of the relatedness of divine and human action within biblical
narratives underlies his exposition of the doctrine of
election.[52]

The question remains, however, as to whether Barth
is attempting too much, as to whether his literary analysis is
capable of bearing the weight of an underlying electedness
of Judas. David Ford expresses the question thus:

> In his eagerness to see all rejection enclosed in Jesus' death
> and overcome in his resurrection, Barth presses the typol-
> ogy of Judas with Paul so as to support the possibility of an
> ultimately favourable verdict on Judas. Yet the two grim
> New Testament versions of Judas' death clearly make no
> attempt to remove in this way the sting of finality from
> Judas' fate. Barth is intent on enveloping Judas in salvation
> whatever his crime...and in doing so not only tries to know
> more of God's purposes than can be elicited from the story
> but also does violence to its realism, which does not let any
> general understanding of salvation gloss over Judas' final
> responsibility for his action.[53]

No serious reading of this small print passage could conclude that it was ever Barth's intention to 'gloss over Judas'
final responsibility for his action' but, more profoundly,
David Ford seems to have missed the point.[54] The focus of
Barth's literary analysis in this section is not a juxtaposing of

---

[52]'It is clear, therefore, that the main hermeneutical support for his
doctrine of election that Barth offers is a literary analysis of certain
biblical stories in such a way as to find the will of God making sense of
the interweaving of good and evil by creating the master pattern, Jesus'
death and resurrection, in which the relation of evil to good is finally
defined' (Ford, 'Barth's Interpretation,' 67).
[53]Ford, 'Barth's Interpretation,' 85.
[54]'Neither in his discussion of Judas nor in his discussion of Israel as a
form of the one community of God...does Barth affirm any more nor
any less than he is compelled to affirm for every man in the light of
Jesus Christ' (Colwell, *Actuality and Provisionality*, 266).

Judas and Paul, it is rather a juxtaposing of both Judas and Paul with Christ:

> (b)etween them both, between Judas and Paul, stands Jesus Christ...and the rejection of Judas is the rejection which Jesus Christ has borne, just as the election of Paul is in the first place His election.[55]

For pneumatological as well as epistemological reasons, Barth's hermeneutical commitment is to respond to the text in its 'final form'. At one level his literary analysis derives from this hermeneutical commitment. But Barth's hermeneutical commitment is christological as well as pneumatological, and never the one without the other, and the form and manner of his literary analysis derives also from an acknowledgement of the christological focus of the text.[56]

On the one hand this christological hermeneutic can be seen simply as the outcome of a commitment to interpret the text of Scripture according to its own content. Far from seeking to establish some special hermeneutic applicable only to Scripture, Barth suggests that hermeneutics in general should be specific to particular texts: hermeneutics are prescribed by content.[57] But on the other hand Barth's christological hermeneutic is pneumatological inasmuch as it is informed by the church's hearing of Scripture. As Nigel Biggar observes, '(i)n the end, for Barth, the canon by which the Bible is interpreted is the christological "story" as narrat-

---

[55]CD II/2:480.

[56]'While the Bible says many things in different ways, its coherent center is the Word of God definitely identified as Jesus Christ' (Wallace, 'The World of the Text,' 10).

[57]'Our present concern is to establish that when we have to do with revelation as the content of the biblical word and with the hermeneutics prescribed by this content, we are not dealing with a mysterious thing apart which applies only to the Bible. Biblical hermeneutics must be guarded against the totalitarian claim of a general hermeneutics. It is a special hermeneutics only because hermeneutics generally has been mortally sick for so long that it has not let the special problem of biblical hermeneutics force its attention upon its own problem. For the sake of better general hermeneutics it must therefore dare to be this special hermeneutics.' (CD I/2:472).

ed by Nicaea and Chalcedon'.[58] It is the community of faith
that is given by the Spirit to hear, to recognize and to confess
the Christ who is the content and focus of the biblical text.
Since the story thus heard is true, albeit not verifiable by so-
called 'detached' historical method, it is recognized as the
story that defines and interprets all stories.[59] Christianity is
inevitably and unashamedly a meta-narrative, a universal
story, a story of stories. But it is such, not in an imposed or
imposable totalitarian sense; it is such as it is given to be
heard; it is such through a Spirit-dependent resonance and
persuasiveness.[60]

It is because this story of the Cross and Resurrection
of Christ is the story that defines and interprets all stories
that it also defines and interprets this story of Judas. The
παραδοῦναι of Jesus by Judas cannot be considered other than
in the context of the divine παραδοῦναι. The rejection of Judas
cannot be considered other than in the context of the
rejection borne by Christ. The *No* of Judas cannot be
considered other than in the context of the divine *No* that has
been overwhelmed by the divine *Yes*. On this basis we are
certainly not permitted to presume an ultimately favourable
verdict for Judas, or for any other man or woman. Mercy
that can be presumed upon is no longer mercy. The living
God is irreducibly the one who loves in *freedom*. But neither
are we permitted to presume the opposite. As a story
defined and interpreted by the gospel story the story of

---

[58]Nigel Biggar, *The Hastening that Waits: Karl Barth's Ethics* (Oxford:
Clarendon Press, 1993) 122.

[59]'...the story of Jesus must...be interpreted as the midpoint of time,
deriving from the universal horizon of the creation of the world and of
humankind in the likeness of God, and pointing towards the universal
horizon of an eschaton in which the human and non-human creation
together reach their appointed goal' (Watson, *Text*, 153).

[60]'There is, we claim, a universal story. It begins at the beginning (if not
before), goes on to the end and then does not stop. There is a Grand
Narrative. It is the creative, redemptive and eschatological narrative,
centred on the passion, death and resurrection, and developed
outwards in all possible directions. It is the workings of God in and
with the whole cosmos, and it can be spoken, at least a little, because it
has revealed its formal structure in the Word—the creative word and
the redemptive word, which (who) is Jesus Christ.' (Sara Maitland, *A
Big-Enough God: Artful Theology* (London: Mowbray, 1995) 115.)

Judas cannot issue in an abandoning of all hope. The living God is irreducibly the one who *loves* in freedom.

> The Church will not then preach an *apokatastasis*, nor will it preach a powerless grace of Jesus Christ or a wickedness of men which is too powerful for it. But without any weakening of the contrast, and also without any arbitrary dualism, it will preach the overwhelming power of grace and the weakness of human wickedness in the face of it. For this is how the "for" of Jesus and the "against" of Judas undoubtedly confront one another. We may not know whether it led to the conversion of Judas or not, but this is how it always is in the situation of proclamation.[61]

---

[61]*CD* II/2:477.

Chapter 9

(PROBABLY) THE GREATEST STORY EVER TOLD?

Reflections on Brueggemann's The Bible and Postmodern Imagination.

Trevor A. Hart

There are a number of reasons for choosing to interact in this essay with Walter Brueggemann's *The Bible and Postmodern Imagination*.[1] The first is apparent enough. Brueggemann's avowed purpose is 'the liberation of the biblical text for the church in a new situation, for interpretation, proclamation, teaching and practice.'[2] A consideration of what Brueggemann himself insists is a provisional set of proposals[3] thus fits neatly within the chosen focus for this volume of essays. Other reasons have to do with a significant overlap between the central themes of the book and some of the foci of my own recent research, especially with regard to issues of epistemology, approaches to the biblical text, and the deployment

---

[1]W. Brueggemann, *The Bible and Postmodern Imagination*: Texts Under Negotiation (London: SCM, 1993).
[2]Brueggemann, *The Bible and Postmodern Imagination*, vii.
[3]Brueggemann, *The Bible and Postmodern Imagination*, ix.

of the category of imagination in theology. Precisely because
I deem the book to be doing something vitally important, the
points at which I find myself either differing from some of its
assumptions and conclusions or desiring to press harder for
clarification are articulated here with some vigour. What
follows is thus a mixture of description of and critical reaction to Brueggemann's case. It should be read, however, as
issuing from within a broad appreciation of his project, and
in the relatively unambitious hope of pushing the discussion
which he has initiated further.

Of Stories, Taxi Cabs, and Tigers' Tails

'It is now clear to many of us, in the academy and in the
church, that we are in a quite new interpretive situation that
constitutes something of an emergency.'[4] Thus Brueggemann's essay opens, with an attempt to locate itself and its
purpose within the now familiar grand narrative of post-
modernity. To the extent to which he endorses this story
Brueggemann can hardly avoid participating in the self-
referentially corrosive risk which seems to be endemic to the
genre: a grand narrative to surpass all grand narratives,
which yet announces the deserving demise of all grand
narratives; a culturally particular perspective privileged so
as to convince everyone that no culturally particular
perspective may be; and so on. To be sure Brueggemann
himself insists that he is not seeking actually to advocate or
even endorse a post-modern position. Post-modernity is not
something to welcome, 'but simply something to acknowledge as the inescapable context in which we live and
interpret.'[5] Yet there is in truth little sense of reluctant
resignation or of making a virtue out of an unwelcome
necessity in this volume. The way in which Brueggemann
himself narrates the cultural evolution of the post-Enlight-
enment Western world leaves a clear impression that (so far
as his own particular set of concerns goes) the advent of
post-modernity has heralded more benefits and opportuities
than it has inflicted collateral damage. In part this is due to

---

[4]Brueggemann, *The Bible and Postmodern Imagination*, 1.
[5]Brueggemann, *The Bible and Postmodern Imagination*, ix.

his (typically post-modern) eclecticism, picking up whatever lies to hand and using it for particular ends, and conveniently overlooking the truth embodied in the (variously attributed) quip that an argument is not like a taxi cab; you can't just pay it off when you reach your chosen destination. There may well be some genuine benefits and opportunities for Christian theology in the post-modern world; but if we choose to lay hold of the tiger's tail we may eventually find that letting go safely is less easy than we thought.

Let us be reminded of the various landmarks around which the plot of the post-modern narrative is woven. Following Toulmin and others Brueggemann reminds us of the cauldron of chaos and uncertainty (intellectual and political) out of which the spirit of modernity was summoned in a bid to establish order, stability, and hence security. In a cosmos from the geographical centre of which humans had only recently been unceremoniously deposed they now laid decisive claim to the intellectual centre, and thereby to an understanding which granted them power; power over their world, but also (notoriously and perniciously) over one another. What began as a quest for the liberation of the individual from oppressive ideologies and political tyrannies rapidly succumbed to the temptation to fend off existential anxiety by imposing models of rationality and morality. This was done in the name of a disinterested objectivity which was, in reality, anything but. People were told (in no uncertain terms!) exactly what the truth which would set them free was, and, by inference, what things must now be deemed unreasonable, irrational, unacceptable. These same newly discovered canons of universal truth and light were in due course carried beyond the borders of their European home-land in the wake of (and as part of the intellectual underpinning for) the imperialistic establishment of colonies in the non-western world. The 'light' of En-lightenment was not to be selfishly hoarded, but shed abroad for the benefit of all peoples. Alternately, 'the new intellectual hegemony of male certitude...fostered a political-economic hegemony, whereby the "disinterested," "objective" ones at the centre could dominate the margin.'[6]

---

[6]Brueggemann, *The Bible and Postmodern Imagination*, 5.

Heirs to a Broken Promise

The eventual application of a hermeneutic of suspicion to Enlightenment claims to offer resources for freedom, progress and general human well-being in the world issued largely from a profound disillusionment with the actual outcomes after more than a century and a half in which its promises and its strategies had held sway. As a result, Brueggemann contends, we are today witnessing the final death throes of the white, male, Western perspective which has dominated human ways of thinking about and being in the world for too long. This perspective, which laid confident claim to an eternal, universal, certain, and liberating truth, in reality managed to sustain itself only by force, thereby becoming a perverse mirror image of that mediaeval synthesis of knowledge and power which it originally sought to supplant. It has now been revealed to have been little more than a culturally particular viewpoint, one imaginative construal of reality among many others, and one which unjustly privileged the interests of some groups at the very definite expense of others.

As heirs to a broken promise and an oppressive regime the advocates of post-modernity have sought to carry out a root and branch recanting of the dogmas of their modernist forebears. Brueggemann explicitly endorses and adopts Toulmin's catalogue of cultural shifts towards a privileging of the oral over the written, the particular over the universal, the local over the general, and the timely over the timeless.[7] When, therefore, he himself turns to offer an account of the sort of theological voice which may be heard in this new reformed environment it is in these very same terms: 'We voice a claim that rings true in our context, that applies authoritatively to our lived life. But it is a claim that is made in a pluralism where it has no formal privilege.'[8] Theology, together with every other branch of human knowing, must reckon with the impossibility of 'voicing large truth' in the post-modern world. There can only be small, local, contextually relative claims, made not in the old oppressive arrogant spirit of modernity, but in humility and

---

[7]Brueggemann, *The Bible and Postmodern Imagination*, 6.
[8]Brueggemann, *The Bible and Postmodern Imagination*, 9.

mutual respect. There can be no absolute claims because there is no transcendent arbiter. In the absence of such a shared principle of adjudication, claims to a truth which is perspective-transcendent could only be established by force, and hence through conflict. Unless we are to repeat the long and tortuous history of imperialistic subjugation of the other (which the modernist project simply perpetuated in a more subtle but ruthlessly efficient version) we must therefore embrace a tolerant pluralism as the environment for the church's attempts to interpret Scripture and to articulate a distinctively Christian construal of 'reality.' In such an environment there can be shared stories, an open exchange of outlooks, a respectful dialogue among equals in the market-place of perspectives and the universe of faiths. What there cannot be is an imperialistic attempt to seize the intellectual or moral high ground. Any claim we make must necessarily be prefaced by a tacit qualifier indicating its essentially local nature and limited ambitions. (Probably) the best lager in the world. (Probably) the greatest story ever told.

The Importance of Imagining Otherwise

Part of the interest and importance of Brueggemann's book lies in his attempt to rehabilitate imagination as a key epistemic category for the new perspectival approach to theological knowing and interpretation which he considers now to be an inevitable and necessary development.

He begins with a familiar point about language and its relation to reality. Language, he insists, is not secondary to reality, a mere tool for describing something already given to experience. Rather language is involved in constructing the reality and shaping the experience which it also describes. This, however, is also an activity in which we must identify the activity of imagination. Once we realise this we must proceed to deconstruct the regnant imaginative construction (which until now has successfully presented itself variously as 'hard fact' or 'common sense' or some such invulnerable quantity), thereby deposing the established power interests which it masks. One of the defining characteristics of imagination is its capacity to challenge and subvert the apparently given. It is 'the capacity to picture, portray, receive, and practice the world in ways other than it appears to be at first glance when seen through a dominant, habitual, unexamined lens.'[9] Imagination ever goes beyond the given, subverts the given, constructs a possible counter-given. This, Brueggemann suggests, is the chief task to which Christians (presumably alongside others in other traditions in a post-modern context) are now called. Our task is to 'imagine otherwise,' to liberate ourselves from the illusion of certainty generated by the modernist project and to explore other possible ways of seeing things.

This transformative 'counter-imagination of the world'[10] will not be arbitrary, but will be funded, nourished, authorised by resources drawn from the textual reservoir of Scripture. Here we find stories, images, symbols which demand to be voiced and made sense of, which point us towards a 'proposed world' which directly challenges the 'presumed world,' and which encourage us to become citizens of the one rather than the other. Yet the notion of 'a proposed world' must be handled carefully if we are to harness the force of a genuinely post-modern (rather than modern) imagination. We cannot proceed apace to imagine a new big picture of things with which to replace the old. This would simply be to repeat modernity's errors, as it in its turn repeated the errors of pre-modernity. The vicious circle must be broken. Our task is precisely to break out of the old imperialistic pattern. Modernity is in terminal decline precisely because it has suffered from a failure of imagination—both in the sense that its particular imaginative construal of reality has failed to deliver on its promises, and in as much as it has failed to recognise itself *as* an imaginative construct (with all the corrigibility, provisionality and humility which this entails) rather than a positivistic given. Again, therefore, post-modern imagination (which Brueggemann favours) must limit itself to the fashioning of smaller, more local and less ambitious versions of 'reality.'

---

[9]Brueggemann, *The Bible and Postmodern Imagination*, 13.
[10]Brueggemann, *The Bible and Postmodern Imagination*, 20

An Imaginative Collage of Biblical Bits and Pieces

This leads us directly to the shape of Brueggemann's proposals for the uses of Scripture within the community of faith. The task which must be ongoing in the church, he tells us, is the fashioning of an 'evangelical infrastructure;' namely, a 'system or network of signs and gestures that make social relationships possible, significant, and effective' which is rooted identifiably in the evangel, and which functions to 'heal, redeem and transform.'[11] This infrastructure will furnish an alternative to the hitherto dominant infrastructure of consumerism. As a properly post-modern enterprise, such an infrastructure will not be allowed to become a new, territorially ambitious grand-narrative. Instead it will be an essentially local construction, imagined by a particular worshipping community in the midst of all its particular questions, expectations and assumptions. Furthermore it will not be a totalitarian whole imposed on the congregation from above (*i.e.*, by the minister!). It will be under continuous construction, a process arising out of the juxtaposition and imaginative mixing together of a particular congregation and particular biblical texts.

The task of the minister, therefore, is not and cannot be to bring a ready-made system or 'world' before the congregation for validation and acceptance. This is oppressive not only with regard to the congregation (who must be furnished with resources and then allowed to engage in their own imaginatively constructive project) but equally with regard to the text. Here again the post-modern privileging of the particular, the local, the other must be heeded to the full. What this means in practice is focusing always on particular texts, and allowing them to speak with the full force of their particularity even when that may come to us as something strange and even scandalous. We must not violate the text by subjugating it to some overarching doctrinal or moral schema or principle (whether those of systematic theology or historical-critical methodologies). We must let it speak with its own distinctive and possibly odd voice, for it precisely in this oddness that its potential to transform our patterns of

---

[11]Brueggemann, *The Bible and Postmodern Imagination*, 27.

thought and practice lies. In the context of worship, one expected outcome of which is the transformation of worshippers' lives through the seizing of their imaginations and the inculcation of alternative visions of the real and the possible, what the minister is called to do is to 'speak the text in its full power.'[12] This will be achieved by being faithful to the text's essential otherness, rather than allowing it to be subsumed within or domesticated by the taken-for-granted world which the congregation brings with it into the sanctuary. In this way, focusing on one text at a time, treating the Bible as an 'army of metaphors,'[13] the congregation's imaginations will be stimulated and funded with bits of biblical material out of which they must fashion a new construal of the way the world is and may yet be. This moment of 'liminality'[14] furnishes the opportunity and context for a genuinely transformative encounter with the Spirit.[15] The shape of the resultant collage will not be random precisely because it is rooted in the Bible which itself hints at a certain coherent pattern; but the collage itself must constantly be remade, worked out afresh by each local congregation rather than heteronomously given.

Brueggemann offers some metaphors for the use of the biblical text in the life of the church. It functions as a compost pile; not itself the place of growth, nor the manual which tells the gardener about his plants and how best to handle them; but that biodegradable matter which stimulates growth when mixed together with the soil and seeds of our present life. Second, biblical texts are fed (together with all manner of other material) into a subliminal zone of imagination which is both shaped by social context and yet also irreducibly personal. The particular semantic outcomes, therefore, do not fall within the domain of responsibility of the one who voices the text. His or her task is simply to ensure that it is voiced in the most lively and forceful manner possible. Third, the Bible is to reality what a script is to a drama. This model seeks a third way between the

---

[12]Brueggemann, *The Bible and Postmodern Imagination*, 24.

[13]Brueggemann, *The Bible and Postmodern Imagination*, 90.

[14]Brueggemann borrows this notion from Victor Turner's *The Ritual Process: Structure and Anti-Structure* (Chicago: Aldine, 1969) 94-130.

[15]Brueggemann, *The Bible and Postmodern Imagination*, 91.

rigidity of objectivism (and its hermeneutical counterpart in biblicist 'propositionalism') and the chaotic flux of relativism since 'a good company can render that script in a variety of different ways, so that the same script in fact can yield many different plays, depending on the freedom and imagination of the players.'[16]

In what remains of this essay I want to offer some critical responses to different parts of Brueggemann's case in the hope of clarifying and thereby furthering the essential project in which he is engaged.

Paddling on the Wrong Side of the Rubicon?

The precise status of post-modernity in relation to the modern remains ambiguous. There are those who would deny it any distinct existence, preferring to view it as an anhypostatic aspect of modernity itself. Brueggemann shows his awareness of this discussion. He also protests his desire to sit lightly with respect to the categories themselves. Yet his book embraces some at least of the key axioms of post-modernity and welcomes them as an advance over what preceded it. One of the problems in the case which he develops is the way in which, at certain significant junctures at least, he appears still to be resorting to strategies or standpoints of the sort which he allegedly wishes to leave behind and thinks he has left behind. One might suppose this itself to be a thoroughly post-modern thing to do, borrowing freely from incommensurable traditions and fashioning a random intellectual pastiche. Why feel bound by coherence and consistency in the new, liberated post-modern environment? But in fact this is not the feel that Brueggemann's text evokes at all. He is trying to argue a case concerning appropriate strategies for interpreting Scripture in the church, and draws on what he deems to be the genuine and irrevocable advances of post-modern under-standing in order to do so. The inconsistencies, where they appear, seem more likely to be the result of not really having crossed the Rubicon at all: paddling instead in the shallows

---

[16]Brueggemann, *The Bible and Postmodern Imagination*, 65.

on the near side, admiring the views across the water, yet from a viewpoint afforded by more familiar ground.

One indication that Brueggemann has not himself entirely broken with the spirit of modernity is apparent in the very way in which he narrates his tale. There is, we might say, a persistently problematic use of the first person plural. '*We* are now in a new interpretive environment.' 'It is now clear to many of *us* that' this is the case. As a result '*our* modes of theological interpretation from the recent past are less and less pertinent.' And so on. Nicholas Lash offers some prudent advice about such generous inclusivity. '(W)henever the word "we" is thus being waved around, three questions are in order: whom do those waving it have in mind? Whom do they suppose themselves to have in mind? Whom should they have in mind?'[17] The particular point here, of course, is that such tacit baptising of the wider human community into the local crisis of one segment of Western late capitalist culture is open to all those charges of imperialism, globalization, failure to acknowledge and privilege the legitimate otherness of the other etc. which post-modern analyses love to identify as specks in the eyes of others. No doubt Brueggemann would acknowledge, if challenged, that the problems which he lists as characteristic of the new situation for the church's interpretation of Scripture are in fact not problems at all for many Christians, not least in those parts of the world where the church seems to be growing most rapidly. Indeed he effectively says as much when he insists that the story which he tells is purely descriptive of 'the great social reality of our time and place'.[18] Yet he makes no more of the matter than this; in other respects his account is fairly typical of Western analyses in its failure actually to explore the social realities of other times and (more significantly) places, and in its apparent assumption that the perspective of the modern-going-on-post-modern West is where the really serious action is to be identified. That may be so; but the post-modern paradigm itself allows us no serious reason for

---

[17] N. Lash, *The Beginning and the End of 'Religion'* (Cambridge: CUP, 1996) 213.

[18] Brueggemann, *The Bible and Postmodern Imagination*, 18.

supposing so, and every reason for supposing otherwise. Is this, we might ask, not simply another instance of the West's insistence on exporting its particular problems and crises to locations where they do not properly belong?

A second area of seeming ambiguity and inconsistency is Brueggemann's attitude to metanarratives and 'grand stories.' Again, while he claims not to be con-cerned to advocate Lyotard's characterisation of post-modernity as rooted in incredulity towards metanarratives, Bruegge-mann's own theological proposals are couched in terms which explicitly favour the local over the universal, the small, unassuming and inherently negotiable over the large and ambitious. Furthermore, it is clear that he values the supposed shift which has occurred in this regard, and in particular its deconstruction of the previously dominant paradigm, reducing it from the status of 'just the way things are' to 'one (not especially congenial) way of looking at the world.' But this is precisely where the problem arises. For it becomes clear as the book progresses that a significant part of its agenda has to do not with making necessary adjust-ments to the new post-modern condition at all (although doubtless the book does have to do with this). Rather, it shares an agenda with some of Brueggemann's earlier work,[19] an agenda which making certain carefully chosen post-modern moves serves very nicely, but which is in itself anything but post-modern in spirit. Take, for example, the following statement: 'If (the) evangelical infrastructure is not carefully constructed, the Christian congregation will rely on the dominant infrastructure of consumerism, and will not even discern until very late (too late) that the infrastructure of consumerism contains little good news.'[20] The selection of an alternative terminology here ought not to disguise what is being said. For all the prior indications that big is bad, and that a post-modern approach must finally be rooted in an ideologically pluralistic spirit of openness to other perspect-ives, what we have in the second chapter of this book in particular is a very clear appeal to one specific 'grand story'

---

[19]See e.g. W Brueggemann, *The Prophetic Imagination* (Minneapolis: Fortress Press, 1978).
[20]Brueggemann, *The Bible and Postmodern Imagination*, 27.

(that furnished by one dominant strand of biblical imagination) and an attempt to privilege it lock, stock, and barrel
over the decaying consumerist perspective of modernity.

Brueggemann urges, as we have already seen, that
the 'evangelical infrastructure' does not come ready made,
and is not imposed heteronomously on the church. It is fed
into the congregational imagination in the form of biblical
bits and pieces to do its fertilising work. This leaves it unclear whether it is 'big stories' as such (*i.e.*, stories which in
some sense claim a capacity to make overarching sense of
human life in its various aspects) which are the problem, or
simply 'big stories' which are imposed on others in a hetero-
nomous manner (*e.g.*, upon a particular congregation by a
minister representing 'The Church'), or perhaps stories
which are themselves 'big' in the sense of being inherently
imperialistic or possessed of a universalistic momentum. If
the former, then it is not at all clear that the fashioning of a
local 'big story' is a desirable project. If the second, then it
must be said that the degree to which what is fed in 'hints at'
an overall coherent pattern and thereby shapes the resultant
democratically imagined product is likely to be quite
considerable. If we reckon seriously with the socially located
nature of imagination, then it may turn out to be the case
that those who 'fund' that imagination are still exercising a
considerable degree of influence over the imagined result.
Heteronomy need not be brazen. But, to return to where we
began, it seems in fact that Brueggemann's interest is quite
specifically in securing the advancement of an 'evangelical'
over a 'consumerist' perspective on human existence. This
may be an aspiration with which many will sympathise; but
it is hardly in itself an embodiment of the post-modern
spirit. His motive is altogether too evangelistic for that.
There is little hint anywhere in his book of the post-modern
declaration of war on 'totality,' or the construal of truth and
morality as little more than local conventions, pragmatically
necessary for social stability, but ultimately inventions for
which we must take responsibility and which we are at
liberty to modify by mutual agreement.

The logic of post-modernity, when pushed through
with rigour, goes way beyond the measured dismantling of
the naive illusions of modernity. It leads, ultimately, to a

deliberate nihilism, to 'the corrosive rhetoric of an apocalyptic pessimism which not only encourages feelings of
paralysis but points, in the longer term, to the possible
demise of humanity itself'.[21] Brueggemann clearly wants
what Richard Kearney refers to as an 'ethical imagination' in
which the endless flux and vicious circles of post-modern
uncertainty, the 'euphoric frissons of apocalyptic mirror-
play'[22] are finally checked by the demands which the face to
face relation with the other makes on the self. Although
Brueggemann cites Kearney's book (briefly) his upbeat
account of the potential benefits of post-modernity betray
little awareness of its (post-modernity's) ethically corrosive
turn in the eventual deconstruction not only of the de-
centred self, but of the other for the well-being of whom we
are responsible. One aspect of Kearney's analysis which
ought to have seized Brueggemann's attention further is the
conspiratorial linkage which he perceives between the post-
modern exaltation of the pseudo-image over reality and that
very consumerist hegemony which Brueggemann himself
wishes to see overthrown. At these and other points his
account seems unaware of the inherently problematic nature
of any simple reference to 'post-modern imagination.' If the
description is not oxymoronic it is certainly needful of a
more subtle analysis and some very careful qualification.

'Woe to Me if I Voice Large Truth'?

These are not, of course, the words which Paul himself used,
(1 Cor. 9:16), a fact which serves very nicely to provoke the
next point. Brueggemann's case concerning the evils of
epistemological objectivism is mostly well made and well
taken. The recognition that all products of human knowing
are essentially perspectival, that all are fundamentally
shaped by a 'human coefficient,' is vital, and can only transform our attitudes and our strategies with respect to knowing and interpreting, to receiving the perspectives of others,
and to articulating our own perspectives in relation to them.
Gone are the days when claims to truth could be made via

---

[21]R. Kearney, *The Wake of Imagination* (London: Routledge, 1988) 361.
[22]R. Kearney, *The Wake of Imagination*, 364.

an arrogant, impatient, careless and, in the strict sense, irresponsible (*i.e.*, admitting no personal responsibility) appeal
to brute facts, universal truths of reason, and the like. This
certainly drives us to a more cautious, humble, and provisional account of our own standpoint. In Polanyi's analysis
(to which Brueggemann refers us) this means that every
factual claim bears before it a tacit fiduciary qualifier. 'X is
the case' always means 'I believe X is the case' or 'X appears
to be the case from where I am standing.' What Brueggemann apparently misses in Polanyi, however, is his capacity
to combine such frank admission of the perspectival nature
of all knowing with an equal insistence on the legitimacy of
charging our truth claims with 'universal intent.' Polanyi, in
other words, has no qualms about 'voicing large truth,' the
very thing which Brueggemann claims we are no longer
(epistemologically or ethically) in any position to do.

Brueggemann insists that no perspective may any
longer be granted 'formal privilege.'[23] If this means merely
that no perspective may be treated as an epistemic absolute,
and institutionalised in forms which attempt to impose it on
others in the name of some alleged absolute objectivity, and
'to silence by force all alternative or dissenting opinion'[24]
then clearly this is true. When Brueggemann proceeds to
claim 'Localism means that it is impossible to voice large
truth,'[25] however, we must be clear what is and is not
implied. 'All one can do is to voice local truth and propose
that it pertains elsewhere.'[26] But is this not, in effect,
proposing 'large truth,' i.e., truth which is not supposed to
be true only for a particular context, but also beyond that
context ('elsewhere') even when it is not recognised? If so it
seems that Brueggemann is nonetheless unsure on what
grounds, if any, such a proposal might actually be made. A
perspectival approach to intellectual dialogue, he suggests,
'holds before the conversation a certain posture on reality.
This posture does not claim to be objectively true, but it
claims to be a position where one will stand at cost and at

---

[23]Brueggemann, *The Bible and Postmodern Imagination*, 9.
[24]Brueggemann, *The Bible and Postmodern Imagination*, 9.
[25]Brueggemann, *The Bible and Postmodern Imagination*, 9.
[26]Brueggemann, *The Bible and Postmodern Imagination*, 9.

risk, so that in the end, the test of its validity is no longer logic or fact, but the expenditure of one's own life, which is the only thing that finally has worth.'[27] Without wishing to detract in the slightest from the force of what he says here about the persuasive force of self-commitment unto death we can, and I think must, query the basis on which he effectively reduces the criteria for comparison of perspectives to this. The willingness of adherents to stake their lives on their cause cannot be the sole (nor even the primary) index of its warrant.

'The truth,' Brueggemann tells us, 'is that ... we are in a situation in which all the rival claims are present to us at the same time, without any transcendent arbiter. Even if we wish it were different, it is not'.[28] But, calling the bluff of Brueggemann's position, we can proffer an alternative (rival) perspective on this situation. The truth that all knowing is perspectival, that no position can claim to be 'objectively true' in the sense of being able to identify the statements which it makes about reality with the actual shape of reality itself, quite apart from its appeal to a ridiculous model of the ideal of human knowing (what on earth would it mean for statements to be 'objectively true' in this sense?) may be conceded. It does not, however, lead ineluctably to the further concession that there is no 'transcendent arbiter' by which rival claims may be adjudicated. Nor does it render necessary the sort of resigned pluralism which is nervous about advocating its own claims to truth over against rival claims, lest it be deemed imperialistic and oppressive.

If we return to Polanyi we find an account of a proper realist *objectivity* which nonetheless eschews the naive *objectivism* described above. Polanyi's point is that there *is* a 'transcendent arbiter;' namely, the shape of reality itself as we encounter and are laid hold of by it. He abandons the characteristic post-Cartesian account of human knowing in which perspective serves to distance us from the real (so that in the final analysis we 'know' and have to do with perspectives alone), and insists instead that the linguistic, conceptual and other tools with which our per-

---

[27]Brueggemann, *The Bible and Postmodern Imagination*, 10.
[28]Brueggemann, *The Bible and Postmodern Imagination*, 10.

spectives furnish us are precisely our means of extending ourselves into the world and coming to know it. Of course this means that in a situation where various competing perspectives are available, some will serve as better and more reliable standpoints, sets of tools, etc. with which to know the real. Our moral obligation as knowers in such circumstances is not to endorse all perspectives equally, or to refuse to make serious comparative judgements between them, but precisely to seek the perspective which affords the most satisfactory means of engaging with reality, which furnishes (we must finally say) the most true account of things, or the account which seems to make most sense of our experience of the real. Thus our engagement (through the mediation of our perspectives) with reality itself serves to enable us to make relative and comparative judgements about competing ways of seeing things. We indwell, using Polanyi's metaphor, a particular perspective in the final analysis precisely because it seems to open up more fruitful and satisfying inroads to the real, than other possible standpoints.

Much more could be said about Polanyi's epistemology and its relevance for Brueggemann's case.[29] For our purposes, the essential point is that it is not only possible but a moral imperative to 'voice large truth,' at least in the sense of advocating one's own perspective in the market place of available products, precisely because one believes it to furnish a better grasp on the shape of the real and therefore wishes to make it available to other seekers after the truth. We have an obligation to speak; an obligation laid upon us by reality itself, and by our fellow humans. It is in this relationship of intellectual commitment to a truth which seizes us from beyond ourselves, this declaration of 'universal intent' (the claim that what we know in this way is not merely 'the truth for us' but makes contact with a properly objective reality), that we transcend our subjectivity.

For someone committed, as Brueggemann appears to be, to a position which is ontologically realist (which assumes that 'the universe and most of what goes on in it are

---

[29]For a fuller account see Trevor Hart, *Faith Thinking: The Dynamics of Christian Theology* (London: SPCK, 1995) Chapter 3.

completely independent of our thoughts'[30]) a nervous, in-offensive relativism which tacitly prefaces its claims with '(probably)' is not the only alternative to objectivism. Polanyi's 'I believe' (which is precisely *not* a statement of nervous reserve but of confident trust) offers a healthier qualifier which both takes account of perspectival factors yet grants us a genuine capacity to transcend our subjectivity.

The relevance of this discussion for Christian theology would seem to be obvious. The calling to the church is precisely to 'voice large truth;' large both in the sense of a truth which encompasses every aspect of human life and in the sense of being firmly possessed of universal intent. The Lord whom Christians serve is no tribal deity. He is Lord of every aspect of life, and of every life (whether he is recognised as such or not). In proclaiming the gospel, the good news concerning this Lord and his world, therefore, the church cannot pull its punches on truth. It must not succumb to talk of 'Christian values,' thereby tacitly conceding a merely local status for what it has to say, but must speak simply and openly about what it believes to be true in God's world. It will not suppose in doing so that this truth is 'objectively' true in the epistemic sense; *i.e.,* obvious to anyone who deigns to consider the matter. But, so far as I am aware, relatively few, if any, Christians have ever thought that about the gospel. Christians have always supposed that faith was a vital factor in knowing this particular truth. To some extent what the breakdown of confidence in the project of modernity has done is simply to show us the extent to which the same is true in other epistemic contexts also.

The danger in the suggestion that there is no transcendent arbiter (rather than that there is no human perspective which may serve as such) is that an epistemology rooted in such a claim will not suffice to undergird the church's mission of bearing its gospel into all the world, but threatens instead ultimately to subvert it. In particular, it overlooks the essential nature of Christian faith as a response to a self-revealing initiative on the part of a personal God, a revelation which while it may not be of a positivistic sort nonetheless lays hold of human persons in such a way as to trans-

---

[30]T. Nagel, *The View From Nowhere* (Oxford: OUP, 1986) 92.

form them, and places them under a moral obligation to speak of it. Neither our theologies nor the forms of our Christian life are to be confused with this self-revealing reality itself: they are human responses to and interpretations of it. As such they remain partial and provisional; yet in our personal engagement and encounter with God we are able to weigh their relative value as appropriate forms through which to bring to expression the inexpressible. Those symbols, images, words and practices which seem to us best to do this are the ones we shall share with others in the missionary task, not so that they might embrace the symbols themselves, but precisely so that through their mediation they might come to see and to experience for themselves the reality mediated.

The Accountability of Imagination

Brueggemann's endorsement of the category of imagination is to be welcomed. Theologians, especially in the Western tradition, have too often simply tracked a wider cultural suspicion and suppression of the category. Analyses such as that of Mary Warnock have revealed how nonsensical such an attitude is, given the inseparability of imaginative activity from every aspect of human knowing.[31]

Imagination is, as Brueggemann reminds us, potentially a subversive capacity. It is powerful in rendering 'alternities' possessed of transformative energy, refusing to leave us content in the face of the given, constantly reminding us how things might be better than they currently are or seem to be. One of the most sustained appeals to the imagination is to be found in Ernst Bloch's *The Principle of Hope* where he traces the power of daydreams to lay hold of a 'real possible' and to project hopes which drag us forward in their wake, energising us to create the conditions for their eventual realisation.[32] In similar vein Steiner reflects on the power of language to fashion counter-factual visions, to contradict the given descriptions of reality in such a way as

---

[31]Mary Warnock, *Imagination* (London: Faber, 1976).
[32]Ernst Bloch, *The Principle of Hope* (Oxford: Blackwells, 1986).

to facilitate a different way of taking that reality.[33] All this is grist to Brueggemann's mill, although he draws on more proximate sources such as Green[34] and Bryant.[35]

Imagination, though, we must remind ourselves, is also the source of fantasy and untruth. We cannot, therefore, simply hand over our custody of reality to a faculty which is free to construct without constraint. This is certainly not what Brueggemann intends. His appeal is precisely to a version of imagination which recognises both a certain givenness in the 'other' of reality and a constructive, interpretative, imaginative grasping of the other, a locating of it within a wider network or pattern of relationships through which we make sense of it. Hence he appeals to Green's appeal to Warnock's appeal to Wittgenstein and his notion of 'seeing an aspect of' a thing, or seeing something 'as' a particular sort of thing. It is our capacity to go beyond the (alleged) bare sensory input in perception (for example) and, in the very moment of knowing, to interpret or make sense of it; to locate it in or recognise it as part of a wider scheme which is not itself present or given in the thing itself. That objects can be located within more than one such pattern is, of course, the very point that perspectivism (as Brueggemann dubs it) wishes to draw to attention. Thus Brueggemann furnishes us with a series of different ways of taking the Gulf War of 1991: *as* the defence of cheap oil, *as* a maintenance of order by the international community, *as* the defence of the state of Israel, and so on. 'Formally,' he writes, 'any one of these "ases" has as much credence as any other. None has privilege, and there is no ultimately right definition.'[36] Again, I would want to accept part of this statement, but to submit other parts to some further examination.

We might begin by noticing an important distinction to which Green draws our attention very helpfully.[37] There are some examples of alternative 'construals as,' he reminds us, where the same object actually belongs quite legitimately

---

[33]G. Steiner, *After Babel* (2nd ed.; Oxford: OUP, 1992).
[34]Garrett Green, *Imagining God* (San Francisco: Harper and Row, 1989).
[35]David J. Bryant, *Faith and the Play of Imagination: On the Role of Imagination in Religion* (Macon: Mercer University Press, 1989).
[36]Brueggemann, *The Bible and Postmodern Imagination*, 15.
[37]See Green, *Imagining God*, 58.

within more than one pattern, where it is a shared compon-
ent of two or perhaps more patterns. This is the case, for
example, with the famous duck-rabbit used by Wittgenstein
in the *Philosophical Investigations*, which can be seen equally
legitimately as a duck or rabbit. The alternative ways of seeing the object may be incommensurable, but they are not in
this case incompatible. It is perfectly proper and necessary to
insist in this instance that 'there is no ultimately right
definition.' There is more than one appropriate answer to the
question 'what is this?' There are, however, other instances
of our attempts to recognise pattern, to make sense of a thing
by imaginatively 'going beyond' and tracing its wider
significances within a broad network of connections, where
alternative construals are in reality competitors with one
another, and where one such construal makes better sense of
the thing than others. Our 'seeing as' can be mistaken. We
think we are perceiving one thing only to discover
subsequently that it does not fit the space we had slotted it
into in our imaginative framework. To use Green's example,
the face which we glimpse across a crowded room is not,
after all, that of our friend, and we are embarrassed by
having called out a greeting in our misrecognition. Or, again,
I may construe my wife's actions as expressing one set of
intentions when 'in fact' they express something quite
different (her quiet and withdrawn mood proves not to have
to do with anything I have said or done, but to be
symptomatic of preoccupation with some difficult problem
at work for example). In cases such as these it makes little
sense to suggest that 'there is no ultimately right definition,'
although it may remain strictly true that absolute certainty
eludes us even when reasonable doubt has been allayed.

In situations where we face competing construals, I
suggest it is incumbent upon us to seek out the most satisfying of the available options. For reasons already articulated I
believe it to be possible to do so. Not all alternatives are
equally uncertain or equally unsatisfying. We must acknowledge the vital function of imagination in granting an
intuitive grasp of patterns and networks which lie beyond
the imagining agent, which inhere in some sense in the deep
structures of reality itself. That we cannot ever pin these
down precisely or absolutely, that even our best attempts to

image them will be subject to distortion and inadequacy, all this can be admitted. But we should not suppose all imaginative attempts to lay hold of the real to be equally inadequate, or underestimate the capacity of the real to seize our imagination. The particular example which Brueggemann offers is confusing rather than clarificatory in this respect, since it combines the possibility of competing and non-competing construals of the event in question. While it would be possible for the differing views of the Gulf War which he lists to be competitive, it would be equally possible for all of them to be true as pertaining to different organisational levels of one overall pattern (what Green calls 'vertical' as opposed to 'horizontal' compatibility)[38].

Back to the Bible

I want, finally, to make a handful of brief and relatively undeveloped responses to Brueggemann's specific proposals for the use of the biblical text in the church. I do so not as a biblical scholar concerned to protect certain vested methodological interests, but as a theologian interested in the text as a primary source and norm for theological reflection.

Brueggemann's proposed model of the Bible taken as the script for a drama seems to me to have some potential for further development. It corresponds interestingly to Dorothy Sayers' exploration of God's creativity in terms of the human analogy of playwright and drama, although she does not specifically address the role of the Bible as such.[39] For her the relevant 'text' or script is the structure of created reality itself which may be interpreted in different ways by different actors, some performances being more in accordance with the script than others. For Sayers, then, the point which this metaphor is intended to illuminate is the relationship between a certain fixity or givenness in reality (the objective form of a carefully composed text) and the variable ways in which that might be taken or interpreted by creatures who find themselves on the 'stage' (the performers).

---

[38]Green, *Imagining God*, 59.
[39]Dorothy L. Sayers, *The Mind of the Maker* (London: Methuen, 1941).

Brueggemann's proposal that *as Bible : reality so script : drama* moves in a different direction, and begs further clarification.

His precise proposal is 'that we "take" reality as a drama, and that we see the text as a script for that drama'.[40] A script, or *the* script? This is one issue which arises immediately. Most dramas, while they may be rendered in many different ways, nonetheless have only one script, and that script functions to prescribe certain limits to the reality of the drama itself. Yet Brueggemann has stressed time and again through his book the point that 'reality' itself cannot be known in any absolute manner, and that the function of the Bible is to furnish one possible construal of reality among others. The model script: drama, therefore, does not work at this point. It may be, though, that he intends something rather different; that 'reality' in the sense of what lies beyond our construals is bracketed out of the picture, and that the drama/reality to which he refers us is the phenomenologist's 'perceived reality' beyond which we may not probe. Then the model works much better. Then the script (biblical text) serves to shape the drama (reality as experienced 'Christianly') which we as Christians perform in our lives. This is fine, but if it is an accurate rendering of Brueggemann's intention then the status of 'reality' needs to be clearer in his account. And, given the discussion of his book up to this point, the question of that other 'reality,' the one which lurks in the wings so to speak, and the question of the relationship between the script and it, will not go away for long. Unless the drama which we play out in our lives as Christians is one which fits appropriately within the theatre of creation, and unless the script serves to enable this, then we are merely playing out a pretence and, to borrow from Paul (this time more accurately) are 'most to be pitied of all people' (1 Cor. 15:19). Perhaps an extension of the model, *e.g.*, drawing on Shakespeare's historical plays, would serve to clarify the point. For here we have three terms in the relationship: a reality (what actually happened); the script (already one configuration of what actually happened among numerous possible configurations); the performance /drama in which players seek to bring to life what actually

---

[40]Brueggemann, *The Bible and Postmodern Imagination*, 65.

happened through a rendering of the given script. No model is ever perfect, but some issues surrounding Brueggemann's proposal which would benefit from further clarification.

My remaining points can be made briefly. First, the suggestion that privileging particular 'little' texts is necessarily the same as allowing them to speak with their own voice and is a route to liberation and freedom from hermeneutical tyranny seems to have decided limits. If historical-critical method has taught us anything it is surely that the form of the biblical texts which have been transmitted to us are the result of many centuries of development, interpretation and reinterpretation within the life of Israel. Where it is possible to isolate a 'little text' from its wider textual context and allow it to speak with its 'own' (possibly scandalous and offensive) force or voice, literary theory forces the question whether such a privileging of this (or indeed any other) particular form of the text is not rather arbitrary. Could it not be asked whether the decision to do so (which amounts to little more than an alternative interpretative convention) does not itself do violence to the larger textual wholes fashioned and handed on by later theological editors whose work added to the cumulative semantic force of the text and, thereby, its capacity to fund imagination in particular ways?

Second, liberating certain 'little' texts from the overarching framework of interpretation which we call the canon may actually facilitate less than liberative and healing uses of the text. Imagination is in itself a morally neutral capacity, and can be fed with and stimulated by good and bad alike. To 'voice' as a text Joshua 1–12, in certain human contexts, without the qualificatory voicing of texts more centrally related to the gospel message itself would seem likely to amount to an irresponsible and potentially dangerous use of the text. There is a serious danger of such a strategy resulting in a levelling of all bits of text so far as their significance is concerned, and the development of a new form of that 'proof-texting' which manages to justify just about anything 'from the Bible.' If a particular text is not informed and restrained by its wider biblical context then it will certainly be informed by some other context or set of factors. To return to a point made earlier, imagination is creative only within certain limits. It cannot create *ex nihilo*, but modifies the stuff which it receives from elsewhere. The really significant consideration is the reservoir of images, stories and the like made available to it which shape its capacity to create. Brueggemann's claim that the one who funds imagination by voicing texts can only feed them into 'the zone of imagination,' and cannot be held responsible for the imagined outcomes seems somewhat naive in this respect. The one who selects and juxtaposes these basic building blocks, and who must be supposed to be aware at least of the broader shared contexts shaping the exercise of imagination, must actually be supposed to be in a position of considerable power. There could be a significant danger that, rather than facilitating a genuinely 'democratic' imaginative exercise, we simply allow the substitution of the ideological preferences of individual 'fund managers' for the wider voice of the church catholic.

Finally, Brueggemann's suggestion that Christians' imaginations are funded by bits and pieces from the biblical text and are thereby enabled to construct an alternative whole out of these parts must reckon more fully with insights into the way imagination works afforded by the analyses of Warnock, Green and others. What these suggest (drawing on gestalt psychology, paradigm theory etc.) is that new wholes (*i.e.*, overall patterns) are not built up from a gradual accumulation of fragments. Rather, the shift to a new construal, a new way of 'seeing as,' happens all at once as our imagination *lays hold of a pattern in its entirety* and is consequently able to make sense of the fragments as belonging to this pattern precisely by locating them in it. The model which Green (following Kuhn) supplies for this is precisely that of a religious conversion in which someone suddenly sees familiar things in an entirely new way because a new wider framework of meaning has been substituted for the old. What this would suggest is that while the contents of a Christian 'world' may constantly be under modification at the local and particular level, the broader pattern within which this refunding occurs will have to be there from the outset if it is genuinely to be a *Christian* configuration at all. It may be, in other words, that we are not able to part company with big pictures, but only to choose among those which are presented to us for consideration.

Chapter 10

IS THE BIBLE HERMENEUTICALLY SELF-SUFFICIENT?

Geoffrey Grogan

Article VI of the *Thirty-nine Articles* of the Church of England reads:

> Holy Scripture containeth all things necessary to salvation: so that whatsoever is not read therein, nor may be proved thereby, is not to be required of any man, that it should be believed as an article of the Faith, or to be thought requisite or necessary to salvation. In the name of the holy Scripture we do understand those Canonical Books of the Old and New Testaments, of whose authority was never any doubt in the Church.

Other Reformation Confessions contain something similar. There is no doubt that this element in Reformation theology was historically conditioned, and that it was directed against the claim that Church tradition needed to be received as authoritatively interpretative of or even, at times, supplementary to, the teaching of the Bible.

In practice the principle, along with the complementary concept of the perspicuity of Scripture, was applied in such a way that the Bible was treated as a self-interpreting book, in the sense that it contained the Holy Spirit's own interpretative keys. In his commentary on 2 Peter 1:20[1] Calvin writes approvingly of the idea that the Holy Spirit is a Self-interpreter while doubting that this is what this particular passage means. If the books of the two testaments, and they alone, are God-breathed and therefore authoritative for the faith and practice of the Christian Church, this would certainly appear to rule out both the necessity for and the appropriateness of any other sources of revelation. How does this affect the hermeneutical task?

I. Implications for hermeneutics

Two phrases in the Article quoted above are of some hermeneutical importance: 'read therein' and 'proved thereby'.

Without doubt, the work of Kant has affected all subsequent epistemological discussion. In particular, the idea that the mind simply receives stimuli and contributes nothing in the course of that reception has lost credibility in the course of the last two centuries. This has influenced the researcher's attitude to his task in such widely diverse fields as history and the physical sciences. The mind's own contribution has, of course, received strong emphasis in modern literary criticism and especially in structuralism.

There can be no doubt that our minds are active and make a significant contribution to our understanding when we read texts, including Scripture. In other words, we come to our reading with a 'pre-understanding'. Must we then say that, because a purely objective reading is impossible, we must abandon the attempt to secure it? No! To cite a somewhat parallel case, we may hold that inspiration applies to the books of the Bible 'as originally given,' and we may do so in the full knowledge that we do not possess the original autographs and that even the painstaking work of the textual critic cannot give us the guarantee of word-for-word textual certainty.

Just as the textual critic will work hard to get as close as he can to the original, so the Biblical interpreter may seek

---

[1]D.W. and T.F. Torrance (eds.), *Calvin's Commentaries: The Epistle of Paul the Apostle to the Hebrews and the First and Second Epistles of St. Peter* (trans. by W.B. Johnston, Edinburgh: St. Andrews Press, 1963) *ad loc.*

the highest level of objectivity in his reading of Scripture. This will involve frank recognition of his bias and other elements of pre-understanding and a humble willingness to hear the word of God afresh. It is important of course for us to be aware that although we may recognise this in theory, we may yet be somewhat unaware of the actual contents of our own pre-understanding.

What about 'proved thereby'? Proof involves argument and therefore reason. What place has reason in understanding Scripture? It would be incredible to maintain that reason can have no function at all in our interpretation of Scripture, for the Bible itself contains arguments designed to persuade its readers, and the prophets and apostles, in their spoken ministries, addressed the minds of their hearers. J.I. Packer,[2] quotes Bernard Ramm as saying,[3]

> With reference to logical forms our Lord used *analogy*, Luke xi.13; *reductio ad absurdum*, Matt. xii.26; *excluded middle*, Matt. xii.30; *a fortiori*, Matt. xii.1-8; *implication*, Matt. xii.828; and *law of non-contradiction*, Luke vi.39.

Packer comments, 'The list could be extended'.

II. The Trinitarian basis of Biblical sufficiency

The sufficiency of Scripture has a Trinitarian basis. It is related to the sufficiency of Christ, for in him the Word of God became incarnate and God's revelation in him, 'the faith that was once for all entrusted to the saints' (Jude 3), built on and interpreting the earlier revelation in the Old Testament, was given authoritative written form through the work of the apostles whom he had appointed to this task. It is also related to the work of Christ at the cross, for this has itself a once-for-all character, and, as Paul argued so cogently in his Epistle to the Galatians, it needs no supplementation by human effort.

---

[2] J.I. Packer, *'Fundamentalism' and the Word of God* (London: Inter-Varsity Fellowship, 1958) 93.
[3] *The Pattern of Authority* (Grand Rapids: Eerdmans, 1957) 1.

It is also related to the person and work of the Holy Spirit. It was he who inspired the writers and it is he who acts as the great Interpreter. In fact, we might go further and say that he is really the only interpreter, for all understanding of the truth in Scripture is due to his work in the minds and hearts of believers. Behind the work of the Son and the Spirit is the sending Father (Gal. 4:4-6).

III. The Bible's own internal hermeneutical principles

It is obvious that we cannot abandon the hermeneutical task altogether. The Bible was written and first read in a very different age from our own. We live at a considerable distance from its people historically, culturally, and, for most of us, geographically. We need to hear the word of God in terms of its relevance for us in our own time and place and culture. A Bible bereft of any hermeneutical principles whatever would be like a chest full of great treasure to which nobody possessed the key.

What the Reformers really stood for was the fact that the Bible contains the basic principles by which it is to be under-stood. These principles of interpretation are therefore just as much 'given' as is the doctrine of inspiration itself. In relation to hermeneutics, this is true both at the grammatico-historical and at the theological levels of interpretation.

In grammatico-historical terms, we discover that the Bible is just like other literature. It uses the normal grammar of the Hebrew, Aramaic and Greek languages. Certainly it has its own technical terms, but the sense of these may be gathered from a study of the contexts in which they occur, and very often, in any case, they are simply special developments from their meaning in normal use. The figures of speech which are familiar to us from other literature occur also in the Bible, and the illustrations used are, more often than not, homely and easy to understand. The symbolism of Scripture too may be learned by careful attention to the text.

The element of distancing that we have already noted certainly presents us with some problems but not in such a way that the main truths taught in the Bible are obscured. It is remarkable, for example, how few of the parables of our Lord present us with major difficulties of understanding at this level, for most of them deal with very homely situations and are easily transferred from one culture to another. Even if they did present insuperable problems, we could find the truths they express through stories given propositional form elsewhere in the Bible.

In theological terms, too, the Bible may often yield its secrets to the unsophisticated reader, who is content that his understanding should be built up gradually as he becomes used to the Biblical way of thinking, the way one passage comments on and builds upon another, the way the great themes of Scripture inter-relate and enrich each other, and the way all the theological material of the Old Testament comes in the New Testament to be focused on Christ.

Certainly there are passages of difficulty, even of great difficulty. Here though the principle we normally apply in other literature applies. We interpret the obscure in the light of the clear. Every Bible passage must be considered in relation to its context and in its theological relationship to its total literary context in the Bible as a whole. What all this amounts to, then, is that God has so constituted our minds that all of us have a basic understanding of the principles of verbal communication and so are equipped for reading the written revelation of God. Perspicuity does not mean that every sentence is clear but that there is a clarity about the whole, and that the gospel and its truths which are necessary to salvation, shine out clearly.[4]

This is not to suggest that there may not be an obscurity that amounts to complete bafflement. If a reader comes to the Bible with a set of ready-made presuppositions that belong to a totally non-Christian or anti-Christian outlook, there may be a perplexity not simply about details, but in relation to the gospel itself. Just as in other literature a certain sympathy with the material is needed for full understanding, so it is with the Bible, for this sympathy is

---

[4]G.C. Berkouwer, *Holy Scripture* (Studies in Dogmatics) (Grand Rapids: Eerdmans) 272-274, points out that the Reformers were not unaware of the fact that the Bible contains problems for the reader but that they laid great stress on the clarity with which it presents the gospel.

(paradoxically) both a pre-condition of and a product of the work of the Holy Spirit in the mind and heart of the reader. We need to be ready to learn to understand God and the meaning, purpose and goal of life quite differently from hitherto, and that is rarely easy.

We may say all this, however, and yet recognize that there are issues that need to be thought through concerning certain types of material of possible hermeneutical value. A.N.S. Lane, in addressing the significance of the Post-Reformation slogan, *Sola Scriptura*, discusses the relevance of many of these.[5] To these issues we must now address ourselves.

IV. The function of Church tradition

1. It is a safeguard against excessive individualism
The 'right of private judgement' does not mean the right of everyone to an idiosyncratic view of Scripture's meaning. It is the Holy Spirit who leads us into truth, and we are not justified in twisting Scripture to give it a meaning to our own liking. To take note of long-standing church tradition is in fact a safeguard against the excesses of unbridled individualism. If we find ourselves arriving at a view of a passage quite at variance with hermeneutical tradition, then we need to be particularly self-critical.

After all, the church is a Divinely-created institution. The Princeton School of theologians is well-known for its particularly strong emphasis on the inspiration and authority of Scripture, and so the words of one of its leading representatives, Charles Hodge, are all the more worth considering. He says:[6]

> It is not denied that the people, learned and unlearned, in order to the proper understanding of the Scriptures, should not only compare Scripture with Scripture, and avail

---

[5]'Sola Scriptura? Making Sense of a Post-Reformation Slogan,' in P.E. Satterthwaite and D.F. Wright (eds.) *A Pathway into the Holy Scripture* (Grand Rapids: Eerdmans, 1994) 297-327.
[6]C. Hodge, *Systematic Theology* (London, Nelson, 1871) I. 184.

themselves of all the means in their power to aid them in their search after the truth, but they should also pay the greatest deference to the faith of the Church. If the Scriptures be a plain book, and the Spirit performs the functions of a teacher to all the children of God, it follows inevitably that they must agree in all essential matters in their interpretation of the Bible.

The Reformers greatly valued contributions made to the understanding of the Bible by many of the Fathers, and they wrote with respect, although not uncritically, of men like Cyprian and Athanasius, of Chrysostom and Ambrose, and, most of all, of Augustine. This is understandable, for, as J.N.D. Kelly says:[7]

> almost the entire theological effort of the fathers, whether their aims were polemical or constructive, was expended upon what amounted to the exposition of the Bible. Further, it was everywhere taken for granted that, for any doctrine to win acceptance, it had first to establish its Scriptural basis.

The main purpose of statements of Biblical sufficiency during the Reformation period was to make it clear that all church tradition must come under the judgement of Scripture, not to reject it altogether.

It would be a mistake, too, to think that this principle was formulated in a purely reactionary spirit. It was important in its own right, not simply in the context of sixteenth-century religious debate. The Reformers' reverence for Scripture was great. and issued in a deep concern to live by it and under it, to study and expound it and to seek reformation of the Church by it. 'Respect for Scripture as the Word of God, as a lamp for the feet and a light on everyone's path was a decisive element, rather than opposition to ecclesiastical interpretation.'[8]

2. It provides helpful summaries of Biblical truth
Protestants have frequently been somewhat negative not only towards the Schoolmen and other Mediaeval Catholic

---

[7]J.N.D. Kelly, *Early Christian Doctrines* (London: A. & C. Black, 1960) 46.
[8]Berkouwer, *Holy Scripture*, 272.

authorities but also, in general, towards the Fathers, blaming them for the development of the two-source concept, the idea that authoritative teaching comes to us both through Scripture and tradition. It is, however, only right that we should seek sympathetically to understand what were the reasons, often very good, why certain stages in this development took place.

The conflict with Gnosticism was very important in this respect, for the Gnostics appealed to the Scriptures for their doctrines, although they applied their own eccentric hermeneutical principles to the understanding of the Bible. A reading of Irenaeus, *Against Heresies*, in which, in refuting them, he often refers to the views of the Gnostics, shows just how essential to the theological health of the Church the work of the anti-Gnostic fathers was.

It was necessary then for men like Irenaeus and Tertullian to emphasise the true understanding, what Irenaeus called 'the canon of the truth 'and Tertullian 'the rule of faith,' the main points of the Christian faith, which had come down from the earliest days of the church. By 'canon of the faith,' Irenaeus meant 'a condensed summary, fluid in its wording but fixed in content, setting out the key-points of the Christian revelation in the form of a rule'.[9]

It is true that Irenaeus began to contrast tradition with Scripture, but this contrast was never in their content but rather in their form. Here, in the apostolic hermeneutical tradition, was the genuine interpretative principle, to be distinguished from Gnostic distortions of Biblical truth. There was a strong emphasis on the apostolicity of the tradition, and a recognition that the classic form of apostolic truth was to be found in the Scriptures themselves.

For centuries there was no thought of tradition and Scripture being set over against each other in the sense that the former might be thought to contain more than the latter. Writing of the period up to AD 451, Kelly says, 'Throughout the whole period, Scripture and tradition ranked as complementary authorities, media different in form but coincident

---

[9]Kelly, *Early Christian Doctrines*, 37.

in content'.[10] So long as tradition is regarded as under the supreme authority of the Scriptures, it may supply a *regula fidei* which may be helpful, but this is not to be considered absolutely indispensable. We may however find in the great Creeds and Confessions that have come down from the past much that is true to Scripture and is of real theological value.

3. It needs to come under the judgement of Scripture

The Christ of the Gospels clearly recognised the authority of Old Testament Scripture. Just as clearly, he rejected much Rabbinic tradition as a corruption or even evasion of Biblical teaching, while it needs to be recognised that some of his teaching coincided with or related well to it.[11]

It is not surprising then that the same situation arose again at the Reformation. The truth is that tradition is always something of a mixed bag. The Reformers raised objections to many of the traditions honoured by Mediaeval Catholicism. On the other hand, there were times when they could quote Aquinas or other Schoolmen with approval.

What really bothered the Reformers was the fact that gradually over the centuries doctrines had developed which had no clear warrant in Scripture, and which were justified by an appeal to tradition, treated, in relation to these doctrines, as an authority independent of Scripture. As Berkouwer puts it,[12]

> The Reformers wished to protest against that independence and range of influence. The sentiment was not that of an anti-historical revolt but that of a desire for preservation and continuity. They saw that the gospel itself, so clear in Scripture, was being obscured and even modified by these traditional doctrinal accretions.

---

[10]Kelly, *Early Christian Doctrines*, 47. Kelly writes helpfully on this whole process of development in his chapter, 'Tradition and Scripture,' 29-51. See also B.S. Childs, *Biblical Theology of the Old and New Testaments* (London: S.C.M. Press, 1992) 31-32.

[11]How much may be discerned from H.L. Strack and P. Billerbeck, *Kommentar zum New Testament aus Talmud und Midrasch* (München: Beck, 1922-28 and 1956-61).

[12]Berkouwer, *Holy Scripture*, 303.

V. The function of the living teaching of the Church

The teaching of the Church has an important function in relating Biblical truth to present-day issues. The authoritative teaching of the Bible needs to be applied to the real issues faced by people in an ever-changing world. This means that we cannot be satisfied with an exegesis which does not pass into exposition and application.

The living teaching of the church should compel attention to the relevance of Scripture. This is what we find in the use made of the Old Testament by Christ and by the New Testament writers, especially in such formulae as 'it stands written' and 'What does the Scripture say?' because this kind of language underlines the contemporary nature of its relevance.

It also makes creative use of Church tradition. The Christian Church today has a long history. Many of its preachers have informed access to the literary deposit of this through their training. Whether he actually quotes them or not, the preacher's understanding, and through him the understanding of his congregation, may be much enriched by a study of the expository and theological works of writers like Chrysostom or Calvin as well as from the Nicene Creed or the Westminster Confession of Faith and the practical theology of the Puritans.

It needs, however, to come under the judgement of Scripture. Rabbinic tradition, 'the tradition of the elders,' clearly arose out of a praiseworthy desire to show how the ancient Mosaic law might apply in changed circumstances. Unhappily, though, it hardened into a tradition which became as sacrosanct as the written Law itself. Christ's independence from this brought a breath of fresh air into the whole business of interpreting the Old Testament and especially its Law. Not only did he set his own authoritative interpretation over against the traditions, but he also subjected them to criticism from the standpoint of Old Testament Scripture.

VI. The function of charismatic utterances

This is of course a controversial issue in today's church. Because some of the charismata like prophecy, tongues (when interpreted), words of knowledge and of wisdom, are verbal and meaningful, it is important to think about their relationship to the Biblical revelation. They may be acceptable as exposition and application of Biblical truth. This would of course put them on a par with the normal teaching ministry of the church, which we have already considered.

They may also be acceptable as local as distinct from universal revelation. Much depends on the claims made for them. If a 'prophecy' is treated as a word for the whole modern church, and especially if it is circulated in written form, this is surely an implicit claim to be equivalent to Scripture, although it could perhaps be argued that it is intended only for a particular age and not for the Christian church in its whole history. The danger, of course, is that even at the local level they could assume an importance in practice which gives them too much weight in comparison to the weight given to Scripture. Many examples of such occurrences could be cited.

They too must be judged on the basis of Scripture. Scripture recognises the existence of false prophets (e.g., in Deut. 13; Jer. 23:9-40; Matt. 24:24-25; 2 Thess. 2:9-12; Rev. 13:11-17) and it prescribes procedures for testing prophecies, some of which are related specifically to the Christian era (Matt. 7:15-23; 1 Cor. 14:29; 1 Tim. 4: 1-5; 1 John. 2:22-23; 4:1-6). At a period in church history when claims to prophecy and other forms of Spirit-given are made quite frequently, it is of vital importance that everything should be tested.

VII. The function of Christian experience

It is important that we do not set Scripture and experience over against each other too sharply. Timothy George reminds us that 'the principle of *Sola Scriptura* has traditionally been referred to as the "formal principle" of the Reformation as opposed to the "material principle" of justification by faith alone. This distinction, however, is misleading insofar as it suggests that the Reformers approached the Bible as a theological axiom or philosophical prolegomenon rather than as the living and powerful oracle of God'.[13] As living and powerful, it deeply affects our experience.

Christian experience is the sphere in which the inner testimony of the Spirit operates. Is the Bible a sufficient revelation of God without spiritual illumination and subjective sympathy? No, for this would be to accord to reason the function which is proper only to the Spirit of God. Because the Bible is the product of the Spirit's inspiring work, it is intrinsically clear and sufficient for salvation, but sin clouds the mind of the unregenerate reader and hardens his heart. Through sin, our natural inclination is not to listen to nor to obey God's word. There needs to be a work of the Spirit within the reader's heart and mind.

What then does the Holy Spirit do? His inner testimony means that he enables us to recognise, in reading it, that the Bible is in truth God's word and not simply the product of human minds. As Berkouwer puts it:[14]

> Genuine perspicuity is the intrinsic intelligibility for the believing sinner; verification of Scripture takes place in the heart. One can only speak of perspicuity in a confession of faith.... According to the Reformers. the force behind this connection of Message and words was the power of the Spirit.

In the same passage, he underlines the fact that this message comes through the words of Scripture and not independently of them.

E.A. Dowey, Jr., well expresses the theological appropriateness of the dual nature of the Spirit's work in relation to the Bible as seen by the Reformers and particularly as emphasized by Calvin. He says:[15] 'By...confirming the author through the inner witness and identifying both as the 'same Spirit' Calvin binds together a high objective evaluation of the Bible with the principle that 'God alone is a

---

[13]*Theology of the Reformers* (Leicester: IVP, 1988) 314.
[14]Berkouwer, *Holy Scripture*, 275.
[15]*The Knowledge of God in Calvin's Theology* (Grand Rapids: Eerdmans, 1994) 107.

suitable witness for his own word'. Christian experience confirms the relevance of Scripture to the Christian life. The heart of the Christian believer may recognise a need that Biblical teaching meets and his faith and obedience will certainly discover its relevance. Without doubt too situations may arise in the life of the Christian which cast light on Scripture, for its appropriateness to the situation may give even its meaning a new sharpness and clarity of definition.

Experience, of course, needs to submit to the creative and controlling influence of Scripture. It should not be given a negative function in relation to Scripture. If our experience and Scripture do not tally, it is not impossible that we have misunderstood Scripture. On the other hand, it may well be that our experience needs to come into line with Scripture. God's Word constantly creates experience and judges it.

VIII. The function of general revelation

General revelation gives us a recognition of God as our Creator, Provider and Judge. Scripture itself recognises this in passages like Psalm 19, Acts 14:15-17 and Romans 1:18-21. This means that, even without Scripture, we do not live in a world which contains no light from God. Creation is eloquent about its Creator, recognising that the God who created also provides food, drink and shelter for his human creatures. There is also an inner witness of God to confront the conscience with the facts of responsibility, judgement and retribution from God.

As Paul recognises in Romans 1, the apprehension of this revelation has become distorted by sin. Humanity, confronted with evidence of God, has worshipped gods; confronted with the responsibility to live righteously, we have turned to sinful acts. The contents of the natural revelation are also to be found in Scripture, for this too teaches that he is our Creator, Provider and Judge.

General revelation has its place, but does not teach the distinctive truths of the Christian gospel. A.N.S. Lane says of general revelation and of 'natural' human knowledge that they are legitimate theological sources, but he goes on to state that,[16] 'one important qualification needs to be made. They are sources for the Christian theologian; they are not sources of Christian revelation.' The historical revelation which came to its climax and fulfilment in Christ and which is recorded in Scripture embodies the great truths of salvation which are absent from the general revelation.

IX. The function of reason

God has endowed us with rational faculties. It is true that these have been deeply affected by sin, but regeneration affects the whole person and we are enabled through it to think about the things of God to his glory and with a new clarity. It is a serious error to treat revelation and reason as necessarily antithetical, for the rational faculties of the godly person have important functions.

Reason has an ordering function, and we see this in the way the New Testament writers handle the Old Testament. To take a very simple example, we note how they see examples of the same principle in different parts of that earlier revelation, as, for instance, in Hebrews 11, where people of faith are brought together from different parts of the Old Testament. This therefore is an encouragement to the theologian and to the ethicist to systematize the material for purposes of deeper understanding.

Reason also relates Scripture to other realms of human knowledge. The Bible touches many other areas of human study such as history, the social sciences and the psychology and philosophy of religion. At such points the Christian specialist in the field concerned will seek integration of Biblical insights with those of the subjects of his or her special interest.

Reason has, however, stepped outside its proper sphere if it rejects what is given in the Biblical revelation. When we come to any literature, we do so with minds deeply influenc-ed and shaped by our previous experience and education. If we are to learn anything new, however, we must approach reading matter that is new to us with at least

---

[16]'Sola Scriptura,' 305.

a certain openness, a willingness to learn. This is supremely true of the Bible because of its status as Divine revelation. Because of this it comes to us, not only with a claim to be heard but also to be believed and obeyed.

X. The function of philosophical concepts and systems

Philosophical concepts and sometimes major parts of a philosophy have been employed in the interpretation of Scripture. One may instance the influence of Platonic and Aristotelian thought on certain forms of patristic and scholastic theology, or the influence of Hegelianism, Kant-ianism, Evolutionism, Existentialism, Marxism and Linguist-ic Philosophy on much modern theology. The many varieties of modern theology and their historical development can be attributed in some real measure to the changes in philosophical thinking.[17] Sometimes it may seem that a philosophical principle coincides with a Biblical concept. Augustine's gratitude to the Neoplatonists for teaching him the spirituality of God prior to his Christian conversion is a famous case in point. Even Paul quoted from pagan poets.

From an apologetic standpoint, there can be value in this, but great caution needs to be employed. When Philo attempts to show that Moses and Plato speak with one voice and when Bultmann claims the New Testament as the first great classic text of Existentialism, warning lights should flash in the Christian mind. It is easy enough, when one finds similarity or coincidence at a few points, to begin to use a philosophy as a major tool for understanding the whole Bible, with disastrous results.

Whatever may be said about Paul's quotations from Menander and Epimenedes, it is clear that he used these only as illustrations of truths otherwise known from revelation and did not employ them in any general hermen-eutical fashion. The example of Tertullian is, of course, a salutary one here, for his explicit rejection of philosophy was

[17]There is an exploration of this in relation to Modern Theology in G.W. Grogan, 'Modern Theology and the Evangelical Faith' in *TSF Bulletin* 49 (Autumn 1967) 1-9.

not matched by sufficient self-awareness and self-criticism. None of us however can throw stones at him. Is any one of us completely Biblical in our thinking?

Of course, there have been some philosophers, such as Van Til, Dooyeweerd and Gordon Clark, who have sought to construct their philosophical systems on the basis of Biblical presuppositions, and their work has been of real value, especially in the realm of apologetics. But their work too needs to be treated with at least some degree of caution, lest a system should take over and ride roughshod over some aspects of Biblical thought. To value the work of Dooyeweerd is one thing, but to be a fanatical Dooyeweerd-ian is another!

XI. The function of Biblical scholarship

Obviously Biblical scholarship has to be employed if most people are to be able to read the Bible at all. Good Biblical translation is impossible without Biblical scholarship, and, because no two languages have exactly equivalent vocab-ularies or grammatical patterns, translation always involves an element of interpretation. This happened, of course, even within the period of Biblical revelation, for the Septuagint is used extensively by the New Testament writers, and so, through this, the knowledge and skills of its translators found a place within the Bible itself.

This should therefore warn us against a naive or over-rigorous application of the principle that the Bible is self-interpreting. A little thought reveals that faithful translation of the text works within the principle rather than outside it, for its concern is to make the all-sufficient text of Scripture available in a way 'understood of the people'. Not only so, but, as we have seen, perspicuity does not apply so much to individual passages but to the clear under-standing of the great gospel truths.

Textual criticism has its place, too, for, if we accept the authority of Scripture, it is important for us to seek an authentic text as far as possible. In this realm, too, it is the gospel that matters supremely, and it is widely accepted that no doctrine of the gospel rests on a disputed text. It is important though that both the translator and the textual scholar should be very self-critical and be aware that their own theological presuppositions affect their work.

The disciplines of Biblical scholarship are certainly not to be despised. For instance, the links of the Old Testament covenant language with the language and forms of ancient Near Eastern treaties, and the Graeco-Roman background to the concept of adoption in the New Testament may help to give greater fullness of meaning to our understanding of these ideas in Scripture. In this way, our basic conception of God's truth, which may certainly be arrived at without awareness of this background, can be much enriched.

XII. Conclusion

One of the results of becoming a Christian should be that we are brought to a new self-understanding. We recognise how imperfect we are, how liable both to sin and to err. For this reason, we should welcome the insights of others into the meaning of Scripture, while recognising that they too are fallible. Most of all, we need to be constantly on guard against reading into Scripture was has simply come out of our own minds.

The article by A.N.S. Lane, referred to earlier,[18] stresses that we should not indulge in over-rigorous application of the sufficiency principle, and the point is well made. The present article seeks to complement this by warning of the danger of reading the text without self-criticism. Without letting it exercise a paralysing influence on our necessary hermeneutical task, we should do well to take seriously the question of Berkouwer, when he asks, 'Do we hear in God's Word that which we already know, that is, the images, feelings and presuppositions of our own hearts?'[19] Much depends on our facing this question with honesty.

---

[18]See note 4 above.
[19]*Holy Scripture,* 107.

Chapter 11

GOD IN DIALOGUE[1]

Paul Helm

Introduction

Any thoughtful reader of the Bible is struck by the fact that it contains, side by side, two quite different languages about God. On the one hand there is activistic language; for example, God has ears and he hears, he has a nose and he smells, he expresses emotions such as anger and jealousy, compassion and mercy. We think that we can cope with this sort of language pretty well; it is not literal language, we say, God does not really have a nose or ears, he is not really given to fits of anger or jealousy; though we may become somewhat uneasy at the idea that he is not given to fits of compassion and mercy either.

But there is more to such activistic language than references to parts of the body and to various emotions; God is active in history; he participates in the Scriptural narrative. He comes down to his people; he is near, and then far off; he asks questions, seemingly in ignorance; he works miracles; most perplexingly of all, he changes his mind; he even

---

[1]This article is based upon the Griffith Thomas Lecture, delivered in Wycliffe Hall, Oxford, on 15th November 1994.

changes his mind having implied that he will not change his mind. Many are uneasy about treating this sort of language as a series of *facons de parler*, and surely this uneasiness is justified. It is unsatisfactory to say that God is not active in history he is only 'active;' that he does not work miracles but he only 'works' miracles; that he does not change his mind he only 'changes' his mind; he does not become Incarnate he only 'becomes' Incarnate.

We may gloss these scriptural expressions about the activity of God with varying degrees of confidence. The need to gloss them, and the confidence that we can do so, arises from the presence in Scripture of the other language about God. There are numerous expressions in the Bible which are, or imply, general features of God's character which seem to be at odds with the anthropomorphic language that we have just been considering. For example, Psalm 139 teaches that God's knowledge of the Psalmist is very extensive indeed, and it would surely be unwarranted to suppose that while God's knowledge of the Psalmist was very extensive, his knowledge of you and me was not; that the Psalmist was in the privileged position of being known through and through, while you and I escape. Similarly, one thinks of the claim of Paul that God works all things after the counsel of his own will, or of the writer to the Hebrews that God's promises are immutable; there are similar general express-ions of the infinity and eternity and power of God.[2]

Unqualified language about the knowledge or power or changelessness of God is often said by historians of doctrine to be the invention of the Greeks, specifically of Plato and the Neoplatonists, and to have found its way into the language of Christian theology through such thinkers as Augustine. But this cannot be correct. Perhaps Augustine was responsible for re-expressing and systematising such general, unqualified expressions about God, and perhaps the tools which he used to effect this systematisation owed a lot to the Neoplatonists, but it is a mistake to think that Augustine (or anyone else) imposed such language onto

---

[2] I shall assume, partly for ease of exposition, that such unqualified language about God implies that he is timelessly eternal.

Christian thought. Our Bible, as we have seen, is full of such language, and Augustine's Bible was just the same.

Some Proposed Solutions

I propose to review some proposed solutions to this problem, the problem of the two languages, as we might call it, and to offer my opinion as to why some of these work better than others. But I do not wish to be so bold as to offer a definitive solution to this difficult cluster of issues; I will be satisfied if I can engage you to think about this problem for yourselves, and if I am able to suggest some profitable lines of enquiry.

(1) Maurice Wiles and the Providence of God

In his Bampton Lectures, *God's Action in the World*,[3] Maurice Wiles defends what he believes to be a necessary consequence of theism, namely a 'unitary view of the world'. On such a view, according to Wiles, the whole process of the bringing into being of the world, the total universe, is one act of God.

Here I am not concerned with whether this view of Wiles is plausible or tenable, but with the consequences of such a view for the activistic language of the Christian religion, and in particular of the Bible. However, I cannot forbear to say that there is nothing inconsistent in supposing both that the universe proceeds from the one will or decree of God and that some of these events which occur in the universe are, when measured by human experience, unparalleled or unprecedented. It is no more consistent to argue from the one will of God that we should abandon the concept of a miracle than that we should abandon, say, the concept of a distinct species of thing. The one will of God is capable of creating both ants and armadillos, and of causing both the flowering of a shrub and the burning of a bush.

But let us suppose that what Wiles says is a tenable view. The God portrayed cannot, on this view, be the God of religion, intervening, responding, answering, learning, or

---

[3](London: S.C.M. Press, 1986).

forgetting, because the idea of divine intervention, of action and reaction in the history of mankind, is ruled out in an *a priori* fashion. Wiles' position would, in effect, cut the Gordian knot of the two languages by denying to God the power to act and to react in human affairs. So, in terms of our dilemma, Wiles' views seem to commit him to saying that only the general, unqualified, and relatively abstract language about God could conceivably be true of him. About the activistic language, all of it, Wiles must say that it is mythical, or primitive, or anthropomorphic, or in some other way off-centre. And this is surely an unsatisfactory result.

(2) J.R. Lucas and the Vulnerability of God

In his book, *The Future*,[4] and a paper, 'The Vulnerability of God',[5] John Lucas places great emphasis upon divine vulnerability, a view of God which arises from his account of the nature of the universe as a perpetual becoming. According to Lucas, God is temporal, for though he transcends time, he is not timeless. Such a view does justice to the interventionist God of scripture (p.210), who intervenes in the world, as Lucas puts it 'doing things, saying things, hearing prayers, and sometimes changing His mind' (p.214).

For Lucas, it is a part of the view of God as an interventionist God that he takes risks with the order which he has created and which he sustains. Because of God's lack of physical limitations, and his omnipresence, he is better placed than anyone else could be to know what each of us has decided, and is going to do. But his knowledge is not complete, nor can it be. For instance Lucas says that God cannot know many things about him, John Lucas, 'since I have not made up my mind about many things, and do not know myself what I am going to do' (p.221). As Lucas rightly points out (p.222) divine foreknowledge is incompatible with libertarian freedom. So, Lucas thinks, if God is going to enter into personal relations with his creatures, then they need freedom to be themselves, freedom to make mistakes. God, like ourselves, does sometimes get things

---

[4](Oxford: Blackwell, 1989).
[5]In *The Philosophy in Christianity* ed. Godfrey Vesey (Cambridge: C.U.P. 1989).

wrong in his predictions of what others will do, and he repents, that is, he changes his mind as a consequence (p.223). Yet the fallibility and vulnerability of God do not in any way derogate from his perfection (p.224).

So what Lucas is offering us is the other horn of the dilemma of the two languages than that favoured by Maurice Wiles; he stresses the personal, activistic, interventionistic character of God; but at the expense of God's immutability, his omniscience, his control of the entire created and providential order. So that those parts of Scripture which assert such things will require re-interpretation in accordance with Lucas's activistic hermeneutic. While we ought to do full justice to the activistic language of Scripture, the cost of doing so is surely too great if it means that we must reinterpret the other language of Scripture in the radical fashion that Lucas proposes.

So far we have glanced at two solutions to our problem, two Oxford solutions, each of which comes down on one side of the problem or the other. But this is clearly unsatisfactory. How shall we then proceed?

(3) T.V. Morris and Epistemic Possibility
In his book on the metaphysics of the Incarnation, *The Logic of God Incarnate*,[6] T.V. Morris is faced with the problem of how the God-man can be tempted. Temptation seems to involve liability to fall, but liability to fall also seems to be inconsistent with the impeccable divine nature of the God-man. In order to meet this problem Morris has recourse to what he calls epistemic possibility. It is sufficient to meet the case, Morris argues, that the Son of God believes himself to be liable to fall, even though, from a strictly metaphysical point of view, he cannot fall. Believing this, the Son will then use every effort not to succumb to the temptation, efforts which (unbeknown to him) are bound to succeed. This is what Morris says:

> Jesus could be tempted to sin just in case it was epistemically possible for him that he sin. If at the times of his reported temptations, the full accessible belief-set of his earthly mind did not rule out the possibility of his sinning,

---

[6](Ithaca, New York: Cornell University Press, 1986).

> he could be genuinely tempted, in that range of conscious-
> ness, to sin....In order that he suffer real tempt-ation, then,
> it is not necessary that sinning be a broadly logical or
> metaphysical possibility for Jesus; it is only necessary that
> it be an epistemic possibility for him. (p.148)

Opinions will differ on whether appealing to epistemic
possibility in the case of Jesus Christ does what Morris intends it to do. As far as I can see, it contains at least one fatal
flaw. Not only is Jesus portrayed as not knowing the outcome of some period of conflict, say the temptation by Satan
in the wilderness, but such ignorance seems to involve Jesus
in the belief, for example, that it is possible, really possible
and not merely epistemically possible, that he succumbs to
temptation. It may be that Jesus is ignorant, but the further
thought that he is actually mistaken is surely too hard for a
Christian to swallow.

Yet even though this solution may not be altogether
acceptable in the case of the Incarnation, it may have other
uses. Perhaps the relation between our two languages about
God is that the activistic language is the language of human
ignorance; because the Children of Israel were ignorant of
the divine intentions, they represent God as coming down to
them and delivering them from the bondage of Egypt when
it was all along part of his immutable decree to do so.

This is a promising line of thought for *some* cases of
activistic and interventionistic language about God in Scripture. God may appear to change his mind because we are
simply unaware of the divine mind. But will it help us with
all cases? Surely not. If we take as a particularly interesting
example the story of the Lord's prediction of Hezekiah's
death (Isa. 38) it is precisely because God tells Hezekiah that
he will die that we have difficulty when he changes his mind
in response to Hezekiah's prayer. While Morris's approach is
of some help, it will not take us all the way.

(4) William Alston and Dialogue

If we suppose that Isaiah is speaking, as a prophet, in the
name of God what we have in the story of Hezekiah is a
fragment of divine-human dialogue. And so it may be helpful if we take a little time to explore the nature of such

dialogue. William Alston has raised the question of whether dialogue is essentially temporal and hence out of bounds for a God who is both timeless and omniscient. Alston concludes that it is not;[7] a timeless, omniscient God can perform acts, including conversational acts, he can even make replies in time, provided that such a God is not omnidetermining, provided that he has not 'decided every detail of His creation, including all the putatively free choices and actions of human beings' (pp.147-8). This looks promising; if we can establish the consistency of dialogue with divine timelessness, or at least with divine changelessness, even if we have to forgo the idea of an omnidetermining God, we would go some way to showing the Scriptural record to be consistent, even if we cannot go all the way. Let us think about the problem in terms of changelessness.

Conversational dialogue obviously entails the possibility of making a reply to whatever has been said. But can a changeless God make a reply to what has been said to him? An obvious objection is that if God is changeless he cannot come to intend to say anything after some event in time, and that replies are necessarily after what is replied to. Or so it may seem. But Alston argues that this is a contingent feature of replies; that something would equally well be a reply if it were contemporary with what it were a reply to.

> If I could be so closely tied to you as to apprehend your cry while you are in the act of producing it, and if I were able to offer my consolation (or at least do the most immediate part of this, the volition) at that very same moment of apprehension, would I not still be responding to your cry? (p.155)

So let us suppose that, as far as the nature of dialogue is concerned, there is nothing odd about a changeless reply. Could a changeless deity make such a reply? Alston says that God's utterance could be performed as a reply to Moses, but not as a piece of genuine dialogue; for a genuine dialogue requires that the one replied to 'stands over against' God as something independent of his will, something intro-

---

[7]*Divine Nature and Human Language* (Ithaca, New York: Cornell University Press, 1989) 153-4.

duced into the situation by the initiative of another, something to which He has to adjust His conduct, something that requires a special *ad hoc* 'response' on His part. Thus if what Alston calls the *uttered as a reply* condition is to be sufficient for genuine dialogue, we must specify that what is responded to is, to some degree, independent of the responder's will (p.158).

If what Alston says about changelessness and the possibility of dialogue is correct then, assuming divine omniscience, to every piece of human dialogue there changelessly exists a specification of the reply in the divine mind; the reply does not exist as a reply until it is uttered, but the specification of the reply exists changelessly. What the changeless deity does in entering into dialogue is not to formulate a reply but to utter in time what is timelessly prepared as a reply. He does not formulate a response upon being addressed; he simply issues his timelessly-ready response at the appropriate time.

Suppose that the person does believe that such a timeless reply exists. Of course he does not know what the reply is, but he believes that there is one. And the fact that he believes that there is such a reply means that he believes something which is not normally regarded as a condition of dialogue between people. For it is a normal condition of human dialogue, of its mutual 'openness,' that A does not know what B will say until B formulates and utters his thought; and that B formulates and utters his thought believing that A does not already possess a reply to it. There are cases where A knows B so well that he is able to anticipate how he will react. But such knowledge is highly fallible and incomplete.

So dialogue in the divine-human case must contain the important feature that, in virtue of divine changeless omniscience, the human partner in the dialogue believes that God changelessly knows what has not yet come into his own mind, and has a reply ready and waiting. This is sufficient to upset the mutuality which Alston seeks to preserve in divine-human dialogue (p.153). It is God's changeless knowledge of my reply and of his changeless answer to my reply which logically entail what he will utter as a reply to me.

And because this is true, the partner in dialogue is entitled to believe it.

The perfect mutuality of dialogue may be constrained not only by one of the partners controlling the dialogue, or by one of the partners knowing in advance the outcome of the dialogue, but by anyone knowing its outcome in advance where at least one of the partners believes this. But what precisely is the constraint? It is a constraint upon the openness of dialogue, in that the dialogue cannot be perfectly open if its outcome is known or knowable in advance. If one of the participants, or a spectator, knows (by whatever means) how the dialogue will turn out, then the dialogue cannot be perfectly 'open'.

So perfectly mutual dialogue appears to require not only two independent participants, neither of whom wholly controls the responses of the other, but two participants neither of whom knows in advance the decisions of the other nor has a reply already prepared. Dialogue is compromised where one of the partners controls the other, and also where one of the partners knows the outcome of the dialogue in advance, as would happen if one of the partners is an omniscient God. The degree of compromise is the greater if the human partner in the divine-human dialogue also knows that God knows what response the human partner will make, even if the partner himself does not yet know this, because he has not yet made up his mind.

So far we have looked at four different approaches to our problem, the approaches of Wiles, Lucas, Morris and Alston. Each of these seems to have important defects; either because of their hermeneutical consequences as far as biblical interpretation is concerned, or because they fail to convince as arguments for the proposed solution to our dilemma. For the remainder of this paper I wish to consider two further approaches which seem to have more promise.

(5) The Idea of Divine Accommodation

The idea of divine accommodation is an important theme in Jewish and Christian theology, as Stephen Benin has recently reminded us.[8] Anyone familiar with the theology of John Calvin will have been struck by the prominence that he gives to the idea of divine accommodation.[9] Not surprisingly, perhaps, Benin says that Calvin is almost unequalled in Jewish and Christian thought in his exploitation of accommodation, employing it to explain

> the relationship between a sublime deity and his mundane creation and creatures; the authority of Scripture; the importance of the Word and not institutions in religious life. Finally, it provided a method by which the book of Scripture could be read along with the book of nature (p.197).

It is with the first of these uses that we are concerned here. Writing of those scriptural passages where God is said to repent, Calvin says:

> What, therefore, does the word 'repentance' mean? Surely its meaning is like that of all other modes of speaking that describe God to us in human terms. For because our weakness does not attain to his exalted state, the description of him that is given to us must be accommodated to our capacity so that we may understand it. Now the mode of accommodation is for him to represent himself to us not as he is in himself, but as he seems to us....So we ought not to understand anything else under the word 'repentance' than change of action.....Therefore since every change among men is a correction of what displeases them, but

---

[8]*The Footprints of God: Divine Accommodation in Jewish and Christian Thought* (Albany: SUNY Press, 1993).

[9]David Wright has written extensively on this theme: 'Calvin's Pentateuchal Criticism: Equity, Hardness of Heart and Divine Accommodation in the Mosaic Harmony Commentary,' *Calvin Theological Journal* 21 (1986) 33-50; 'Accommodation and Barbarity in Calvin's Old Testament Commentaries' in A.G. Auld (ed.), *Understanding Poets and Prophets. Essays in Honour of George Wishart Anderson* (J.S.O.T. Supplement Series 152) (Sheffield: J.S.O.T., 1993) 413-27; 'Calvin's "Accommodation" Revisited' in P. De Klerk (ed.), *Calvin as Exegete* (Grand Rapids: Calvin Studies Society, 1995) 171-90; 'Calvin's Accommodating God' forthcoming in W H Neuser(ed.), *Calvinus Sincerioris Religionis Vindex* (Kirksville: Sixteenth Century Journal Publishers, 1996/97). See, also, Ford Lewis Battles, 'God Was Accommodating Himself to Human Capacity,' *Interpretation* 31 (1977) 19-38 and Paul Helm, 'John Calvin on Divine Accommodation,' *The Baptist Review of Theology*, 4 (1994) 41-53.

> that correction arises out of repentance, then by the word
> "repentance" is meant the fact that God changes with
> respect to his actions. Meanwhile neither God's plan nor
> his will is reversed, nor his volition altered; but what he
> had from eternity foreseen, approved and decreed, he
> pursues in uninterrupted tenor, however sudden the
> variation may appear in men's eyes.[10]

What I think Calvin means in passages such as this is that
God accommodates himself to human spatio-temporal
conditions, by the use of sensory, figurative, anthropomorphic language about himself. The movement is from
God to mankind; such accommodation is an act of divine
condescension and grace. It may seem that what Calvin says
about God representing himself means that the language of
accommodation is a teaching aid and nothing more.

But for Calvin such language is more than that. Yet
Calvin is not a reductionist; he is not a proponent of what
has come to be called 'metaphorical theology'. The very fact
that we know certain expressions to be divine accommod-
ations implies that it is possible to think of God in non-
accommodated ways, even though Calvin stresses that when
we think of God in such ways, God 'as he is in himself,' we
cannot fully grasp what we think of.

A better way to understand what Calvin is saying is
to think in terms of the idea of two standpoints, the divine
and the human. Christian thought about God and the world
must always reckon with two standpoints, that of the
transcendent creator, and that of the time-bound and space-
bound creature. When Calvin (and the long tradition of
speaking in this way in Christian and Jewish thought)
invokes accommodation, it is to cater for the fact that God
condescends to speak in terms which creatures with a time
and space bound standpoint need if they are to respond
appropriately.

For at the heart of the idea of divine accommodation
as Calvin uses it is a logical point; that it is a logically
necessary condition of dialogue involving the creaturely
standpoint that such people should act and react in time. If

---

[10]*Institutes of the Christian Religion* trans. F.L. Battles (London: S.C.M.
Press, 1960) 1:18:13.

dialogue is to be real and not make-believe, then God cannot represent himself as being only immutable, for then dialogue, real dialogue, would be impossible.

We may begin to explore this idea of two standpoints a little by first thinking of two physical standpoints. A building may be viewed from more than one standpoint from, let us say, the respective standpoints occupied by two individuals. But while any building, in order to be viewed, must be viewed from some standpoint, any viewer could occupy the standpoint of any other viewer, and there is an infinity of such standpoints.

Temporal standpoints are somewhat different from spatial standpoints because of the unidirectionality of time, and the consequent idea that what has happened cannot now not have happened. While you could occupy my physical standpoint (if I vacate it) you cannot now take up Napoleon's temporal standpoint and perhaps you never could have.

Anyone who occupies a human standpoint necessarily occupies some temporal standpoint or other. If God is timelessly eternal then he is necessarily so, and so he could not occupy any temporal standpoint. So it is necess-arily the case that God, if he is timelessly eternal, cannot translate his standpoint into ours, nor can we translate ours into his.

The contrast in the standpoints can be brought out starkly as follows. From our standpoint God's creation is continuously unfolding; the state of the universe at time $t1$ does not logically necessitate the character nor even the existence of any phase at $t2$ or later, even though there are discovered regularities between different past phases, and promised continuations of them, for as long as the created order persists. So from our perspective the Creator may be said to be continuously creating the universe, in that there is more universe today than there was yesterday. But from the divine standpoint, since today includes yesterday and tomorrow, what is created is one temporally extended universe.

Theologians sometimes ask if creation is continuous, and whether a sharp distinction can be made between creation and the providence of God. Perhaps asking these questions in this way betrays a confusion of thought. From the standpoint of the timeless Creator the creation is never 'over and done with,' because something can only be over and done with if it is past, and so in time. So creation is one eternal act, the one act of creation, and from the divine standpoint it never ceases to be, any more than it starts to be. But from the human standpoint the creation is unfolding, developing; so divine providence, or one aspect of divine providence, can by us creatures be seen in the regular temporal unfolding of creation's latent powers.

Suppose that God wishes to convey some truth about himself to his creatures existing in space and time; in particular, some truth about his relation to them, seeking to elicit a response from them. Then it would seem that he is bound to represent the matter to his creatures in the only terms which they are going to be able to comprehend, in terms of action in space and time. It is not simply that God chooses, for the sake of pedagogic effectiveness, to accommodate himself to humankind, but that he *must* accommodate himself in these ways if he is faithfully to represent his relations to humankind to human beings themselves. The 'must' here is an ontological or meta-physical 'must'. Given the metaphysical distinction between timeless creator and time bound creature there is nothing else for it than that he represent himself to them in such ways. So the activistic language of Scripture is the language of divine accommodation.

Let us briefly consider three types of objection to this idea of divine accommodation as an answer to the problem of the two languages.

1. *The problem of priority.* I have set forth an account of the two languages in terms of two different standpoints, each not reducible to the other. But which standpoint has priority? Here it is necessary to distinguish between what I shall call ontological priority, and evidential or epistemic priority. The ontological priority must go to the story as told from the divine standpoint, since that standpoint is the one of him who is the creator and sustainer of all that is. It is only in virtue of his say-so that there has come into existence any other standpoint than his own. But as far as our knowledge of God is concerned the human standpoint must take priority over the divine. We think our way into the Christian

faith, normally, through learning of the divine words and actions as they have occurred in our space-time world.

But to say that the human standpoint has epistemic or evidential priority, that we first learn of the divine activity as mediated through this standpoint, is not to say that our knowledge of God is necessarily restricted to such divine words and actions in space and time. To say this would be to suppose that we could have no knowledge of God other than that of such space-time activity. But this is not the case. As we saw at the outset of our enquiry, Scripture presents us with two accounts; an account of what goes on in space and time, and an account about the divine nature as such. The extent to which these assertions about the divine nature as such give us unqualified knowledge of the divine nature, and the extent to which the language is analogical, are matters of legitimate dispute, which would take us too far afield all that I can say here is that I can see no insuperable objection to the thought that such language can give us real, though limited, knowledge of God.

2. *The problem of relativism.* Some may take fright at my idea of two irreducible standpoints, a human and a divine, because they fear that it is taking us in a relativistic direction. Let us suppose that God, from his eternal standpoint, wills

> (1) that the bush burn in the presence of Moses on a particular day

and that Moses knows, on that particular day

> (2) the bush is burning here and now

Are the two states of affairs represented by (1) and (2) respectively, contradictory or incompatible in some way? Relativism is the doctrine that truth is relative to a person's position, or set of beliefs, or intellectual context. Is it relativistic in this sense to suppose that it is true for God that he knows that the bush is burning on some date while Moses knows, on that date, that the bush is burning now? Hardly, for given God's knowledge that Moses sees the bush burn on some particular day, and his knowledge of certain other states of affairs, it follows as a matter of logic from what he knows eternally that he knows that when on that date Moses sees the bush burn, he is seeing the bush burn now.

Philosophers of religion have frequently debated the question of whether a timeless God can know facts in

precisely the same sense in which temporal creatures know.
If God is timeless, can he know what I am doing now? How
can God, who is timeless, know what time it is now? Some
say that he cannot, and so cannot be omniscient, since if he
cannot know what time it is now then there are truths which
he does not know, and cannot know. Some say that God and
a creature can know the same truths, but have different
ways, necessarily different ways, of expressing these truths.
And still others argue that the use of temporal indexical
expressions such as 'now', 'then', 'yesterday', 'today' and so
on is indicative not of a different mode of knowledge, but of
a different kind of know-how. The use of such expressions
helps us, creatures in time, to handle temporal concepts, and
to find our way around the temporal order in an efficient
way, but it does not provide a distinctive kind of knowledge
of time. And so what God lacks when he does not know
what time it is now is not knowledge but power, in the same
way that someone who does not know how to change a
bicycle-tyre lacks power.

   Which of these various stratagems, if any, com-
mends itself to us as a way of coping with the apparent
irreconcilability of divine knowledge and human knowledge
ought not to affect our attitude to the idea of the two
standpoints. For our question is not, does God know
precisely what we know, but is God's knowledge of the
created order inconsistent with our knowledge of it,
inconsistent to the extent that we have to adopt some form of
relativism? Why should we think this?

3. *The problem of make-believe.* Despite all that has been said
about the two standpoints one may still be left with the
nagging feeling that the divine action and reaction in the
world which the Scriptures recount is only shadow action,
and that the real action, or inaction, takes place from the
divine standpoint. We may ask, does God really change his
mind, or not?

   But why should we think that the only true account
of reality is that expressed from the divine side? Surely the
point is that when we ask, does God really change his mind?
this question is elliptical in character. For what we are really
asking is, does God really change his mind *when his action is
considered from the human standpoint*? And the answer to this

question is clearly 'Yes, he does'. For as far as biblical theism is concerned there is no standpointless truth of the matter; anything that occurs must be considered from either the divine standpoint or the human, but not from neither.

We have been trying to put a philosophical gloss on what I take to be the idea of divine accommodation as we find it in John Calvin. I am not for one moment suggesting that he had all such points in mind himself, but rather that such an approach is the best answer that we have so far considered to the problem of the two languages.

Nevertheless, despite these defences to objections, and important though the doctrine of accommodation is, and the doctrine of the two standpoints, I do not believe that the idea of accommodation solves our problem with Hezekiah.

(6) Change and Intention.

In the story of Hezekiah's sickness and recovery the Lord tells Hezekiah that he will die and then, in answer to a prayer from Hezekiah about this, promises his recovery. Here is a case not simply of God changing his mind, but of him changing his mind having implied that he will not change his mind. What are we to make of this? Can this be made consistent with what the Bible elsewhere says about God's immutability and steadfastness? If God is steadfast, how could God's first utterance, that Hezekiah will not recover, be sincere? For only if it is believed to be sincere could it cause Hezekiah to pray for his own recovery. If God were simply *making as if* to bring about the death of Hezekiah, while all the while not intending it, then there would be no reason for anyone, including Hezekiah himself, to pray for his recovery. But if God is sincere in what he says, does he not really change his mind when Hezekiah prays? And if he does change his mind, then is not God changeful?

Perhaps an answer to at least some of these questions can be gained if we think about intentions, and ask: could the entire incident of Hezekiah and his recovery be encompassed within one indivisible divine intention, or must we resort to a series of intentions formed as God reacts to successive circumstances?[11] There is reason to believe that we *can* talk about indivisible intentions, along the following lines.

The prophet's utterance, 'Hezekiah will not recover', can be understood as occurring within a framework of conditions or promises, and as having, under certain circumstances, the force of a warning or a threat. In understanding this we may find help from an analogy. Under certain circumstances, the sentence of a judge in a court of law may be an appealable sentence, where (say) a court of appeal exists, and leave to appeal against the sentence is granted. If the judge says to the convicted man, 'you will serve ten years', he is sentencing him to a certain term of punishment. But in circumstances which are appealable, the convicted man will serve his full term only if any appeal that he may make against his sentence is unsuccessful. The judge's sentence, like the Lord's pronouncement about Hezekiah, may seem from its grammatical features to be final and unconditional. Yet its place within a particular legal framework, say within a covenantal framework, makes it tacitly conditional, liable to overturn through appeal. Given a framework of divine promises to answer prayer, the divine utterance, 'Hezekiah will not recover,' is to be regarded as conditional in character. In terms of the analogy that we have been using, God is both the sentencing judge and the appeal judge. So what God intends, the one unchanging intention, might be (rather cumbersomely) expressed as, 'that Hezekiah will recover from sickness having expressly indicated that Hezekiah will die if his recovery is not requested, knowing that as a matter of fact his recovery will be requested'.

So that provided we are prepared to place God's various utterances to Hezekiah (and any similar utterances) within a covenantal framework, something that is surely congenial with the biblical picture of God's relations to Israel and with wider humanity, then the language of change and variability applied to God, can be rendered consistent with his unchangeableness, the unchangeableness of his covenant

---

[11]The following paragraphs are closely related to Paul Helm, 'Omnipotence and Change,' *Philosophy* 51 (1976) 454-461.

promises. What God says to Hezekiah is sincerely intended, but it is not irrevocable if Hezekiah prays for some other outcome within a covenantal framework such as that suggested.

Conclusion

We have been reviewing various ways of tackling the dilemma posed by the fact that biblical language about God implies both that he changes and that he is changeless. By a process of elimination I have tried to argue that both horns of this dilemma can be grasped if we understand that the relevant divine utterances, the utterances that imply that God changes, occur within a covenantal framework which, despite their unconditional surface grammatical form, makes them tacitly conditional in character. I have not argued that this is the only way of tackling the dilemma, but that it is the best way of all those that we have reviewed here. Moreover it is an attractive approach to anyone who is prepared to give the biblical idea of the covenant a central place in thought about God.[12]

---

[12]Cf. *The Westminster Confession of Faith*, ch.7 ('Of God's Covenant with Man'): 'The distance between God and the creature is so great, that although reasonable creatures do owe obedience unto him as their Creator, yet they could never have any fruition of him as their blessedness and reward, but by some voluntary condescension on God's part, which he hath been pleased to express by way of covenant'.

Chapter 12

THE CHURCH AND STATE RELATIONSHIP: SOME ECCLESIOLOGICAL OPTIONS

Tim Bradshaw

The question of the relationship between church and state was of immense importance during the nineteenth century and gained a high public profile. The rise of the Free Churches and the development of their theology of separation led to debates over disestablishment and education which were central issues at general elections, up to 1906. Thereafter the issue seems to have died down. However, it may rise again as the monarchy mutates and a new monarch awaits, who may wish to change the mode of establishment by incorporating a multi-faith dimension into it. The constitutional bar on Roman Catholic monarchs has been raised as an anomaly which presses for a cutting of the establishment in the United Kingdom. From the church side, a motion was brought to General Synod by Bishop Colin Buchanan in 1995, advocating the cutting of the constitutional link between the Church of England and the state.[1] What principles are at stake, and what options are open in the British context?

---

[1] For the arguments deployed, see Colin Buchanan, *Cut the Connection* (London: Hodder, 1995).

State control of the Church

The Church needs to be free to govern itself. That is a primary claim. It was the reason for the Scottish Disruption of 1843. 'The thing we deprecate,' said Thomas Chalmers, 'is the authority of the civil magistrate in matters of religion'.[2] Chalmers did not object to state endowment funding ministers, assisting the church in terms of resources. This was a matter of the church being recognised by the state and given help, very different from the state claiming to create the church and make decisions for it. The state's acceptance and support of the church is the proper form of establishment, and this is to be applauded since such a system is needed for the church to diffuse the faith nationally, an aim which can never be fulfilled by 'the Voluntary System, or by what has been termed the System of Free Trade in Christianity'.[3] The church must be free in appointing its leaders and in theological teaching, matters of religion. Otherwise the patronage of the state is only to be welcomed and will allow the gospel to be ministered as widely and effectively as possible since the resources for this will be made available.

The Oxford Movement was triggered by the same concern. The Church of England, according the Tractarians, was catholic and apostolic, but since the Reformation had fallen into an Erastian thrall whereby a Parliament containing men who had no concern for the church could take part in legislation affecting her. Keble's Assize Sermon 1829 had summoned the Church of England to look to her own apostolic credentials and dignity. The Church was the Church of Christ, not a department of state. *The Tracts for the Times* sought to work out this truth and to reclaim the religious power and dignity of the visible church. Newman in his tract *The Catholic Church* wrote: 'Are we content to be accounted the mere creation of the State, as schoolmasters and teachers may be, or soldiers or magistrates, or other

---

[2]*Lectures on the Establishment and Extension of National Churches* (1838) in *The Works of Thomas Chalmers* (1836f.) vol.18, pp.194ff., taken from David Nichols, *Church and State in Britain Since 1820* (London: Routledge, 1967) 48. Sadly David Nichols, vicar of Littlemore and eminent theologian of church and society, died in the summer of 1996.
[3]In Nichols, *Church and State*, 43.

public officers? Did the State make us? Can it unmake us? Can it send out missionaries? Can it arrange dioceses? Surely all these are spiritual functions...'.[4] Newman's submission to Rome was in no small measure fuelled by such criticism of the established church. The Church of England was insufficiently free to govern herself, and her credentials as the church catholic in England were compromised.

Later in life, as a Roman Catholic and making a defence of his secession to Rome despite the intellectual problems attached to that move, Newman voiced his belief that the Anglican establishment weakened the church, 'for the Nation drags down its Church to its own level'.[5] The church, if too tied to the national government risks becoming a kind of moral department of state, absorbing the mores of society. The church will be persuaded to revise its doctrinal and ethical teaching so as to 'keep in touch with society,' a kind of ecclesial reductionism. The pressures on the church to dilute Christian teaching are evident in such matters as marriage and divorce, on sexual ethics, on the uniqueness of Christ in the face of claims for multi-faith worship and practice at Commonwealth celebrations in Westminster Abbey. The Churches of England and Scotland, each established in different modes and each somehow specially charged to provide the moral and spiritual lead to the people, whereas Newman predicted that a counter-flow of ethos would operate and that the Church would come under the influence of the social mores rather than vice versa.

David Wright has pointed out that this is a deep temptation to established churches facing decline, 'the perpetuation of an imperialistic Christendom mentality in maintaining the identification of the church with the broader community at the cost of the distinctiveness of Christian faith and life'.[6] The end result of seeking to act as an un-

---

[4]In Nichols, *Church and State*, 49.

[5]*Apologia Pro Vita Sua* (The two versions of 1864 & 1865) (London: Oxford University Press, 913) 396. Newman argues that the current weak state of the Roman Catholic Church in England means that on balance it should not seek to harm the Church of England, although the balance could change. The present state of relations between the two churches he regards as 'that of an armed truce.'

[6]'Editorial,' *Scottish Bulletin of Evangelical Theology* 13 (1995) 2.

critical and undemanding chaplain to the nation will be 'to baptise sub-Christian morality',[7] as David Wright puts it. The Church's need for freedom from being subject to other powers corresponds to the core apostolic doctrine that Jesus is Lord, and anything qualifying that rule of Christ in and over his Church must be rejected. 'The crown rights of the redeemer' must take precedence over the rights of a temporal ruler and a temporal legislature. The Church must be free to conduct itself so as to accord with the will of Christ, to be the servant of Christ in the world.

Undoubtedly since the Scottish Disruption and the Assize Sermon, the Church of Scotland has gained its independence of state interference in appointments and church government. The Church of England has gradually gained independence from the rule of Parliament, although there remain the closest constitutional ties. Nevertheless in what has been called a 'Constantinian Church,' the question is whether there is sufficient eschatological tension possible between the Church of England and the nation of England, given the structural integration of Church with society. In practice, it must be said, the Church of England has stood against governments of the day over issues of social justice and become unpopular with politicians for this interference in secular affairs. It is in the area of personal moral behaviour that the Church is criticised for drifting uncritically with the prevailing currents of moral relativism, for fear of causing offence by being 'judgemental'.[8] A confusion seems to have taken root between judging individuals and judging patterns of behaviour in this regard.

---

[7] *Ibid.*, 3

[8] A recent classic example of this was the report, roundly castigated by General Synod, *Something to Celebrate* (London: Church House Publishing, 1995), in which the working party of the Board for Social Responsibility affirmed the value of a very wide range of cohabitation and radical domestic arrangements which have evolved in society since the 1960s. This was fiercely criticised for its purely sociological approach and moral indifferentism.

State Assisted Church

It is arguable that there are in fact three established churches in the United Kingdom. Obviously the Kirk and Church of England are established, albeit in different modes. But the Roman Catholic Church is deeply integrated into the social and economic fabric of the nation through its state funded schools, of which there are now more than Anglican schools in England. The tax payer funds Roman Catholic schools which exist primarily to foster the faith of Rome, and hence which will take in only a strictly limited number of non Roman Catholics. The state subsidy going towards Roman Catholic education is massive, and would be considered a form of establishment in other countries. Indeed it is through its policy of placing schooling as the priority, a policy ad-vocated by Manning, that has seen the burgeoning of the Roman Catholic cause in Britain this century. Similarly Roman Catholic teacher training colleges have been estab-lished and are funded by the state, as with the various forms of chaplaincies in the services and health service.

This exemplifies perhaps the most advantageous form of relationship with the state for a church. The church is wholly free to govern itself and yet receives considerable finance from the state to fund a modern system of education which it could never afford on its own. Such an arrangement would have been acceptable to Thomas Chalmers who want-ed a free church but one recognised and valued by society, which would support church influence in many ways. 'The one great religious beneficiary of the 1944 Education Act,' according to Adrian Hastings, 'was the Roman Catholic Church, as indeed it had already been of the 1902 Act.... It greatly enlarged the size of the Catholic middle class and the proportion of Catholics going to the university...'.[9] Their church school system has also enabled Roman Catholics to maintain a greater hold on their children through their development. This form of what can be called state support,

---

[9] Adrian Hastings, *A History of English Christianity 1920-1990* (London: SCM, 1991) 421. Hastings explains that the 1944 Act, coupled with Anglican complacency and optimism, led to the giving up of Anglican Church schools on a large scale, 'disastrous for the Church of England' (p. 422).

and legal establishment of a kind, confers pure benefit on a church with no loss at all of ecclesiastical control.[10]

When church schools exist to further the aims and propagate one denomination, and to protect the children of that denomination from contamination from the values of secular society, certain questions arise regarding the relative benefit and cost to the society which funds such a privilege. Obviously, there are areas of the UK in which serious social division exists along religious lines. Ulster is the prime example, and some parts of Scotland another. The pressing social need for children across the sectarian divide to share a common educational experience would seem to outweigh the claim of one religious group to exercise its freedom to separate development. A system which amounts to educational apartheid in a context of mutual suspicion hinders improved relations in the future and condemns the rising generation to continual sourness. From the state's perspective such an arrangement can therefore become undesirable. Current agonising over state funded Muslim schools in some of the large urban conurbations reflects fears of reinforcing ghetto areas, sealed off culturally from contact with people or values of the majority of society. It is hard to see how this could not turn out to be too high a risk for society to fund.

This leads one to ask whether such religious schools, of whatever denomination, if narrowly constructed to take only members of one church, are 'christian' in concept or merely sectarian. Exclusivist schooling, and teacher training, in the name of the Gospel, seems to offend firstly the ecumenical commitments of all denominations to do nothing separately that might be done together. But, secondly, the definition of the church implied by strictly denominational schools becomes problematic. If we take Avery Dulles' well known list of 'models of the church', which seems most appropriate in this connection? He lists the church 'as': institution, mystical communion, sacrament, herald and servant. Should the church be promoting itself as an

---

[10]State funded, Church controlled, schooling has been such a highly prized and consistent goal of the Curia throughout this century as to cause it to lose sight of other crucial factors. See e.g. K. Scholder, *The Churches and The Third Reich* (London: SCM, 1987) 146ff. on the Vatican Concordat with Hitler.

institution, with its own government and values, in the midst of a liberal democracy, a state within a state, but dependent on taxpayers' subsidy? One must doubt whether the church should use such schooling as its evangelistic tool, as herald. The concept of mystical communion hardly squares with the bureaucratic structures of mass education. The church as sacrament begs the question 'sacrament of what?'. The only category from Dulles' list which seems to suit a nationwide education system by a single denomination is that of servanthood.

The missionary endeavour of churches often comes in the shape of education, the provision of education, to people who otherwise would not receive it, by the church. This is a servant model of provision, of giving to those in need. There may well be the complementary motive of spreading the faith in through the provision of education, although to make acceptance of the gospel, or worse the denomination, a condition of entry verges on a modern version of simony. The church, in an effort to serve the community, provides a kind of education with an ethos which people may want to take up, that could be a servant model of church education. This claim, however, hardly stands up if access to the schooling is restricted almost wholly to children of that denomination. The critical question is whether what is a de facto apartheid mode of education can truly be said to be 'christian'. Should any policy which leads to social fragmentation and mutual suspicion be supported by a church? The question of power and a christian understanding of its exercise in relation to care for all humanity raises its head here.

An inversion of this problem can occur in church institutions which have accepted state help and, by a process of symbiosis, gradually lose their christian distinctiveness and become secular. This can be illustrated again from the field of education, this time from the Anglican policy towards the many church schools it controlled prior to the 1944 Education Act. Hastings' account[11] of Butler's policy in framing the Act was to produce legislation that would edge most of the Anglican schools into full state control, while

---

[11]See Hastings, *English Christianity*, 418-422.

offering Catholics terms which they might grumble about but accept. This was achieved by offering a choice between controlled schools or aided schools. The former were effectively taken over by the government, the latter retained church control. Anglicans would have had to raise massive sums to opt for the latter and so generally opted for the former. William Temple justified his decision in terms of avoiding segregation and of seeking to produce a Christian ethos throughout the state sector. The Church of England developed no policy for training teachers or catechists, and in effect trusted the secular state to maintain a loosely christian ethos in erstwhile Church of England schools. Hastings' view of the Anglican policy in response to Butler's calculation is that 'the quickly advancing secular consensus of middle England in the sixties owed a great deal to the educational choices made in the 1940s'.[12]

The field of health care can also exemplify the quandary for church policy towards society. Historically the church provided the motivation to care for the sick and the means to do so. The modern liberal democracy has taken over this role, although the system of state funded chaplaincies in hospitals retains something of an acknowledgement of spiritual need. In Germany there are still church hospitals, funded by the state.[13] The hospice movement provides an interesting example of a movement arising from within practical Christianity in the middle of this century to meet the perceived neglect of the terminally ill in the state system of medical care. St. Christopher's Hospice was founded by the Christian doctor Cicely Saunders who had been influenced by the work of the Irish Sisters of Charity at St. Joseph's Hospice, Hackney, begun at the turn of the century. The success of St. Christopher's spread, issuing in hospices all over the country, rooted in the broadly Christian ethos of care, and attracting state funding. Now, however, there are clear signs of a creeping secularisation of

---

12*Ibid.*, 421.

13Interestingly it was the Lutheran hospital at Kaiserswerth, run by the community of deaconesses and Pastor Fliedner, which did much to give Florence Nightingale her vision for a renewed nursing profession.

the hospice movement.[14] If hospice care becomes merely a technique, rather than an exercise of caring, this will be another example of Weber's 'routinization of charisma'.[15] If the spiritual dimension does become marginalised or secularised, hospices will need to be reinvented.

Hendrikus Berkhof has an interesting treatment of this regular phenomenon of Christian good works being taken over by the secular state in the process of history. 'Sanctification and secularisation,' he thinks, 'progress together. With his sanctification of society the Spirit evokes an ambiguous and internally contradictory world, a society which is busy cutting down the gospel tree from which it is picking its fruits'.[16] The Christian dynamic should, and often does, produce moral fruit in a society which in turn is copied, or taken over, by the governing authorities at which point the ethos which produced the good is removed. The need for a new initiative begins again, in a somewhat Hegelian dialectic.

This phenomenon of secularisation of even specifically Christian institutions has happened with dramatic force in tertiary education, where trust deeds of colleges such as Keble, Oxford, set up with definite Christian intent, have been changed to water down the avowed intention of the founders and visionaries who worked to build the college. Church of England colleges, formerly teacher training colleges, have retained the name but allowed the Christian ethos intended at the outset to dissipate. This is so for evangelical and catholic Anglican traditions.[17] The Church of England therefore gives its label to twelve colleges, while consenting

---

[14]See Ann Bradshaw, 'The Spiritual Dimension of Hospice: The Secularization of an Ideal,' *Social Science & Medicine* 43 (1996) 409-419; and D. Field, *Nursing the Dying* (London: Routledge, 1989).

[15]M. Weber, *The Protestant Ethic and the Spirit of Capitalism* (London: George Allen & Unwin, 1976) 182.

[16]H. Berkhof, *Christian Faith: An Introduction to the Study of the Faith,* translated by Sierd Woudstra (Grand Rapids: Eerdmans, 1979) 514f.

[17]The General Synod Report *An Excellent Enterprise: A Report by the Working Party on the Church Colleges of Higher Education* (London: Board of Education of General Synod, 1994) tells a story of colleges which are wholly independent of the Church in anything but name, and with no policies towards fostering a Christian mind through the syllabus.

to their total autonomy and secularised character, calling this
'an excellent enterprise'. The only agency which can seek to
implement policies of such institutions are their boards of
trustees or governing bodies, generally lay and clerical
church members. Such groups have evidently been unwilling or unable to implement or press for a Christian vision for
the institution for which they are trustees. The Church of
England General Synod, at the advice of its Board of Education, in November 1994 voted not to develop any policy
for the training of RE teachers in Church schools by the
colleges, although this had been recognised as a critical need
in schools. Roman Catholic policy is precisely the reverse.

State assistance to church institutions can lead to
powerful denominational institutions, with single minded
policies to build up the denominational strength and powerfully seek to mould young minds through teacher training
and schooling. It can also lead to a nominalism and a
resigning of all control and any policy in teacher training,
tertiary education, and school influence. For an established
church, it must be said, it is easy to go along the track of
realising an identity of sacred with secular rather than an
identification which preserves Christian distinctiveness,
seeking both to serve and inculcate a moral ethos. This way
of looking at such church influence in society has been
defended by John Habgood[18] on the grounds that the majority ethical view in society is a broadly christian one, that of
the many who indulge in 'believing without belonging'.[19]

Pannenberg pointed out recently that the state has at
times been ahead of the church in shaping policy for the
church, instancing the 'need to recall that the emperors from
the time of Theodosius were themselves professed Christians, and they sometimes did more for the Church than leading bishops and theologians to restore peace and provide for
the flourishing of the Christian community'.[20]

The Anglican mode of church schooling as provid-
ing, at best, a very light dusting of moral tone, may also have

---

[18]*Church and Nation in a Secular Age* (London: DLT, 1983).
[19]The sub-title of Grace Davie's book *Religion in Britain Since 1945:
Believing Without Belonging* (Oxford: Blackwell, 1994).
[20]Wolfhart Pannenberg, 'Christianity and the West: Ambiguous Past,
Uncertain Future,' in *First Things* 48 (December 1994) 18.

a negative impact on pupils in terms of specific Christian faith and spirituality: social mores may benefit slightly at the cost of real faith.[21] If this is true then the Church of England must take stock of the dual aim of its educational enterprise, since one counters the other. Kierkegaard's criticism of 'Christendom' relates to its replacement of the Gospel by a pale substitute of cultural mores, which acts as an inoculation against true faith.

> For this is the end of the State Church, which under the form of care for men's souls cheats them out of the highest thing in life, that in them there should come into being the concern about themselves, the want, which verily a teacher or priest should find according to his mind; but now, instead of this, the want (and precisely the coming into being of this want is life's highest significance for a man) does not come into being at all, but having been satisfied before it came into being, it is prevented from coming into being.[22]

This is the classic criticism of implementing the Christian faith as if it were a system to be taught rather than a faith to be caught, or teaching the good works while bracketing the importance of personal faith. Church enterprises requiring substantial state funding may turn out inevitably to fall under this criticism.

The Nature of the Church's Influence on Society

The purest form of church influence on society surely is that which comes through the outworked faith of the believers. The pre-Constantinian church, simply through life and worship, had an impact on its social context. There was no policy to take over the power structures of society, but an

---

[21]The researches of Leslie Francis, for example, *Religion in the Primary School: A Partnership between Church and State?* (London: Collins, 1987) indicate that controlled schools impart a negative spiritual influence on pupils; only the aided Roman Catholic schools impart some positive influence towards Christianity.

[22]S. Kierkegaard, *Attack Upon Christendom* in R. Bretall (ed.), *A Kierkegaard Anthology* (Princeton: Princeton University Press, 1973) 444.

indirect influence was exerted through the care shown by Christians associated with the God of Jesus Christ. The evangelical revival begun by Wesley and Whitefield in 1740 gradually fuelled a renewal of the moral level of a society which had the institution of an established church mandated to take pastoral care of the nation.[23] The dialectical pattern suggested by Berkhof with his fruit and tree analogy seems to ring true to the path of history. Grass roots movements do shift expectations of conduct and produce institutions, which in turn can lose their original spirit.

Church institutions need the spiritual life and work of the faithful rather more than public subsidy if they are to remain Christian and spiritually uplifting. Death steals up swiftly otherwise, and the institutions become mere power structures of the world, rather than representing the kingdom of God. Gladstone regarded the decree of the first Vatican Council, 1870, declaring the Pope infallible *ex cathedra* and consolidating his jurisdiction worldwide as 'ordinary, immediate and truly episcopal', as a claim to worldly power over the consciences of Roman Catholic citizens of the nations of the world. Newman's response to Gladstone's *Expostulation* was to assure the British of the priority of conscience over Papal decree, since the Papacy had learned its lesson since the corruption of the Middle Ages and was now thoroughly ethical and would not seek to enforce anything immoral on Roman Catholics.[24]

Nevertheless the claim to infallibility is a huge one and de facto creates an empire of subjects who have a temporal ruler—and that is the problem. It cannot be said that Gladstone is answered by saying that believers owe a duty to God above that of the state, it is a duty to an earthly governor claiming immense spiritual insight and authority. That is what sent shock waves through Europe and so upset Gladstone, that an alternative human government could seek to impose its will on citizens who lived in democ-

---

[23]Ford K. Brown, *Fathers of the Victorians* (Cambridge: CUP, 1961).

[24]For an account of the story, cf., John R. Page, *What Will Dr Newman Do? John Henry Newman and Papal Infallibility 1865-1875* (Minnesota: Michael Glazier, 1994). Nichols has a substantial excerpt of Newman's defence of the decree and its possible effects on the conscience of good citizens (*Church and State* 171ff.).

racies.[25] Newman's pragmatic apologetic, that no clash of loyalty would be likely to happen, did not meet the problem of principle about power and allegiance.[26] Gladstone's fear was of control, rather than influence, being exercised by a denomination.

The Anglican view developed in the last century by Coleridge and Maurice regarded the church as the spiritual heart of the nation, and the established church, shaped to be as open as possible to as many as possible, was that church. The Roman error was to confuse the church with the state, making the former the governing power over the latter, but Coleridge and Maurice demurred, emphasising that the nation is also a God-given society with its own proper sphere of activity. The Protestant error is the sectarian and voluntaristic one, setting the church against the society. All the various denominations have a grip on some dimension of the truth of the church. Christ is the transformer of culture has made atonement for the whole world, the Lamb of God who takes away the sin of the world, and baptism is the declaration of this salvation. The church's task is to enable the world to realise the kingdom of Christ in the world, and hence Maurice's practical involvement with Christian Socialism and education. To leave education, for example, to the secular spirit is to abandon students to the commercial principle: the church plays a vital role in bringing the spiritual dimension to such enterprises.[27]

Maurice's defence of establishment may fail to convince today, although his notion of the place of the church within society and its need to transform society might be critically appropriated, and today that surely must be through an ecumenical mode of operation. John Habgood

---

[25] An interesting example of a possible clash of allegiance today could be that of birth control. How should a government health minister, recently converted to Roman Catholicism, implement UK policy at an international conference on this matter? Education policy could be an equally difficult matter.

[26] The Roman Catholic Director General of the BBC, Charles Curran, shows this remained the case. See his autobiography, *A Seamless Robe* (London: Collins, 1979) 347.

[27] See William J. Wolf (ed.), *The Spirit of Anglicanism* (Edinburgh: T & T Clark, 1982).

argued that 'some sort of de facto ecumenical establishment seems not only possible but desirable'.[28] This sounds easy enough for the Anglican, but cannot be an ecclesiological option for the Free Churches such as the Baptists and Congregationalists whose polity since the Reformation has been specifically 'separatist,' desiring to separate any church structures from those of the state, including financial subsidy.

The separatist position, which became enshrined in the constitution of the USA in reaction to the English model, cuts away all structural integration but does not advocate a strict dualism of the church against the world. Rather the influence of Christ in society and the world should be that of regenerate individual believers whose opinions and life styles indirectly have transform social structures. The means through which this might happen is that of democratic process, so that elected politicians might exercise a Christian influence on policy making at various levels in society. The nature of any Christian influence should be personal. This approach seeks to avoid the pitfalls of the church becoming an institution dealing in power and enforcing itself on others in society, the Constantinian error which fundamentally altered the nature of the faith and blunted its eschatological radical edge.

Whether a politician, elected on the basis of a party political platform and not having a specifically Christian mandate, has a right to influence policy in a Christian direction may be debatable. In a democracy should the politician not consider every view as equally important to represent, why should a Christian perspective gain a preference when it has no special mandate? If a Muslim or Jewish local councillor or MP allowed a religion to influence political decisions, much complaint might be expected from the electorate. *A fortiori* is this the case with a secret movement such as Opus Dei or the Masons. This radical model of Christian influence may have rather less in the way of democratic rectitude than may have been assumed. The example of the USA is that since no religion is acknowledged as belonging the state, although a large majority of the population are

---

[28]*Church and Nation* 108.

professedly Christian, all religious claims are to treated as of equal importance, hence the bizarre phenomenon of Satanist army chaplains alongside all the others!

The church may seek to offer a 'prophetic' influence to those who govern the state, trying to issue a word in due season about questions of social justice through the mass media. This should in theory be rather difficult for an established church to do, since its structures are involved in the governing process, bishops sitting in the House of Lords for example.[29] This enterprise is a dangerous game for churches. They can begin to sound like a mildly left wing party of opposition, mouthing a social critique on matters such as housing and prisons in which they have little competence. Worse still, this role of comfortable prophet can seem to contrast with practical inaction by the church in the areas it is urging action by the government.

What is the Church of England, as a national institution, for example actually doing about prisoners released into hopeless situations? Is it investing in hostels for such people, or merely telling others to act? The discarnate word from the prelate to the governing authorities carries little conviction and may mislead the church into thinking that 'speaking out' discharges the Christian duty. The other great problem with such policy is that it relies on the media which in turn has its own axes to grind and will manipulate things accordingly. The result is an image of a liberal Church of England with a social gospel, highly damaging and demoralising for the largely orthodox people in the pews. The policy of 'speaking out' regularly on only social issues seems questionable, often posturing, and counter productive.[30]

---

[29]It must be said that in practice the Church of England is almost certainly more unpopular with the government than any other denomination, a notable instance of such disfavour being Archbishop Runcie's 'Falklands Sermon' and its refusal of triumphalism.

[30]Keith Clements has many words on this subject in his *Learning to Speak: The Church's Voice in Public Affairs* (London: T & T Clark, 1995).

The Church in the Liberal Society

Churches will find that their action will be their best sermons to the nation, and that prophetic words of criticism are best addressed to the church: such at any rate seems to be the more biblical pattern. Judgement begins inside the household of God. The middle of this century, marked by the 1944 Education Act, saw an optimism about the path social mores and institutions were taking. Liberal democracy with its standards of decency and care for the weak evidently could manage without the church's help in education as it had taken over in the field of health and social services. A kind of Kantian morality seemed set fair, a Protestantism without the embarrassment of God, or the Comtean 'Catholicism without Christianity'. Christian insights had been given and now harvested, the fruit picked from the tree, and institutions could develop from that point.

The close of the twentieth century sees no such complacent picture. Liberal democracies are in crisis over their values and community ties. Alastair MacIntyre has shown that liberal democracy after virtue has developed into an emotivist culture, without norms and without coherent community.[31] The church may also be living in the same way, 'by schisms rent asunder, by heresies distressed,' endlessly debating about social issues and often distracted from the focus on the God of Jesus Christ.

David Nichols identified the problem of liberal democracy as not being self-resourcing in terms of an ethical basis over thrity years ago,[32] and said in 1967 that the privileged position of the Church of England has been so eroded as to render it merely one church among several in a plural society. He would today no doubt have added the multi-faith dimension to his description. Before accepting the secular liberal state as sufficient, we first need to look at its basis. The secular ideal can become another kind of religion and an intolerant ideology. At least Christianity of the Anglican variety now has a track record of toleration which may not be provided by secularist civic substitutes. Nichols cites T.S. Eliot:

---

[31] *After Virtue* (London: Duckworth, 1992).
[32] In the Introduction to his *Church and State*.

'As political philosophy derives its sanction from ethics, and ethics from the truth of religion, it is only by returning to the eternal source of truth that we can hope for any social organisation which will not, to its ultimate destruction, ignore some essential aspect of reality'.[33]

The pure pragmatism of much modern government, concerned mainly to massage public opinion into returning a political party back into power, confirms this dictum starkly.

The effort to establish politics as an autonomous activity goes back, Nichols points out, at least as far as Machiavelli, and according to this way of organising society the rules by which it is played emerge during the playing of the game. Whereas a game has an ordered aim, politics needs to decide the goal towards which it is working, and surely here politics depends on ethics.[34] If ethics ultimately depends on religion, as Nichols and more recently MacIntyre powerfully argue, then a flourishing church life is vital for politics, for deciding what society is for and how its aims should be achieved. Nichols' view contradicts that of Habgood in holding that establishment is hindering the church's mission to promote true faith, and misleading the Church of England into hanging on to much too wide a brief. 'The Church's concern is, in this sense, a limited one; its business is religion.'[35] The Church cannot be expected to cope with the whole panoply of modern health, education, welfare, recreation and all the other needs and expectations of people. Nichols believes that the values of society come through the faith and character of individuals, and that the liberal state has no values of its own to offer, 'the liberal house cannot ultimately stand on its own, and the foundations which the sceptic can provide are made of sand'.[36]

Society needs the church and the church needs to know that before withdrawing further into the shadows, or awkwardly apologising for its own existence and fitting its message to the emotive contemporary feel. No doubt it

---

[33]T.S. Eliot, *The Idea of a Christian Society* (London: Faber & Faber, 1939) 63.
[34]Nichols, *Church and State* 15.
[35]*Ibid.*, 23.
[36]*Ibid.*, 24.

weakens itself by continued division and powerful claims against the validity of other churches, proselytism by negative campaigning. The question of the monarchy's future, now at the centre of public debate, hopefully will stimulate the churches to see how a further coming together and sharing of power can create some fresh theological and practical synthesis. The Church of England is damaged by the present system of establishment which loads it with state concerns it can ill afford to handle, by distracting it from its primary pastoral task, by perpetuating a false self-confidence gained from the fondness of folk religion of most of the population.

Establishment, as currently constituted and practised, dilutes the specifically Christian mission of the Church of England[37] and alienates a major segment of Non-conformity. Disestablishment, if radical, would be a declaration that this is a secular society *in principle*, which, for reasons given by Nichols, may not be wise or proper move for the good of society. The debate about the monarchy and the possibility of its going Roman Catholic presses the issue of an ecumenical soft version of establishment, cut free from the crown since a Roman Catholic monarch, out of sacramental communion with most of the Christian citizenry, would be a symbol of division rather than inclusivity, which was always the aim of the Elizabethan settlement. The lack of a confessional identity on the part of the Church of England alone among the denominations, save perhaps the Baptists, locates it as 'catholic' in the pre-Reformation sense, fitting it for a role with other churches as an ecumenicised established church on the Scottish, rather than English, model.[38]

---

[37]O'Donovan describes the Church of England's mode of addressing the nation as that of bracketing the fact of being a Christian Church for fear of using assumptions not shared by much of the nation, clearly a disastrous mistake or loss of nerve probably caused by the established status. See *Resurrection and Moral Order* (Leicester: IVP 1986) 20-21. The Recent Roman Catholic publication on social ethics avoids this, its avowed audience being its own community of faith with others 'overhearing' what is said; surely the latter model is vastly superior and indeed more helpful and welcome by society at large, the majority of which identify themselves as culturally Christian in any case if opinion polls are to be believed.

[38]Indeed developments are afoot in Scotland for uniting the mainline churches, including the established Church of Scotland.

Chapter 13

EGALITARIANISM AND HIERARCHY IN THE BIBLICAL TRADITIONS

Richard Bauckham

Egalitarianism and hierarchy are two opposed forms of thinking about the structures of human society and the ordering of human relationships. For hierarchical thought, human beings are fundamentally unequal, such that some are entitled to power and privilege over others. The rule of superiors over inferiors is justified either by nature or by divine decree or both. Some humans may be considered to be by nature inherently superior to others and thus designed by nature to rule their inferiors. This is how, for example, Aristotle justified slavery, and how many nineteenth-century Europeans justified their empires. Alternatively or additionally, hierarchical structures of domination and subordination may be justified by divine ordination. Thus, in much medieval thinking about both ecclesiastical and secular political and social hierarchy, the model was of a hierarchy in which God, as the ultimate source of all power, devolved power downwards, in the first place to the pope and/or the emperor, and subsequently through lower levels of God-given authority. By contrast, for egalitarian thought, human beings are fundamentally equal, such that none is entitled to status and privilege above others. Insofar as the exercise of power and authority by some is necessary, it is justifiable only as a responsibility to be exercised on behalf of all and in the interests of all. Egalitarian thought has inspired the modern search for democratic structures which can place power ultimately in the hands of all people equally and can ensure that rule is exercised with responsibility to and for all.

The most powerful critique of hierarchy is currently the feminist one.[1] Since it is a critique which in many cases extends to the role of the Bible as promoting and sanctioning hierarchy, it is an appropriate point of entry to a consideration of this issue as a biblical hermeneutical issue. The feminist critique, of course, focuses on patriarchy, the hierarchical ideology which in western Christian societies has sanctioned not only the domination of some men over others, but also the domination of men in general over women in general. The feminist critique further recognizes that, in traditional western Christian thought, these structures of domination in human society belong to a broader hierarchical ideology, which envisages all of reality in a hierarchical structure. The overall hierarchical structure is: God–man–woman–nature. In this structure the man–woman hierarchy is legitimized and strengthened by its place in a wider cosmic hierarchy. Male rule over women is justified by seeing men as closer to God and more rational, while women are closer to nature and more physical. The man–woman hierarchy coheres in this way with the hierarchies of human rule over the rest of creation and of the superiority of reason to body, both of which have played key roles, along with patriarchy, in the western tradition.

It is evident that traditional ideas of God are implicated in this overall hierarchical scheme of thought about cosmic reality and the structures of human society. In the feminist critique, traditional Christian ideas of God belong to the patriarchal system and provide ideological support for it. The image of God as male reflects and reinforces the rule of man over woman. When God is imaged as King or Father, images of male rule are projected onto the deity. ('Father' is

---

[1]The kind of feminist critique of hierarchy which is briefly outlined here is common to most feminist thought: for very different examples see R.R. Ruether, *Gaia and God: An Ecofeminist Theology of Earth Healing* (London: SCM Press, 1993); D. Hampson, *After Christianity* (London: SCM Press, 1996).

as much an image of male domination as 'King' is. The father rules his family, and ancient kings often called themselves the fathers of their nations.) The feminist critique of masculine language and imagery for God is badly misunderstood if it is taken to involve only the issue of gender. The critique combines the issues of gender and hierarchical domination, which, according to feminists, have been inseparable in western Christian tradition. Male images of God portray not merely a divine male but a divine patriarch, who rules at the summit and source of the whole structure of patriarchal hierarchy. Hence much feminist theology rejects traditional ideas of divine transcendence, which seem to set God above us and so sanction a generally hierarchical way of thinking.

There can be little doubt that much of the western Christian tradition is vulnerable to this feminist critique of hierarchy, though it is arguable that there have also been significantly egalitarian trends in the tradition. The aim of the present chapter is not to discuss the tradition, but rather to argue that the Bible itself should not be regarded as the source and guarantor of western hierarchical ideology. It is a mistake to read through the lens of hierarchical thinking, as much of the western Christian tradition in the past has read it and as much feminist theological criticism today reads it. The overall direction of biblical thought, it will be argued, is egalitarian. Its tendency is not in support of but away from hierarchical structures in human society, and biblical images of God's rule function not to legitimate human hierarchy, but to relativize or to de-legitimize it.[2]

Two biblical strategies

It is certainly not the case that advocacy of egalitarian social structures is everywhere apparent in the Bible. What can, however, be argued is that running through the biblical

---

[2]Unfortunately, space prevents an account of biblical thought on the relation of humans to the rest of creation, which would be important in a full discussion of the issue.

traditions is a strongly egalitarian *direction* of thought,[3] operating especially to critique relationships of privilege, which give one person or class privileges or rights at the expense of others who lack them. This egalitarianism takes, in both testaments, two different forms. One form is radical opposition to hierarchical relationships and structures. It de-legitimizes such structures altogether and requires egal-itarian relationships and structures instead. The other, less radical form accepts hierarchical structures while trying to ensure that they operate for the good of all, rather than for the particular benefit of the privileged. Instead of radical opposition to hierarchy, this second form of egalitarianism is a strategy of relativizing and transforming hierarchy. Since it involves a pragmatic acceptance of hierarchical structures as a starting-point, its egalitarian *direction* can be missed by a static reading of the texts which fails to observe the dynamic of biblical thought. But when this second attitude to hier-archy is recognized as tending in an egalitarian direction, then the two forms of egalitarianism can be seen to be alter-native strategies aiming in the same direction. The strategy of radical opposition to hierarchy and the strategy of relativization and transformation of hierarchy are alternative routes towards the same goal.

Both strategies can be observed in both testaments. The difference between the testaments lies in the main focus of the issue of egalitarianism in each case. In the Old Testa-ment, egalitarianism is expressed primarily in the form of the economic equality of family households, while the form of hierarchy which has to be addressed is the political hier-archy constituted by the monarchy. In the New Testament, egalitarianism is expressed primarily in the form of the equality of individuals in the family of faith, while the form of hierarchy which has to be addressed is that of the house-hold. This is not to say that equality of individuals is in no way a concern in the Old Testament, or that political hier-archy is never addressed in the New Testament. But as a relative difference of focus, the contrast just stated is valid

---

[3]For the hermeneutical principle of discerning the direction of biblical thought, see R. Bauckham, *The Bible in Politics: How to read the Bible politically* (London: SPCK, 1989) 103.

and will enable us to observe how the two biblical strategies in relation to equality and hierarchy are both operative in both testaments, though taking different forms because of the different foci of the issue in the two testaments.

Old Testament

In the Old Testament, the *source* of the egalitarian direction lies in the event which made Israel YHWH's people: the Exodus.[4] The powerful memory of the Exodus, which reverberates through Israel's traditions of faith, was a memory of liberation from slavery. As slaves in Egypt, the Israelites had been at the bottom of a strongly hierarchical social structure, which stretched from the divine Pharaoh, who exercised absolute sovereignty by virtue of his relation to the gods, down to foreign slaves like the Israelites. The value of persons decreased as one moved down the scale. At the Exodus, YHWH took the side of the slaves against the divine Pharaoh, overturned the hierarchy, and by emancipating the slaves set his face against oppressive structures based on privilege. The God of the Exodus was clearly not the kind of god who devolved power and privilege downwards from a divine king. The God of the Exodus was the God of freed slaves, and therefore the ideal of society which arose from the Exodus was that of a people always mindful of the fact that they had been slaves, (*e.g.*, Exod. 23:9; Lev. 19:33-34; 25:42; Deut. 24:18). Such a people should not set up the kinds of structures of privilege and exploitation from which they themselves had suffered. They should form a community free of oppressive structures, and with provisions to protect any who might be vulnerable to exploitation. In this way the Exodus was the source of a radically egalitarian ideal, frequently forgotten but always there to be recovered and applied in criticism of hierarchy and privilege.

In pre-monarchical Israel the egalitarian ideal seems to have achieved a reasonable—in its historical context, remarkable—degree of practical realization. The *form* which egalitarianism took was the basic economic equality of

---

[4]See, *e.g.*, P.D. Hanson, *The People Called: The Growth of Community in the Bible* (San Francisco: Harper & Row, 1987) 20-24.

family households. In this structure the individual featured primarily as a member of a household: the three-generational family unit, of varying size. While this is alien to a modern egalitarian perspective, the Israelite perspective focuses on the household because this was the economic unit. It is above all an economically realistic form of egalitarianism, recognizing that, since power and privilege come from the accumulation of wealth, real equality must have an economic base. The prevalent modern notion that equality in democratic rights can coexist with large-scale economic inequality would have made no sense to anyone in ancient societies, which fully recognized that wealth is what gives some people status and power over others.

In the agrarian society of early Israel, the individual could not normally be economically self-sufficient. The economic unit was the family group, working together, in often harsh conditions, to make a living from its plot of land. The essential need was that each family should have its own portion of land, sufficient for subsistence and inalienable. Israelite law was designed to ensure that land could not pass permanently out of the kinship group in which it passed down by inheritance.[5] If people were obliged, through debt, to sell land, there were provisions for the re-demption of land by relatives, while in the jubilee year all land should revert to its original family. Of course, there could be no mathematical equality of economic resources. But accumulation of land—by which some families grow wealthier and others lose their livelihood—should not, according to the law, happen. When it did happen, in disregard of the law, the prophets denounce it (*e.g.,* Isa. 5:8; Micah. 2:1-2).

Even in this system of inalienable family landownership, some people will be unable support themselves. The three groups, repeatedly mentioned in the laws and the prophets as paradigmatic, are widows, orphans (*i.e.,* categories of people who, if they owned land, could not work it themselves) and resident aliens (*i.e.,* foreign workers who did not own land). Israelite laws in a variety of ways make provision for the support of these people who fall outside the household economic structure. The focus on the house-

---

[5]See, *e.g.,* Hanson, *The People Called,* 63-65.

hold is not therefore to the exclusion of individuals. Most individuals are considered as integral to family units with collective economic resources, but the whole society must take responsibility for those who are not in this position.

This land-based form of egalitarianism has an important theological basis in the idea that the land is the land YHWH has given to his people, who hold it in trust from him. He has apportioned it fairly to provide for the support of all of his people. To deprive Israelites of their family inheritance of land is, in effect, to challenge God's rule over his people. God's rule over Israel is intimately related to God's gift of the land to Israel, since in the ancient world kings were commonly considered to own the whole land they ruled. This was the basis on which they could demand taxes from the land their subjects held by their permission, or even reappropriate the land for their own use.[6] In Israel's case, since God is the king who owns the land, there seems no place for a human king. With the absence of a human king went the absence of the other social strata of wealth and privilege that monarchy entailed in ancient practice. God's sole kingship over his people was the foundation for an egalitarian, non-hierarchical structure opposed to human monarchy and the structures of inequality associated with it.

Of course, early Israel had leaders, especially for military purposes, but the so-called judges had no court and founded no dynasty: the opportunities for power and privilege to become entrenched were avoided. The theocratic principle is expressed by Gideon when the people invite him to rule as king: 'I will not rule over you, and my son will not rule over you; YHWH will rule over you' (Judg. 8:22-23). Even more revealing of the anti-monarchical principle of Israel's egalitarian tradition is the account of the origins of the monarchy in 1 Samuel 8. Israel wishes to abandon her distinctive non-monarchical egalitarianism and have a king 'like the other nations' (8:5), thereby rejecting YHWH's rule over them. In a remarkable warning Samuel spells out what human kingship means: subjection to absolute monarchy,

---

[6]This is what Ahab does in 1 Kings 21, bringing him into direct conflict with YHWH's own rule over his people.

and the growth of a military and bureaucratic elite made rich at the expense of the peasantry (8:11-17). In the climactic summary—'you will be his slaves' (8:17)—Samuel implies that Israel will, in effect, be reversing the Exodus, rejecting the liberating kingship of YHWH in favour of the enslaving rule of a human monarch like Pharaoh. Since this time they are choosing oppression with their eyes open, YHWH will not hear their cry for deliverance as he did at the Exodus, but leave them to the fate they have chosen (8:18). In this passage we see how clear-sighted the Israelite tradition of radical opposition to monarchy was about the evils of political hierarchy as it actually developed in Israel: the growth of a rich landowning class, the draining of resources from the peasantry to support the elite, the impoverishment of many of the peasantry, the radical inequality of status and wealth. We can also see clearly why monarchy was seen to threaten the Israelite ideal of a free society of equals, subject only to the liberating rule of YHWH.

From a pragmatic point of view no doubt there was a certain inevitability about the development of monarchy, if Israel was to survive in a world of strong, centralized states. Stable, centralized political structures that were not monarchical and hierarchical had not been invented. It is not surprising that the monarchy is accepted in much of the Old Testament. But it is accepted with major qualifications. In other words, the second strategy of ancient Israelite egalitarianism comes into play. While the first strategy opposes human monarchy as incompatible with YHWH's sole rule, the second attempts to co-opt the monarchy to the service of YHWH's rule over his people. This involves relativizing monarchy's pretensions to absolute power: in Israel, YHWH's people, the king is *not* to rule like the kings of other nations. It also involves insisting that the king's function is to serve his people (*cf.*,1 Kings 12:7). The strategy is to attempt to ensure that, since there is hierarchy, it should be as far as possible benevolent hierarchy, serving not the interests of the privileged but the interests of all, especially the most vulnerable.

Three different examples of this strategy will suffice. First, the only passage about kingship in the Mosaic law (Deut. 17:14-20) envisages a king who is as unlike the kings of the nations and as much like the ideal 'judges' of pre-monarchical Israel as possible. The king is not to exalt himself above his fellow-Israelites, but to rule *as one of* his people. The king's power and privileges are relativized to the extent of requiring, if it were conceivable, an egalitarian form of monarchy. Here the second strategy is so radically applied as to be virtually the first strategy in disguise.

Second, Psalm 72, a coronation psalm, provides, as one might expect, an idealized version of the monarchy. However, this is not an idealization that cloaks oppression, but an idealization that demands justice. The two interwoven themes of the psalm are the prayer that the king should execute God's righteousness for his people and the prayer for the prosperity of the king's reign. It is clear that the prosperity is conditional on the justice, which, since it is God's justice, is justice for the poor and the needy, deliverance for the oppressed, support for the weak and vulnerable (Ps. 72:2, 4, 12-14). The king is not to be the summit of a hierarchy of oppression, in which the poor and the vulnerable are at the bottom. On the contrary, the king's prime duty is to protect and to support the poor and the vulnerable. This is an entirely practicable ideal, since, as the highest judicial authority, the king had the unique power to intervene on behalf of those denied their rights in local courts, where the powerful could all too easily bend justice to their interests. If the king's highest authority were aligned with God's concern for the disadvantaged, then the king could be the hope of justice for the poor. Of course, there is no earthly sanction to ensure that the king fulfils this ideal, but should he do so, monarchy, by adopting the concerns of God's rule, justifies itself as the servant of God's rule. It is no accident that this monarchical ideal became the messianic hope for a king who would execute justice for the poor (Isa. 11:4).

Third, the ideal, such as we see in Psalm 72, of a king who implements God's righteousness, especially in protecting the needy and the vulnerable, is the criterion by which the prophets assessed the actual kings of Judah and Israel, found many of them severely wanting, and pronounced

God's judgement on them.[7] For example, Jeremiah praises Josiah for judging the cause of the poor and needy, but condemns his son Jehoiakim for thinking that being a king consists in building palaces at the expense of his people (Jer. 22:13-17). The prophets never fully accepted the entrenched privilege of a royal dynasty, because for them YHWH remains the true king of his people who intervenes in judgement to remove kings and royal houses who fail to rule as his anointed. Again we see the relativization of royal power and pretensions by means of belief in divine sovereignty.

New Testament

In the New Testament the *source* of the egalitarian direction lies initially in Jesus' understanding of God's fatherly concern for each individual person, and subsequently also in the Christian conviction that this love of God was enacted in Jesus' death for each individual, such that one's brother or sister must be valued as one for whom Christ died.

Jesus appropriated the radical egalitarian tradition of Israel,[8] but instead of focusing on the image of God as king (making Israelites all equally his subjects), he preferred to think of God's rule in terms of the image of God as Father, making all Israelites equally his children, brothers and sisters to each other. (The use of 'brother' for 'fellow-Israelite' is already an Old Testament usage, but one which comes into its own in the New Testament through the unprecedented extent to which Jesus privileged the image of God as Father.) The family image becomes primary. Instead of the egalitarianism of family units in early Israel, Jesus was concerned with the equality of family members in the renewed community of Israel, envisioned as a family of faith.

It is very striking that, in this context, Jesus disallows human fathers. Just as in the radical form of Old Testament egalitarianism, the equality of all Israelites under the sole

---

[7]See, *e.g.*, P. D. Miller, 'The Prophetic Critique of Kings,' *Ex Auditu* 2 (1986) 82-95.

[8]On what follows see, in more detail, R. Bauckham, 'Kingdom and Church according to Jesus and Paul,' *Horizons in Biblical Theology* 18 (1996) 4-13.

rule of YHWH means there cannot be a human king in Israel, so in Jesus' teaching, representing the radical form of New Testament egalitarianism, the equality of all means there cannot be human fathers. Among the new relationships Jesus establishes in the community of his disciples, the renewed Israel, fatherhood is pointedly excluded (Matt. 23:9; Mark 3:35; 10:29-30). It is excluded because it represents hierarchical authority in the family. (The mother's authority over small children did not significantly survive their coming of age, whereas the father held authority over all family members.) Jesus abolishes patriarchal authority in the renewed Israel because patriarchal authority belongs exclusively to God. This is the necessary corollary of his transposition of the Israelite egalitarianism of divine kingship into the familial image of God's rule as his fatherhood.

Also indicative of Jesus' radical vision of a society without status or privilege is the way he makes those who had the lowest status or lacked any status in hierarchical society the paradigms or models of what it means to belong to the kingdom of God. He makes slaves the paradigm for status in the kingdom of God, when he acts as a slave to his disciples by washing their feet, and requires them to do the same for each other (John 13:3-15). He makes the poor—*i.e.*, the destitute, who lack any reliable means of support—the paradigm for status in the kingdom of God, when he pronounces them blessed, as those to whom the kingdom belongs (Matt. 5:3; Luke 6:20). And since children had no social status at all, he makes them the model for the lack of status which all must accept on entering the kingdom of God (Matt. 18:1-4; Mark 10:13-16). If the kingdom of God belongs to slaves, the destitute and children, then others can enter the kingdom only by accepting the same lack of status. The kingdom of God makes all equal by requiring all to come down to the level of the lowest. In this way Jesus envisages and implements an egalitarianism in radical opposition to the hierarchical structures of his contemporary society.

In the churches of the Pauline mission, which are the churches about which we know most in this respect, Jesus' radical egalitarianism made a strong impact. Christians were a family of faith, brothers and sisters to each other, relating to each other without the structures of privilege and status which subordinated one to another in society around them. This egalitarianism was one of the strikingly counter-cultural features of early Christianity and is classically expressed in Galatians 3:28, which declares the typical relationships of inequality and privilege (Jew/Greek; slave/free; male/female) to have no validity in Christ (*cf.*, 1 Cor. 12:13; Col. 3:11).

While in many respects this egalitarianism successfully resisted the highly hierarchical structures of the early churches' social environment,[9] the strategy of radical opposition to such structures was not uniformly applied. As in the Old Testament, another strategy also evolved, in which the hierarchy was not rejected from the outset, but relativized and transformed. Whereas in the Old Testament the hierarchy in question was monarchy, with the political and social structures it entailed, in the New Testament the focus is especially on the hierarchy of the household. This is natural in view of the nature of the early Christian communities, but it also means that the relationships within the household are especially the focus of the tension between egalitarianism and hierarchy in the New Testament: the egalitarianism of the new household of faith has to be related to the hierarchical structures of the old households to which many of its members still belong. (A revealing point at which the two languages of household relationships are juxtaposed is when Paul asks Philemon to receive Onesimus 'no longer as a slave but more than a slave, a beloved brother' [Philem. 16].)

The second strategy can be seen most clearly in the 'household codes' of Colossians (3:18-4:1), Ephesians (5:21-6:9) and 1 Peter (2:18-3:7), which address Christians in the roles they played in the three main forms of relationship within the household: husbands and wives, parents and children, masters and slaves. All three relationships were understood in contemporary society in strongly hierarchical terms: the husband, the parent and the master have authority; the wife, the child and the slave are subordinate. Hierarchical subordination in the household was normally thought essential to order in society, and Christians must

---

[9]For other aspects of it in the Pauline literature, see Bauckham, 'Kingdom and Church,' 16-20.

have felt strong pressure not to be seen to be disrupting this order. They were in fact accused of breaking up households, in cases where, for example, a wife became a Christian but her husband did not (cf., 1 Cor. 7:13-14; 1 Pet. 3:1-2). In such cases Christian faith unavoidably entailed an act of insubordination: a wife had to reject her husband's gods in order to follow a faith of which her husband disapproved. It is understandable, therefore, that Christians, who could not avoid public disapproval of such breaches of hierarchical order, might wish to reaffirm as far as possible the general hierarchical structure of household relationships.

In the advice given in New Testament letters to the superior partner in each of the hierarchical relationships of the household we can observe attempts to relativize and to transform the hierarchy. There are (1) attempts to relativize the hierarchy by reference to God's or Christ's authority. Masters are told not to threaten their slaves 'for you know that both of you have the same Master in heaven' (Eph. 6:9; cf., Col. 4:1). Christ's authority here relativizes the human master's, just as in the Old Testament God's kingship can relativize the power of a human king. (The contrast between the two strategies can be seen by comparing this passage with Matthew 23:10. There, from the fact that the disciples have 'one master, Christ' it follows that there may be no human masters among them. In Ephesians and Colossians masters are still called masters, but their subordination to Christ the master of all his Christian slaves relativizes their authority.)

There are also (2) attempts to ensure that the hierarchical relationships operate benevolently and beneficently, not oppressively or exploitatively. The person in authority is instructed to exercise it for the good of the subordinate, not in his own interests. Thus, whereas wives are told to be subject to their husbands, husbands are not told to rule their wives but to love them (Col. 3:19; Eph. 5:25; 1 Pet. 3:7), and in one case the nature of the love required is developed by means of an elaborate comparison with Christ's love for the church (Eph. 5:25-33). Just as in the Old Testament human kingship can be accepted on condition that it serves the purposes of God's rule, so here the husband's authority is acceptable only insofar as it follows the pattern of Christ's love for his people.

Most interesting is (3) the attempt to transform relationships of dominance and subordination into relationships of *mutual* subordination. The household code in Ephesians 5:21-6:9 puts all the hierarchical relationships of the household under the introductory rubric: 'Be subject to one another out of reverence for Christ' (5:21). The meaning is certainly not that some should be subject to others, but rather that there should be mutual subjection. The principle is not worked through in the case of the first two relationships (wives/husbands; children/fathers) but affects the third in a remarkable way. When slaves have been instructed to 'render service with enthusiasm, as to the Lord, not to human beings' (6:7), masters are told to 'do the same to them' (6:8). This can only mean: render service to them, serve them as slaves, as they do you. This is a radical transformation of hierarchy, which, taken fully seriously, would take the second strategy beyond itself and destroy hierarchy. At this point the egalitarian direction of the second strategy clearly converges with that of the first.

This last example is one of the best illustrations of the difference that discerning the direction of thought in a text, as in the biblical texts as a whole, can make to interpretation. On a static interpretation this text (Eph. 5:21–6:9) is likely to be read as simply endorsing hierarchy, but such a reading cannot do justice either to 5:21 or to 6:9a. A static interpretation cannot acknowledge the real tension in the text between the hierarchical structures which are accepted and the principle of mutual subordination which aims to transform them into non-hierarchical structures. A dynamic reading finds precisely in this tension a direction of thought away from hierarchy towards egalitarian relationships of mutual service. The tension in the text authorizes readers to follow its egalitarian direction further than the text does.

Divine rule and human society

It remains to draw conclusions about the Bible's use of God-language in relation to our issue. When the Bible depicts God in images of masculine hierarchical power and authority—King, Lord, Father—how do these images function in relation to the structures of human relationships and society? They certainly do not function to legitimate human hierarchies. It is not at all the case that the Bible depicts the divine King or Father as the summit of cosmic hierarchy which includes the subordination of women to men, slaves to masters, and subjects to kings. Quite the opposite. These images, though drawn from human hierarchy, come to be used as symbols of what is utterly unique to God: that transcendence of God over all creatures which puts all humans on the same level of equality before God their Creator and Lord.

Thus, in the radical strategy of opposition to hierarchy, that God is king or father means that no human should claim royal or patriarchal authority. To call God king is to recognize that all humans are equally his subjects. To call God father is to recognize that all humans are equally his children. It is to forbid humans to claim any status or privilege above their fellows.

Even in the more compromising strategy, the effect of divine kingship or fatherhood is not in the direction of legitimating or bolstering human hierarchical power, but of relativizing it. It is accepted that Israel has a royal dynasty, but the king must remember that he and his subjects are equally subject to God's authority. It is accepted that there are Christian masters and slaves, but masters must remember that they are slaves of Christ no less than their slaves are. The tendency is to the levelling of hierarchy, not the entrenching of it.

Chapter 14

HOMOSEXUAL TERMINOLOGY IN 1 CORINTHIANS 6:9: THE ROMAN CONTEXT AND THE GREEK LOAN–WORD

Bruce W. Winter

Introduction

Among the many subjects to which David Wright has turned his scholarly attention, the contentious issue of homosexuality and the Bible features more than once in his list of learned publications. In this chapter it is being suggested that the *Romanitas* of Corinth has not been taken into account when discussing matters affecting early Christians there, including attitudes to homosexual conduct. This is also true of the use of words, because the Romans transliterated Greek sexual terminology into Latin for conduct related to their citizens of which they did not approve. Important light is thereby thrown on the meaning of μαλακός (*malacus*) which helps in turn in deciphering the significance of ἀρσενοκοίτης which was the other term Paul used. He also provided a soteriological key which had important implications for the interpretation and application of 1 Corinthians 6:9-11 to the pastoral needs of Corinthian Christians.

The Roman context

Roman Corinth

First century Corinth was not a Greek city but a Roman colony. This is reflected not only in the fact that its town plan of 44 BC was Roman with its typical centuriation,[1] but also that its Roman architecture and buildings made no concessions to its Greek past. Its administration followed Roman conventions, its inscriptions were Latin, and so were the coins it issued.[2] Those who founded Roman Corinth named the colony *Colonia Laus Julia Corinthiensis* and 'they avoided the more common–*ius* or–*us* ethnic, which implies that the Italian colonists wished to distinguish themselves from the original Greek inhabitants of the city.'[3]

An Argive petition only recently come to light and relating to the federal imperial cult of Archaia at the end of the Principate of Claudius and the beginning of Nero's reign, complained about the Corinthians because they did not 'respect the high authority of the ancient laws and customs' of the Greeks, but 'rather those which it seems they took over from the sovereign city' (409C).[4] As a colony it saw itself 'as a community that traditionally originated from Rome, could be regarded as an extension of Rome itself,...[and] then exuberantly claim to form part of the grandeur and majesty

---

[1]See D.G. Romano, 'Post-146 B.C. Land Use in Corinth, and Planning of the Roman Colony of 44 B.C.', *The Corinthia in the Roman Period*, Supp. J.R.A. (1994) 9-30. On Roman town plans and buildings see E.J. Owens, 'Roman Town Planning' in ed. I.M. Barton *Roman Public Buildings*, Exeter Studies in History 20 (Exeter: University of Exeter, 1989) ch. 1 and E.J. Owens, *The City in the Greek and Roman World* (London and New York: Routledge, 1991).

[2]M. Amandry, *Le Monnayage des duovirs corinthiens*, BCH Supplement 15, Paris (1988).

[3]D. Engels, *Roman Corinth: An Alternative Model for the Classical City* (Chicago: University of Chicago Press, 1990) 69 citing *CIG* 1 no. 106.

[4]*The Letters of Julian* no. 28. For its first–century dating and discussion see A.J.S. Spawforth, 'Corinth, Argos and the Imperial Cult: Pseudo-Julian, letters 198' *Herperia* 63.2 (1994) 211-32 which was reproduced as an abbreviated form in 'The Achaean Federal Imperial Cult: Pseudo–Julian Letters 189', *Tyn.B.* 46.1 (1995) 151–68.

of Rome'.[5] Had Roman Corinth valued the heritage of its Greek predecessor which had not functioned as a city for a century,[6] then the payment of heavy tribute for extravagant entertainment for the provincial imperial cult would not have been required of Argos, so the citizens of the latter city argued (409C). The reference to the expensive purchase of bears and panthers for its 'hunting shows' and not for gymnastic or musical contests shows Corinth's preferences were for the former which was a Roman innovation and not part of Greek culture (παιδεία) (409A). 'Corinth's control of the Isthmian games provided another means by which the city could act as a pro–Roman focal point in Achaian life'.[7] They were one of the three most important religious and athletic festivals in Greece and were held biennially. Every four years the Caesarean Games and the Imperial Contests were held, having begun in the time of Tiberius to honour the imperial family. The Ceasarean and Imperial contests provided opportunities to compete for the best encomium to the emperor and his family. Upon these ancient Greek games they consciously stamped *Romanitas*.[8]

While there were other Roman colonies in Archaia culturally none had quite the 'strong gravitational pull' towards things Roman that Corinth had.[9] Corinth was self–consciously Roman in its outlook and cultural preferences and was 'the centre of *Romanitas*' in Greece.[10]

---

[5]E.T. Salmon, *Roman Colonization under the Republic* (London: Thames and Hudson, 1969) 136.

[6]W. Willis, 'Corinthusne deletus est?' *BZ*, 35 (1991) 233-41 and the important reply by D.W.J. Gill, 'Corinth: A Roman Colony of Achaea' *BZ*, 37 (1993) 259-64 who assembled and interpreted the evidence showing that civic discontinuity was what was really meant.

[7]S.E. Alcock, *Graecia Capta: The Landscapes of Roman Greece* (Cambridge: CUP, 1993) 169.

[8]Engels, *Roman Corinth*: 51–2.

[9]E.T. Salmon, *Roman Colonization under the Republic*, (London: Thames and Hudson, 1969) 136.

[10]A. Spawforth and P. Cartledge, *Hellenistic and Roman Sparta: A Tale of Two Cities*, (London: Routledge, 1989) 104.

Roman law in Corinth and homosexuality

An Argive petition concerning Corinth states what was true in Roman colonies. Roman law operated in them—'in reliance on the laws they now have, they claim that their city has gained the advantages since they received the colony from Rome' (409D), laws which it indicates elsewhere are not those of ancient Greece but rather 'those which it seems they took over from the sovereign city' *i.e.*, Rome (409A). As homosexuality came under Roman criminal law it is important that we first examine this before we proceed to discuss attitudes to it, on the premise that Roman society was greatly influenced by Roman law.[11]

In a recent work on criminal law in Rome, Robinson in his chapter 'Sexual Offences' devotes a section to homosexuality as an offence.[12] The *lex Scantinia* (*c.* 149 BC) named after a plebeian tribune, Scantinius, is said to have dealt with homosexuality.[13] It is known to have been invoked 100 years later. In a letter to Cicero in September, 50 BC Caelius indicates that a charge has been made under that law as part of a vexatious campaign against him. At the same time he charged Appius in public under the same law, and notes with some satisfaction 'the scandal of it has given Appius more pain than the fact of his being charged'.[14] It was clearly in operation a century and a half later in the reign of Domitian where Suetonius reports that the emperor 'administered justice scrupulously and conscientiously' and cites as an example that he 'condemned several men of both orders [senatorial and equestrian], offenders against the Scantinian

[11]See J. Crook, 'Introduction' *Law and Life in Rome* (Ithaca, New York: Cornell University Press, 1967) ch. 1 where he argues that compared with English society the Romans were much better acquainted with their law and this certainly was true where Roman law dealt with marriage and sexuality.

[12]O.F. Robinson, *The Criminal Law of Ancient Rome* (London: Duckworth, 1995) ch. v, 70–1.

[13]See S. Lilja, *Homosexuality in Republican and Augustan Rome* (Helsinki: Societas Scientiarum Fennica, 1982) 112–21 who sought to argue the law was not concerned with homosexual crimes. See note 18 below for a comment on her own admission of the difficulties of her case.

[14]Cicero, *Letters to Friends* 8.12 and 14. On vexatious litigation see D.F. Epstein, *Personal Enmity in Roman Politics 218–43 BC* (London: Routledge, 1987) 90–100.

Law'.[15] When Augustus had earlier legislated in the general area of sexuality,[16] the law 'defined all sexual intercourse with people of either sex who fell under the law as *stuprum*, a word which was in general use for any irregular or promiscuous sexual acts'[17] or what was known as 'debauchery', *e.g.*, *stuprum cum masculo* as in the following case. According to Quintilian, writing at the end of the first century, a legal case could be argued where someone 'debauched a free–born citizen (*ingenuum stupravit*) and the latter hanged himself, but that was no reason for the author to be awarded capital punishment as having caused the death; he will instead pay 10,000 sesterces, the fine imposed by law', 4.2.69.[18] Roman law protected the rights of its free–born citizen (*ingenuus*).

> The qualification 'free–born' highlights the fundamental difference between the attitude of Athenians and Romans...on this matter [homosexuality]. Whereas Solon had forbidden slaves to partake in homosexual practices, at Rome it was only slaves and other non–citizens who could legitimately be used for them; and could be used without restraint. There was something sacred about the person of a Roman citizen.[19]

Roman Corinthian attitudes to homosexuality

The Argive petition reminds us that the Corinthians followed the Roman 'custom' (νόμιμος), 409C. What would the

---

[15]Suetonius, *Domitian* 8.
[16]For a full discussion of the legislation see L.F. Raditsa, 'Augustus' Legislation concerning Marriage, Procreation, Love Affairs and Adultery' *ANRW* II. 13 (1980) 278-339 and more recently J.E. Grubbs, '"Pagan" and "Christian" Marriage: The State of the Question' *Journal of Early Christian Studies* (1994) 361-412.
[17]S. Treggiari, *Roman Marriage: Iusti coniuges from the Time of Cicero to the Time of Ulpian* (Oxford: Clarendon Press, 1991) 264.
[18]Lilja, *Homosexuality in Republican and Augustan Rome* 133 is forced to concede in her conclusion that all would be well for her interpretation of the *lex Scantinia* 'if Quintilian had not referred to [this] law' cited here which in effect undermines her thesis.
[19]L.P. Wilkinson, *Classical Attitudes to Modern Issues: Population and Family Planning; Women's Liberation; Nudism in Deed and Word; Homosexuality* (London: Willima Kimber, 1979) 136–7. See Petronius, *Satyricon*, 9–11, Juneval, 6.33–7.

attitude of the élite members of Roman Corinth have been to homosexuality?[20] Lucian reflects the concerns of the Romans about homosexuality when he wrote in a dialogue that it would be better that a woman invade the provinces of male wantonness (homosexuality) 'than that the nobility of the male sex should become effeminate and play the part of a woman' (ἢ τὸ γενναῖον ἀδρῶν εἰς γυναῖκα θηλύνεσθαι), *Amores*, 28.[21]

How do we account for the élite's literary tastes on homosexuality? Wiedemann observes 'In Latin poetry on homosexual themes, the characters frequently have Greek names, and the object of the poet's love is not a respectable boy of citizenship status but a *declassé* or a slave.'[22] The sexual penetration of male slaves, some of whom were specifically purchased for the purpose, was approved by the Romans. However, Cato rebuked them because in Rome 'pretty boys fetched more than fields'.[23] In Roman Corinth Charicles was said to be 'only fond of the wrestling schools because of his love of "passive partners" (παιδικός)'.[24]

In Roman political oratory, including forensic rhetoric, homosexual passivity which was equated with effeminacy was the butt of humour and hubris. 'In the particular process of defining and enforcing the importance of masculinity in

---

[20]For a discussion of this issue see my 'Gluttony and Immorality at Élitist Banquets: The Background to 1 Corinthians 6:12–20' *Jian Dao* 7 (January, 1997) 55–67 where I suggest that the ethics being argued for are by young Roman male citizens, and for a wider discussion of ethical permissiveness covering all of 1 Cor. see my 'Élitist Ethics and Christian Permissiveness', *After Paul left Corinth: The Impact of Secular Ethics and Social Change* (Grand Rapids: Eerdmans, 1998) ch. 4.

[21]θηλύνω=become soft, *i.e.*, to actually become a passive homosexual. γυναῖκα is a derivative of ὁ γύννις = an effeminate male.

[22]T. Wiedemann, *Adults and Children in the Roman Empire* (London: Routledge, 1989) 30–1. Polybius, 31.25.4–5.

[23]E. Eyben, *Restless Youth in Ancient Rome* (ET London: Routledge, 1995) 245.

[24]Lucian, *Amores* 9. παιδικός=*pedico*, a passive homosexual. Cf. *P.Tebt.* 104 l. 20 (92 BC) where the marriage contract forbids the husband 'to have a male passive lover', παιδικὸν ἔχειν.

Roman culture, public speakers found an easy target for their insecurities in the person of the effeminate male.'[25]

There was the open liaison between C. Vibius Maximus, a Prefect of Egypt (107-12 AD), and a 'still beardless...and handsome youth' who dined and travelled with him, rather attended the school and the gymnasium.[26] He was a seventeen year old *ephebus*. The 'shameless conduct of the young man coming out of the bedchamber alone showing signs of intercourse with him', and appearing before the assembled gathering who were waiting to give the *salutatio* to the Prefect, told against him in the advocate's speech. The young lover accompanied the Prefect to the praetorium and travelled with him on his assize around Egypt and 'once accustomed to his shame this handsome and rich youth gave himself airs and became so impudent...in the presence of every one and laughed long and freely in the middle of the clients'. The recording in such detail evidence that substantiated a homosexual liaison would only be apposite if the criminal act of the penetration of a young Roman citizen was among the charges being brought against Maximus. Because of his overall conduct he subsequently suffered *damnatio memoriae* with his name being removed from public monuments.[27]

---

[25]A. Corbeill, 'Moral Appearance in Action: Effeminancy', *Controlling Laughter: Political Humor in the Late Roman Republic* (Princeton: Princeton University Press, 1996) ch. 4, citation 130. In this excellent chapter Corbeill demonstrates 'Extant evidence strongly supports the notion that our constructed effeminate male constitutes a real category of person to whom distinguishing and distinctive codes of behaviour can be ascribed', 131.

[26]These activities epitomised education, Lucian, *Amores*, 45.

[27]Maladministration was also alleged in *P.Oxy.* 471 (second century AD) where two columns are missing. If the charges were vexatious, then allegations of effeminancy would be apposite, Corbeill, 'Moral Appearance in Action: Effeminancy', 148 and not a charge of *muliero*, an act of *pedicatio* perpetrated against a boy which was presumably being brought under the *lex Scantinia*. R. Syme, 'C. Vibius Maximus, Prefect of Egypt' *Historia* 6 (1957) 484 refers to the various charges 'notably and lavishly the scandal of a *puer delicatus*' citing this papyrus and epigraphic evidence.

The sexual loan-word

Discussions of sexual terminology need to be more nuanced than is sometimes the case in New Testament studies. Nowhere is this more needed than in the debate that has surrounded the two words used by Paul in 1 Corinthians 6:9 for homosexuality. The problems are highlighted by the vast number of words and allusions to sexual conduct as the work by J.N. Adams on *The Latin Sexual Vocabulary* shows.[28] The *Sitz im Leben* is important. Terms used in *De Medicina* by the medical writer Aulus Cornelius Celsus in the reign of Tiberius, or the famous Galen in the following century, on sexual anatomy and activity, will be very different from those scratched on the walls of Pompeii which advertised the most ancient of trades. The discussions in Petronius' *Satyricon* or Apulaeus' *Metamorphosis or the Gold Ass*, which are in the *genre* of the salacious historical novel, will again use more ribald terms.[29] Geographical and cultural differences can account for variations in terms or different meaning assigned to the same term between Greece and Egypt, as Monserrat's work shows.[30]

Religious contexts also influenced choices where a more restrained *vox propria* would be used. Such language would not be found in graffiti in Pompeii or Herculaneum. The Jewish works of Philo of Alexander who was Paul's contemporary and *The Sentences of Phocylides* provide examples. 'Transgress not for unlawful sex the natural limits of sexuality. For even animals are not pleased by intercourse of male with male.'[31]

---

[28]London: Duckworth, 1982.

[29]See ed. J. Tatum, *The Search for the Ancient Novel* (Baltimore: Johns Hopkins University Press, 1994) and ed. G. Schnaling, *The Novel in the Ancient World* (Leiden: E.J. Brill, 1996).

[30]D. Monserrat, *Sex and Society in Graeco–Roman Egypt* (London: Kegan Paul, 1996) esp. 107–8 on the different uses of πόρνη, παιδικός and ἑταιρίς in the different geographical locations.

[31]*The Sentences of Phocylides* ll. 190–1. Κύπρις is used to describe an unlawful sexual act. Cf. Lucian, *Amores* 22 for the same animal analogy.

The Latin borrowing of Greek sexual terminology

Cultural susceptibilities and moral attitudes play a highly significant role in the choice of terms as Adams' important observation shows.

> Forms of perversion [to the Roman mind]...tend to be ascribed particularly to foreign people, and those perversions may be described by a word from the foreign language in question. Various words to do with homosexuality in Latin are of Greek origin (*pedico, pathicus, cinaedus, catamitus*; cf. *malacus*)...But the sexual organs and ordinary sexual behaviour did not attract loan-words.[32]

Loan-words can then provide an indicator that the Romans did not endorse activities represented by these terms.[33]

The meaning of μαλακοί in 1 Corinthians 6:9

The borrowing of the Greek term, μαλακος, is something of an indicator of what the Romans thought of the activity to which it refers. The word refers to 'a soft person'. The fact that it is in the masculine gender in the semantic field of sexuality is significant, because the 'transfer to a male of terms strictly applicable to a female suggests effeminacy of the referent with extreme forcefulness.'[34] A private letter requests 'Also send us Zenobius, the effeminate, τὸ μαλακόν, with drums and symbols and castanets, for he is wanted by the women for sacrifice: let him wear as fine clothes as possible', *P.Hib.* 1.54 (3rd century BC). It was said that 'a man's character could be known from his looks and when 'a rake' (κίναιδος) is brought in, even though his hands bore the signs of hard agricultural work, it was declared 'He is effeminate' (μαλακός ἐστι), Diogenes Laertius 7.173.[35]

---

[32]Adams, *The Latin Sexual Vocabulary*, 228. For discussion of these terms for a 'passive homosexual' see nn. 24 and 36 in this chapter.

[33]Although Celcus, *De Medicina* 6.18.1 comments on the superiority of the Greek sexual vocabulary to that current in Latin, he himself did not introduce loan–words. The reality was that the Greeks had not established any uniform terminology, Adams, *The Latin Sexual Vocabulary*, 227.

[34]Adams, *The Latin Sexual Vocabulary*, 116.

[35]See also Vettius Valens, (Teubner, 1986) 115 *l.* 31 μαλακὸς ἔσται.

Plantus, *The Braggart Warrior*, provides a good example of the meaning of μαλακός in its transliterated form. Periplectomenus who boasts of his youth, offers his services 'in every situation'. He could be a legal counsellor, the gayest dinner guest, a peerless parasite [client], or an incomparable cook. Finally he parades himself as a receptive homosexual, using the terms *cidaedus* and *malacus*. 'There is no dancer who can dance as seductively as I' (*tum ad saltandum non cidaedus malacus aequest atque ego*), line 668. The reference to this is unmistakable, as he combines it with the term *cinaedus* (κίναιδος).[36] There was the powerful myth that 'Any person who touched the stone of a *kinaidion*–fish[37] will become impotent or carries the stone unwillingly will become soft', (μαλακίζομαι) i.e. 'made effeminate'. Gleason points out that we learn what was deviant *i.e.*, what made the person effeminate. It was not the gender of the sexual object—'A man who actively penetrates and dominates others whether male or female, is still a man'. He may engage in active homosexual penetration but he is not 'soft'.[38]

Plutarch writes 'that the one who uttered the abuse was charged with effeminate practices (μαλακία) and the subsequent discussion contrasting him with a lady—'she refrained from [sexual] "commerce" with men, though you are a man' (πλείω χρόνον ἐκείνην ἀπ' ἀνδρὸς οὖσαν ἢ σε τὸν ἄνδρα), *C. Gracchus*, 4.4.[39] Vettius Valens writes 'a hermaphrodite is a catamite, an effeminate' (ἀνδρόγαμος ἔσται κίναιδος, μαλακός) who belongs to those who are regarded as lusting unnaturally (πασχητιῶν).[40]

---

[36]μαλακία and κιναιδεία are almost synonymous, Plutarch, *C. Gracchus* 4 and Dio Cassius, 58.4. The latter term orginally meant 'dancer' but because of his sexual orientation came to mean a passive homosexual, J. Colin, 'Juvénal, les baladins et les rétiaires d'après le MS d'Oxford', *Atti delle Accademia delle Scienze di Torino*, 87 (1952-53) 329-35, and Corbeill, 'Moral Appearance in Action: Effeminancy', 135-39.

[37]The term is also used of fish, Pliny, *Natural History*, 32.146.

[38]M.W. Gleason, *Making Men: Sophists and Self–Presentation in Ancient Rome* (Princeton, Princeton University Press, 1995) 65 citing, Kyranides 1.10.49–67.

[39]Corbeill, 'Appearance in Action: Effeminacy' 148.

[40]Vettius Valens, *Anthologies*, 113, 22. *Cf.*, Lucian, *Amores*, 26 where 'the man who makes attempts on a young man of twenty seems to me to be

In addition to using another standard term, κίναιδος as a synonym for μαλακός, there was the word παθικός. It refers to those who are sexually passive in a homosexual relationship. It was transliterated by some authors into Latin as *pathicus* where it also described the passive homosexual.[41]

What is an antonym for μαλακός? Literary sources provide indications of how an individual author may choose to express the dichotomy of homosexual roles. In Philo of Alexandria's discussion of pederasty he suggests that 'in former days the very mention of it was a great disgrace, but now it is a matter of boasting not only to the active but the passive partners' (οὐ τοῖς δρῶσι μόνον, ἀλλὰ καὶ τοῖς πάσχουσιν), *Spec.* III. 37. He used first a metaphor that was not inherently sexual to convey the meaning.[42] The verb δράω is descriptive, meaning 'to be active', while πάσχω means 'to be affected' by passions or feelings. In Lucian, *Amores*, 27 the 'active lover' is ὁ διαθείς and the passive person, the 'one who has been outraged' (τῷ ὑβρισμένῳ) which reflected his view that homosexual intercourse gave no pleasure at all to the young passive person whereas in a heterosexual liaison equal pleasure is enjoyed.

Is Paul's antonym for μαλακός in 6:9 the term ἀρσενοκοίτης? In an excellent article concentrating on the latter term, David Wright refuted the interpretation that it referred to 'male sexual agents', *i.e.*, male prostitutes for either male or female clients, but rather to a male who lies with another male. He also drew attention to the neglected linguistic connection with the LXX translation of Leviticus 18:22, μετὰ ἄρσενος οὐ κοιμηθήσῃ κοίτην γυναικός and especially in 20:13 where the word order of the latter's prohibition is ὅς ἂν κοιμηθῇ μετὰ ἄρσενος κοίτην γυναικός.[43] It is against a male who 'beds' or lies in bed with a male as he would with

---

unnaturally lustful (πασχητιάω) and pursuing an equivocal love' because as he explained he is fully grown and covered in bodily hair.
[41]Corbeill, 'Appearance in Action: Effeminacy' 137 and Adams, *The Latin Sexual Vocabulary*, 189–90. See Juvenal, 2.99.
[42]Adams, *The Latin Sexual Vocabulary*, 193.
[43]'Homosexuals or Prostitutes? The Meaning of ΑΡΣΕΝΟΚΟΤΑΙ (1 Cor. 6:9, 1 Tim. 1:10) *Vigiliae Christianae* 38 (1984) 125–53.

a woman.[44] The verb κοιμάω with μετά was also used in Classical Greek to refer to having sexual intercourse with another person.[45] Paul is seen to have invented the word ἀρσενοκοίτης by combining two words from Leviticus 20:13.[46] ἄρσενικος meaning 'male'=ἀρρένικος and the former is the less Attic form of the adjective ἀρρενικός.[47] Paul joins this with κοίτη which means 'bed' and of itself had sexual connotations, (*i.e.*, Num. 5:20)—he uses the term in Romans 13:13 to denote sexual debauchery. Did he read the LXX and as an interpreter of Scripture combine the two words from Leviticus 20:13, because it expressed a particular role in homosexual intercourse?

Given the Romans preoccupation with 'the nature of the masculine self' over against effeminate behaviour by males,[48] the meaning of ἀρσενοκοίτης for a male engaging in sexual penetration of another male would be explicable for a Corinthian audience. Furthermore, with the citing of the term μαλακός first with its very strong connotations of passive homosexuality, one would have expected a word describing an active homosexual. It was not a reference to a male prostitute. If Paul had been seeking a term the LXX chose ὁ πορνεύων in Deuteronomy 23:17, and this would have provided him with an appropriate one, *cf.,*1 Corinthians 6:15.[49] If ἀρσενοκοίτης had meant something other than an active homosexual person, Paul would be proscribing only passive

---

[44]Cf. Lucian, *Dialogue with the Courtesans*, 6.1 'make someone into a woman' (τὸ γυναῖκα γενέσθαι ἐκ παρθένου). The concept of turning someone into a woman by penetration, i.e making them effeminate, reflects the major Roman concern about homosexuality of its citizens.

[45]A person spends a night in bed with a female prostitute μετά χαμαιτύπτης τὴν νύκτα κοιμᾶσθαι, Timocles, *Comicus* 22.2.

[46]It is not possible to state categorically that one author invented a word because as the CD Rom of the *TLG* has shown it is not the case that some New Testament words were not *hapax legomena* since almost the entire body of literary texts from Homer to the sixth century AD can now be searched. Newly discovered papyriological or epigraphic evidence always makes it possible that the word may be pre-Pauline.

[47]*P.Oxy.* 38 (first century AD).

[48]Corfeill, 'Appearance in Action: Effeminacy' 128.

[49]The word for the female prostitute ἡ πόρνης appears six verses later. ὁ πόρνος could be used of a male prostitute, Athenaeus, *Deip.* 13 572.

homosexuality, and therefore simply be reflecting the values and attitude of Roman society on this issue.

The interpretation offered helps answer the question why Paul used two words to describe homosexual persons in 1 Corinthians 6:9, rather than one general term. He used two to refer to passive and active persons in homosexual inter-course because ancient literature expressed such a dicho-tomy in discussing it. It has been shown that the Latin trans-literation of the Greek term is an indicator that passive homosexual sexual activity did not have Roman endorse-ment for its citizens. The Roman did not condemn active penetration provided it was not with a Roman citizen. Un-like Roman society, Paul proscribed both for Christians.

Homosexuality in a wider context

Other Corinthian Christians' sexual mores

It should be observed that there was a *laissez–faire* attitude to sexuality and its expression prevailing amongst some in the Corinthian church. In 1 Corinthians 6:12-20 when Christian young men took the *toga virilis* they attended a banquet to gorge themselves with food and to fornicate with female prostitutes on the grounds that on coming of age 'all things are permitted'. It was fornication with a prostitute which established a one flesh relationship which concerned Paul and not adultery that was the outcome of the evening spent in banqueting.[50]

The Christian man who was involved in an incest-uous relationship in 1 Corinthians 5:1ff. was not condemned for what was a criminal offence under Roman law; whether this was because he was of such status that his fellow Christians could not prosecute because they did not possess

---

[50]For evidence for the use of this stock phrase and young men who were no longer subject to authority and my argument that the mis-deamour was fornication, see my 'Gluttony and Immorality at Élitist Banquets: The Background to 1 Corinthians 6:12–20', 80–1, 85–90.

equal or higher status as has been argued, or action was not taken because he was a high status person, is uncertain.[51]

Some Christians exercised their right to recline in the idol temple (1 Cor.8:9-10). I have suggested that this privilege was for Roman citizens in Corinth and was connected with the imperial games in Isthmia. There, the President of the Games invited these élite members of Corinth to dine on a number of occasions as his guests and this provided an opportunity for them to sit down to eat and drink and rise up to play (10:7-8). On these grand occasions no expense was spared and the provision of 'after dinners' as they were described involved liaisons with prostitutes from 'travelling' brothels.[52]

In 1 Corinthians 15:32-4 Paul rebukes their misdemeanours resulting from corrupting influence of bad company. The context of the citation from Menander's *Thais* in 15:33 is sexual intercourse with prostitutes. Their life-style was inappropriate, epitomised as it was by the 'unholy trinity' of gluttony, drunkenness and promiscuous behaviour, behaviour epitomising that of their compatriots.[53]

Given that Paul never hesitated to challenge different forms of promiscuous behaviour among the Christians, it is significant that a case or cases of homosexual intercourse is not one of the sexual lapses with which he has to deal, even though he noted originally 'such *were* some of you' (6:12a).

Pastoral and theological dimensions

Paul sees the need to name homosexual activities among sexual sins in 6:9. While active homosexual intercourse was tolerated in certain circumstances in Roman Corinth, Christians must not add them to the list of other sexual mores which some had defended with the dictum 'for me everything is permitted' in 6:12 and 10:23. Gentile Christians may have shared the same attitude on active homosexual

---

[51] A.D. Clarke, *Secular and Christian Leadership in Corinth: A Socio–Historical and Exegetical Study of 1 Corinthians 1–6*, (Leiden: E.J. Brill, 1993) 77–88.

[52] See 'Civic Rights' in my *Seek the Welfare of the City: Early Christians as Benefactors and Citizens*, First–Century Christians in the Graeco–Roman World (Grand Rapids & Carlisle: Eerdmans & Paternoster, 1994) ch. 9.

[53] See my 'Christian Permissiveness' for the detailed argument.

intercourse with their secular Roman counterparts, but despised passive activity while accepting its practice on the person of non–citizenship status. This may be another reason why Paul does not use a general term to describe homosexuality but indicates a prohibition on active as well as passive homosexuality.

In all the preoccupation with semantic investigations into homosexual terms in 1 Corinthians 6:9–11, as significant as they are, three important matters can easily be overlooked. For Paul, to continue to describe a Christian in terms of what he or she had been would be highly inappropriate theologically and pastorally, because he considered that a Christian is not a person who *is* 'washed, sanctified, justified', 'but (ἀλλά) *was* washed, but (ἀλλά) *was* sancitified, but (ἀλλά) was justified in the name of the Lord Jesus Christ and in the Spirit of our God' at their conversion, 6:11. He uses the aorist tense and the strong adversative ἀλλα to introduce crucial salvational terminology which is meant to convey emphatically the effectiveness of Christ's work in completely distancing a person at conversion from their past by cleansing, making holy and acquitting. Therefore, the use of the term 'homosexual Christian' would have been a contradiction in terms for Paul, in the same way it would be a denial of God's saving work to continue to describe a person as an 'adulterous Christian' who had committed this sexual act prior to conversion—an activity also condoned by men generally in Roman Corinth—or in terms of their previous activity, *i.e.*, drunkenness, idolatry, theft, etc..

Practising homosexuals, as well as practising fornicators and adulterers were not the only persons to be excluded from the inheritance of the Kingdom. Paul does not differentiate them from idolaters, thieves, covetous people, drunkards, and extortioners, although the former offenders would be seen to be sinning against their own bodies (1 Cor. 6:18). Just as Roman society discriminated against passive homosexuals, there has been the problem of double Christian standards when it comes to exercising pastoral care and discipline on the basis of 6:9–11. The singling out of sexual behaviour alone, and homosexual conduct in particular, to the virtual exclusion of other conduct, much of which is rife in our own day, cannot be justified if full weight is given to the application of the passage in the church.

Finally, there is the matter of biblical interpretation for which 1 Corinthians 6:9–11 provides an important example of a factor neglected in some exegesis. The passage appears to sit rather awkwardly between vexatious litigation[54] and young men indulging their appetites for food and sex at private dinners under the banner of liberation occasioned by assuming the *toga virilis*. However, it repeats and expands a crucial theological referent in 5:11 concerning conduct that excluded Christians from the covenant community. This enlightens our understanding of the issue resting behind 6:1-8.[55] Paul's succinct comment in 6:9-11 on the persons excluded from the Kingdom explains the reasons for his stance on subsequent issues for Christians, including fornication (6:12-20), avoiding adultery (7:2, 5), covetousness related to social mobility (7:17-24), and idolatry (10:14).

1 Corinthians 6:9-11 is a short statement which is extremely important in the interpretation of the subsequent discussion. In their treatment of sections of 1 Corinthians or other New Testament books in which there is extensive discussion, scholars need to be alert to the presence of theological building blocks or referents that have been put in place, such as 6:9-11. These need to be incorporated into the interpretation of subsequent passages as part of the overall theological framwork of the letter. It has been the hallmark of David Wright's careful work as a scholar that, in his theological and historical studies, he has been alert to the important interpretative principal of theological referents. His scholarly discussions of homosexuality, including the outworking of his considered judgement on the meaning of ἀρσενοκοίτης in 1 Corinthians 6:9, have been no exception.

---

[54]See my 'Civil Litigation in Secular Corinth and the Church: The Forensic Background to 1 Corinthians 6:1–8) in ed. B. Rosner *Understanding Paul's Ethics: Twentieth–Century Approaches* (Grand Rapids and Carlisle: Eerdmans and Paternoster, 1995) ch. 3.
[55]The financial penalties suffered in such vexatious litigation may well be the reason why Paul accuses them of 'defrauding' a fellow Christian, 6:8 cf. 5:10. G.D. Fee, *The First Epistle to the Corinthians* (Grand Rapids: Eerdmans, 1987) 243 suggests this is an example covered by the broad term 'thief'.

Chapter 15

EVANGELICALS AND ESCHATOLOGY: A CONTENTIOUS CASE

Stephen Williams

David Wright outstandingly combines scholarship, church-manship and evangelical commitment. Amongst his long-standing concerns, and one close to his heart, is the social dimension of Christian witness and endeavour. Back in 1979, he edited papers from the significant National Evangelical Conference on Social Ethics, held in the previous year.[1] His continued commitment to the matters which occupied him there was indicated in a powerful editorial in the *Scottish Bulletin of Evangelical Theology*.

> '...How commonly,' he asked, 'does the designation "Calvinist" imply for the modern evangelical in Scotland the particular theological perspective which most obviously dis-tinguished the Reformed from other varieties of sixteenth-century Protestantism? This was, of course, the vision of the godly ordering of the whole of society. It is likely to be a poor history of the Reformation that fails to single out the shaping of the total life of the community according to the will of God as perhaps the most distinctive mark of Calvinism.'[2]

---

[1] D.F. Wright (ed.), *Essays in Evangelical Social Ethics* (Exeter: Paternoster, 1979).

[2] 'Rediscovering a (Scottish) Evangelical Heritage,' *SBET* 4 (1986).

He proceeded to lament (i) *'the paucity of evangelical contributions on the broad front of Christian socio-political responsibility;'* (ii) *'our non-involvement with wider evangelical developments in this field;'* (iii) *'the inadequacy of our common evangelical "line" on socio-political issues'.*

He made brief, but valuable, proposals for remedying this deficiency. But I shall not follow here the trajectory of these proposals. Rather, I shall use as a springboard his remarks under the second of the points above. The 'wider evangelical developments' which he instantiated here were those embodied in the Lausanne Covenant. In particular, he cited the Grand Rapids consultation, held under the aegis of the Lausanne movement and the World Evangelical Fellowship, in 1982. The report came out later that year, and Bruce Nicholls edited the papers published three years later.[3]

I make no apology for revisiting these documents twelve to fifteen years on. It is surprising how little progress has been made in some evangelical circles since then, in key areas of this discussion.[4] Our quarry in this essay is just one of the issues, namely, the relation of eschatology to social responsibility. More specifically, we are interested in the bearing of our beliefs about the relation between the present and the future on our social engagement. Although the brief labours that follow are expended mostly on clearing ground and blocking off routes, it is in the hope that the high road of social action be traversed with as little impediment, and as much confidence, as theology can contribute.

The question of continuity

At Grand Rapids, intra-evangelical disagreements surfaced in relation to eschatology.[5] There is one point in his report on

---

[3]John Stott chaired the drafting committee of the report, entitled *Evangelism and Social Responsibility: An Evangelical Commitment* (Exeter: Paternoster, 1982). Bruce Nicholls edited the papers entitled *In Word and Deed: Evangelism and Social Responsibility* (Exeter: Paternoster, 1985).

[4]This was particularly impressed on me at a conference last year where some of the Lausanne issues were re-run in a company where one would not expect it. And this was no isolated instance.

[5]For the context of the consultation, see p.9 of the report. Page numbers to various works will occasionally be placed in the text of this essay, where it is clear which work is cited.

the consultation where John Stott noted inability to agree. This was in the area of eschatology. Representatives of the three millennarian positions (amillennialism, premillennialism and post-millennialism) at the consultation had no desire to address those differences directly. But while there was common ground on the matter of 'eschatological motivation for evangelism and social responsibility' (p.38), the question of whether 'the final Kingdom [will] enjoy some continuity with its present manifestation,' or whether 'the future [will] be discontinuous with the present...' evoked disagreement (p.40). The disagreement bore on social action. 'Those who have the assurance of this continuity find in it a strong incentive to social and cultural involvement' (p.42).

The force of this disagreement emerged when the consultation papers were eventually published. 'History and Eschatology' had occupied a day of the discussion and Peter Kuzmic's paper, in particular, focused the issue that will interest us.[6] But the issue came up in other papers. Its importance, and the significance of Kuzmic's subsequent contribution, were stated early and clearly in David Bosch's paper, where he described premillennialism as a negative influence on social involvement, a trend that had hindered understanding.[7] We will concentrate on what Kuzmic said.

When Peter Kuzmic laid out the three main options on the millennial question, he expended by far the most time on premillennialism. This was on account of its supposedly deleterious social consequences. On the one hand, he granted that 'there are varieties of premillennialism leading to significantly varied practical and behavioural consequences' (p.141). But he took it that 'premillennialism's underlying philosophy of history has almost inevitable negative consequences for Christian social responsibility,' citing Donald Dayton and Timothy Weber in support (pp.142-44). On this view, only when Christ returns are there decent prospects for the earth; evangelism is our task until then. Kuzmic protested against this purely futuristic eschat-

---

[6]Peter Kuzmic, 'History and Eschatology: Evangelical Views' in *Word and Deed*.

[7]David J. Bosch, 'In Search of a New Evangelical Understanding' in *Word and Deed*, 71f.

ology and neglect of the reality of the Kingdom already come, whose blessings are meant to include social blessings.

Tied to the neglect of realised eschatology is the emphasis on a 'radical break between the present earth and the awaited "new heaven and earth." Such teaching of total discontinuity sees the present completely unredeemable and under judgement of divine destruction, and the "new earth" to be a kind of a new *creatio ex nihilo*'. (p.151). And so, as well as affirming realised eschatology, Kuzmic affirmed a continuity between this earth and the next, without denying discontinuity. 'We are to work for a better world already here and now, knowing that everything that is noble, beautiful, true and righteous in this world will somehow be preserved and perfected in the new world to come' (p.151). In his support, he cited those who stand in the Dutch Calvinist tradition (Berkouwer, Berkhof and Hoekema) and Calvin himself. He concluded by pressing for a connection between eschatology and ethics, whereby both the presence of the Kingdom and the promise of its consummation in some continuity with this earth would ground, or help to ground, our social as well as our personal ethics.

I shall not pursue the case against premillennialism here. But let us look at the case for continuity. It is particularly interesting to notice the role played, in recent evangelical debate, by a text Kuzmic highlighted in support of his position, namely, Revelation 21:24-26. We encounter this text more than once in this collection, *e.g.*, in the contribution by Vinay Samuel and Chris Sugden.[8] They, too, embed reference to the text in a wider argument for continuity, on the analogy of the resurrection of the body. The practical consequence of this latter belief is that we must deal with people here and now according to their bodily reality, according to the 'series of integrated relationships' in which we live. They press on as follows. 'Such an understanding of transformation equally applies to our stewardship of creation....All the Old Testament concepts of the Kingdom of God are in terms of a renewed earth' (p.209). One conclusion

---

[8]See Vinay Samuel and Chris Sugden, 'Evangelism and Social Responsibility: A Biblical Study on Priorities' in *Word and Deed*, 209, though they refer to Revelation 21:22-24.

is that the values expressed in 'good works performed within the structural relationships of human history....are heavenly values which will last for ever. So too the works which express these values inasmuch as they belong to the new age, will find their fulfilment in that age' (p.210). So Kuzmic is not a voice crying in the wilderness. But there are difficulties.[9]

Difficulties
The prominence given, in recent years, to Revelation 21:24-26, is rather curious. Anything approaching exegetical consensus on this text, either within or without the evangelical community, is unlikely in the near future. Not that this should preclude staunch advocacy of a particular option. Nor that we should throw up our hands in hermeneutical despair. It is just that we are on precarious ground.

A number of commentators affirm in general that Revelation 21 teaches the continuity of the new with the present heaven and earth, albeit in transformed mode, and they affirm in particular the support Revelation 21:24-26 gives to this standpoint. But the contrasting approaches can be illustrated by three examples chosen from the decade or so before the Grand Rapids conference.

Leon Morris took John to be 'concerned with spiritual states, not with physical realities,' his description of 'a complete transformation of all things' making use of 'the language of heaven and earth for he has no other language'.[10] He had earlier glossed 'there was found no place for them' (*i.e.,* earth and sky, or earth and heaven, Rev. 20:11) as meaning 'they were completely destroyed'. He found the bringing of the glory and honour of the nations into the new Jerusalem (21:26) hard to understand. Shortly afterwards, George Eldon Ladd, in his commentary on Revelation,

---

[9]There is a number which I shall not pursue here.*e.g.,* the analogy with the resurrection of the body is difficult to sustain effectively. The person and the body are relatively simple compared to the heterogeneous mass of things that constitute 'the world.' Another issue is the semantics and significance of the linguistic distinction between two Greek words for 'new,' *kainos* and *neos*.

[10]Leon Morris, *The Revelation of St. John: An Introduction and Commentary* (London: Tyndale. 1969) 242f.

argued that the element of discontinuity was stronger in the New than in the Old Testament, as exemplified by the closing chapters of Revelation.[11] On 21:1, he observed: 'The abolition of the sea suggests that there is practically no substantial continuity between the old fallen and the new redeemed order, but that the old order is completely swept away and replaced by something altogether new and different'. True, 21:5 'suggests the renovation of what already exists. But it is improbable that the apocalyptist was much concerned about such details; his attention is fixed on the coming of the new order'. Finally, we refer to Robert Mounce's commentary published in 1977.[12] He concluded that neither the language of 21:1 nor rabbinic commentary enabled us to decide between 'renovation of the old or a distinctly new creation'. On 21:24, he remarked that the 'imagery of the Apocalypse must of necessity be concrete and spatial, but its significance is inevitably spiritual'.

I am not expressing agreement or disagreement with anything in these comments. But they indicate the controversial nature of appealing to Revelation. However, the difficulty is compounded—and it is this that constitutes the main difficulty, in our present context—when the application of Revelation 21:24-26 is made in detail. Consider these words of Hoekema, to whose work Kuzmic appealed.

> that whatever people have done on this earth which glorified God will be remembered in the life to come (Rev. 14:13). But more must be said. Is it too much to say that, according to these verses, the unique contributions of each nation to the life of the present earth will enrich the life of the new earth? Shall we than perhaps inherit the best products of culture and art which this earth has produced?[13]

The questions are rhetorical, expecting respectively negative and affirmative answers. Having cited Hoekema, Kuzmic

---

[11]G.E. Ladd, *A Commentary on the Revelation of John* (Grand Rapids: Eerdmans, 1972) 271ff.

[12]Robert H. Mounce, *The Book of Revelation* (Grand Rapids: Eerdmans, 1977). Note that references in this essay are not to the most recent commentaries for we are not entering the exegetical arena directly.

[13]A. Hoekema, *The Bible and the Future* (Exeter: Paternoster, 1979) 286.

affirmed that 'we are to appreciate and co-operate with non-Christians where in the areas of science, art, literature, philosophy, and social work they are producing what may well be found on the new earth' (p.152).

To parrot Hoekema: is it too much to ask what we mean here? Transformed Constables? Revised Brontes? Reconstructed *Summae Theologiae*? And what about the mass of our social work, geared towards containing social problems? Now some may get impatient with such questions and argue as follows. Scripture is not in the business of, and theology has no responsibility for, such specific description. If one pursues my line of questioning, with its uneasy hint of mockery, one may be found in contempt of God himself, who bids us believe in continuity and transformation, but not on the strength of our ability to conceptualise. It would be a truly fatal attitude to Scripture and to the whole theological task if statements of faith were subjected to this kind of demand for conceptual precision.

Such a demurral contains much that is serious, valuable and true. But it does not detract from the force of our questions. For talk of literature, art and science is introduced not by Scripture, but by advocates of continuity. Such specificity is the alleged entailment of a theologically sensitive exegesis of Scripture, which provides an incentive for action. The Christian effort in literature, art, science, philosophy and social work, and the Christian appreciation of non-Christian literature, art, science, philosophy and social work, is enhanced by such a reading of Scripture. So it is claimed.

However, the claim is deeply problematic. It raises the question of whether works which, it may be conceded, are perhaps not destined for such a specific form of consummation, somehow lack a motivational dimension that the others possess; of whether Christians engaged in art, innocent of the potential eschatological destiny of their products, lack the motivational edge possessed by the continuists.[14] We can extend the line of questioning beyond examples

---

[14]It is worth scrutinizing interpretations of the disappearance of the sea (Rev. 21:1), to see if they have any logical bearing on our present responsibilities towards the marine environment. The discussion usually carried on does not go in for distinctions between motives, incentives, grounds, reasons etc. So I am using the word 'motive' very loosely.

principally from the world of human commerce and human artifacts. When the 'continuism' which surfaced at Grand Rapids was challenged in an article in *Transformation*, in 1990, Miroslav Volf offered a rebuttal on behalf of the continuist position.[15] According to Volf, 'important and unambiguous New Testament statements...explicitly support the idea of an eschatological transformation of the creation'. This is not based just on a text from Revelation. The text Volf himself took up was Romans 8:21, where Paul refers to the liberation of creation. Citing F.F. Bruce in his support, Volf commented: 'The liberation of creation—i.e. of the whole of sub-human nature, both animate and inanimate—*cannot occur through its destruction but only through its transformation*' (p.29). As heretofore, transformation and continuity are mutually implicative notions. But does the turn to Romans help?

The fact is that Bruce's own formulation is open to serious questioning, when he requires that we interpret the apocalyptic language of Revelation via these 'more prosaic statements'.[16] The loose comparative in this claim is a stumbling-block when one considers the insistence of a C.H. Dodd, for instance, that this language is 'poetic' and 'as little as possible dependent on any particular metaphysic'.[17] However, we need not at all enlist Dodd to make the point that counts here. Volf's emphatic reference to 'the *whole* of sub-human nature' indicates equally emphatically the problem with his own position. For what about the animals? Volf seems committed not only to the position that there will be animals on the new earth. He seems committed to the belief that these will be transformed animals from the present earth, and the prospect of transformed particular animals— not just those of the last generation—is meant to furnish some kind of incentive for caring for them. Is this *reductio ad absurdum* not just the logic of Volf's own insistence?

[15]M. Volf, 'On Loving with Hope: Eschatology and Social Responsibility,' *Transformation* (7.3) 1990. He was replying to my article, 'The Partition of Love and Hope: Eschatology and Social Responsibility,' in the same issue.
[16]F.F. Bruce, *The Epistle of Paul to the Romans: An Introduction and Commentary* (London: Tyndale, 1963) 170, n.2.
[17]C.H. Dodd, *The Epistle of Paul to the Romans* (London: Hodder & Stoughton, 1932) 132f.

It is intriguing to watch Charles Hodge in action on this passage. Hodge was a robust transformationist, arguing the Reformed position against Lutheran annihilationist interpretations of the future of the universe.[18] In his commentary on Romans, he interprets 8:21-25 along similar lines, although he does not shrink from insisting on Paul's poetical vein. It may be thought that he ducks the question about animals that arises from his own interpretation of the creation (κτίσις) that is to enjoy eschatological liberty. But he does make the programmatic assertion, in a sentence picked up by John Murray in his later commentary, that the words 'the whole creation' are 'so comprehensive, that nothing should be excluded which the nature of the subject and the context do not show cannot be embraced within their scope'.[19] 'The nature of the subject,' in addition to 'context,' invites pause. The issue before is not whether Scripture speaks of the eschatological transformation, as opposed to the annihilation, of the present cosmos. The issue is what continuity can be inferred from transformation; how alleged continuity constitutes the destiny of particulars; and how or whether our perception of the destiny of particulars affects our treatment of them. In addressing this further, we now need to chart rather deeper and wider theological waters.

Deeper reaches
Volf's riposte to the criticism of continuism was vigorous. He went beyond reference to Romans and to exegesis. He agreed that although one could logically marry a contrary conviction, one that maintained discontinuity, with social action yet, theologically, there are insuperable difficulties. The central one is this: 'The expectation of the eschatological destruction of the world (and of everything human beings have created in it) is not consonant with belief in the value and goodness of creation: what God will annihilate must either be so bad that it is not possible to redeem it, or so insignificant that it is not worth being redeemed. It is hard to believe in the intrinsic value of goodness of something that

---

[18]Charles Hodge, *Systematic Theology*, vol.3 (New York: Scribner, 1873) 851-855.
[19]Charles Hodge, *Commentary on the Epistle to the Romans* (Edinburgh: Andrew Eliot/James Thin, 1875) 268.

God would completely annihilate'. Thus, 'one can believe in the intrinsic goodness of creation only if one believes in eschatological transformation rather than destruction' (p.30).

This argument, however, gets into serious difficulty if it is offered, as it is, from within an evangelical perspective. This is clear when we consider the question of universalism. What is of most value, what is the pinnacle of goodness in God's creation? Humanity. Yet, on the non-universalist view, some humans reap destruction. Supposing one synecdochically substituted that which is of greatest importance in the world (humanity) for 'the world' in the sentence quoted from Volf. Then it reads: 'The expectation of the eschatological destruction of the human being...is not consonant with belief in the value and goodness of creation'. That spells universalism. One presumes that, on Volf's wording, it is immaterial whether one believes in annihilation or in everlasting punishment. In either case, the supremely valuable is not redeemed. Yet, the fact is the desperate eschatological destiny of part of the human race does not mean that it initially lacked created goodness or value. Then, *a fortiori*, why should putative destruction be inconsistent with goodness and value in the case of 'the world'?

Of course, there is a ready answer to all this. Some humans eventually go beyond redemption. Humans may be destroyed when and because they allow their inherent goodness and valuableness to be negated by sinfulness. Participation in a fallen world does not disqualify from redemption, but responsibly sinning within it does. But if Volf's position is something like this, note that the implication of his reasoning is not just the negative—that the participation of the good and the valuable in the fallen world does not disqualify it from redemption. It is the positive—what is created good and of value thereby qualifies for eschatological redemption. Which surely means that all the hamsters that ever were will be transformed eschatologically, their annihilated non-appearance being inconsistent with their created goodness. More: this fact gives us an additional incentive to comb out the hair of the loosehaired variety, lest the tangles cause consternation.

I do not mean to trivialise in any way. Hamsters are not insignificant. It is part of the greatness of God that not a hamster feels pain, discomfort or consternation without our heavenly father knowing and caring. There is something important at stake here: the bearing of eschatological hope on the particulars of social action which concretely constitute our earthly responsibility. It is as though the more specific or concrete our asseverations on eschatological hope, the more we have the problem of relating that hope to earthly particulars in the way under scrutiny. Now there is a wider problem here, not confined to the form in which we have encountered it in the Lausanne context. We find Volf, in his essay, appealing to Oliver O'Donovan's treatment of 'Eschatology and History' in *Resurrection and Moral Order*.[20] Here, as we might expect, theo-logical reasons for belief in transformation, are lodged within a firm conceptual structure. We turn to it at this juncture, because it broadens our enquiry out of its original context in the Lausanne debates, while keeping us close to the biblical material.

O'Donovan's treatment turns out to be problematic along lines that we can identify from our enquiry. Introducing his general thesis, he argues that the resurrection of Christ is theologically central for ethics, since 'it tells us of God's vindication of his creation and so of our created life'. He adds that 1 Peter is 'the most consistently theological New Testament treatise on ethics'. Its great declaration of living hope through the resurrection 'proclaims the reality of the new life upon which the very possibility of ethics depends' (p.13). A second reference to 1 Peter, in Part One of the work, conducts to its conclusion the argument that 'Christian ethics, like the resurrection, looks both backwards and forwards, to the origin and to the end of the created order. It respects the natural structures of life in the world, while looking forward to their transformation' (p.58). All this is exemplified in 1 Peter, which opens with a declaration of hope, and moves on to such things as ethics of government, labour and marriage. O'Donovan avers that 'a hope which envisages the transformation of existing natural structures cannot consistently attack or repudiate those structures,' though the institutions need redemption.

---

[20]Oliver O'Donovan, *Resurrection and Moral Order: An Outline for Evangelical Ethics* (Leicester: Apollos, 1994).

The transformation envisioned here is eschatological, including a comprehensive dimension of future redemption. But again the Bible is unconvincingly used in the advancement of a theological thesis about transformation, which logically seems to entail some form of continuity, although O'Donovan does not commit himself here. For nothing in Petrine hope clearly envisages such an eschatological transformation; the question of eschatological transformation is, as far as this letter goes, irrelevant to Peter. Even after investigating the Jewish background to 1 Peter, to see whether Petrine hope is really as otherworldly as it *prima facie* appears, the epistle meets with stony silence any who would enquire, on its basis, and with deep theological intent, whether natural institutions are to be abolished or transformed. Nothing in resurrection hope shapes its ethics in that particular respect.

O'Donovan does, of course, seek a broader biblical basis for his theological ethics than what he finds in 1 Peter. He may object that Petrine hope must be assimilated to wider New Testament hope; when it is so assimilated, we can read into the logic of Petrine hope an entailment as to the transformation of natural structures. The *locus classicus* is Romans 8. O'Donovan speaks of transformation here, when God redeems the whole of creation, which must, as a whole, fulfil a God-given purpose. '...This fulfilment is what is implied when we speak of the "transformation" of the created order' (p.55). '...We must understand "creation" not merely as the raw material out of which the world as we know it is composed, but as the order and coherence in which it is composed' (p.31). 'Creation is the given totality of order which forms the presupposition of historical existence. "Created order" is that which neither the terrors of chance nor the ingenuity of art can overthrow' (p.61).

We quote these words to indicate O'Donovan's emphasis, which runs out (as far as it interests us) in the conviction that Petrine and more generally biblical natural structures of natural life in this world, qua part of the created order, must be destined for eschatological transformation. It is important to remember that, while O'Donovan steers studiously clear of having transformation entail the kind of strong continuities we have encountered, his 'fulfilment' is opposed to eschatological annihilation.

However, the language of 'wholeness' or 'totality,' while aptly characterising biblical eschatological promises *per se*, hinders, rather than helps, when pressed into the service of grounding ethics, in the mode that we are encountering here. O'Donovan consistently refers to the eschatological destiny of humankind, treating humanity as a 'whole'. Yet, he appears to reject universal salvation. So the humanity to whom a glorious destiny is promised is not the sum total of all individuals. On the meaning of redemption for the non-human creation, he professes agnosticism but, obviously, when one considers botanical or zoological natural *history*, sum total, again, is scarcely an option.

'Natural structures' or 'institutions' are not the same as either people or biological organisms. How should we take them as some sort of whole, in some kind of generic solidarity? What could it mean to say that they are destined for trans-formation, by virtue of their participation in a larger whole? One thinks of legal structures (more exactly, perhaps, logical provision for justice), generically a feature of political society as God has established it in this world, the promotion of justice being a central biblical theme. It is only at a stratospheric level or generalization that one could insist that we must term what happens to them 'transformation' rather than 'abolition;' indeed, one might deny the right to do so at all. The claim that there is some sort of wholeness to creation destined for trans-formation, according to biblical witness, is compatible with agnosticism on the question of whether the massive natural structures which we indwell have any kind of eschatological future.

Ex professo, O'Donovan's motive for retaining 'transformation' language is, in the first place, the preservation of whatever Scripture means when speaking of *fulfilment* in the eschaton. But on that score we must say this: in Scripture we are summoned to live our lives on this earth in relation to a host of things that may simply, like heaven and earth, 'pass away'.[21] Our behaviour in their regard is not

---

[21]With this reference, I am not committing myself to any particular exegesis of this verse.

characteristically governed by our perception of their destiny, and the onus is on those who are theologically reflective about it to specify in some detail why the theological logic of biblical eschatology leads us to insist on transformation and on its importance in relation to specific moral conduct. The eschatological status of the structures and institutions in question is so opaque that it is hard to see how the conviction that there is a whole to be redeemed affects our ethics within them. A response to some of these charges is not difficult to anticipate (though I shall not rehearse it), but it seems to me that an unsatisfactory unclarity remains. Our difficulties with eschatological wholes and earthly particulars surely remain.

Caution

In drawing to a conclusion I want to be very cautious about the direction of my own argument and a trifle non committal on its conclusions. For until one has come to terms with the powerful tradition of Dutch Calvinism on the pertinent questions, one ought to suspend judgement.[22] Those of us who cannot manage Dutch are debarred from access to the crucial theological contributions of Abraham Kuyper on this point, not to mention those of others in his tradition. Kuyper has invested this tradition with such weight that those of us who are linguistically below par ought to keep an open mind on the subject that has detained us. Still, I want to advert briefly to two who stand in that tradition: G.C. Berkouwer and Hendrikus Berkhof.[23] My self-imposed caution is partially, though not entirely, matched by an element of caution in these authors too, which we ought to notice.

Berkouwer, despite compelling reservations about the terms on which Reformed theologians of eschatological transformation argued their case against the Lutheran

---

[22]Douglas Schuurman noted some of the sources here in *Creation, Eschaton and Ethics: The Ethical Significance of the Creation-Eschaton Relation in the Thought of Emil Brunner and Jürgen Moltmann* (New York: Peter Lang, 1991) 157, n.12.

[23]Both Kuzmic and Hoekema appealed to these two. Interestingly we may at times be attracted to some form of continuism by work which lacks hermeneutical discussion, like that of Richard Mouw, especially *When the Kings Come Marching In* (Grand Rapids: Eerdmans, 1983).

theology of annihilation in the seventeenth century, clearly throws in his lot with the former.[24] Faced with the choice of Thurneysen's highly concrete description of continuity and Brunner's rejection of its dogmatic content, he opts for the first. Against Brunner's superficially laudable agnostic restraint, Berkouwer says: 'If he is completely correct about this, why do the Old and New Testaments not talk about an "x"—an unknown quantity—instead of arousing these various concepts of what the new heaven and the new earth will be like and talking about the longing for the creation for freedom from its perishability? The need for sobriety in talking about these matters ought not to lead one to overlook the equal need for certainty' (p.232). 'If he is completely correct' indicates a note of restraint in Berkouwer's dissent from the position he rejects. Still, caution is tempered with conviction.

Without prejudice to Berkouwer's wider discussion on these points, it should be pointed out that there are two difficulties attached to the formulation quoted. First, the New Testament *does* sometimes point to an unknown 'x'.[25] Second, we encounter here an hermeneutical question about eschatological statements, unaddressed at this point, which

---

[24]G.C. Berkouwer, *The Return of Christ* (Grand Rapids: Eerdmans, 1972), 219ff. This was translated and edited from the Dutch original. Reference to the seventeenth century debate allows us to make a point which is also relevant to Volf's strictures on those who *expect* cosmic annihilation. Note how J. Moltmann, in his opposition to the Lutheran tradition, seems not to deny the *possibility* of annihilation, only its positive *expectation*. See Moltmann, *God in Creation* (London: SCM, 1985) 86-93. The latter signifies an attitude to Creator and creation not necessitated by the former. I may be misinterpreting Moltmann here, but one should not jump to the conclusion that permitting and expecting annihilation amount to the same thing.

[25]I am thinking here less of the extent to which individual texts, like 1 John 3:2, might be pressed in the service of such a claim, than of a sustained discussion such as 1 Corinthians 15.35ff. I cannot exegete that here, but it seems to me that attention to the logic of the argument, and the distinction between *sarx* and *soma*, even in the wider Pauline context, warrants our description of the spiritual body as an unknown 'x.' However, I believe that this should be qualified by, and is consistent with, a credal affirmation of the resurrection of the body. It would take too long to say how and why!

also needs more thorough attention in contemporary evangelicalism. The question we ask of Berkouwer is this. If what
is to be transcends our ability to conceive it, what words
should be used to describe it? What compelling objection is
there if Scripture were held to take the finest that we can
imagine, stating its eschatological message of wonderful
consummation in those terms, as a substitute for stating an
abstraction that signifies our lack of knowledge? Is that so
foreign to the way that the language and imagery of the
Bible works?[26]

Our second figure, Berkhof, is rightly prepared at
least to cast a peripheral glance in the direction of this question at this point, briefly discussing the relationship of faith
to imag-ination, in *The Christian Faith*.[27] In this work, Berkhof
seems to modify or to qualify tacitly, but significantly, the
'continuist' position taken in an earlier and well-known
work, *Christ, the Meaning of History*.[28] In *The Christian Faith*
Berkhof will not be dogmatically forced into a choice
between these following possibilities.

> We can say that our culture provides the scaffolding for the
> coming structure, a scaffolding that will later be torn down
> again. It is also possible, however, to view our culture as
> providing the building materials for a coming kingdom.

He settles finally for 'the fact that all of cultural development
will prove to be meaningful in the light of eternity. But that
is the limit of what can be said about eternity' (p.539). That is
a good way short of the strong continuism which launched
our investigation in this essay. Berkhof is not remote from
the following conviction, although he does not sanction it.
While continuity may indeed be a rich prospect as far as we
are con-cerned, whatever the eschaton delivers, if it be found
that we made over-literal deductions from the biblical data
in respect of continuity, will not strike us an impoverish-

---

[26]The phrase is borrowed from G.B. Caird, *The Language and Imagery of
the Bible* (London: Duckworth, 1980), whose third part treats
eschatology.

[27]H. Berkhof, *Christian Faith: An Introduction to the Study of the Faith*
(Grand Rapids: Eerdmans, 1979) 539.

[28]See the third edition of this (London: SCM, 1966). Note also a brief
study: H. Berkhof, *Well-Founded Hope* (Richmond: John Knox, 1969).

ment, a disappointment in the direction of putatively unbiblical annihilationism. It will strike us in its transcendent majesty. How can it not, when God will be all in all?

Conclusion

> Hear O Israel, the Lord our God is one. Love the Lord your God will all your heart and with all your soul and with all your mind and with all your strength. This is the first and greatest commandment. And the second is like it: Love your neighbour as yourself.[29]

These non-identical but twin commandments are set in the realm of grace, in Old Testament as in New. The whole of the Christian life of faith and of love is set in the light of hope.[30] One cannot conceive of Christians engaging in social action detached from an eschatological context. But neither can one conceive of a limit to what the love of God and neighbour should, and should desire to, accomplish—a limit, for example, set by the possibility of non-continuity between present and future. Such is the nature, power and mandate of love that it demands great rigour on the part of the proponents of transformation and continuity, versus annihilation and discontinuity, to demonstrate that their incentive is *required* by full-orbed biblical Christianity in order to undertake our social responsibilities to the greater glory of God. My own conviction, for what it is worth and which I shall not elaborate here, is that the mandate for social responsibility is adequately secured by love, within a more general eschatological framework than our continuists allow.[31]

David Wright may not welcome, and may dissent from, the tentative conclusion of this essay. What he will undoubtedly welcome is the suggestion that the matter would be profitably pursued by continued enquiry about the

---

[29]I am conflating the Matthean and Markan renderings of the great commandment here.

[30]Col. 1:5 refers to 'the faith and love that spring from the hope...,' although this is not a standard way of relating the triumvirate.

[31]I certainly do not mean that anything goes in eschatology. For example, I fully agree with emphasizing the 'now' of the Kingdom.

theological basis of the Reformers' theology of social concern, a matter he brought to light in the *SBET* editorial with which we started. Indeed, he has led the way in the matter. He edited *Martin Bucer: Reforming Church and Community* to mark the quincentenary of Bucer's birth.[32] Of his subject, he said: 'It would be difficult to find a sixteenth-century churchman and theologian with more to say to the churches of Europe now living through the disorienting transition between the old order of the Christian establishment and the emergent ex-Christian (rather than post-Christian) pluralistic world' (p.2). Although neither David Wright nor his fellow-essayists pursue Bucer's theology of society and action in connection with his eschatology, we should learn much from Bucer, as from other Reformers, of that passion which drives the true believer to care for God's world, and of the theological sources of that passion.[33] It will all be found to be of such power and profundity that although it may please God that we grow in theological insight as the centuries pass, yet if we perch ourselves on these giant shoulders, we shall have ascended high indeed. It is no wonder that David Wright has recalled us to the Reformation. It is not the least of his contributions to have summoned us to consider our social responsibility in its light. May our deeds, not our theology alone, be enriched by his reminder.[34]

---

[32]D.F. Wright (ed.), *Martin Bucer: Reforming Church and Community* (Cambridge: CUP, 1994).

[33]The first two essays here indicate what we might mine: P. Matheson, 'Martin Bucer and the Old Church' and M. Greschat, 'The relation between church and civil community in Bucer's reforming work.'

[34]In 1956 T.F. Torrance wrote on 'The Eschatology of Love: Martin Butzer,' in *Kingdom and Church: a Study in the Theology of the Reformation* (Edinburgh: Oliver & Boyd, 1956). He noted Bucer's comment on the Isaianic reference to the new heavens and new earth, which is 'magis de Ecclesiae innovatione et foelicitate spiritali, quam de futuro mundi statu, immutationeque corporali' (p.88). Both his comparative studies and the work on Bucer now in progress deserve careful study by those interested in the theological and eschatological foundations of social concern.